VOLUME MEASURES

1 tsp	**90ml** (3fl oz)	**300ml** (10fl oz)	**900ml** (1½ pints)
2 tsp	**100ml** (3½fl oz)	**360ml** (12fl oz)	**1 litre** (1¾ pints)
1 tbsp (=3 tsp)	**120ml** (4fl oz)	**400ml** (14fl oz)	**1.2 litres** (2 pints)
2 tbsp	**150ml** (5fl oz)	**450ml** (15fl oz)	**1.4 litres** (2½ pints)
3 tbsp	**200ml** (7fl oz)	**500ml** (16fl oz)	**1.5 litres** (2¾ pints)
4 tbsp = **60ml** (2fl oz)	**240ml** (8fl oz)	**600ml** (1 pint)	**1.7 litres** (3 pints)
75ml (2½fl oz)	**250ml** (8fl oz)	**750ml** (1¼ pints)	**2 litres** (3½ pints)

LIQUID VOLUME MEASURES

½ cup	120ml (4fl oz)
⅔ cup	150ml (5fl oz)
1 cup	250ml (8fl oz)
2 cups	450ml (15fl oz)
2½ cups	600ml (1 pint)
4¼ cups	1 litre (1¾ pints)

DRY MEASURES

1 CUP FRESH BREADCRUMBS	60g	2oz
1 CUP BULGUR WHEAT	115g	4oz
1 CUP FLOUR	115g	4oz
1 CUP COUSCOUS	175g	6oz
1 CUP ICING SUGAR	175g	6oz
1 CUP PEARL BARLEY	200g	7oz
1 CUP BUTTER	225g	8oz
1 CUP UNCOOKED RICE	225g	8oz
1 CUP WHITE/BROWN SUGAR	225g	8oz

MasterChef

KITCHEN BIBLE

MasterChef

KITCHEN BIBLE

CONTENTS

John Torode

Having had the honour of working on MasterChef for over 12 years now, I have tasted some of the most fantastic food and watched many people fulfil their dreams. Food has changed and evolved over the years: we've moved from nose-to-tail eating to molecular gastronomy; from foams, airs, and splodges and splashes on the plate to the trend for serving "burnt" things. You'll find some of each style in this book. But before you try to reach the dizzying, restaurant-standard cooking heights of the amazing cooks who have toiled in the MasterChef kitchens, you need to know the basics.

This book is for everybody, from kitchen novices to truly adventurous and advanced cooks. It will guide you through the basics: how to joint a bird, make a custard, or create pasta dough. It will also equip you with the classic recipes that need to be in every cook's notebook: how to make a proper, fail-safe cake, simmer a stock, or make a light chocolate mousse. This book is full of skills, techniques, and tips you can perfect to become the cook you want to be. Even if you just want to learn how to chop an onion well, or perfect the ever-so-tricky Italian meringue made with sugar syrup, it's all here.

Should you aspire to cook dishes from the finals of MasterChef, there are recipes from many of the ambitious and creative MasterChef finalists to inspire your cooking and show you how to take it to another level. This is where you will find the open lasagnes, French-style macarons, and even a couple of airs and foams, if you fancy that sort of thing. Some of the recipes – particularly those from the most recent years – are very elaborate, with many component parts and advanced techniques that challenge the most ambitious cooks, but give them a go as they are all doable.

To be a better cook, the best tip I can give anyone is that you have to practise: pick a few recipes, and cook them over and over again. Like a piece of music, the more you practise, the better it will be. Or, as a great golfer once said, "The more I practise, the luckier I get!"

Enjoy and good luck! Practise practise practise.

Gregg Wallace

The most expensive commodity I know of is knowledge. You either pay somebody clever for it or you learn expensive lessons through your own mistakes. Here are two things I wish someone had told me years ago.

Know your olive oil. Most of us who cook know we use olive oil for cooking and virgin olive oil for salad dressings. Even though millions of bottles are sold I rarely find anybody who knows what extra virgin and virgin olive oils are. Both are the first press, only oil with less than 1 per cent acidity can be called extra virgin.

Please, please, please use a sharp knife. It is blunt knives that slip. All my bad cuts come from blunt knives, not sharp ones.

Now, my background as a greengrocer has served me well when it comes to knowing my fresh produce. So here are some lessons for you from me.

If you want to cook great potato dishes, use the right spud. For chips you need starchy, for mash you want floury, for a gratin you should use waxy. Two decent all-rounders are the Maris Piper and, my favourite, the King Edward. And a new potato is only new if you can rub the skin off with your thumb; if you can't, it's just a salad potato.

Everything else that you will ever need to know in the kitchen about fruit and veg – and meat, fish, grains, cakes, and all the rest – is in this book. From tips for new cooks, such as how to cut veg, to the high-end stuff, like making hollandaise sauce, it's all here.

And lastly, here's a treasure I've gleaned directly from my work on MasterChef over the years. Taste. Taste. And taste again. It's only through knowing how a food should taste, and how that flavour and texture changes with every stage of the cooking process, that you will develop the skills and refined palate of a great cook.

You may not be able to use all this knowledge straight away, so make space for it in that big brain of yours – and keep this book safe, of course – for use at a later date. One day, I promise you, it will all come in handy.

Gregg

MODERN CLASSIC RECIPES

WELL-LOVED
MODERN CLASSICS
THAT ALL GOOD
HOME COOKS
SHOULD KNOW.

Bouillabaisse

Originally nothing more than a humble fisherman's soup using the remains of the day's catch, this is now a famous dish. Use the fish bones and heads and the prawn shells to make the stock, if you have time.

PREPARATION TIME **20 minutes** • COOKING TIME **45 minutes** • **SERVES 4**

4 tbsp **olive oil**

1 **onion**, thinly sliced

2 **leeks**, thinly sliced

1 small **fennel bulb**, thinly sliced

2–3 **garlic cloves**, finely chopped

4 **tomatoes**, skinned, deseeded, and chopped

1 tbsp **tomato purée**

250ml (8fl oz) **dry white wine**

1.5 litres (2¾ pints) **fish stock** or **chicken stock**

pinch of **saffron threads**

strip of **unwaxed orange zest**

1 **bouquet garni**

salt and freshly ground **black pepper**

1.35kg (3lb) mixed **white and oily fish** and **shellfish**, such as red gurnard, John Dory, monkfish, red mullet, heads and bones removed, peeled raw prawns, and cleaned mussels

2 tbsp **Pernod**

8 thin slices of day-old **French bread**, toasted, to serve

FOR THE ROUILLE

125g (4½oz) **mayonnaise**

1 **bird's eye chilli**, deseeded and roughly chopped

4 **garlic cloves**, roughly chopped

1 tbsp **tomato purée**

1 Heat the oil in a large saucepan over a medium heat. Add the onion, leeks, fennel, and garlic and fry gently, stirring frequently, for 5 minutes, or until the vegetables are softened but not coloured. Add the tomatoes, tomato purée, and wine and stir until blended.

2 Add the stock, saffron, orange zest, and bouquet garni. Season to taste with salt and pepper, and bring to the boil. Reduce the heat, partially cover the pan, and simmer for 30 minutes, or until the soup has reduced slightly, stirring occasionally.

3 To make the rouille, place all ingredients into a blender or food processor with ¼ tsp salt and process until the mixture is smooth. Transfer to a bowl, cover with cling film, and chill until required.

4 Just before the liquid finishes simmering, cut the fish into chunks. Remove the orange zest and bouquet garni from the soup and add the fish (but not the shellfish). Reduce the heat to low and let the soup simmer for 5 minutes, then add the shellfish and simmer for further 2–3 minutes, or until all the fish is cooked through, the prawns are pink and the mussels have opened. Stir in the Pernod and season to taste with salt and pepper.

5 To serve, spread each piece of toast with rouille and put 2 slices in the bottom of each bowl. Ladle the soup on top and serve.

FISH KNOW-HOW: *see* Bone a round fish through the stomach **p268**
FISH KNOW-HOW: *see* Bone a round fish from the back **p269**
SHELLFISH KNOW-HOW: *see* Clean mussels **p286**
SAVOURY SAUCES AND STOCKS KNOW-HOW: *see* Make fish stock **p484**

Lobster bisque

Rich and undeniably impressive, this makes a satisfying meal on its own, or serve smaller portions before a light main course.

PREPARATION TIME **45 minutes** • COOKING TIME **1 hour 10 minutes** • **SERVES 4**

1 **lobster**, cooked, about 1kg (2¼lb) in weight

50g (1¾oz) **unsalted butter**

1 **onion**, finely chopped

1 **carrot**, finely chopped

2 **celery sticks**, finely chopped

1 **leek**, finely chopped

½ **fennel bulb**, finely chopped

1 **bay leaf**

1 sprig of **tarragon**

2 **garlic cloves**, crushed

75g (2½oz) **tomato purée**

4 **tomatoes**, roughly chopped

120ml (4fl oz) **Cognac** or **brandy**

100ml (3½fl oz) **dry white wine** or **Vermouth**

1.7 litres (3 pints) **fish stock**

120ml (4fl oz) **double cream**

salt and freshly ground **black pepper**

pinch of **cayenne pepper**

juice of ½ **lemon**

snipped **chives**, to garnish

1 Split the lobster in half, twist off the claws and legs, and reserve the shells. Remove the meat from the body, claws, and legs, chop into small pieces, and set aside. Crack the shells with the back of a knife, chop into rough pieces, and set aside.

2 Melt the butter in a large saucepan over a medium heat, add the vegetables, herbs, and garlic, and cook gently for 10 minutes, or until softened, stirring occasionally.

3 Add the chopped lobster shells. Stir in the tomato purée, chopped tomatoes, Cognac, white wine, and fish stock. Bring to the boil and simmer for 1 hour.

4 Leave to cool slightly, then ladle into a food processor. Process the soup in short bursts until the shell breaks into very small pieces. (If you would rather not process the shell pieces, scoop them out before ladelling the mixture into the food processor.)

5 Strain the soup through a coarse sieve, pushing as much liquid through as you can. Strain the soup again, this time through a fine mesh sieve, and return to the heat.

6 Bring to the boil, add the reserved lobster meat and the cream, season with salt and pepper, and add the cayenne pepper and lemon juice to taste. Serve in warm bowls, garnished with chives.

SHELLFISH KNOW-HOW: *see* Clean a live lobster **p282**
SAVOURY SAUCES AND STOCKS KNOW-HOW: *see* Make fish stock **p484**

Minestrone

This substantial soup has almost infinite variations; you can prepare it throughout the year with whatever vegetables and herbs come into season, and discover your favourite combinations.

PREPARATION TIME **20 minutes, plus soaking** • COOKING TIME **1 hour 45 minutes** • **SERVES 4–6**

100g (3½oz) **dried white cannellini beans**

2 tbsp **olive oil**

2 **celery sticks**, finely chopped

2 **carrots**, finely chopped

1 **onion**, finely chopped

400g (14oz) can **chopped tomatoes**

750ml (1¼ pints) **chicken stock** or **vegetable stock**

salt and freshly ground **black pepper**

60g (2oz) small **short-cut pasta**

4 tbsp chopped **flat-leaf parsley**

40g (1½oz) **Parmesan** or **Grana Padano cheese**, finely grated

1 Put the beans in a large bowl, cover with cold water, and leave to soak for at least 6 hours, or preferably overnight.

2 Drain the beans, place in a large saucepan, and cover with cold water. Bring to the boil over a high heat and boil for 10 minutes, skimming the surface as necessary. Reduce the heat to low, partially cover, and leave the beans to simmer for 1 hour, or until just tender. Drain well and set aside.

3 Heat the oil in the rinsed-out pan over a medium heat. Add the celery, carrots, and onion and fry, stirring occasionally, for 5 minutes or until softened but not browned. Stir in the

beans, chopped tomatoes, and stock, and season to taste with salt and pepper. Bring to the boil, stirring, then cover and leave to simmer for 20 minutes.

4 Add the pasta and simmer for a further 10–15 minutes or until cooked but still firm to the bite. Stir in the parsley and half the cheese, then adjust the seasoning. Serve hot, sprinkled with the remaining cheese.

SAVOURY SAUCES AND STOCKS KNOW-HOW: *see* **Make vegetable stock p484**

Roast tomato soup

It makes such a tremendous difference in flavour when you roast the tomatoes first. They become sweet, and the heat brings out their deliciously deep umami qualities.

PREPARATION TIME **10 minutes** • COOKING TIME **35 minutes** • **SERVES 4**

8 **plum tomatoes**, about 675g (1½lb) in total, quartered

1 **red onion**, cut into 8 wedges

2 **garlic cloves**, unpeeled

3 tbsp **olive oil**

sea salt and freshly ground **black pepper**

1 litre (1¾ pints) hot **vegetable stock**

3 tbsp **sun-dried tomato paste**

1 Preheat the oven to 180°C (350°F/Gas 4) and line a large baking tray with baking parchment. Put the tomatoes, onion, and garlic cloves on the tray, drizzle with oil, and season well with salt and pepper. Roast until the vegetables are soft, caramelized, and slightly browned, removing them from the tray once they are ready. Allow 10–15 minutes for the garlic, 15–20 minutes for the onion, and 25 minutes for the tomatoes. Squeeze the roasted garlic cloves from their skins once they have cooled slightly.

2 Transfer to a blender, add the stock and tomato paste, then whiz until smooth but still slightly chunky. Season with salt and pepper, reheat gently, and serve hot.

FROM **Ordinary** TO **Extraordinary**

Make gluten-free croutons by roasting chickpeas with spices to add a delicious crunch. Preheat the oven to 220°C (425°F/Gas 7). Drain a 400g can of **chickpeas** and pat dry with kitchen paper. Tip into a bowl and mix with 1 tbsp **olive oil** or **chilli oil**, 1 tsp **chilli flakes**, and plenty of **sea salt** and freshly ground **black pepper**. Toss well to coat, spread out on a baking tray and roast for 25 minutes or until crisp, stirring halfway. Allow to cool, then sprinkle a few over each portion of soup, offering the rest in a bowl on the table.

Vichyssoise

Despite its French name, this silky, smooth chilled soup originates from America.
If you make it during winter, remember that it is also wonderful when served hot.

PREPARATION TIME **15 minutes, plus chilling** • COOKING TIME **45 minutes** • **SERVES 4**

30g (1oz) **unsalted butter**

3 large **leeks**, green ends discarded, finely sliced

2 **potatoes**, about 175g (6oz) in total, peeled and chopped

1 **celery stick**, roughly chopped

1.2 litres (2 pints) fresh **vegetable stock**

salt and freshly ground **black pepper**

150ml (5fl oz) **double cream**, plus extra for garnish

2 tbsp snipped **chives**, to serve

1 Heat the butter in a heavy saucepan over a medium heat and add the leeks. Press a piece of damp greaseproof paper on top, cover, and cook, shaking gently from time to time, for 15 minutes, or until the leeks are softened and golden.

2 Add the potatoes, celery, and stock, and season with salt and pepper. Bring to the boil, stirring, then cover and simmer for 30 minutes, or until the vegetables are tender.

3 Remove the pan from the heat and leave to cool slightly, then process in a blender until very smooth, in batches if necessary. Season to taste with salt and pepper, and allow the soup to cool completely before stirring in the cream. Chill for at least 3 hours before serving.

4 To serve, pour into serving bowls. Drizzle a little cream over the top of each bowl of soup, sprinkle with chives, and season with pepper.

FROM **Ordinary** TO
Extraordinary

Transform into a dramatic layered starter or canapé. At the end of step 1, divide the leeks between 2 saucepans. In step 2, add **1 potato** to the first saucepan, and **1 orange-fleshed sweet potato** to the second, then follow the recipe as directed, dividing the remaining ingredients evenly between the saucepans. To serve, chill glasses (or shot glasses if using as a canapé) and add the green-coloured soup to fill half of each glass. Gently spoon on the orange-coloured soup to form the top layer.

SAVOURY SAUCES AND STOCKS KNOW-HOW: *see* Make vegetable stock **p484**

Eggs Benedict

This classic brunch dish is typically served with a slice of ham, or with smoked salmon for Eggs Royale. Homemade hollandaise sauce adds a luxurious touch.

PREPARATION TIME **20 minutes** • COOKING TIME **20 minutes** • **SERVES 4**

vinegar, for poaching

8 large **eggs**

4 **English muffins**

butter, for spreading

FOR THE HOLLANDAISE

2 tbsp **white wine vinegar**

4 **egg yolks**

115g (4oz) **unsalted butter**, melted

salt and freshly ground **black pepper**

juice of ½ **lemon**

1 First make the hollandaise sauce. Heat the vinegar in a small pan and allow to bubble until it reduces by half. Remove from the heat, add 2 tbsp water, then whisk in the egg yolks one at a time.

2 Return the pan to a very low heat and whisk continuously until the mixture is thick and light. Remove from the heat and gradually whisk in the melted butter. Season to taste with salt and pepper, and stir in the lemon juice.

3 Fill 2 large saucepans with water and a drop of vinegar, then bring to a gentle boil. Crack the first egg onto a small plate, then carefully slide into one of the pans. Repeat with

3 more eggs in the first pan, and the remaining 4 eggs in the second. Allow each egg to poach for 3–5 minutes, using a slotted spoon to gently scoop the whites of the eggs over the yolks. Once set, remove the eggs using the slotted spoon, and drain on kitchen paper.

4 Meanwhile, preheat the grill on its highest setting, split each muffin in half, and toast both sides.

5 Butter each muffin half and place 2 on each serving plate. Top each half with a poached egg and spoon the hollandaise sauce over the top.

FROM **Ordinary** TO **Extraordinary**

Reinvent this brunch classic by adding **hot-smoked salmon** under the eggs and using **rich brioche buns** (see p455) instead of muffins. To liven up the hollandaise, substitute **yuzu juice** for the lemon juice.

EGGS AND DAIRY PRODUCTS KNOW-HOW: *see* Poach eggs **p433**
SAVOURY SAUCES AND STOCKS KNOW-HOW: *see* Make hollandaise **p491**

Cheese soufflés

The most popular savoury soufflé is a simple cheese creation such as this. Any hard cheese can be used, but choose one with a fairly robust flavour, such as mature Cheddar, or try a mixture of Gruyère and Parmesan.

PREPARATION TIME **20 minutes** • COOKING TIME **30–35 minutes** • **SERVES 6**

45g (1½oz) **butter**

45g (1½oz) **plain flour**

225ml (8fl oz) **milk**

salt and freshly ground **black pepper**

125g (4½oz) **mature Cheddar cheese**, finely grated

½ tsp **French mustard**

5 large **eggs**, separated

1 tbsp grated **Parmesan cheese**

1 Preheat the oven to 190°C (375°F/Gas 5) and put a baking tray in the oven. Grease six ramekins.

2 Melt the butter in a small saucepan, stir in the flour until smooth, and cook over a medium heat for 1 minute. Whisk in the milk until blended, then bring to the boil, stirring constantly, until thickened and smooth. Remove the pan from the heat, season to taste with salt and pepper, and stir in the Cheddar cheese and mustard.

3 Gradually stir in 4 of the egg yolks into the cheese sauce. The remaining egg yolk can be saved for another recipe.

4 In a large, clean bowl, whisk all the egg whites together until stiff peaks form. Stir 1 tbsp of the whisked egg whites into the cheese mixture to "loosen" it, then gently fold in the rest using a large metal spoon.

5 Divide the mixture between the ramekins. Place them on the baking tray and bake for 10 minutes, or until the soufflés are puffed and golden brown. Serve at once, sprinkled with Parmesan cheese.

FROM **Ordinary** TO **Extraordinary**

Try making a **hot roast tomato–basil sauce** to serve with the soufflés. Roast the tomatoes as for Roast tomato soup (see p15), but blend the mixture without adding stock or tomato paste. Add a **small handful of basil leaves**. Reheat gently and serve in jugs.

EGGS AND DAIRY PRODUCTS KNOW-HOW: *see* Whisk egg whites **p431**
EGGS AND DAIRY PRODUCTS KNOW-HOW: *see* Bake a soufflé **p434**

Quiche Lorraine

The key to success here is not to overcook the quiche, but remove it from the oven while it still has a slight wobble when shaken gently. Overcooked quiche will be rubbery in texture.

PREPARATION TIME **35 minutes, plus chilling** • COOKING TIME **35 minutes** • **SERVES 4–6**

FOR THE PASTRY

225g (8oz) **plain flour**, plus extra for dusting

115g (4oz) **unsalted butter**, cubed

1 **egg yolk**

FOR THE FILLING

200g (7oz) **bacon lardons**

1 **onion**, finely chopped

75g (2½oz) **Gruyère cheese**, grated

4 large **eggs**, lightly beaten

150ml (5fl oz) **double cream**

150ml (5fl oz) **milk**

freshly ground **black pepper**

1 To make the pastry, place the flour and butter in a food processor and blend until the mixture resembles fine crumbs. Add the egg yolk and 3–4 tbsp of chilled water, enough to make a smooth dough. Turn out on a floured surface and knead briefly. Alternatively, rub the butter into the flour with your fingers until crumbly, then add the egg yolk and water. Cover and chill for at least 30 minutes. Preheat the oven to 190°C (375°F/Gas 5).

2 On a lightly floured surface, roll out the pastry and line a 23cm (9in) deep flan tin, pressing the dough to the sides. Prick the base of the pastry and line with greaseproof paper and baking beans. Bake blind for 12 minutes, then remove the paper and beans, and bake for a further 10 minutes, or until lightly golden.

3 Meanwhile, heat a large frying pan and dry-fry the lardons for 3–4 minutes. Add the onion, fry for a further 2–3 minutes, then spread the onions and bacon over the pastry case. Add the cheese.

4 Whisk together the eggs, cream, milk, and black pepper, and pour into the pastry case. Place the tin on a baking tray and bake for 25–30 minutes, or until golden and just set. Allow to set, then slice and serve while still warm.

FROM **Ordinary** TO **Extraordinary**

Make **stunning individual cone-shaped quiches**. Preheat the oven to 180°C (350°F/Gas 4). Cover six ice-cream cones in tin foil, fold 6 **filo pastry sheets** in half, and wrap 1 folded sheet around each cone. Brush with **melted unsalted butter** and bake for 3 minutes, or until crisp. Cool on a wire rack. Make a half quantity of the filling, as directed, then bake in an ovenproof baking dish for 15 minutes, or until lightly set. Serve spoonfuls of filling inside each cone, then add a **crisp-fried bacon rasher** to each, so it sticks out of the cone.

DOUGH, PASTRY, AND CAKE KNOW-HOW: *see* Blind bake **p462**

Omelette aux fines herbes

Hold your nerve here; as so often with egg-based dishes, the best omelettes are served still soft and tender and, if anything, slightly under-cooked.

PREPARATION TIME **5 minutes** • COOKING TIME **6 minutes** • **SERVES 4**

1½ tbsp each chopped **chives**,
flat-leaf parsley, **tarragon**, and **chervil**,
mixed together

100g (3½oz) **unsalted butter**

12 **eggs**

salt and freshly ground **black pepper**

a few **chive stalks**, to garnish

1 Heat an omelette pan or frying pan and melt one-quarter of the butter.

2 For each omelette, break 3 eggs into a small bowl and beat them lightly with a fork. Add some seasoning and one-quarter of the mixed chopped herbs. Pour into the warmed omelette pan. As the omelette starts to set around the outside, draw the set egg into the centre and tilt the pan so that the raw egg fills the space. When almost set, stop stirring, and cook for a further 30 seconds until the omelette is golden brown underneath, but the top is still creamy.

3 Fold the omelette by tilting the pan and shuffling the omelette forward – it should roll up like a large cigar. Roll it onto a warm plate and garnish with a few fresh chive stalks on the side. Repeat for the remaining 3 omelettes, melting fresh butter before cooking each one.

Croque monsieur

A wonderful brunch or lunch, with extra creaminess from the cheese sauce.

PREPARATION TIME **15 minutes** • COOKING TIME **10 minutes** • **SERVES 4**

400g (14oz) **Gruyère cheese**

60g (2oz) **unsalted butter**, plus extra for spreading

2 tbsp **plain flour**

2 tsp **Dijon mustard**

150ml (5fl oz) **milk**

8 slices of **white bread**

8 thin slices of **ham**

1 Preheat the grill on its medium setting. Cut 115g (4oz) of the cheese into thin slices and grate the rest.

2 Melt the butter in a saucepan over a low heat. Remove from the heat and stir in the flour. Return to the hob and cook for 1 minute. Remove from the heat again and stir in the mustard and milk. Return to the hob and cook, stirring until thick and smooth. Stir in the grated cheese, and set aside until ready to use.

3 Toast 4 of the bread slices under the grill on 1 side only. Turn over and spread the untoasted sides lightly with butter and top with the ham and cheese slices. Press the remaining 4 slices of bread on top and spread with the cheese mixture.

4 Grill until the cheese is bubbling and golden brown. Serve at once.

Lobster thermidor

This wonderful dish relies on an irresistibly indulgent wine, Gruyère, and cream sauce, thickened by reducing it quickly over a high heat.

PREPARATION TIME **25 minutes** • COOKING TIME **20 minutes** • SERVES 4

2 cooked **lobsters**, about 675g (1½lb) each

paprika, to garnish

lemon wedges, to serve

FOR THE SAUCE

30g (1oz) **butter**

2 **shallots**, finely chopped

120ml (4fl oz) **white wine**

120ml (4fl oz) **fish stock**

150ml (5fl oz) **double cream**

½ tsp **English mustard**

1 tbsp **lemon juice**

2 tbsp **parsley**, chopped

2 tsp **tarragon**, chopped

salt and freshly ground **black pepper**

75g (2½oz) **Gruyère cheese**, grated

1 Cut the lobsters in half lengthways. Remove the meat from the claws and tail, along with any coral or meat from the head. Cut the meat into bite-sized pieces. Clean out the shells and reserve.

2 To prepare the sauce, melt the butter in a small saucepan, add the shallots, and fry gently until softened but not browned. Add the wine and boil for 2–3 minutes, or until the liquid is reduced by half.

3 Add the stock and cream and boil rapidly, stirring, until reduced and slightly thickened. Stir in the mustard, lemon juice, and herbs, then season to taste with salt and pepper. Stir in half the cheese.

4 Preheat the grill on its highest setting. Add the lobster meat to the sauce, then divide between the lobster shells. Top with the remaining cheese.

5 Place the lobsters on a foil-lined grill pan and grill for 2–3 minutes, or until bubbling and golden. Sprinkle with a little paprika and serve hot with lemon wedges.

Moules marinières

Mussels have a wonderful depth of flavour, which needs only gentle flavouring and this simple base recipe to reveal itself. Serve with a crusty baguette to mop up the fabulous juices.

PREPARATION TIME **20 minutes** • COOKING TIME **10 minutes** • **SERVES 4**

60g (2oz) **unsalted butter**

2 **onions**, finely chopped

1.8kg (4lb) fresh **mussels**, cleaned

2 **garlic cloves**, crushed

600ml (1 pint) **dry white wine**

4 **bay leaves**

2 sprigs of **thyme**

salt and freshly ground **black pepper**

2–4 tbsp chopped **parsley**

1 Melt the butter in a large, heavy, lidded saucepan. Add the onion, and fry gently until softened but not browned. Add the mussels, garlic, wine, bay leaves, and thyme, and season to taste with salt and pepper. Cover, bring to the boil, and cook for 5–6 minutes, or until the mussels have opened, shaking the pan frequently. If you do not have a large enough saucepan for all the mussels, divide the ingredients between 2 pans instead.

2 Remove the open mussels with a slotted spoon, discarding any that remain closed. Transfer the mussels to warmed bowls, cover, and keep warm.

3 Strain the liquid into a pan and bring to the boil. Season to taste with pepper, add the parsley, pour it over the mussels, and serve at once.

FROM **Ordinary** TO **Extraordinary**

Switch up the flavours to make spicy **Vietnamese-style mussels**. Follow the recipe as directed, but substitute **shallots** and **shredded lime leaves** for the onions, bay leaves, and thyme. Add 1 finely chopped **lemongrass stalk**, 1 finely chopped **bird's eye chilli**, and 1 thumb of **fresh root ginger**, peeled and finely chopped. Omit the wine, and instead add the **juice of 1 lime**, 2 tbsp **soy sauce** and 1 tsp **fish sauce**. Substitute the parsley for **coriander**.

SHELLFISH KNOW-HOW: *see* Clean mussels **p286**

Fisherman's pie

There are few one-pot meals more comforting than this. The fish and shellfish can easily be varied depending on what is readily available – check sustainable fishing lists online for up-to-date buying advice and inspiration.

PREPARATION TIME 25 minutes • COOKING TIME 50 minutes–1 hour • SERVES 4

500g (1lb 2oz) **floury potatoes**, such as **King Edward** or **Maris Piper**, peeled and cut into chunks

salt and freshly ground **black pepper**

450ml (15fl oz) **milk**

100g (3½oz) **unsalted butter**, plus extra for topping

300g (10oz) raw **prawns**, shells on

400g (14oz) fresh **haddock** fillets

200g (7oz) undyed **smoked haddock** fillets

4 **black peppercorns**, lightly crushed

1 **bay leaf**

several sprigs of **flat-leaf parsley**

4 tbsp **plain flour**

squeeze of **lemon** juice

2 tbsp **double cream**

4 tbsp chopped **flat-leaf parsley**

pinch of **cayenne pepper**

1 Place the potatoes in a large saucepan with cold salted water. Boil for 10–15 minutes, or until the potatoes are tender when pierced with a knife; drain well. Mash until smooth, then beat in 150ml (5fl oz) of the milk and 60g (2oz) of the butter. Season to taste with salt and pepper. Set aside.

2 Meanwhile, remove the prawn heads and shells, reserving the shells. Devein the prawns and set aside.

3 Put the fresh and smoked haddock in a frying pan with the remaining milk. Gently simmer for 10 minutes, or until the fish flakes easily. Use a slotted spoon to remove the fish from the pan and set aside.

4 Add the prawn shells, peppercorns, bay leaf, and parsley to the pan and simmer over a very low heat for 10 minutes.

5 Meanwhile, preheat the oven to 220°C (425°F/Gas 7). Melt the remaining butter in a saucepan over a medium heat. Sprinkle in the flour and cook, stirring, for 1 minute. Remove from the heat. Strain the milk and gradually stir into the butter mixture. Return to the heat and simmer until the sauce thickens, stirring all the time. Add the lemon juice and cream, and season to taste with salt and pepper. Stir through the chopped parsley, cayenne, and prawns, and flake in the fish, discarding skin and any bones.

6 Spoon the fish mixture into the pie dish, top with the mashed potatoes, and dot with a little extra butter. Place the dish on a baking tray and bake for 20–25 minutes, or until the topping is golden and the filling is hot when you test the centre with a knife. Remove the pie from the oven and serve immediately.

FISH KNOW-HOW: *see* Bone a round fish through the stomach **p268**
FISH KNOW-HOW: *see* Bone a round fish from the back **p269**
FISH KNOW-HOW: *see* Skin a fillet **p273**
SHELLFISH KNOW-HOW: *see* Prepare prawns **p286**

Salade niçoise

A modern tweak on the southern French original, using seared tuna steaks. If you prefer, use good-quality tuna canned in olive oil, drained and broken into flakes.

PREPARATION TIME **25 minutes** • COOKING TIME **10 minutes** • **SERVES 4**

12 baby **new potatoes**, halved

salt and freshly ground **black pepper**

150g (5½oz) **green beans**, trimmed

4 x 150g (5½oz) **tuna steaks**

150ml (5fl oz) **extra virgin olive oil**, plus extra for brushing

8 **anchovy fillets in olive oil**, drained

1 **red onion**, finely sliced

250g (9oz) **plum tomatoes**, quartered lengthways

12 **black olives**

2 **Romaine lettuce hearts**, trimmed and torn into pieces

8–10 **basil leaves**

4 **eggs**, hard-boiled

FOR THE VINAIGRETTE

2 tsp **Dijon mustard**

1 **garlic clove**, finely chopped

3 tbsp **white wine vinegar**

juice of ½ **lemon**

1 Put the potatoes in a saucepan of lightly salted water, bring to the boil and boil for 6 minutes. Add the beans and boil for a further 3–4 minutes, or until just tender. Drain and quickly place the vegetables into a bowl of ice water.

2 Preheat a ridged griddle pan over a medium-high heat. Brush the tuna steaks with 1–2 tbsp olive oil and season to taste with salt and pepper. Sear the tuna steaks for 2 minutes on each side. The centres will still be slightly pink. Set the tuna aside. Drain the potatoes and beans and set aside.

3 Combine the vinaigrette ingredients in a bowl. Whisk together and season to taste with salt and pepper.

4 Place the potatoes, green beans, anchovies, onion, tomatoes, olives, lettuce, and basil in a large bowl. Drizzle with the vinaigrette and gently toss.

5 Divide the salad between 4 plates. Peel and quarter each egg and add them to the plates. Cut the tuna steaks in half and arrange two halves on top of each salad.

VEGETABLES KNOW-HOW *see* Trim, wash, and dry salad leaves **p369**
EGGS AND DAIRY PRODUCTS KNOW-HOW *see* Soft- and hard-boil eggs **p432**

Salmon fishcakes

These have a sophisticated touch of heat from horseradish and spring onions, and great aromatics from dill and lemon.

PREPARATION TIME **30 minutes, plus cooling and chilling** • COOKING TIME **30 minutes** • **SERVES 6**

450g (1lb) **potatoes**, peeled and cut into chunks

900g (2lb) **salmon fillets**, skinned and boned

1 **onion**, halved

2–3 **bay leaves**

1 tsp **black peppercorns**

4 **spring onions**, finely chopped

2 tbsp **horseradish cream**

salt and freshly ground **black pepper**

juice and zest of 1 unwaxed **lemon**

large handful of **dill**, chopped

pinch of **cayenne pepper**

FOR THE COATING

225g (8oz) fresh **breadcrumbs**

2 tbsp snipped **chives** (optional)

2 tbsp chopped **parsley** (optional)

plain flour, for coating

2 **eggs**, lightly beaten

sunflower oil, for frying

1 Place the potatoes in a saucepan of cold water and boil for 20 minutes, or until very tender. Drain, mash, and set aside.

2 Place the salmon in cold water with the onion, bay leaves, and peppercorns. Bring to the boil, simmer for 2 minutes, then turn off the heat and leave to cool for 20 minutes. Drain well, discarding the cooking liquid, and cool.

3 Flake the salmon into a large bowl. Fold in the cooled mashed potatoes and all the other fishcake ingredients. Mix well and shape into 12 round cakes. Ideally, chill for 1 hour before coating.

4 Mix the breadcrumbs with the herbs, if using. Put the flour, eggs, and breadcrumbs into separate shallow bowls. Coat the first fishcake in flour and then in the egg. Finally, roll it in the breadcrumbs so that it is completely coated. Repeat for the remaining fishcakes. Return to the fridge to chill for a further 30 minutes, if possible.

5 Heat the sunflower oil in a frying pan and fry the fishcakes for 3–4 minutes on each side, or until crisp and hot through. Drain on kitchen paper and serve while hot.

FISH KNOW-HOW *See* Bone a round fish through the stomach **p268**
FISH KNOW-HOW *See* Bone a round fish from the back **p269**
FISH KNOW-HOW *See* Skin a fillet **p273**

Sea bass in a salt crust

This does not taste overly salty, just beautifully well-seasoned, and retains all its juices within the crust. Serve with garlic mayonnaise and baby new potatoes.

PREPARATION TIME **5 minutes** • COOKING TIME **22–25 minutes** • **SERVES 4**

1 whole **sea bass**, about 1.3–2kg (3–4½lb),
trimmed and gutted, but not scaled

1kg (2.2lb) **coarse sea salt**

1–2 **egg whites**

splash of **water**

1 Preheat the oven to 220°C (425°F/Gas 7). Rinse the fish inside and out and pat dry with kitchen paper. Spread a layer of salt onto a large piece of foil on a baking tray. Lay the fish on top. Moisten the remaining salt with the egg whites and a splash of water if necessary. Pack this mixture on the fish to completely encase it.

2 Bake in the oven for 22–25 minutes. Lift the fish onto a serving dish. Take to the table and carefully chip off any remaining salt crust. Using clean utensils, peel away the skin and serve the fish straight from the bone.

FISH KNOW-HOW: *See* Gut a fish through the stomach **p266**

Scallops with pancetta

Searing scallops well without over-cooking them is an essential skill in a cook's armoury. The combination of seafood with pork is an Iberian favourite and a truly successful marriage.

PREPARATION TIME **5 minutes** • COOKING TIME **10 minutes** • **SERVES 4**

a knob of **butter**

1½ tbsp **olive oil**

salt and freshly ground **black pepper**

12 fresh **king** or **queen scallops**

150g (5½oz) **pancetta**, cubed

1 Heat a non-stick frying pan over a medium-high heat. Add the butter and 1 tbsp of olive oil.

2 Season the scallops and add to the pan. Sear for 1–2 minutes on one side until golden, then turn over and cook on the other side for 1–2 minutes more, turning the first scallop that went into the pan first and quickly working your way to the last one. Remove from the pan with a slotted spoon, and set aside to keep warm.

3 Add the remaining olive oil to the same pan, tip in the pancetta, and cook for 5–8 minutes until crispy. When cooked, tip over the scallops to serve, along with any juices from the pan. Serve immediately.

SHELLFISH KNOW-HOW: *See* Prepare scallops **p287**

▲ Sea bass in a salt crust

ALL ABOUT
ROAST
BEEF

Rich, hearty, and, if cooked correctly, melt-in-the-mouth, roast beef is a true classic.

Roast rib of beef

PREPARATION TIME **10 minutes** • COOKING TIME **1 hour** • **SERVES 4, PLUS LEFTOVERS**

2.25kg (5lb) **rib of beef**, bone in (use 2 ribs)

olive oil, to coat

salt and freshly ground **black pepper**

1–2 tbsp **wholegrain mustard**

1 Preheat the oven to 200°C (400°F/Gas 6). Rub the beef with olive oil and season with salt and black pepper.

2 Sit the beef in a roasting tin with the bones on the underside, and rub the mustard over the fatty area. Roast in the oven for about 15 minutes until it begins to brown, then reduce the oven temperature to 180°C (350°F/Gas 4). Roast for a further 1 hour, or until cooked to your liking (see overleaf).

3 Remove the beef from the oven and leave to rest in a warm place for about 20 minutes. Slice and serve with crispy roast potatoes, Yorkshire puddings, horseradish sauce, and seasonal vegetables of your choice (see pp38–39). Remember to save your beef bones for making stock.

Beef essentials

Use this chart to identify the best beef cuts for roasting, and how long to cook each for the perfect result.

Beef roasting chart

CUT	DESCRIPTION
Rump/popeseye	From the top of the leg, this has a coarser grain than sirloin but nevertheless yields a good roasting joint. Rump steak is preferred by many to sirloin for its fat content.
Topside/top rump	Boneless, less expensive, and leaner than sirloin but still good for roasting and grilling/frying. When sliced very thinly it is called minute steak.
Sirloin	Tender and marbled with fat, this yields one of the most popular steaks and the best roasting joint of beef on the bone, with a covering of fat. Without the bone, this joint cooks a little quicker.
Fillet	Extremely tender, but can be very lean. The whole fillet, the centre portion called Châteaubriand, and the tapering end or tail are usually roasted but can also be braised. Steaks are often cut thicker, so adjust cooking times.
Ribeye	The trimmed main muscle from the forerib yields a good marbled joint and a tender steak (ribeye/entrecôte).
Brisket	The element of fat makes it a good braising joint. Also good for curing. Slices can be fried but must be served pink or they will toughen.
Forerib	From the shoulder end of the sirloin, this is a less expensive, but excellent bone-in joint for roasting and braising.
Silverside	For braising, this lean joint needs moisture to prevent it from drying out. Slices are suitable for quick cooking only if served pink; sometimes sliced thinly into minute steaks.
T-bone steak	A large, tender cut, including the sirloin and fillet on either side of the bone.
Flank/skirt	Has long fibres and connective tissue so needs either slow cooking or quick frying. Cut across the grain. If flash-fried it must be served very pink or it will toughen.
Thick flank and thin flank	These cuts can be rolled into a joint, sliced, or diced for braising and stewing, or minced.
Rib/short rib/runner	Chunks of rib bone with meat and fat attached. Stew to make a hearty, rustic dish.
Chuck/blade	With a variety of marbling and connective tissue, these shoulder cuts are superb for braising, stewing, and mincing.

ROAST

Rump joint: 190°C (375°F/Gas 5). 20 min per 450g (1lb) plus 20 min for rare; 25 min per 450g (1lb) plus 25 min for medium; 30 min per 450g (1lb) plus 30 min for well-done.

Roast topside joint as rump joint.

Sirloin joint bone-in: Preheat oven to 230°C (450°F/Gas 8). Roast for 25 min. Reduce heat to 190°C (375°F/Gas 5), then roast 12–15 min per 450g (1lb) for rare; 20 min per 450g (1lb) for medium; 25 min per 450g (1lb) for well-done. Rest 20–30 min. Boneless sirloin joint: Preheat oven to 190°C (375°F/Gas 5). Roast 20 min per 450g (1lb) plus 20 min for rare; 25 min per 450g (1lb) plus 25 min for medium; 30 min per 450g (1lb) plus 30 min for well-done. Rest 20–30 min.

Whole fillet, Châteaubriand, and fillet tail: Preheat oven to 230°C (450°F/Gas 8). Brown meat in hot oil in a frying pan, then place in oven. Roast for 10–12 min per 450g (1lb) for rare; 12–15 min per 450g (1lb) for medium; 14–16 min per 450g (1lb) for well-done. Rest 10 min.

Roast ribeye joint as rump joint.

Brisket joint: Preheat oven to 180°C (350°F/Gas 4). Pot-roast for 30–40 min per 450g (lb) plus 30–40 min.

Roast forerib joint as bone-in sirloin joint.

Not recommended.

Not recommended.

Not recommended.

Not recommended.

Not recommended.

Not recommended.

Maximize flavour

1 When preparing beef for roasting, remove the meat from the refrigerator in advance to allow it to come to room temperature. Preheat the oven. Brush the meat with oil and scatter over fresh herbs, such as thyme or rosemary. Alternatively, you could make multiple cuts into the fat and stick slivers of garlic and herbs inside. Position the meat, rib-side down, in a roasting tin and place in the oven.

2 After 20 minutes, reduce the oven temperature (see chart, left), then continue roasting for the calculated amount of time (about 2 hours or more, depending on the size), basting occasionally to keep the meat moist and flavourful.

Beef essentials

It's important to leave your meat to rest – and you can use the resting time to perfect the classic roast beef trimmings.

Test and rest

The most accurate way to test that your roast is done is by inserting a meat thermometer (50°C/120°F for medium rare). Before carving, leave the roast to stand for 15–30 minutes, covered with kitchen foil. Letting the meat rest after roasting allows the muscles to relax, so the juices are retained within the meat and carving is easier. The meat will not go cold during this time – as long as it is covered and not cut into, it will stay hot inside. This leaves plenty of time for you to turn your attention to the all-important trimmings.

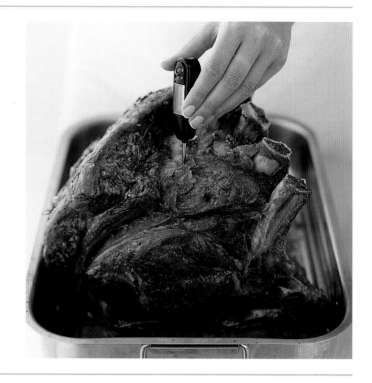

Yorkshire puddings

PREPARATION TIME **20 minutes**
COOKING TIME **25–35 minutes**
SERVES 6

125g (4½oz) **plain flour**

pinch of **salt**

2 **eggs**

300ml (10fl oz) **milk**

1–2 tbsp **sunflower oil** or **corn oil**

1 Preheat the oven to 220°C (425°F/Gas 7). Sift the flour into a bowl and add the salt. Make a well, pour in the eggs and a little milk. Stir the mixture, adding the flour gradually, then the remaining milk. Whisk with a balloon whisk, then refrigerate for 30 minutes.

2 Add a little oil to each hole of the bun tin and put in the oven for 5 minutes. Remove, then pour in the batter. Cook for 20–30 minutes, until risen and crisp.

Crispy roast potatoes

PREPARATION TIME **25 minutes**
COOKING TIME **40–55 minutes**
SERVES 4

900g (2lb) **floury potatoes**, such as **Maris Piper**, peeled and quartered

sea salt

1 tbsp **plain flour**

4 tsp **olive oil**

1 Preheat the oven to 220°C (425°F/Gas 7). Put the potatoes in a pan of salted water, boil then "nearly" cook over a medium heat for 10–15 minutes. Drain, then return to the pan.

2 Add the flour, put the lid on, and shake the pan. Put the oil in a large roasting tin, and pop it in the oven until hot. Remove from the oven and add the potatoes one by one, turning each in the oil. Add the salt and return to the oven for 30–40 minutes, until golden.

Horseradish sauce

PREPARATION TIME **10 minutes**
MAKES 250ML (8FL OZ)

75g (2½oz) fresh **horseradish**, grated

1 tsp **English mustard**

1 tbsp **white wine vinegar**

1 tsp **caster sugar**

juice of ½ **lemon**

150ml (5fl oz) **double cream**

salt and freshly ground **black pepper**

1 Put all the ingredients in a large bowl and whisk to a soft peak consistency by hand, or with an electric hand whisk. Season to taste with salt and pepper.

2 Spoon into a serving bowl and chill until you are ready to serve.

Beef Stroganoff

This is a rich dish, so serve it on a bed of plain rice, or buttered noodles, with a crisp green salad.

PREPARATION TIME **15 minutes** • COOKING TIME **25 minutes** • **SERVES 4**

675g (1½lb) **fillet**, **rump**, or **sirloin steak**, trimmed

3 tbsp **plain flour**

salt and freshly ground **black pepper**

1 tbsp **paprika**, plus extra for sprinkling

60g (2oz) **unsalted butter** or 4 tbsp **olive oil**

1 **onion**, thinly sliced

225g (8oz) **chestnut mushrooms**, sliced

300ml (10fl oz) **soured cream** or **crème fraîche**

1 tbsp **French mustard**

lemon juice

1 Thinly slice the steak into 5cm (2in) strips. Season the flour with salt, pepper, and paprika, then coat the beef strips in the flour.

2 Heat half the butter or oil in a deep frying pan. Add the onion and fry over a low heat for 8–10 minutes, or until soft and golden. Add the mushrooms and continue to fry for a few minutes, or until the mushrooms are just soft.

3 Remove the onions and mushrooms and keep warm. Increase the heat and, when the pan is hot, add the remaining butter or oil, put in the beef strips, and fry briskly, stirring, for 3–4 minutes.

4 Return the onions and mushrooms to the pan and cook, stirring, for 1 minute.

5 Reduce the heat, stir in the cream and mustard, and cook gently for 1 minute; do not allow the cream to come to the boil.

6 Season with salt and pepper, then add lemon juice to taste. Serve immediately.

Châteaubriand with béarnaise

A traditional dish that cannot be bettered.

PREPARATION TIME **15 minutes** • COOKING TIME **20 minutes** • SERVES 2

450g (1lb) **Châteaubriand** (beef fillet, centre cut)

salt and freshly ground **black pepper**

50g (1¾oz) **butter**

2 tbsp **olive oil**

FOR THE BÉARNAISE SAUCE

100ml (3½fl oz) **white wine**

2 tbsp **white wine vinegar**

1 **shallot**, finely chopped

1 tbsp chopped **tarragon**

2 **egg yolks**

100g (3½oz) **unsalted butter**, cubed

1 Preheat the oven to 230°C (450°F/Gas 8). Make the béarnaise sauce: combine the wine, vinegar, shallot, and half of the tarragon in a small pan and boil until reduced to 2 tbsp. Pour this into a heatproof bowl set over a pan of barely simmering water. Stir the egg yolks into the mixture one at a time. Continue to stir constantly as you gradually add the butter, allowing one piece to melt before adding the next, until the sauce thickens. If the sauce curdles, beat in a few drops of water. As soon as all the butter has been incorporated, remove the sauce from the heat and strain. Add the remaining tarragon and season with salt and pepper. Keep warm.

2 Season the beef with black pepper. Heat the butter and oil in a heavy frying pan. When the butter stops foaming, add the beef, and brown well on all sides.

3 Transfer to the oven and roast for 10–12 minutes. Remove from the oven and allow to rest in a warm place for 8–10 minutes (for medium-rare). If preferred, leave it to rest for longer (up to 20 minutes).

4 Slice the beef into rounds and serve with the warm béarnaise sauce.

Steak au poivre

Use black peppercorns for more warmth, or green for a sharper note.

PREPARATION TIME **10 minutes** • COOKING TIME **12 minutes** • SERVES 4

4 **sirloin** or **fillet steaks**, 225g (8oz) each

½ tsp **mustard powder**

1–2 tsp **black** or pickled **green peppercorns**, crushed

2 tbsp **sunflower oil**

4 tbsp **sherry** or **brandy**

150ml (5fl oz) **crème fraîche**

1 If using fillet steak, flatten slightly with a meat mallet or rolling pin. Sprinkle the steaks with the mustard, then press the peppercorns firmly onto both sides.

2 Heat the oil in a frying pan over a high heat, and fry the steaks for 2–3 minutes on each side for rare, 4 minutes for medium, and 5–6 minutes for well done. Remove from the pan, wrap in foil and leave to rest in a warm place.

3 Stir the sherry into the pan juices, add the crème fraîche, and simmer gently, stirring, for 2–3 minutes, or until just reduced. Serve the steaks with the sauce.

MEAT KNOW-HOW *See* Cook steaks to perfection **p324**

Boeuf bourguignon

Make sure the beef is not cut too small here, as large pieces give the best, juiciest result. Ideally, ask a butcher to cut it for you, or buy the meat in one piece and cut it yourself, as pre-cut packages of braising steak are often in much smaller pieces.

PREPARATION TIME **25 minutes** • COOKING TIME **2 hours 30 minutes** • **SERVES 4**

175g (6oz) **streaky bacon rashers**, chopped

1–2 tbsp **olive oil**

900g (2lb) lean **braising steak**, cut into 4cm (1½in) cubes

12 small **shallots**

1 tbsp **plain flour**

300ml (10fl oz) **beaujolais**, or other red wine

300ml (10fl oz) **beef stock**

115g (4oz) **button mushrooms**

1 **bay leaf**

1 tsp **dried herbes de Provence**

salt and freshly ground **black pepper**

4 tbsp chopped **parsley**, to garnish

mashed **potatoes**, to serve

1 Preheat the oven to 160°C (325°F/Gas 3). Fry the bacon in a non-stick frying pan until lightly browned. Drain on kitchen paper and transfer to a casserole.

2 Depending on how much fat is left from the bacon, add a little oil to the pan if necessary so that you have about 2–3 tbsp. Fry the beef in batches over a high heat, transferring to the casserole as they brown.

3 Reduce the heat to medium and fry the shallots. Transfer to the casserole with a slotted spoon and stir the flour into the remaining fat in the frying pan. If the pan is quite dry, mix the flour with a little of the wine or stock. Pour the wine and stock into the frying pan and bring to the boil, stirring constantly until smooth.

4 Add the mushrooms, bay leaf, and dried herbs. Season to taste with salt and pepper and pour the contents of the pan over the meat and shallots in the casserole. Cover and cook in the oven for 2 hours, or until the meat is very tender.

5 Garnish with chopped parsley and serve with a side of mashed potatoes.

SAVOURY SAUCES AND STOCKS KNOW-HOW *See* **Make beef stock p485**

Steak and kidney pie

A traditional pie that deserves a revival. Serve it with English mustard, fluffy parsnip and potato mash, and lightly steamed shredded greens.

PREPARATION TIME **20 minutes** • COOKING TIME **2 hours 15 minutes** • **SERVES 4**

3 tbsp **plain flour**, plus extra for dusting

salt and freshly ground **black pepper**

500g (1lb 2oz) lean **braising steak**, cut into 2cm (¾in) pieces

175g (6oz) **ox kidney**, trimmed and diced

3 tbsp **sunflower oil**

1 large **onion**, chopped

1 large **carrot**, chopped

115g (4oz) **button mushrooms**, halved

350ml (12fl oz) **beef stock**

1 **bay leaf**

½ tsp **dried thyme**

1 tbsp **Worcestershire sauce**

1 tbsp **dark soy sauce**

350g (12oz) **rough puff pastry**

lightly beaten **egg**, to glaze

1 Season the flour well with salt and pepper. Toss the steak and kidney in the flour, shaking off any excess.

2 Heat 2 tbsp of the oil in a large non-stick frying pan and fry the steak and kidney in batches over a high heat until browned on all sides. Transfer the meat to a large saucepan.

3 Add the remaining oil to the frying pan, and fry the onion and carrot over a medium heat for 5 minutes. Add the mushrooms and cook for 3–4 minutes, or until beginning to brown, stirring frequently.

4 Transfer the fried vegetables to the saucepan along with the stock, bay leaf, thyme, Worcestershire sauce, and soy sauce. Bring to the boil, reduce the heat, cover with the lid, and simmer gently for 1½ hours, or until the meat is tender.

5 Using a slotted spoon, transfer the meat and vegetables to a 1.7 litre (3 pint) pie dish. Add enough gravy to cover, reserving the remainder. Leave to cool.

6 Preheat the oven to 200°C (400°F/Gas 6). Roll out the pastry on a lightly floured surface to 5cm (2in) larger all round than the dish. Cut a 2cm (¾in) strip from around the pastry, brush the rim of the dish with water, and place the strip on the rim. Brush the strip with water. Place the pastry over the dish and press the edges down to seal against the pastry strip below. Trim and knock up the edge with the back of a knife, then crimp all round. Make a hole in the middle for steam to escape. Make leaves out of the pastry trimmings and use to decorate.

7 Brush the pastry with beaten egg. Place the pie on a baking tray and bake for 25 minutes, or until the pastry is puffed and dark golden. Serve with the remaining gravy reheated and offered separately.

DOUGH, PASTRY, AND CAKE KNOW-HOW *See* Rough puff pastry **p456**
DOUGH, PASTRY, AND CAKE KNOW-HOW *See* Roll out puff pastry **p459**
DOUGH, PASTRY, AND CAKE KNOW-HOW *See* Trim and decorate pastry **p463**

Osso buco

This classic, rich veal stew from Milan is flavoured with garlic and salty anchovies, and is traditionally served with Risotto alla milanese (see p100).

PREPARATION TIME **15 minutes** • COOKING TIME **1 hour 45 minutes** • **SERVES 4**

3 tbsp **plain flour**

salt and freshly ground **black pepper**

4 thick **veal osso buco** slices (from shank)

60g (2oz) **unsalted butter**

4 tbsp **olive oil**

4 **garlic cloves**, chopped

½ **onion**, chopped

4 tbsp **tomato purée**

about 120ml (4fl oz) **beef stock** or **water**

4 tbsp chopped **flat-leaf parsley**

2 **anchovy fillets in oil**, drained and chopped

grated zest of 1 unwaxed **lemon**

1 Season the flour with salt and pepper, then roll the veal in the flour and shake off any excess.

2 Melt the butter with the oil in a large flameproof casserole. Add the veal, fry for 5 minutes, or until browned on all sides. Remove and set aside. Add the garlic and onion to the casserole and fry gently, stirring occasionally, for 5 minutes, or until softened but not browned.

3 Stir in the tomato purée, stock or water, and salt and pepper to taste, and bring to the boil. Reduce the heat to low, cover the casserole and simmer for 1½ hours, or until the veal is tender. Check as it cooks and add more liquid, if necessary. The gravy should be thick but not stiff.

4 To serve, combine the parsley, drained anchovy fillets, and lemon zest in a bowl. Stir the mixture into the casserole and serve immediately.

VEGETABLES KNOW-HOW *See* Peel and chop garlic **p363**

ALL ABOUT
ROAST
LAMB

Perfect this Sunday lunch favourite by adding lots of flavour with punchy garlic and fragrant rosemary.

Roast leg of lamb

PREPARATION TIME **15 minutes** • COOKING TIME **1 hour 45 minutes** • **SERVES 6, PLUS LEFTOVERS**

2kg (4½lb) **leg of lamb**

4 **garlic cloves**, peeled and halved

handful of fresh **rosemary sprigs**

salt and freshly ground **black pepper**

600ml (1 pint) hot **vegetable stock**

1 tsp **redcurrant jelly**

1 Preheat the oven to 200°C (400°F/Gas 6). Spike the lamb leg evenly all over with the point of a sharp knife, then stuff the garlic cloves and small sprigs of rosemary into the holes (see p48). Season the lamb all over with salt and black pepper.

2 Sit the leg of lamb in a roasting tin, and roast in the oven for about 15 minutes, until it begins to brown. Reduce the oven temperature to 180°C (350°F/Gas 4), and continue to roast for a further 1 hour (for rare), basting it with its juices halfway through the cooking time; allow 1½ hours for well done. Remove the lamb to a large plate, cover with foil, and leave to rest in a warm place for 15 minutes while you make the gravy.

3 To make the gravy, tilt the roasting tin at a slight angle, and skim off any fat. Sit the tin over a high heat on the hob or stovetop. Add the stock and redcurrant jelly, and bring to the boil, scraping up any bits from the bottom of the tin with a wooden spoon. Reduce the heat slightly, and simmer, stirring all the time, for 5–8 minutes. Taste, and season if needed. Carve at the table, and serve with roast or creamy mashed potato, fresh mint sauce, and seasonal vegetables.

Lamb essentials

Use this chart to identify the best lamb cuts for roasting, and how long to cook each. Then perfect the classic accompaniment: mint sauce.

Lamb roasting chart

CUT	DESCRIPTION	ROAST
Leg	On the bone or boned and rolled, the hind leg is a prime roasting cut. Half leg joints are either fillet (rump) end or shank end. Can be boned and butterflied for barbecuing. Tender steaks and chops (gigot chops) are cut from the leg or chump (rump). Diced boneless leg meat is suitable for kebabs and stews.	Leg steaks and chops (2.5cm/1in thick): Preheat oven to 200°C (400°F/Gas 6). Brush meat with butter or oil and roast for 30–45 min. Leg joint, bone-in or boneless: roast for 25–30 min per 450g (1lb), then rest 5 min per 450g (1lb).
Saddle	A prime bone-in roasting joint from the back of the lamb, consisting of both loins joined together. The fillet/filet mignon is a tiny tender muscle underneath the backbone, cooked whole.	Roast saddle as leg joint.
Loin	The most tender muscle above the backbone. Joints can be left on the bone or boned and rolled. Loin chops include the loin eye; double loin chops include the fillet and sometimes kidney. Barnsley chops, sliced through the whole loin, include the loin eye and fillet on either side of backbone. Butterfly/Valentine steaks are nearly sliced through and opened out to form thin, heart shapes. Noisettes/medallions are small, round loin steaks.	Roast loin and Barnsley chops as leg steaks and chops. Not recommended for butterfly steaks. Loin joint: Preheat oven to 220°C (425°F/Gas 7). Brown joint on all sides, then roast for 8–10 min; rest for 5–10 min.
Best end of neck	From the fore end of the loin, best end gives cutlets when sliced through the bone. The neck fillet makes a good mini-roast. When trimmed of fat, and the chine bone is removed, best end becomes a rack. If the rib ends are exposed it is called a French rack. Two racks leaning together form a guard of honour; two formed into a circle and stuffed make a crown roast.	Roast neck fillet and cutlets as leg steaks and chops. Roast rack of lamb as loin joint. Roast crown roast, guard of honour, and best end joints as leg joint.
Shoulder	May be the whole shoulder, or halved into blade end or knuckle end, and bone-in or boned and rolled, sometimes with stuffing. Cut into chops or steaks, on or off the bone, and into boneless dice, which can be quite fatty.	Shoulder joint, bone-in or boneless: Preheat oven to 200°C (400°F/Gas 6). Roast for 20–30 min per 450g (1lb) plus 30 min. Rest for 30 min.
Shank	A tasty cut from the end of the fore and back legs needing long, slow cooking. Back leg shanks are the plumpest.	Not recommended.
Breast	A cheaper cut from under the ribs. If boned, good for stuffing and rolling.	Not recommended.
Flank	Tougher cut suitable for stuffing and slow cooking, or for mincing.	Not recommended.
Scrag end	Slices of neck on the bone; sometimes boned and diced.	Not recommended.

Maximize flavour

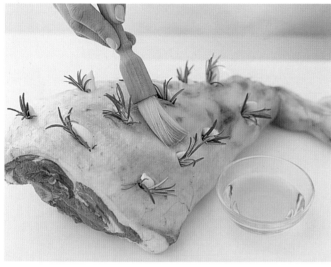

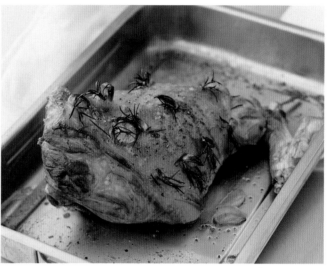

1 Using a sharp knife, make deep slits over the joint 5cm (2in) apart. Press halved garlic cloves deep into the holes with some rosemary tips. Brush the meat with oil or melted butter, and season with black pepper and salt.

2 Place the lamb in the roasting tin in the middle of the oven and roast as per instructions (see chart, opposite). Remove from the hot oven, cover with foil, and let rest for 20–30 minutes.

Mint sauce

PREPARATION TIME **10 minutes**
SERVES 4

handful of **mint leaves**, finely chopped

1–2 tsp **sugar**

1 tbsp **white wine vinegar**

1 Put the mint in a serving bowl and add the sugar and vinegar. Set aside to infuse for 10 minutes.

2 Stir well to make sure the sugar has dissolved, then taste and adjust the seasoning, adding more sugar or vinegar, if needed.

Shepherd's pie

Traditionally, this recipe would be cooked on Monday with meat left over from a Sunday roast. This version is topped with a leek-enhanced mash.

PREPARATION TIME **30 minutes** • COOKING TIME **30 minutes** • SERVES 4–6

675g (1½lb) raw **minced lamb** or precooked **leftover lamb**, finely chopped

2 tbsp **sunflower oil**

1 large **onion**, chopped

1 **garlic clove**, crushed

2 **carrots**, sliced

90ml (3fl oz) **dry red wine**

2 tbsp **plain flour**

250ml (8fl oz) **lamb stock** or **gravy**

1 tbsp **Worcestershire sauce**

2 tbsp chopped **flat-leaf parsley**

1 tbsp **rosemary**, finely chopped

salt and freshly ground **black pepper**

FOR THE POTATO AND LEEK MASH

900g (2lb) **floury potatoes**, such as **King Edward**, peeled and cut into large chunks

2 large **leeks**, cut in half lengthways, sliced

60g (2oz) **unsalted butter**

150ml (5fl oz) **milk**, warmed

1 To make the leek mash, place the potato chunks in a large saucepan, cover with water, and bring to the boil. Boil for 12 minutes, then add the leeks, and cook for a further 5 minutes, or until the vegetables are tender, and drain.

2 Mash the potatoes and leeks and return them to a low heat. Stir in the butter and milk and season to taste with salt and pepper. Preheat the oven to 200°C (400°F/Gas 6).

3 To make the filling, if using minced lamb, fry it in a large frying pan over a medium-high heat, stirring, for 5 minutes, or until lightly browned and all the grains are separate. Pour off the fat, remove the meat from the pan, and set aside.

4 In the same pan, heat the oil. Fry the onion and garlic, stirring for 3–5 minutes, or until softened, then add the carrots. Add the cooked mince or chopped precooked lamb to the pan and stir together.

5 Add the wine, increase the heat to high, and cook for 2–3 minutes. Stir in the flour once the wine has evaporated. Stir in the stock, Worcestershire sauce, parsley, and rosemary, and season to taste with salt and pepper. Bring to the boil, then reduce the heat to low, and simmer for 5 minutes.

6 Spoon the filling into a large ovenproof dish and top with the potato and leek mash. Place the dish on a baking tray and bake for 30 minutes, or until the mash is golden. Leave to rest for 5 minutes, then serve straight from the dish.

VEGETABLES KNOW-HOW *See* Mash potatoes **p374**

Rack of lamb with flageolet beans and herbs

This cut of lamb is expensive, and so deserves to be cooked well. This recipe will produce tender, juicy, and flavoursome cutlets. Serve with new potatoes.

PREPARATION TIME **15 minutes** • COOKING TIME **40 minutes** • **SERVES 4**

1 **rack of lamb** with 8 cutlets

½ tbsp **olive oil**

a few **rosemary sprigs**, leaves finely chopped

salt and freshly ground **black pepper**

150ml (5fl oz) hot **vegetable stock**

1 tsp **redcurrant jelly**

400g can **flageolet beans**, drained

handful of **mint leaves**, finely chopped

1 Preheat the oven to 200°C (400°F/Gas 6). Smother the lamb with the oil, sprinkle over the rosemary, and season well with salt and pepper. Sit the rack in a roasting tin and put in the oven to roast for 40 minutes for pink lamb, or longer if you like your meat well done.

2 Remove the lamb from the roasting tin and keep warm, covered with foil, while you prepare the beans. Place the tin on the hob over a medium to high heat, add the stock, and bring to the boil. Reduce to a simmer, stir in the redcurrant jelly until dissolved, then stir through the flageolet beans and simmer gently for 5 minutes. Remove from the heat and stir through the mint.

3 Slice the rack into 8 cutlets and serve with the beans.

FROM **Ordinary** TO **Extraordinary**

Impart an extra punch of flavour to the lamb with a **panko-herb crust**. Combine 75g (2½oz) **panko breadcrumbs** with 6 tbsp **mixed fresh herbs** (such as **thyme**, **parsley**, **rosemary**, or **mint**). Remove the lamb from the oven 10 minutes into the cooking time, coat with a little extra olive oil, press the panko-herb mixture on to the surface of the meat, then return it to the oven for another 30 minutes. Just before serving, process the bean mixture in a food processor to create a **smooth flageolet purée** to contrast with the crunch of the crusted lamb.

ALL ABOUT
ROAST
PORK

Shards of super-crisp crackling giving way to succulent, tender meat is roast pork perfection.

Roast pork loin

PREPARATION TIME **20 minutes** • COOKING TIME **1 hour 45 minutes** • **SERVES 6, PLUS LEFTOVERS**

2kg (4½lb) **boneless pork loin**, skin scored

4 **garlic cloves**, grated or finely chopped

handful of **black olives**, pitted and finely chopped

pinch of **dried oregano**

sea salt and freshly ground **black pepper**

olive oil, to coat

1 Preheat the oven to 220°C (425°F/Gas 7). Lay the pork out skin-side down. Mix the garlic, olives, and oregano in a bowl, and season with salt and black pepper. Rub the mixture in a line down the middle of the pork, then roll the pork up tightly and secure with string. Sit the roll in a large roasting tin, cut-side down. Rub all over with olive oil, then rub sea salt into the cuts.

2 Roast the pork in the oven for about 20 minutes until the skin is really golden and crispy for perfect crackling. Reduce the oven temperature to 190°C (375°F/Gas 4), and continue to roast for a further 1 hour to 1¼ hours until the pork is cooked through. Remove to a large plate, and leave to rest in a warm place for about 15 minutes.

3 Cut the pork into slices, and serve with gravy made with the pan juices, apple sauce (see p57), crispy roast potatoes (see p39), and seasonal vegetables – and a generous piece of crackling for each portion.

Pork essentials

Use this chart to identify the best pork cuts for roasting, and how long to cook each. Then perfect the art of crackling and apple sauce, too.

Pork roasting chart

CUT	DESCRIPTION	ROAST
Leg	The hind leg is a prime but lean roasting joint, bone-in or boned and rolled. Leg steaks are lean, boneless slices; escalopes (schnitzels) are thinner. Cubed boneless leg is suitable for kebabs and stir-frying.	Leg joint: Preheat oven to 220°C (425°F/Gas 7). Roast for 30 min, then reduce heat to 160°C (325°F/Gas 3) and cook for 23 min per 450g (1lb). Rest for 20–30 min.
Chump	From the rump end of the back, this yields a roasting joint that is usually boned and rolled, as well as the largest of the pork chops.	Roast chump joint as leg joint.
Loin	Tender loin joints are sold on the bone with skin on, and also boned and skinless. Rack is a joint from the fore end of the loin, sometimes with the skin on; two racks tied together and stuffed become a crown roast. Loin is cut into chops, with bone, and into steaks, which are slices with a covering of fat on one side.	Roast loin joint and rack as leg joint.
Belly	A fatty cut, boned and rolled as a joint, or sliced/diced for grilling and frying or marinating and slow-cooking. Spare ribs, trimmed from inside the belly, are a popular cut for marinating and grilling or baking.	Spare ribs and slices: Preheat oven to 180°C (350°F/Gas 4). Roast for 20–30 min, then coat with marinade/sauce and roast for a further 10–15 min until well glazed. Or slow-roast at 160°C (325°F/Gas 3) for 1–1½ hours, basting with liquid or sauce; increase heat to 200°C (400°F/Gas 6) and roast for 20–30 min to brown and glaze. Belly joint: Preheat oven to 220°C (425°F/Gas 7). Score skin and rub with salt. Roast for 20 min, then reduce heat to 150°C (300°F/Gas 2) and cook for 3–4 hours.
Shoulder	Shoulder/hand/blade joint may be on the bone or boned and stuffed; slow-roast for delicious flavour. A steak is a succulent slice of shoulder; a chop includes some bone. Diced, boneless, forequarter meat is suitable for stews.	Shoulder/hand/blade joint: Preheat oven to 220°C (425°F/Gas 7). Score skin and rub with salt. Brown for 30 min, then reduce heat to 150°C (300°F/Gas 2) and continue roasting for 3–3½ hours.
Trotters	Need very slow simmering; then they are cooled, stuffed, and grilled.	After cooking and cooling, halve, brush with butter, and roll in breadcrumbs. Roast at 200°C (400°F/Gas 6) for 15–20 min, or until crisp and brown.
Head and cheek/ jowl	Pig's head is mostly used to make brawn. Cheek and jowl are fatty cuts from the head that can be used like belly.	Head: Preheat oven to 190°C (375°F/Gas 5). After braising, protect ears with foil and roast for 30–45 min to colour; remove foil for the last 15 min.
Fillet/tenderloin	A slim, tender, tapering muscle from the hind end of the loin that is usually cooked whole. May be sliced into medallions, which when part-sliced and opened out become Valentine steaks.	Not recommended.
Neck/collar	A well-marbled cut that can be sliced, diced, or cooked as a joint.	Not recommended.

Make perfect crackling

1 Using a very sharp knife, score the rind of a pork shoulder widthways, working from the centre, outwards. Repeat for the other end. Rub the entire shoulder with a little oil, then massage the rind liberally with sea salt.

2 When finished resting, hold the meat with a carving fork and cut just beneath the crackling. Lift away the crackling in one piece. Using kitchen scissors or a sharp knife, cut the crackling crossways in half. Serve alongside the roasted meat.

Apple sauce

PREPARATION TIME **10 minutes**
COOKING TIME **10 minutes**
SERVES 4

450g (1lb) **cooking apples**, peeled, cored, and quartered

2–3 tbsp **caster sugar** (depending on the tartness of the apples)

1 Put the apples in a pan, sprinkle over 1 tbsp of water, then add the sugar. Cover and cook over a low heat for 10 minutes, or until the apples have begun to break down.

2 Stir with a wooden spoon until the sauce reaches your preferred consistency – either a smooth purée or more chunky. Taste and add more sugar, if required. Serve warm or cold with roast pork.

Pork belly with onions and potatoes

A delicious one-pot Sunday roast, which gives up lots of wonderful juices.
Be sure to skim the surface of fat before serving, for the best results.

PREPARATION TIME **10 minutes** • COOKING TIME **1 hour 50 minutes** • **SERVES 6**

1kg (2¼lb) piece of **pork belly**

1 tsp **sea salt**

6 tbsp **olive oil**

3 large **red onions**, each cut into 8 wedges

4 large **potatoes**, cut into wedges

250g (9oz) **chestnut mushrooms**, halved

300ml (10fl oz) **medium-dry cider**

4 **garlic cloves**, chopped

1 heaped tbsp **thyme**

600ml (1 pint) light **vegetable stock**

1 tsp freshly ground **black pepper**

1 Preheat the oven to 220°C (425°F/Gas 7). Score the skin of the pork belly deeply, then rub the salt and 2 tbsp of the oil into it. Transfer to a baking tray and place in the oven for 20 minutes, or until the skin has crisped up. Remove from the oven and reduce the temperature to 160°C (325°F/Gas 3).

2 While the pork is roasting, heat the remaining oil in a large frying pan, add the onions and potatoes, and cook for 10 minutes, stirring constantly. Add the mushrooms and

cook for 5 minutes. Add the cider and cook for 2 minutes. Transfer the mixture to a large baking dish, add the garlic, thyme, stock, and pepper, and combine well. Nestle the pork in the mixture, ensuring the crackling is not covered, and roast in the oven for 1½ hours.

3 Allow to rest for 10 minutes, then cut the pork up with kitchen scissors and serve with steamed broccoli or greens.

FROM **Ordinary** TO **Extraordinary**

Cut through the richness of this pork dish with **quick-pickled apples**. Core **3 tart apples** and cut them, along with **2 shallots**, into 5mm (¼in) wedges. Place in a jar with a few **black peppercorns**, **allspice berries** and **juniper berries**. Bring to the boil 1 tbsp **honey**, 120ml (4fl oz) **white wine vinegar** and 4 tbsp **water**, adding **sea salt** to taste, then pour over the apples and shallots. Let cool to room temperature, then eat immediately, or within 1 week. Store in the fridge.

Honey-glazed ham

A perfect centrepiece for a festive occasion, this roast ham will serve a throng of people and works out as an economical solution for a large group.

PREPARATION TIME **15 minutes** • COOKING TIME **2 hours** • SERVES 8–10

1.5kg (3lb 3oz) boneless **gammon joint**

1 **onion**, quartered

2 **bay leaves**

6 **peppercorns**

handful of **cloves**

finely grated zest and juice of 1 **orange**

3 tbsp set **honey**

1 Place the gammon in a large saucepan with water to cover. Add the onion, bay leaves, and peppercorns. Bring slowly to the boil, then simmer for 1½ hours. Remove from the pan. Allow to cool.

2 Preheat the oven to 200°C (400°F/Gas 6). Using a sharp knife, carefully remove the skin from the ham and discard. Place the ham in a roasting tin, cut a criss-cross pattern in the fat and push a clove into the centre of each diamond. Combine the orange zest, honey, and 2 tbsp of the orange juice, then brush the surface of the ham with the mixture.

3 Bake for 10 minutes, then baste with the remaining glaze. Return to the oven and bake for 20 minutes, or until golden. Allow to rest before carving. Also delicious served cold.

FROM **Ordinary** TO **Extraordinary**

Update this dish with deeply savoury Japanese flavours to make a **miso-glazed ham**. Simmer the gammon as instructed, then make a glaze by mixing together 2 tbsp **miso paste**, 2 tbsp **mirin** and 4 tbsp **ume plum seasoning** or **honey**. Proceed with the recipe as instructed, omitting the cloves.

Cassoulet

This hearty, slow-cooked dish originates from the south of France. Rich and filling, it is an ideal dinner for cold winter evenings.

PREPARATION TIME **30 minutes, plus soaking** • COOKING TIME **3 hours 45 minutes** • **SERVES 4–6**

350g (12oz) **dried haricot beans**

1 tbsp **olive oil**

8 **Toulouse sausages**

250g (9oz) piece of **pancetta** or a whole **chorizo sausage**, cut into small pieces

2 **onions**, peeled and finely chopped

1 **carrot**, peeled and chopped

4 **garlic cloves**, crushed

4 **duck legs**

1 sprig of **thyme**, plus ½ tbsp chopped **thyme leaves**

1 **bay leaf**

salt and freshly ground **black pepper**

2 tbsp **tomato purée**

400g can chopped **tomatoes**

200ml (7fl oz) **white wine**

½ day-old **baguette**

1 tbsp chopped **parsley**

1 Soak the beans in cold water for several hours or overnight. Drain, place in a saucepan, cover with cold water, bring to the boil, and boil rapidly for 10 minutes. Drain.

2 Heat the olive oil in a frying pan and brown the sausages for 7–8 minutes, turning occasionally. Remove from the pan and set aside. Add the pancetta to the pan and cook for 5 minutes. Remove and set aside with the sausages. Add the onions and carrot, and cook gently for 10 minutes, or until soft. Then add three-quarters of the garlic and cook for 1 minute.

3 Preheat the oven to 220°C (425°F/Gas 7). Place the duck legs in a deep roasting dish, prick all over with a fork and roast for 30 minutes. Remove the legs and set aside, reserving the fat left behind in the tray. Reduce the oven to 140°C (275°F/Gas 1).

4 In a heavy casserole, layer the ingredients, beginning with half the beans, then the onions, carrot, sausages, pancetta, and duck legs, followed by the remaining beans. Push the thyme sprig and bay leaf in among everything and season well with salt and black pepper.

5 Mix together 900ml (1½ pints) boiling water with the tomato purée, tomatoes, and wine. Pour into the casserole, cover, and cook in the oven for 3 hours, adding a little extra water if needed.

6 Cut the crusts off the baguette, then tear the bread into pieces and place in a food processor with the remaining garlic. Process into coarse crumbs. Heat 2 tbsp of the duck fat in a frying pan and fry the crumbs over a medium heat for 7–8 minutes, or until crisp and golden. Drain on kitchen paper and stir in the chopped thyme and parsley. Remove the cassoulet from the oven and stir. Sprinkle the breadcrumb topping over in a thick, even layer and serve.

Coarse meat terrine

A great light lunch, this can be made up to 3 days ahead and stored in the fridge. Bring it to room temperature before serving.

PREPARATION TIME **30 minutes, plus pressing** • COOKING TIME **1 hour 30 minutes** • **SERVES 8**

350g (12oz) rindless **streaky bacon rashers**

250g (9oz) **chicken livers**

300g (10oz) **minced pork**

450g (1lb) **minced veal**

1 **onion**, finely chopped

2 **garlic cloves**, crushed

1 tsp **dried oregano**

½ tsp **ground allspice**

115g (4oz) **unsalted butter**, melted

120ml (4fl oz) **dry sherry**

salt and freshly ground **black pepper**

1 Preheat the oven to 180°C (350°F/Gas 4). With the back of a knife, stretch the bacon rashers. Use them to line the terrine dish or other ovenproof dish, leaving the rasher ends hanging over the sides.

2 Mince or chop the chicken livers and mix with the minced pork, minced veal, onion, garlic, oregano, allspice, and melted butter. Stir in the sherry and season with salt and pepper.

3 Spoon the mixture into the dish and fold the ends of the bacon over the top. Cover tightly with foil or a lid, then stand the dish in a deep roasting tin. Fill the tin with enough hot water to reach halfway up the sides of the terrine dish.

4 Cook in the oven for 1½ hours, then remove and cover with fresh foil. Place a weight on top and leave to cool, then chill, for up to 24 hours, then turn out and cut into slices. Serve with slices of warm crusty bread or toast, topped with gherkins or cocktail onions.

Chicken liver pâté

For an impressive finish, set the pâté in individual ramekins, topping each with a few snipped chives.

PREPARATION TIME **10 minutes, plus cooling and chilling** • COOKING TIME **8 minutes** • **SERVES 8**

350g (12oz) **chicken livers**

115g (4oz) **unsalted butter**

150ml (5fl oz) **red wine**

¼ tsp dried **thyme**

10 **chives**, snipped, plus extra for garnishing

salt and freshly ground **black pepper**

1 Rinse the chicken livers and pat them dry with kitchen paper. Trim away any white sinew or greenish portions from the livers with small scissors, then cut each in half.

2 Melt half the butter in a large frying pan over a medium heat until it foams. Add the livers and cook, stirring often, for 4 minutes, or until browned.

3 Add the wine, thyme, and chives to the pan. Bring to the boil then reduce the heat and cook, stirring occasionally for 4 minutes, or until the liquid is reduced and the livers are just cooked through when sliced open.

4 Remove the pan from the heat and leave to cool for 10 minutes. Add salt and pepper to taste, then tip the livers and sauce into a blender, and blend until smooth. Adjust the seasoning if necessary. Spoon the pâté into a serving bowl, pressing it down with the back of the spoon so it is firmly packed, then set aside.

5 Melt the remaining butter over a medium heat, then pour it over the top of the pâté. Chill, uncovered, for at least 2 hours. Serve garnished with snipped chives.

▲ Coarse meat terrine

ALL ABOUT
ROAST POULTRY

The perfect roast bird is a keystone of a good cook, but there are a few tricks for getting it right every time.

Poultry roasting chart

Use these times as a guide, bearing in mind the size and weight of each bird varies. Be sure to preheat the oven before cooking your bird(s), and always check that the bird is fully cooked before serving.

BIRD	OVEN TEMP	COOKING TIME
Chicken	200°C (400°F/Gas 6)	20 mins per 450g (1lb) plus 20 mins
Turkey		
3.5–4.5kg (7–9lb)	190°C (375°F/Gas 5)	2½–3 hrs total cooking
5–6kg (10–12lb)	190°C (375°F/Gas 5)	3½–4 hrs total cooking
6.5–8.5kg (13–17lb)	190°C (375°F/Gas 5)	4½–5 hrs total cooking
Duck	180°C (350°F/Gas 4)	20 mins per 450g (1lb) plus 20 mins
Goose	180°C (350°F/Gas 4)	20 mins per 450g (1lb) plus 20 mins
Poussin	190°C (375°F/Gas 5)	12 mins per 450g (1lb) plus 12 mins

Roast chicken

PREPARATION TIME **15 minutes**
COOKING TIME **1 hour 15 minutes**
SERVES 4, PLUS LEFTOVERS

1.3kg (3lb) **oven-ready chicken**

50g (1¾oz) **unsalted butter**

1 **lemon**, quartered

salt and freshly ground **black pepper**

150ml (5fl oz) hot **vegetable stock** or **water**

1 Preheat the oven to 200°C (400°F/Gas 6). Sit the chicken in a roasting tin, then coat evenly all over with the butter – this ensures crisp, evenly golden skin. Stuff the neck end (see overleaf), push the lemon in the body cavity, and season the chicken all over with salt and black pepper.

2 Roast in the oven for about 1¼ hours until cooked through and golden, basting with the juices 2 or 3 times. To check whether the chicken is cooked, pierce the thickest part of the thighs with a knife. If the juices run clear, it is done; if it is pink or bloody, cook for a little longer. Remove to a large plate, cover with foil, and leave to rest in a warm place for about 15 minutes before carving. Serve with gravy, made with the pan juices, crispy roast potatoes (see p39), and seasonal vegetables.

Poultry essentials

Though it may seem simple, roasting a bird perfectly takes finesse. If it comes with giblets, use these to make the stock for the gravy.

1 Stuff the bird

A stuffing to accompany a bird can be cooked in one of two ways – either stuffed into the neck end (as below) or cooked separately in the oven. If stuffing the bird, stuff it under the skin, rather than into the cavity, as this will ensure that it cooks properly. It will also help to protect the breast meat as it roasts and any butter or fat in the mixture will help to keep the meat moist.

WATERCRESS AND APRICOT STUFFING

50g (1¾oz) **dried apricots**

3 slices **white bread**, processed
into crumbs

50g (1¾oz) **hazelnuts**, skinned

bunch of **watercress**, roughly chopped

Put the apricots in a small pan of water and bring to the boil. Drain and add to the breadcrumbs. Put the hazelnuts into a food processor and process for a few seconds, then add the chopped watercress and breadcrumbs. Process for a few seconds, then season and put into a bowl.

To stuff the bird, lift the flap of skin from around the wishbone area at the neck and draw this back until it exposes as much of the breast as necessary. Carefully push the stuffing in under the skin onto the breast, then pull back the skin to cover it and tuck in under the bird.

2 Baste and cook

1 Preheat the oven (see chart on p70). Paint oil, rub on butter, and season the bird. Place in a pan, pour in 150ml (5fl oz) stock, and put in the middle of the oven. After 15 minutes, reduce the heat to 190°C (375°F/Gas 5).

3 Make gravy

1 Using a large spoon skim off most of the fat from the pan juices. Put the pan over a low heat. Mix 1 tbsp plain flour with 1 tbsp of the bird fat and whisk it into the remaining pan juices.

2 Roast for a further 25 minutes, then baste the bird with the juices in the pan. Turn the bird over onto its breast so that the oven heat can focus on the thighs. Baste the bird again, then continue roasting for another 25 minutes.

3 Turn the bird onto its back and test for doneness. Insert a skewer into the thigh or the thick end of the breast. If the juices run clear, the bird is cooked. If there are traces of blood, continue cooking and test again after 10 minutes.

2 Add 300ml (10fl oz) water or stock and 1 tbsp tomato purée, increase the heat, and bring to a boil, whisking constantly to get rid of any lumps.

3 Strain the gravy through a sieve, into a clean container, for maximum smoothness, then pour into a gravy boat, ready to serve piping hot.

Game bird essentials

Use these techniques to ensure that small, delicate game birds roast evenly. It is also essential to time the cooking properly, so the meat remains moist.

Truss

Trussing smaller game birds, such as quails, before roasting helps them to keep their shape and ensures that each part of the bird cooks evenly, without overcooking any of the bony parts first. Hold the bird, breast-side down, on a work surface, tuck the neck skin under the bird, and cover with the wings. Turn the bird over and pass a length of string under the tail end of the bird. Tie a secure knot over the leg joints. Bring the strings along the sides of the body, between the breasts and the legs, and loop them around the legs. Turn the bird over, so that it is breast-side down again and tie the strings tightly under the body. Bring both ends of the string down between the sides of the body and the insides of the wings. Tie the wing bones at the neck opening so they are tucked securely under the body.

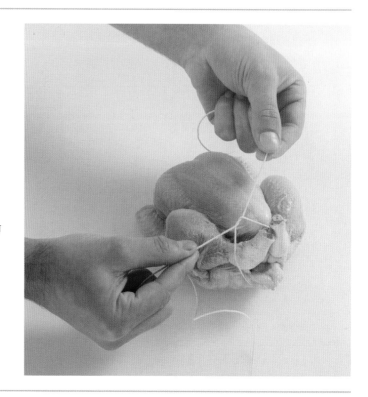

Lard and bard

Larding is the technique of inserting fat deep into meat. This is unnecessary when serving game pink; it is only necessary if you want to cook the meat past that stage. To lard, cut the fat into strips and insert the strips deep into the meat with a larding needle or sharp knife. This task is much easier if the fat has been frozen beforehand. Barding means wrapping the meat in fat before cooking it. You can use bacon and pancetta, for example. Here, game birds are barded by being wrapped in vine leaves and streaky bacon before they are roasted.

Game roasting chart

BIRD	DESCRIPTION	ROAST
Quail	Farmed bird, not hung, so mild-flavoured. Sometimes sold boned and stuffed. Allow 1 bird per person (or 2 if large appetites!).	Put a bay leaf or small sprig of rosemary inside to flavour. Truss bird. Season well. Smear all over with butter. Preheat the oven to 200°C (400°F/Gas 6). Roast 20–25 minutes, basting frequently until tender and just cooked through.
Grouse	Plump with dark flesh and unique gamey flavour, renowned world-wide. Allow 1 bird or 2 breasts per person.	Put half an onion or some herbs inside to flavour. Truss bird. Season well. Rub with oil. Bard breast with bacon. Preheat oven to 200°C (400°F/Gas 6). Roast 35–40 minutes.
Mallard	Dark, rich meat, much less fatty than domestic duck. Allow 1 breast each or 1 bird for 2–3 people.	Put some sage and/or half an onion inside to flavour. Truss bird. Season well. Smear well with butter or duck fat. Preheat oven to 220°C (425°F/Gas 7). Roast 30–35 minutes.
Partridge	Young birds have paler flesh and are more tender. Allow 1 bird per person.	Put a sprig of thyme and/or half a small lemon inside to flavour. Truss bird. Season well. Bard breast with bacon or pancetta. Preheat oven to 200°C (400°F/Gas 6). Roast 40 minutes.
Pheasant	One of the most popular game birds with pale flesh. If hung, has a stronger, gamey flavour. Allow 1 breast each or 1 bird for 2–3 people.	Put half an onion and/or apple inside to flavour. Truss bird. Season well. Rub with oil. Bard breast with bacon. Preheat oven to 200°C (400°F/Gas 6). Roast 50 minutes–1 hour.
Teal	Very small duck with a superb flavour. Allow 1 bird per person.	Push some sage leaves and/or orange slices inside for flavour. Truss bird. Season well. Smear with butter. Preheat oven to 230°C (450°F/Gas 8). Roast 15 minutes, basting frequently.
Wood pigeon	Dark red flesh with a distinctive flavour. Farmed birds (squabs) are fatter and more tender than wild ones. Allow 1 bird or 2–3 breasts per person.	Only roast if farmed. Put a bay leaf inside to flavour. Truss bird. Season well. Smear all over with butter or bard with bacon. Preheat oven to 230°C (450°F/Gas 8). Roast 15 minutes, basting frequently.
Woodcock	Considered one of the finest for flavour, particularly if cooked with entrails intact and head on. Also available drawn. Allow 1 bird per person.	Usually roasted undrawn, but can be drawn first. Season well. Smear all over with butter. Preheat oven to 230°C (450°F/Gas 8). Roast 15 minutes, basting frequently. Serve on toast.

Roast turkey

Turkey can be challenging to cook well, as its size means it can become dry while it finishes cooking through. Follow this recipe for great, moist meat every time.

PREPARATION TIME **15 minutes** • COOKING TIME **3 hours 15 minutes** • **SERVES 6, PLUS LEFTOVERS**

250g (9oz) **unsalted butter**

3 **onions**, 1 finely chopped, 2 peeled and quartered

125g (4oz) **breadcrumbs**

handful of fresh **flat-leaf parsley**, finely chopped

salt and freshly ground **black pepper**

4kg (9lb) **turkey**

1 First, make the stuffing. Melt half the butter in a pan over a low heat, add the chopped onion, and sweat gently until soft. Remove from the heat, stir through the breadcrumbs and parsley, season, and set aside to cool.

2 Preheat the oven to 200°C (400°F/Gas 6). Sit the turkey in a large roasting tin. Season inside and out. Spread the remaining butter over the skin. Stuff the onion quarters into the body cavity, and the stuffing into the neck end. Roast for 20 minutes, then reduce the oven temperature to 190°C (375°F/Gas 5).

3 Cover the turkey loosely with foil, and roast for 20 minutes per 450g (1lb) plus 20 minutes. Baste every hour with juices from the tin. Pierce the bird with a skewer. If the juices run clear, it is ready; if there is any trace of pink, cook for a little longer. Remove the foil for the last 10–15 minutes.

4 Remove the turkey from the tin, and put on a large warmed plate. Cover with foil, and leave to rest in a warm place for 15 minutes. Serve slices of turkey with gravy, roast potatoes, cranberry sauce, and seasonal vegetables.

FROM **Ordinary** TO **Extraordinary**

Ensure perfect moistness by jointing the turkey and **making confit wings and legs** and a **fast-roast crown**. The day before, remove the wings and legs, jointing the legs into thighs and drumsticks (see pp296–97). Place the legs and wings in a dish, sprinkle generously with **sea salt**, freshly ground **black pepper** and **thyme leaves**, cover and place in the fridge. The next day, preheat the oven to 130°C (250°F/Gas ½), scrape off the seasonings from the legs and wings and place in a roasting dish with 500g (1lb 2oz) melted **duck fat**.

Cook for 4 hours, then cover with foil and set aside to keep warm. Fast-roast the turkey crown: increase the oven temperature to 200°C (400°F/Gas 6) and roast for 40 minutes, then cover with foil and roast for another 45 minutes. Cook the stuffing in a separate roasting dish alongside for the final 30 minutes. Carve the crown and serve with the drained, meltingly tender wings and legs, and the crispy stuffing.

Roast quail

As a rule, the darker and leaner the meat of a game bird, the more carefully it needs to be cooked.

PREPARATION TIME **10 minutes** • COOKING TIME **20–25 minutes** • **SERVES 4**

8 quail

½ tsp freshly grated **nutmeg**

salt and freshly ground **black pepper**

small bunch of **sage leaves**

8 **pancetta slices**

2 crisp **dessert apples**, cored and sliced

15g (½oz) **unsalted butter**, melted

2 tsp **demerara sugar**

4 tbsp **calvados** or **cider brandy**

1 Preheat the oven to 200°C (400°F/Gas 6). Season the birds inside and out with the nutmeg, and salt and pepper. Tuck a couple of sage leaves into the cavity, and wrap a strip of pancetta around each bird, tucking the ends underneath.

2 Toss the apples in the butter, sprinkle with the sugar, and place in a roasting tin. Arrange the quail on top of the apples and roast for 20–25 minutes, turning occasionally, until both the quail and apples are golden brown.

3 Lift the quail and apples on to a warmed serving plate. Stir the calvados into the roasting tin to deglaze, boil for 30 seconds, then spoon over the quail to serve. Accompany with roast potatoes and green beans.

FROM **Ordinary** TO **Extraordinary**

Spatchcock and griddle or barbecue the quail for a deliciously smoky flavour. Spatchcock the birds (see p300), seasoning with nutmeg as instructed. Place 1 **sage leaf** on each breast, then cover with 1 **pancetta slice**. Skewer the birds, securing the pancetta in place as you do so. Place the quails on a very hot griddle pan or over a very hot barbecue, turning frequently, for 10–15 minutes or until cooked all the way through. Roast the apples as instructed and serve alongside.

Chicken cacciatore

"Hunter-style chicken" is traditionally served with polenta to soak up the delicious juices, but is also good with Risotto alla milanese (see p100).

PREPARATION TIME **20 minutes** • COOKING TIME **35–40 minutes** • **SERVES 4**

4 **chicken leg quarters**, about 1.5kg (3lb 3oz) total weight

salt and freshly ground **black pepper**

2 tbsp **olive oil**

2 **garlic cloves**, sliced

1 **onion**, chopped

200ml (7fl oz) **dry white wine**

1 **celery stick**, chopped

200g (7oz) **button mushrooms**, sliced

400g can **chopped tomatoes**

150ml (5fl oz) **chicken stock**

1 tbsp **tomato purée**

2 tsp chopped **rosemary**

2 tsp chopped **sage**

8 pitted **black olives**, halved

1 Trim any excess fat from the chicken and season with salt and pepper. Heat half the oil in a large, heavy frying pan and fry the chicken in batches, until browned all over. Remove and keep hot. Pour the excess fat out of the pan.

2 Add the remaining oil, garlic, and onion and fry gently for 3–4 minutes to soften, but not brown. Add the wine and boil for 1 minute. Stir in the celery, mushrooms, chopped tomatoes, stock, tomato purée, and herbs.

3 Return the chicken to the pan, cover, and cook over a low heat for 30 minutes, or until the chicken is cooked through.

4 Remove the lid, add the olives, then cover and cook for a further 5–10 minutes. Serve hot.

SAVOURY SAUCES AND STOCKS KNOW-HOW *see* Make fresh chicken stock **p482**

Coq au vin

Traditionally cooked for longer with a tough old rooster from the farmyard, these days the same flavours still suit our modern, more tender birds.

PREPARATION TIME **30 minutes** • COOKING TIME **1 hour 30 minutes** • **SERVES 4**

2 tbsp **plain flour**

salt and freshly ground **black pepper**

4 **chicken** portions

60g (2oz) **unsalted butter**, finely chopped

125g (4½oz) diced **pancetta**

2 **garlic cloves**, crushed

1 **carrot**, diced

1 **celery stick**, roughly chopped

4 tbsp **brandy** or **Cognac**

750ml (1¼ pints) **red wine**, such as **beaujolais**

1 **bay leaf**

4–5 sprigs of **thyme**

1 tbsp **olive oil**

450g (1lb) **button onions**

1 tsp **soft light brown sugar**

1 tsp **red wine vinegar**

225g (8oz) **button mushrooms**

1 Season the flour to taste with salt and pepper. Coat the chicken with 1 tbsp of the seasoned flour. Melt half the butter in the casserole over a medium heat, add the chicken, and fry gently until golden brown on all sides.

2 Add the pancetta, garlic, carrot, and celery, and fry until softened. Add the remaining flour and cook for 1–2 minutes. Pour in the brandy and wine, stirring to remove any sediment from the bottom of the casserole. Add the bay leaf and thyme, bring to the boil, cover, and simmer for 1 hour.

3 Meanwhile, melt the rest of the butter with the olive oil in a frying pan over a medium heat. Add the onions and fry until just brown. Stir in the sugar, vinegar, and 1 tbsp water.

4 Add the onions and mushrooms to the chicken, and cook for another 30 minutes, or until the chicken is cooked through and the vegetables are tender.

5 Transfer the chicken and vegetables to a hot serving dish, leaving the sauce in the casserole. Discard the bay leaf and thyme. Skim off any excess fat and boil the sauce for 3–5 minutes, or until reduced. Pour over the chicken and serve.

Tandoori chicken

You will get the best results here if you use dark meat chicken pieces, such as thighs and drumsticks, or whole chicken legs. Chicken breasts tend to dry out too easily during the high-temperature cooking required in this recipe.

PREPARATION TIME 10–15 minutes, plus at least 3 hours marinating • **COOKING TIME** 25–35 minutes • **SERVES 4**

8 **chicken pieces**, such as thighs, legs, and breasts, skin removed

groundnut oil or **sunflower oil**, for greasing

60g (2oz) **ghee** or **unsalted butter**, melted

1 **red onion**, thinly sliced, to serve

lemon wedges, to serve

FOR THE TANDOORI MARINADE

1 **onion**, coarsely chopped

2 large **garlic cloves**

1cm (½in) piece **fresh root ginger**, peeled and coarsely chopped

250g (9oz) **plain yogurt**

3 tbsp fresh **lemon juice**

¼ tsp **salt**

1¼–1½ tsp **chilli powder**, to taste

1 tsp **garam masala**

pinch of **ground turmeric**

pinch of **Kashmiri chilli powder**

pinch of **saffron powder**

1 Use a fork to prick the chicken pieces all over, then place them in a non-metallic bowl and set aside.

2 To make the marinade, put the onion, garlic, and ginger in a blender or food processor and blend until a paste forms, scraping down the side of the bowl. Add the yogurt, lemon juice, salt, and the spices, and process again.

3 Pour the marinade over the chicken and rub in well. Cover the bowl with cling film, and leave to marinate in the refrigerator for at least 3 hours, occasionally turning the chicken pieces in the marinade.

4 Preheat the oven to 220°C (425°F/Gas 7) and remove the chicken from the fridge. Put a rack in a roasting pan lined with kitchen foil, shiny-side up, and grease with groundnut oil. Arrange the chicken on the rack then brush with melted ghee or butter. Roast for 20–25 minutes, or until the juices run clear.

5 Preheat the grill on its highest setting. Pour off the juices that have accumulated in the bottom of the pan. Brush the chicken with more ghee or butter and place under the grill for 5–10 minutes, or until the edges are lightly charred. Serve with the onion slices and lemon wedges.

Thai green chicken curry

The heady aromatics in a home-made green curry paste are almost intoxicating.
Do try and make your own paste if you can, as it gives a big lift to the finished dish.

PREPARATION TIME **10 minutes** • COOKING TIME **10 minutes** • **SERVES 4**

1 tbsp **olive oil**

4 skinless, boneless **chicken breasts**, about 140g (5oz) each, cut into bite-sized pieces

2 tbsp **nam pla** (Thai fish sauce)

400ml can **coconut milk**

175g (6oz) **button mushrooms**, chopped

6 **spring onions**, trimmed, with the green part sliced lengthways

salt and freshly ground **black pepper**

chopped **coriander**, to garnish

FOR THE CURRY PASTE

1 heaped tbsp diced **bird's eye chillies**

1 **long green chilli**, deseeded

1 rounded tbsp chopped **galangal**

2½ tbsp chopped **lemongrass**

1 tsp chopped **kaffir lime** zest

1 tsp chopped **coriander root**

1 tsp chopped **red turmeric**

2½ tbsp chopped **red shallots**

2 tbsp chopped **garlic**

1 tsp **yellow beans**

good pinch of finely ground **white peppercorns**

1 First, make the curry paste: put all the ingredients in a blender or food processor with a pinch of salt and blend for 3–4 minutes, adding water 1 tbsp at a time as necessary, until you have a smooth paste.

2 Heat the oil in a large frying pan over a medium heat. Add 4 tbsp curry paste and stir. Add the chicken and stir-fry for 2 minutes, or until lightly browned.

3 Pour in the nam pla and coconut milk and bring to the boil, stirring. Lower the heat, stir in the mushrooms and most of the spring onions, and season with salt and pepper to taste, then simmer for about 8 minutes, or until the chicken is tender and cooked through.

4 Serve hot, garnished with coriander and the remaining sliced spring onions. Any leftover curry paste can be kept in the fridge for up to two weeks in an airtight container: press cling film against the surface of the paste before closing the container.

FROM **Ordinary** TO **Extraordinary**

Serve som tam (green mango or papaya salad) on the side. Grate 140g (5oz) **green mango** or **papaya** with the same amount of **cucumber**. Place in a bowl with 3 finely sliced **spring onions** and a handful each of **coriander** and **mint leaves**. Toast a handful of **unsalted peanuts** in a dry frying pan and add them to the bowl with 1 **bird's eye chilli** and 2 **garlic cloves**, both finely chopped. Separately mix together the juice of 2 **limes** with 2 tbsp **nam pla** and 2 tsp **soft brown sugar** until the sugar dissolves, then toss through the salad. Set aside for 20 minutes, to allow the flavours to combine, then toss again and serve alongside the curry.

FLAVOURINGS KNOW-HOW *see* Prepare herbs **p391**

Seared duck with five-spice and noodles

Ideal for those nights when you're craving something just a little special. This is easy to cook and makes a memorably delicious and filling meal.

PREPARATION TIME **10 minutes** • COOKING TIME **20 minutes** • **SERVES 4**

4 **duck breasts**, about 150g (5½oz) each, skin scored in a criss-cross pattern

2–3 tsp **five-spice paste** or **powder**

knob of **unsalted butter**

2 tbsp freshly squeezed **orange juice**

1 tsp **palm sugar** or **soft light brown sugar**

250g (9oz) fresh **Chinese egg noodles**

handful of **coriander leaves**, finely chopped

1 Rub the duck breasts in the five-spice paste or powder. Melt the butter in a frying pan over a high heat. Add the duck breasts, skin-side down, and cook for about 8 minutes until the skin is golden and crisp. Carefully pour the fat away from the pan, then turn the breasts over and cook on the other side for a further 6 minutes.

2 Remove the meat from the pan, and set aside to rest in a warm place for 10 minutes. Cut into slices, and arrange on a warm plate. Pour away any remaining fat from the pan, then add the orange juice and sugar. Let it simmer for a minute or so over a low heat, scraping up any sediment from the bottom of the pan with a wooden spoon.

3 Add the noodles and toss them in the sauce for a couple of minutes until cooked. Remove from the heat and stir through the coriander. Serve immediately with the warm sliced duck.

FROM **Ordinary** TO **Extraordinary**

Change up the regular noodles into striking **fried noodle nests**. Pour **vegetable oil** to the depth of 4cm (1½in) into a large, deep pan. Divide the noodles into 4 equal portions. Place a 10cm (4in) ring mould into the oil. Carefully lower one-quarter of the noodles into the ring mould, feeding them in so they don't clump together. Fry until crisp and golden, then remove the ring mould and carefully turn the noodle nest with a spatula to cook the other side. Repeat to make 4 nests. Blot on kitchen paper to remove excess oil, and serve the sliced duck and sauce alongside.

PASTA, NOODLES, AND GNOCCHI KNOW-HOW *see* Boil noodles **p470**

Crispy roast duck

This Chinese-style recipe, with its sweet-and-sour top notes, is astonishingly good. It takes some effort, but the burnished, aromatic results are well worth it.

PREPARATION TIME **1 hour 15 minutes, plus drying and resting** • COOKING TIME **1 hour 35 minutes** • **SERVES 4**

1 tsp **five-spice powder**

3 tbsp **oyster sauce**

1 tsp **salt**

1 **duck**, about 1.8kg (4lb)

FOR THE GLAZE

3 tbsp **honey**

1 tbsp **dark soy sauce**

2 tbsp **rice wine** or **dry sherry**

1 Mix the five-spice powder, oyster sauce, and salt, and spread over and inside the duck.

2 Insert a meat hook through the neck end, or tie string around the neck to hang the duck. Place the duck in a colander in the sink, pour a kettle of boiling water over it, then pat dry with kitchen paper. Repeat this pouring and drying 5 times.

3 To make the glaze, put the honey, soy sauce, rice wine or sherry, and 150ml (5fl oz) water in a saucepan, and bring to the boil. Reduce the heat, simmer for 10 minutes, or until sticky, then brush the glaze over the duck until thoroughly coated.

4 Hang the duck over a roasting tin or shallow tray in a well-ventilated place and leave for 4–5 hours, or until the skin is dry.

5 Preheat the oven to 230°C (450°F/Gas 8). Place the duck in a roasting tin, breast-side up, and pour 150ml (5fl oz) cold water into the tin. Roast for 20 minutes, then reduce the oven temperature to 180°C (350°F/Gas 4), and roast for 1¼ hours, or until the skin is crisp and golden.

6 Leave the duck to rest for 10 minutes, then joint and arrange it on a serving platter. Serve at once.

FROM **Ordinary** TO **Extraordinary**

Try serving this with authentic **Chinese smashed cucumber** to add a sharp pop that cuts through the fatty duck. Cut 1 **cucumber** into 10cm (4in) lengths, then halve each lengthways. Smash each piece hard with the flat side of a broad knife, or a cleaver, then break or slice into bite-sized pieces. Toss with a large pinch of both **sea salt** and **sugar**, place in a colander and allow to drain for 30 minutes. Put 2 tbsp **rice vinegar** in a bowl with 1 tsp **sea salt** and 2 tsp **sugar**, and stir until the sugar and salt dissolves. Stir in 1 tbsp each of **sesame oil** and **soy sauce**, then stir in the cucumber, adding **chilli flakes** to taste, if desired. Serve with the duck.

Chicken tikka masala

Famously a British-Indian invention, this is a true crowd-pleaser. Leave out the chilli, if you prefer; it will still be wonderfully spice-flavourful without the heat and will wipe the floor with any shop-bought paste.

PREPARATION TIME **20 minutes, plus marinating** • COOKING TIME **25 minutes** • **SERVES 4**

8 skinless, boneless **chicken thighs**

2 **garlic cloves**, coarsely chopped

2.5cm (1in) piece of **fresh root ginger**, peeled and coarsely chopped

juice of 1 **lime**

1 **red chilli**, deseeded

2 tbsp coarsely chopped **coriander leaves**, plus extra to garnish

2 tbsp **vegetable oil**

1 **red onion**, chopped

1 tsp **ground turmeric**

1 tsp **ground cumin**

1 tbsp **tomato purée**

300ml (10fl oz) **double cream**

1 tbsp **lemon juice**

salt and freshly ground **black pepper**

1 Place the chicken thighs in a single layer in a shallow dish. Put the garlic, ginger, lime juice, chilli, and coriander in a food processor with 1 tbsp of the oil and process to make a paste. Spread the paste over the chicken. Set aside to marinate for 2 hours.

2 Heat the remaining oil in a frying pan, add the onion, and fry until softened and starting to colour. Add the turmeric and cumin, and fry gently for 2–3 minutes.

3 Preheat the grill on its highest setting. Lift the chicken from the dish, reserving any marinade left behind, and place on a foil-lined grill rack. Grill for 5 minutes, or until almost cooked and slightly scorched at the edges, turning once.

4 Stir the tomato purée and cream into the frying pan with any leftover marinade. Add the lemon juice and stir over a medium heat until mixed in. Place the chicken into the pan and baste with the sauce. Simmer for 5 minutes or until the chicken is cooked through. Season to taste with salt and pepper and serve, sprinkled with coriander.

Pappardelle alla bolognese

The rich, meaty, slow-simmered ragù goes well with most types of pasta.

PREPARATION TIME **15 minutes** • COOKING TIME **2 hours** • SERVES **4**

2 tbsp **olive oil**

100g (3½oz) **smoked bacon lardons**

1 **onion**, finely chopped

2 **garlic cloves**, crushed

400g (14oz) lean **minced steak**

115g (4oz) **button mushrooms**, sliced

120ml (4fl oz) **red wine**

2 tbsp **tomato purée**

400g can **chopped tomatoes**

1 tsp **dried oregano**

good pinch of **sugar**

salt and freshly ground **black pepper**

90ml (3fl oz) **double cream**

450g (1lb) **dried pappardelle pasta**

freshly grated **Parmesan cheese**, to serve

1 Heat the oil in a deep, heavy saucepan and fry the lardons for 1–2 minutes. Add the onion and garlic, and continue to fry, stirring occasionally, for 5 minutes, or until softened but not browned.

2 Stir in the beef, breaking up any lumps, then cook for a further 10 minutes, or until it is evenly coloured, stirring frequently until all the grains are separate. Stir in the mushrooms and fry, stirring, for 1 minute. Add the wine, tomato purée, tomatoes, oregano, and sugar. Season to taste with salt and pepper, then bring to the boil.

3 Reduce the heat to very low, cover the pan, and simmer very gently for 1½ hours. Stir occasionally to prevent sticking. Stir the cream into the ragù, cover, and simmer for a further 30 minutes.

4 Bring a large pan of lightly salted water to the boil. Add the pappardelle and simmer for 8–10 minutes, or until cooked but still with some bite. Drain well, spoon the ragù over, and serve with freshly grated Parmesan.

FROM **Ordinary** TO **Extraordinary**

Add a home-made "umami bomb" flavour enhancer to really make your bolognese sauce sing. Place a handful of **dried porcini mushrooms** in a blender and whizz to a powder. Tip into a bowl and stir in 1 finely chopped **garlic clove**, 2 tbsp **sun-dried tomato purée**, 2 tsp **anchovy** or **black olive paste** and 2 tbsp **balsamic vinegar**. Add to the ragù 5 minutes before the end of cooking, 1 tsp at a time, stirring it in and tasting as you go. Store the rest in a jar in the fridge. It will keep for up to 2 weeks. You can add it to almost any savoury dish, when you feel you need just a little more pizzazz.

Spaghetti puttanesca

A famously piquant sauce, this is an ideal, super-convenient store cupboard dish to have in your repertoire. It's much more than the sum of its parts.

PREPARATION TIME **15 minutes** • COOKING TIME **25 minutes** • **SERVES 4**

4 tbsp **olive oil**

2 **garlic cloves**, finely chopped

½ fresh **red chilli**, deseeded and finely chopped

6 canned **anchovies**, drained and finely chopped

115g (4oz) **black olives**, pitted and chopped

1–2 tbsp **capers**, rinsed and drained

450g (1lb) **tomatoes**, skinned, deseeded, and chopped

450g (1lb) **dried spaghetti**

salt

1 Heat the oil in a saucepan over a medium heat, add the garlic and chilli, and cook for 2 minutes, or until the garlic is slightly coloured. Add the anchovies, olives, capers, and tomatoes and stir, breaking down the anchovies to a paste.

2 Reduce the heat and let the sauce simmer, uncovered, for around 10–15 minutes, or until the sauce has thickened, stirring frequently.

3 Meanwhile, bring a large pan of lightly salted water to the boil. Add the spaghetti and simmer for 10 minutes, or until cooked but with some bite. Drain well, toss the with the sauce, and serve.

VEGETABLES KNOW-HOW *see* Deseed and cut chillies **p373**
PASTA, NOODLES, AND GNOCCHI KNOW-HOW *see* Cook dried pasta **p470**

Pasta alla carbonara

The eggs in this recipe are cooked by the heat of the pasta. Make sure to stir in the sauce vigorously, until it thickens (this shows the eggs are cooking) and clings to the pasta.

PREPARATION TIME **10 minutes** • COOKING TIME **10 minutes** • **SERVES 4–6**

450g (1lb) **dried pasta**, such as **tagliatelle**, **spaghetti**, or **linguine**

salt and freshly ground **black pepper**

4 tbsp **olive oil**

175g (6oz) **pancetta** or **cured unsmoked bacon rashers**, rind removed, and finely chopped

2 **garlic cloves**, crushed

5 large **eggs**

75g (2½oz) **Parmesan cheese**, grated, plus extra to serve

75g (2½oz) **pecorino cheese**, grated, plus extra to serve

1 sprig of **thyme**, leaves only, chopped (optional)

1 Bring a large saucepan of salted water to the boil. Add the pasta, and cook for 10 minutes, or until cooked but with some bite.

2 Meanwhile, heat half the oil in a large frying pan over a medium heat. Add the pancetta and garlic, and fry, stirring, for 5–8 minutes, or until the pancetta is crispy.

3 Beat the eggs and cheeses together, add pepper to taste, and the thyme, if using. Drain the pasta well and return to the pan. Add the eggs, pancetta, and the remaining oil, and stir until the pasta is coated. Serve while still hot, sprinkled with the extra cheese and thyme (if using).

PASTA, NOODLES, AND GNOCCHI KNOW-HOW *see* Cook dried pasta **p470**

Lasagne al forno

A great dish to feed a hungry family. Make this up to 2 days ahead, cover, and store in the fridge, then bake when needed.

PREPARATION TIME 25 minutes • COOKING TIME **1 hour 35 minutes** • **SERVES 4**

1 tbsp **olive oil**

1 large **onion**, chopped

2 **celery sticks**, chopped

2 small **carrots**, chopped

50g (2oz) **pancetta**, diced

500g (1lb 2oz) lean **minced steak**

400g can **chopped tomatoes**

1 tsp **dried oregano**

60g (2oz) **unsalted butter**

60g (2oz) **plain flour**

600ml (1 pint) **milk**

salt and freshly ground **black pepper**

150g (5½oz) **ricotta cheese**

12 pre-cooked **lasagne sheets**

50g (1¾oz) **Parmesan cheese**, grated

1 To make the ragù sauce, heat the oil in a saucepan over a medium heat and sauté the onion, celery, carrots, and pancetta for 5 minutes, or until beginning to brown. Add the beef and cook until browned, breaking up with the side of a spoon, until all the grains are separate. Add the tomatoes, oregano, and 150ml (5fl oz) water. Bring to the boil, then reduce the heat and simmer, stirring occasionally, for 40 minutes.

2 Meanwhile, to make the béchamel sauce, melt the butter in a small saucepan over a low heat and stir in the flour. Cook, stirring, for 1 minute, then remove the pan from the heat and slowly whisk in the milk. Return to the heat and cook, whisking, for 2–3 minutes, or until the sauce thickens. Season to taste with salt and pepper, then stir in the ricotta.

3 Preheat the oven to 190°C (375°F/Gas 5). Spread a little béchamel sauce over the base of an ovenproof dish. Arrange a layer of lasagne sheets on top, then add one-third of the ragù sauce in an even layer. Drizzle 1 or 2 spoonfuls of the béchamel over the meat sauce and top with another layer of lasagne.

4 Repeat until all the lasagne and sauce has been used, finishing with a thick layer of béchamel sauce. Sprinkle Parmesan on top and bake for 45 minutes, or until piping hot and the sauce bubbles around the edge.

SAVOURY SAUCES AND STOCKS KNOW-HOW *see* **Make béchamel sauce p489**

Macaroni cheese

The key to perfecting this filling favourite lies in the béchamel sauce: make sure it is smooth, creamy, and packed with a blend of gooey cheeses.

PREPARATION TIME **20 mins** • COOKING TIME **35 mins** • SERVES **4–6**

400g (14oz) **dried macaroni**

salt

85g (3oz) **unsalted butter**

100g (3½oz) fresh **breadcrumbs**

60g (2oz) **plain flour**

1 tsp **mustard powder**

pinch of **ground nutmeg**

400ml (14fl oz) **milk**, warmed

175g (6oz) **Cheddar cheese**, coarsely grated

100g (3½oz) **mozzarella cheese**, drained and finely chopped

60g (2oz) **Parmesan cheese**, coarsely grated

1 Bring a large pan of lightly salted water to the boil. Add the macaroni and boil for 2 minutes less than specified on the packet. Drain well and set aside, shaking off any excess water.

2 Meanwhile, preheat the oven to 200°C (400°F/Gas 6) and grease a large ovenproof serving dish. Melt 30g (1oz) of the butter in a small pan. Add the breadcrumbs, stir, then remove the pan from the heat and set aside.

3 Melt the remaining butter in a large saucepan over a low heat and stir in the flour. Cook, stirring, for one minute, then stir in the mustard powder and nutmeg. Remove the pan from the heat and slowly whisk in the milk. Return the pan to

the heat and bring the mixture to the boil, whisking, for 2–3 minutes, or until the béchamel sauce thickens. Remove from the heat. Stir in the Cheddar cheese until melted and smooth, then add the macaroni and mozzarella and stir.

4 Transfer the mixture to the prepared dish and smooth the surface. Toss the breadcrumbs with the Parmesan cheese and sprinkle over the top. Place the dish on a baking tray and bake for 25 minutes, or until heated through and golden brown on top. Leave to stand for 2 minutes, then serve straight from the dish.

Paella

This colourful rice dish, bursting with seafood and infused with saffron, is a true Spanish-style treat. And, unlike risotto, it does not require constant stirring.

PREPARATION TIME **10 minutes** • COOKING TIME **30 minutes** • **SERVES 4**

1.2 litres (2 pints) hot **fish stock**

large pinch of **saffron threads**

2 tbsp **olive oil**

1 **onion**, finely chopped

2 **garlic cloves**, crushed

2 large **tomatoes**, skinned and chopped

12 peeled, raw **king prawns**

225g (8oz) **squid**, sliced into rings and tentacles

400g (14oz) **paella rice**

85g (3oz) **petits pois**

4 **langoustines** or Dublin Bay prawns

12–16 **mussels**, cleaned

1 tbsp chopped **parsley**, to garnish

1 Pour a little of the hot fish stock into a cup or jug, add the saffron threads, and set aside to infuse. Heat the oil in a paella pan or large frying pan over a medium heat, and fry the onion and garlic until softened. Add the tomatoes and cook for 2 minutes, then add the prawns and squid, and fry for 1–2 minutes, or until the prawns turn pink.

2 Stir in the rice, then stir in the saffron liquid, petits pois, and 900ml (1½ pints) of stock. Simmer, uncovered, without stirring, over a low heat for 12–14 minutes, or until the stock has evaporated and the rice is just tender, adding a little extra stock if necessary.

3 Meanwhile, cook the langoustines in 150ml (5fl oz) simmering stock for 3–4 minutes, or until cooked through. Transfer to a warm plate with a slotted spoon. Add the mussels to the stock, cover, and cook over a high heat for 2–3 minutes, or until open. Remove from the pan with a slotted spoon, discarding any that have not opened. If the paella seems dry, strain in this flavourful cooking liquid, a spoonful of a time, as necessary.

4 Reserve 8 mussels for garnish. Remove the rest from their shells and stir into the paella. Arrange the reserved mussels and langoustines on top, and garnish with parsley.

FROM **Ordinary** TO **Extraordinary**

Make a **saffron and black garlic aïoli** to serve alongside. Soak a pinch of **saffron threads** in a small amount of warm water for 20–30 minutes. Crush 1 **black garlic clove**. Add both to a batch of home-made **mayonnaise** (see p490) and serve with the paella.

SHELLFISH KNOW-HOW *see* Clean mussels **p286**

Pad Thai

This is a simple version of one of Thailand's national dishes. It's quick to cook and utterly irresistible.

PREPARATION TIME **20 minutes** • COOKING TIME **10 minutes** • **SERVES 4**

2 tbsp chopped **coriander**

1 **red bird's eye chilli**, deseeded and finely chopped

4 tbsp **sunflower oil**

250g (9oz) raw **tiger prawns**, peeled

4 **shallots**, finely chopped

1 tbsp **palm sugar** or **light brown sugar**

4 large **eggs**, lightly beaten

2 tbsp **oyster sauce**

1 tbsp **nam pla** (Thai fish sauce)

juice of 1 **lime**

350g (12oz) **flat rice noodles**, cooked according to packet instructions

250g (9oz) **beansprouts**

4 **spring onions**, sliced

115g (4oz) **unsalted roasted peanuts**, coarsely chopped

1 **lime**, cut into 4 wedges, to serve

1 Mix together the coriander, chilli, and sunflower oil in a bowl. Fry half the mixture in a wok over a medium heat, add the prawns, and stir-fry for 1 minute. Remove and set aside.

2 Add the remaining flavoured oil to the wok and stir-fry the shallots for 1 minute. Add the sugar and the eggs, and cook for 1 minute, stirring frequently to scramble the eggs as they begin to set.

3 Stir in the oyster sauce, nam pla, lime juice, noodles, and beansprouts, and return the prawns to the wok. Stir-fry for 2 minutes, then add the spring onions and half the peanuts. Toss everything together for 1–2 minutes, or until piping hot.

4 To serve, divide between 4 individual bowls, scatter the remaining peanuts on top, and serve with lime wedges.

PASTA, NOODLES, AND GNOCCHI KNOW-HOW *see* Boil noodles **p470**

Smoked haddock risotto

Knowing how to make a good risotto is a cornerstone skill for any cook. Be patient as you gradually add the hot stock, stirring all the time, and you will have success every time.

PREPARATION TIME **10 minutes** • COOKING TIME **30 minutes** • **SERVES 4**

1 tbsp **olive oil**

60g (2oz) **unsalted butter**

1 **onion**, finely chopped

1 **celery stick**, finely chopped

200g (7oz) **arborio rice**

150ml (5fl oz) **dry cider**

1 litre (1¾ pints) **chicken stock**

150g (5½oz) fillet of **undyed smoked haddock**, skinned and chopped

50g (1¾oz) **baby leaf spinach**

grated zest and juice of 1 **lemon**

60g (2oz) **Parmesan cheese**, freshly grated

4 tbsp **double cream**

salt and freshly ground **black pepper**

1 Heat the oil and half the butter in a large saucepan. Add the onion and celery and fry over a medium heat for 5 minutes until softened but not browned. Add the rice, cook for a few minutes, stirring constantly until glistening. Add the cider and allow to bubble, stirring all the time, until it has been absorbed. Start adding the stock, a ladleful at a time, allowing the rice to absorb all the liquid before adding more.

2 After about 15 minutes, when the rice is nearly cooked and you have only 1 more ladleful of stock to go, add the haddock and the last of the stock. Cook until the stock is absorbed,

then stir in the spinach and lemon zest. As soon as the spinach has wilted, stir in the lemon juice, Parmesan cheese, the rest of the butter (cut into small pieces), and the cream. Taste and adjust the seasoning.

3 Spoon the risotto on to warm bowls and serve straight away.

FISH KNOW-HOW *see* Skin a fillet **p273**
RICE, GRAINS, AND PULSES KNOW-HOW *see* Make risotto **p449**

Risotto alla milanese

Traditionally served with Osso buco (see p45), this is a great blueprint recipe from which to develop your own risotto creations.

PREPARATION TIME **5 minutes** • COOKING TIME **25 minutes** • **SERVES 4–6**

2 good pinches of **saffron threads**

1.2 litres (2 pints) boiling **chicken stock**

85g (3oz) **unsalted butter**

2 tbsp **olive oil**

1 **banana shallot**, very finely chopped

400g (14oz) **arborio rice**

150ml (5fl oz) **dry white wine**

85g (3oz) **Grana Padano** or **Parmesan cheese**, grated, plus a few shavings for garnish (optional)

salt and freshly ground **black pepper**

1 Put the saffron in a cup with 3 tbsp of the boiling stock and set aside to infuse.

2 Heat the oil with half the butter in a large saucepan. Add the shallot and fry over a low heat, stirring, for 3 minutes until softened but not browned. Add the rice and cook for a few minutes, stirring constantly, until glistening and translucent. Add the wine and simmer gently, stirring all the time, until it has been absorbed.

3 Add the stock a ladleful at a time, allowing the rice to absorb all the liquid before adding more, until the rice is creamy, but still with some bite; this should take about 20 minutes.

4 Strain the saffron liquid into the rice. Stir in with the rest of the butter (in small pieces) and the grated cheese. Taste and season, if necessary. Serve straight away, garnished with a few Parmesan shavings, if using.

FROM **Ordinary** TO **Extraordinary**

Make risotto balls (arancini) filled with oozing mozzarella. The day before, make the risotto as described, and leave to cool, then cover and refrigerate. The following day, stir in 2 lightly beaten **eggs** and quarter 2 **mozzarella balls**. Form a handful of cold risotto into a ball around a piece of mozzarella. Pass each risotto ball through a dish of **plain flour**, then a dish of lightly beaten **egg**, then a dish of **breadcrumbs**, to coat. Place on a plate, cover and refrigerate for 30 minutes, or up to 2 days. To cook, heat 1cm (½in) **light olive oil** over a medium heat in a broad frying pan. Add the risotto cakes and cook for 5 minutes, then turn and cook for a further 5 minutes. Blot off excess oil and serve, with a roast tomato–basil sauce if you like (see p20).

RICE, GRAINS, AND PULSES KNOW-HOW *see* Make risotto **p449**

Ratatouille

The fragrances of Mediterranean garlic, oregano, and olive oil make this the ideal dish for serving at room temperature. A fantastic accompaniment to a high-summer barbecue.

PREPARATION TIME **15 minutes** • COOKING TIME **40 minutes** • **SERVES 4**

4 tbsp **olive oil**

1 **onion**, chopped

1 **garlic clove**, chopped

1 **courgette**, sliced

1 small **aubergine**, about 225g (8oz), cut into 2.5cm (1in) cubes

1 **red pepper**, deseeded, and cut into 2.5cm (1in) pieces

150ml (5fl oz) **vegetable stock**

400g can **chopped tomatoes**

2 tsp chopped **oregano**, plus 2–3 sprigs to serve

salt and freshly ground **black pepper**

1 Heat the oil in a large casserole over a medium heat. Add the onion and cook for 5 minutes, until soft and transparent. Stir in the garlic, courgette, aubergine, and red pepper, and fry for 5 minutes, stirring.

2 Add the stock, tomatoes with their juice, and the chopped oregano to the casserole, and bring the mixture to the boil.

Reduce the heat to low and partially cover the pan. Cook until the vegetables are tender, stirring occasionally.

3 Season to taste with salt and pepper. Spoon the ratatouille into a serving bowl and serve immediately, garnished with oregano sprigs. Alternatively, serve at room temperature, or cool quickly, cover, and refrigerate then serve cold.

VEGETABLES KNOW-HOW *see* Prepare bell peppers **p372**
FLAVOURINGS KNOW-HOW *see* Prepare herbs **p391**

Gratin dauphinois

A gratin rich with cream and fragrant with garlic and nutmeg. Eat it as an accompaniment, or as a simple Sunday supper with a crisp green salad.

PREPARATION TIME **20 minutes** • COOKING TIME **1 hour 30 minutes** • **SERVES 4–6**

900g (2lb) even-sized **waxy potatoes**, such as **Nicola**

salt and freshly ground **black pepper**

600ml (1 pint) **double cream**

1 **garlic clove**, cut in half

freshly grated **nutmeg**

45g (1½oz) **unsalted butter**, at room temperature

1 Preheat the oven to 180°C (350°F/Gas 4). Butter a gratin dish.

2 Peel the potatoes and slice them into even rounds 3mm (⅛in) thick – use a mandolin or a food processor fitted with a fine slicing blade, if you have one. Rinse the potato slices in cold water, drain, and pat dry with kitchen paper or a tea towel.

3 Arrange the potato slices in layers in the prepared dish, seasoning each layer well with salt and pepper.

4 Pour the cream into a saucepan, add the garlic and a good grating of nutmeg, and bring just to the boil. Pour the cream over the potatoes and dot the top with small pieces of butter.

5 Cover with foil and bake for 1 hour. Remove the foil and continue baking for 30 minutes, or until the potatoes are tender when pierced with a knife and the top is golden. Serve hot, straight from the oven.

FROM **Ordinary** TO **Extraordinary**

Make the most of **seasonal vegetables** and bake gratins all year round. Use **celeriac**, **swede**, and **Jerusalem artichoke** in winter, or in summer layer in **fennel**, **kohlrabi**, and **turnips**. In every case, substitute them for half the weight of potato, and follow the recipe as instructed. The dish has infinite variations and will never get boring.

Tabbouleh

Aromatic herbs and sharp lemons lift this Middle Eastern bulgur salad. It's at its best as a side with simple grilled and glazed meats.

PREPARATION TIME **20 minutes, plus standing** • **SERVES 4**

115g (4oz) **bulgur wheat**

juice of 2 **lemons**

75ml (2½fl oz) **olive oil**

salt and freshly ground **black pepper**

bunch of **flat-leaf parsley**

small bunch of **mint leaves**

4 **spring onions**, finely chopped

2 large **tomatoes**, deseeded and diced

1 head of **Little Gem lettuce**

1 Put the bulgur wheat in a large bowl, pour over cold water to cover, and leave to stand for 15 minutes, or until the wheat has absorbed all the water and the grains have swollen.

2 Add the lemon juice and olive oil to the wheat, season to taste with salt and pepper, and stir to mix.

3 Just before serving, pick the leaves from the herbs and finely chop them, discarding any coarse stalks. Mix the parsley, mint, spring onions, and tomatoes into the wheat.

4 Arrange the lettuce leaves on a serving plate and spoon the salad into the leaves.

FROM **Ordinary** TO **Extraordinary**

For a different take, make **crisp tabbouleh fritters**. Make a batter by putting 4 tbsp **chickpea flour** in a bowl and mixing in 2 tbsp **plain yogurt** to make a paste about the thickness of thick double cream. Add a splash of water to thin it out, if necessary. Mix in the tabbouleh. Heat 5mm (¼in) of **light olive oil** in a large frying pan, then add 1 tbsp of the tabbouleh mixture to make a round fritter. Add a few more to the pan, but be careful not to overcrowd it. Cook, turning once, until golden on both sides. Serve with **lemon wedges** and **tahini sauce**, made by mixing 3 tbsp **tahini paste**, 1 crushed **garlic clove** and the juice of 2 **lemons**.

Chargrilled asparagus with hollandaise

Asparagus is one of the most exquisite vegetables, made all the more alluring by its short six-week season. This recipe heightens its flavour by griddling, to intensify the asparagus taste, then adding the creamy sauce.

PREPARATION TIME **10 minutes** • COOKING TIME **10 minutes** • **SERVES 4**

500g (1lb 2oz) fresh **asparagus spears**

1 tbsp **olive oil**

FOR THE HOLLANDAISE

2 tbsp **white wine vinegar**

4 **egg yolks**

115g (4oz) **unsalted butter**, melted

salt and freshly ground **black pepper**

juice of ½ **lemon**

1 Trim the woody ends from the asparagus, then toss the spears in the olive oil. Heat a ridged cast-iron griddle pan. When very hot, add the asparagus and cook for 5–6 minutes, depending on the thickness of the spears, turning often, until lightly charred and just tender.

2 Meanwhile, to make the sauce, heat the vinegar in a small pan and allow to bubble until it reduces by half. Remove from the heat, add 2 tbsp water, then whisk in the egg yolks one at a time.

3 Return the pan to a very low heat and whisk continuously until the mixture is thick and light. Remove from the heat and gradually whisk in the melted butter. Season to taste with salt and pepper, and stir in the lemon juice.

4 Divide the asparagus between serving plates and serve with the sauce spooned over.

VEGETABLES KNOW-HOW *see* Prepare asparagus **p367**
SAVOURY SAUCES AND STOCKS KNOW-HOW *see* Make hollandaise **p491**

Roasted vegetables

Learn how to roast vegetables and this recipe will take you through the year, as you replace these winter roots with fennel or turnips, and the rosemary with oregano, as the year rolls round to the warmer months.

PREPARATION TIME **25 minutes** • COOKING TIME **1 hour** • **SERVES 4–6**

4 tbsp **olive oil**

900g (2lb) **floury potatoes**, such as **Maris Piper**, peeled and quartered

4 **carrots**, peeled and quartered

sea salt

4 **parsnips**, peeled and quartered

4 **banana shallots**, peeled and quartered

1 bulb of **garlic**, separated into cloves but left unpeeled

2 sprigs of **rosemary**, torn into leaves

1 Preheat the oven to 200°C (400°F/Gas 6). Put the oil in a large roasting tin and place it in the oven.

2 Put the potatoes and carrots in a pan of salted water, bring to the boil, then boil for 5 minutes. Add the parsnips and cook a further 3 minutes. Drain well, then return to the pan.

3 Put the lid on the pan and give it a good shake to roughen the edges of the vegetables.

4 Remove the hot roasting tin from the oven. Carefully add the part-cooked vegetables, along with the shallots and garlic cloves, turning each piece over in the hot oil. Sprinkle with the rosemary and season with sea salt. Return to the oven to roast for about 1 hour, turning once, until the vegetables are golden and tender.

Chips

Nearly as quick as opening a packet, mastering the art of deep-frying will stand you in good stead in the kitchen. And give you the world's best chips, of course...

PREPARATION TIME **10 minutes, plus soaking** • COOKING TIME **20 minutes** • **SERVES 4**

900g (2lb) **Maris Piper potatoes**, peeled and cut into thick chips

groundnut oil, for deep-frying

coarse **sea salt**

1 Soak the potatoes in cold water for 10 minutes, drain, and dry thoroughly. Heat the oil to 160°C (325°F) and cook the potatoes, a batch at time, for a few minutes in the oil until soft, but do not brown. Drain on kitchen paper.

2 Increase the heat of the fryer to 180°C (350°F). Return the chips for another 2–3 minutes, until they are brown and crisp. Using a slotted spoon, lift the chips onto clean kitchen paper to drain, and then transfer to a serving bowl. Sprinkle with coarse sea salt and serve hot.

FROM **Ordinary** TO **Extraordinary**

Make **sweet potato chips** in the same way, but do not soak them in water. Instead, toss them with 2 tbsp **cornflour** mixed with 1 tsp **paprika** before the first frying. Serve with **sriracha sauce** alongside a spiced pork chop.

VEGETABLES KNOW-HOW *see* Make chips **p375**

Apple pie

Few puddings are as comforting and universally welcomed. Home-made shortcrust pastry will make a difference here, so do try to make it yourself.

PREPARATION TIME **25 minutes, plus chilling** • COOKING TIME **50 minutes** • **SERVES 8**

350g (12oz) **sweet shortcrust pastry**

4 tbsp **plain flour**, plus extra for dusting

finely grated zest and juice of
1 unwaxed **lemon**

100g (3½oz) **caster sugar**

1 tsp ground **mixed spice**

1kg (2¼lb) **Bramley apples**, peeled
and thinly sliced

2 tbsp **milk**, to glaze

1 Divide the dough into 2 pieces: one piece should be two-thirds of the dough, the other about one-third. On a lightly floured work surface, roll the larger piece into a 30cm (12in) circle and use it to line a 23cm (9in) deep pie plate, leaving any excess to overhang. Cover with cling film and chill for at least 15 minutes. Roll out the remaining dough into a 25cm (10in) circle, place on a plate, cover, and refrigerate.

2 Meanwhile, preheat the oven to 200°C (400°F/Gas 6) with a baking tray inside. Mix the lemon zest and juice, sugar, flour, and mixed spice in a large bowl. Gently toss with the apple slices.

3 Tip the filling into the pie plate. Lightly brush the pastry on the rim of the pie plate with water and place the smaller dough circle on top. Crimp the edges together and cut off the excess pastry. Carefully brush the top of the pastry with milk and cut a few slits with a sharp knife.

4 Put the pie on the hot baking tray in the oven. Reduce the oven temperature to 190°C (375°F/Gas 5) and bake for 50–55 minutes, or until the pastry is golden brown. Leave to stand for 5 minutes, then slice and serve hot.

FRUITS AND NUTS KNOW-HOW *see* Peel and prepare apples **p422**
DOUGH, PASTRY, AND CAKE KNOW-HOW *see* Sweet shortcrust pastry **p457**

Chocolate fondants

A guaranteed smash hit. The vital thing here is split-second timing.

PREPARATION TIME **20 minutes** • COOKING TIME **12–15 minutes** • MAKES **4**

150g (5½oz) **unsalted butter**, cubed, plus extra for greasing

1 heaped tbsp **plain flour**, sifted, plus extra for dusting

150g (5½oz) **dark chocolate** (70% cocoa), broken into pieces

3 large **eggs**

75g (2½oz) **caster sugar**

cocoa powder or **icing sugar**, for dusting (optional)

cream or **ice cream**, to serve (optional)

1 Preheat the oven to 200°C (400°F/Gas 6). Thoroughly grease the sides and base of 4 x 150ml (5fl oz) dariole moulds or ramekin dishes. Sprinkle the insides of each dish with a little flour, turning it around until all the butter is covered with a thin layer of it. Tip out any excess flour. Line the bases of the moulds or ramekins with small discs of baking parchment.

2 Gently melt together the chocolate and butter in a heatproof bowl over simmering water, stirring occasionally. Make sure the the bowl does not touch the water. Allow to cool slightly.

3 In a separate bowl, whisk together the eggs and sugar. Once the chocolate mixture has cooled slightly, beat it into the eggs and sugar until thoroughly combined. Sprinkle the flour over the top of the mixture and gently fold it in.

4 Divide the mixture between the moulds or ramekins, making sure that the mixture does not come right up to the top. At this stage the fondants can be refrigerated for several hours or overnight, as long as they are brought back to room temperature before baking.

5 Bake the fondants on a baking tray in the middle of the oven for 5–6 minutes if using dariole moulds, 12–15 minutes for ramekins. The sides should be firm, but the middles soft to the touch.

6 Run a sharp knife around the edge of the moulds or ramekins. Place a serving plate over each one, and invert the fondant onto the plate. Gently remove the mould or ramekin, peel off the parchment, and dust with cocoa powder or icing sugar, if desired. Serve immediately with cream or ice cream.

FROM **Ordinary** TO **Extraordinary**

For a **salted caramel chocolate fondant**, prepare a batch of **caramel sauce** (see p394), stirring in 1 tbsp **sea salt** as it cools. Pour the sauce into 4 greased hollows of an ice cube tray and freeze overnight. Just before baking the chocolate fondants, place a frozen cube in the centre of each fondant, pushing it down below the surface. Serve with the remaining salted caramel sauce, if wished.

FLAVOURINGS KNOW-HOW *see* Prepare chocolate **p395**

Bread and butter pudding

Careful cooking in a low oven gives the pudding a custardy texture.

PREPARATION TIME **15 minutes, plus soaking** • COOKING TIME **40 minutes** • **SERVES 4**

30g (1oz) **unsalted butter**, plus extra for greasing

5–6 slices of day-old **bread**, crusts removed, about 175g (6oz) in total

60g (2oz) **raisins**

3 **eggs**

300ml (10fl oz) **full-fat milk**

200ml (7fl oz) **single cream**

60g (2oz) **caster sugar**

1 tsp **vanilla extract**

4 tbsp **apricot jam**

2–3 tsp **lemon juice**

1 Lightly grease an ovenproof dish with a little butter. Spread the remaining butter on the slices of bread. Cut each slice in half diagonally, then in half again to form 4 triangles.

2 Place the raisins in the bottom of the dish and arrange overlapping slices of bread on the top. Beat together the eggs, milk, cream, sugar, and vanilla extract. Carefully pour the mixture over the bread and leave to soak for at least 30 minutes.

3 Preheat the oven to 180°C (350°F/Gas 4). Place the dish in a deep roasting tin then pour boiling water into the tin to a depth of 2.5cm (1in). Bake in the oven for 30–40 minutes, until still slightly moist in the centre, but not runny.

4 Meanwhile, put the jam in a small pan with the lemon juice and 1 tbsp water. Bring to the boil, then press the jam mixture through a sieve. Carefully brush or spoon the sieved jam over the surface of the hot pudding.

Rice pudding

This is lovely chilled and served with fruit compôte and cream.

PREPARATION TIME **15 minutes** • COOKING TIME **2 hours–2 hours 30 minutes** • **SERVES 4**

15g (½oz) **unsalted butter**, plus extra for greasing

60g (2oz) **short-grain rice**, such as **Arborio** or **pudding rice**

600ml (1 pint) **full-fat milk**

30g (1oz) **caster sugar**

pinch of ground **cinnamon** or grated **nutmeg**

1 Lightly butter a 900ml (1½ pint) ovenproof serving dish. Rinse the rice under cold running water, and drain well. Pour the rice and the milk into the dish and leave to rest for 30 minutes.

2 Preheat the oven to 150°C (300°F/Gas 2). Add the sugar, stir, then sprinkle the top with cinnamon or nutmeg, and dot with pieces of the butter. Bake for 2–2½ hours, or until the skin of the rice is golden.

Crème caramel

A simple custard gives a delightfully smooth finish to this famous pudding.

PREPARATION TIME **20 minutes, plus chilling** • COOKING TIME **35–40 minutes** • **MAKES 4**

235g (8½oz) **caster sugar**

1 **vanilla pod**

600ml (1 pint) **full-fat milk**

4 **eggs**

4 **egg yolks**

1 Preheat the oven to 160°C (325°F/Gas 3). Pour boiling water into 4 individual ramekins and set aside. Fill a large bowl with cold water. Pour 175g (6oz) caster sugar into a heavy saucepan and place over a low heat, until the sugar has just dissolved. Do not stir; if sugar crystals form at the sides of the saucepan, dip a pastry brush in water and brush the pan above the crystals, taking care not to touch the sugar. Once the sugar has dissolved, increase the heat and boil rapidly, gently swirling the pan until the caramel is golden brown. Place the base of the pan in the bowl of cold water to rapidly cool, to prevent it cooking any further.

2 Working quickly and carefully, empty the ramekins and divide the hot caramel between them. Gently swirl the dishes so that the caramel comes halfway up the sides of each ramekin. Set aside to cool.

3 Using a sharp knife, split the vanilla pod and scrape out the seeds; place both the seeds and pod in a saucepan with the milk, and heat until almost boiling. Remove from the heat and discard the pod.

4 Meanwhile, whisk the eggs, egg yolks, and remaining sugar together in a large bowl. Pour over the warm milk mixture, whisking to combine, then pour this mixture into the ramekins. Place in a roasting tin and pour boiling water into the tin to come halfway up the sides of the dishes. Bake for 25–30 minutes, or until just set in the centre. Remove from the tin, allow to cool, then chill until ready to serve.

5 Gently pull the edges of the custard away from the sides of the ramekin using a fingertip. Place a serving plate over the top of the ramekin and invert on to the plate.

FLAVOURINGS KNOW-HOW *see* Extract vanilla seeds **p392**
EGGS AND DAIRY PRODUCTS KNOW-HOW *see* Separate yolks and whites **p430**

Crème brûlée

Err on the side of generosity here when adding the sugar topping. Too little, and you won't get that tempting "crack" when you dive in with your spoon.

PREPARATION TIME **20 minutes, plus standing** • COOKING TIME **45 minutes** • **SERVES 6**

500ml (16fl oz) **double cream**

1 **vanilla pod**, split in half lengthways

5 **egg yolks**

50g (1¾oz) **caster sugar**

4 tbsp **granulated sugar**

1 Preheat the oven to 140°C (275°F/Gas 1). Place the cream in a saucepan over a low heat. Add the vanilla pod and heat until just simmering, then remove from the hob and set aside to infuse for 1 hour.

2 Whisk the egg yolks and caster sugar together in a bowl until well combined. Remove the vanilla pod halves from the cream, and use the tip of a sharp knife to scrape the seeds into the cream.

3 Whisk the cream into the egg mixture, then strain through a sieve into a jug. Pour the mixture evenly into 6 ramekins. Place the ramekins in a roasting tin and pour boiling water into the tin to come halfway up the sides of the dishes. Bake for 40 minutes, or until just set. Remove from the tin, cool, and chill.

4 Just before serving, preheat the grill to its highest setting. Sprinkle 2 tsp sugar evenly over the top of each pudding and grill until the sugar caramelizes. You can also use a blow torch, if you prefer: sweep the flame gently over the sugar from a slight distances until it caramelizes. Allow to rest for 5 minutes before serving.

FROM **Ordinary** TO **Extraordinary**

There are near-infinite flavour variations to this recipe. Give it **a fragrant Indian style** by using the crushed seeds from 10 **green cardamom pods** instead of the vanilla, then add **rosewater** to taste in step 3, adding it gradually and tasting as you go, as some brands of rosewater are stronger than others. Use **jaggery** instead of granulated sugar for the topping, if you can find it. You could also swap out the vanilla for **lavender**, or even peeled and finely grated **fresh root ginger**.

FLAVOURINGS KNOW-HOW *see* Extract vanilla seeds **p392**
EGGS AND DAIRY PRODUCTS KNOW-HOW *see* Separate yolks and whites **p430**

Chocolate mousse

An elegant way of serving the mousse is in a demitasse with a chocolate teaspoon or mint stick laid on the saucers.

PREPARATION TIME **20 minutes, plus chilling** • COOKING TIME **20 minutes** • MAKES 4

115g (4oz) **dark chocolate** (70% cocoa), broken up, plus extra grated or curled chocolate to serve

1 tbsp **brandy** or **Cognac**

2 **eggs**, separated

35g (1¼oz) **caster sugar**

150ml (5fl oz) **double cream**

1 Place the chocolate and brandy or Cognac in a heatproof bowl over a pan of simmering water, ensuring the bowl does not touch the water. When the chocolate has melted, stir until combined, remove from the heat, and allow to cool slightly.

2 Place the egg yolks and sugar in a large bowl and whisk until thick and creamy. Then whisk in the chocolate mixture.

3 Whip the cream in a bowl until stiff. Gently fold in the chocolate mixture until combined, taking care not to overmix. Whisk the egg whites until stiff, and gently fold into the chocolate mixture.

4 Spoon into individual dishes and chill for at least 2 hours. If you like the mousse soft, take it out of the refrigerator and let it warm to room temperature before serving. Decorate with grated chocolate or chocolate curls before serving.

FROM **Ordinary** TO **Extraordinary**

For a dramatic **Japanese-style update**, make the mousse as instructed, but use **white chocolate** instead of dark chocolate. Add **a yuzu and matcha crumble**: put 60g (2oz) **plain flour** in a bowl with 30g (1oz) **caster sugar** and 1 tbsp **green matcha powder**, then rub in 30g (1oz) **unsalted butter** with your fingertips. Spread out on a baking tray and bake for 15 minutes, stirring halfway through. Leave to cool, then sprinkle over the mousses just before serving.

FLAVOURINGS KNOW-HOW: *See* Prepare chocolate **p395**
EGGS AND DAIRY PRODUCTS KNOW-HOW: *See* Whisk egg whites **p431**
EGGS AND DAIRY PRODUCTS KNOW-HOW: *See* Whip cream **p438**

Lemon tart

Don't let the filling of this tart over-cook in the oven. Remove it while it is still a silky, just-set custard, and before it becomes fully set.

PREPARATION TIME **35 minutes, plus chilling** • COOKING TIME **45 minutes** • **SERVES 8**

FOR THE PASTRY

175g (6oz) **plain flour**, plus extra for dusting

85g (3oz) **unsalted butter**, chilled

45g (1½oz) **caster sugar**

1 **egg**

FOR THE FILLING

5 **eggs**

200g (7oz) **caster sugar**

zest and juice of 4 unwaxed **lemons**

250ml (9fl oz) **double cream**

icing sugar and **lemon zest**, to serve

1 To make the pastry, place the flour, butter, and sugar into a food processor and pulse until it resembles breadcrumbs. Add the egg and process until the pastry draws together into a ball.

2 Roll out the pastry on a lightly floured surface into a large circle and use to line a 23cm (9in) loose-bottomed tart tin. Chill for at least 30 minutes.

3 Prepare the filling: beat the eggs and sugar together until combined. Beat in the lemon zest and juice, then whisk in the cream. Chill until needed.

4 Preheat the oven to 190°C (375°F/Gas 5). Line the pastry case with greaseproof paper, fill with baking beans, and bake blind for 10 minutes. Remove the paper and beans, then return to the oven for another 5 minutes, or until the base is crisp.

5 Reduce the oven temperature to 140°C (275°F/Gas 1). Place the tart tin on a baking tray. Pour in the lemon filling, being careful not to allow the filling to spill over the edges. Bake for 30 minutes, or until just set. Remove from the oven and cool. Serve dusted with icing sugar and sprinkled with lemon zest.

FROM **Ordinary** TO **Extraordinary**

In the winter months, make a **blood orange tart with chocolate pastry** instead. For the pastry, just substitute 3 tbsp of the flour with **cocoa powder**, then proceed as instructed. For the filling, use the zest and juice of 4 **blood oranges** instead of the lemons. Sprinkle the finished tart with **candied peel** instead of lemon zest to serve.

DOUGH, PASTRY, AND CAKE KNOW-HOW: *See* Sweet shortcrust pastry **p457**
DOUGH, PASTRY, AND CAKE KNOW-HOW: *See* Blind bake **p462**

Pavlova

The meringue base for a pavlova should be wonderfully marshmallow-like within.
That is achieved here by using a touch of vinegar in the mixture, which is stabilized
with a little cornflour.

PREPARATION TIME **15 minutes, plus cooling** • COOKING TIME **1 hour 20 minutes** • **SERVES 6**

6 **egg whites**, at room temperature

pinch of **salt**

350g (12oz) **caster sugar**

2 tsp **cornflour**

1 tsp **white wine vinegar**

300ml (10fl oz) **double cream**

strawberries, raspberries, and
blueberries, to decorate

1 Preheat the oven to 180°C (350°F/Gas 4). Line a baking tray with greaseproof paper. Put the egg whites in a large, clean, grease-free bowl with a pinch of salt. Whisk until stiff, then start whisking in the sugar 1 tbsp at a time, whisking well after each addition. Continue whisking until the egg whites are stiff and glossy, then whisk in the cornflour and vinegar.

2 Spoon the meringue onto the baking tray and spread to form a 20cm (8in) circle. Bake for 5 minutes, then reduce the oven temperature to 140°C (275°F/Gas 1) and cook for a further 1¼ hours, or until the outside is crisp. Allow it to cool completely before transferring to a serving plate.

3 Whip the cream until it holds its shape, then spoon it onto the meringue base. Decorate with the fruit and serve.

FROM **Ordinary** TO **Extraordinary**

Try **individual hazelnut meringues with hazelnut spears**. Add 50g (1½oz) **ground hazelnuts** to the meringue mixture at the end of step 1, then pipe or spoon out individual meringues instead of the large version. Bake and fill as directed. For praline spears, put 60g (2oz) **caster sugar** in a heavy-based saucepan with 90g (3oz) **chopped hazelnuts**, place over a medium-low heat and wait until the sugar melts and turns a deep golden brown. Do not stir. Tip onto a silicone sheet and leave to cool, then break into long shards and use to decorate the pavlovas.

EGGS AND DAIRY PRODUCTS KNOW-HOW: *See* Whisk egg whites **p431**
EGGS AND DAIRY PRODUCTS KNOW-HOW: *See* Whip cream **p438**

Blueberry crumble

A classic comfort food recipe, this will bring certain cheer to the table.

PREPARATION TIME **15 minutes** • COOKING TIME **30 minutes** • **SERVES 4**

450g (1lb) **blueberries**

2 large **peaches** or 2 **eating apples**, sliced

grated zest of ½ unwaxed **lemon**

2 tbsp **caster sugar**

FOR THE CRUMBLE TOPPING

115g (4oz) **plain flour**

75g (2½oz) **unsalted butter**, cut in small pieces

60g (2oz) **rolled oats**

100g (3½oz) **demerara sugar**

1 Preheat the oven to 190°C (375°F/Gas 5). Spread the blueberries and peaches over the base of a shallow ovenproof dish and sprinkle with the lemon zest and caster sugar.

2 Sift the flour into a bowl. Add the butter and rub in with your fingertips until the mixture resembles breadcrumbs. Stir in the oats and sugar. Spoon over the fruit to cover completely and press down gently with the back of a spoon.

3 Place the dish on a baking tray and bake in the oven for 30 minutes, or until golden. Leave the dish to cool briefly before serving.

Pecan pie

Deliciously moreish, this wonderful nutty pie deserves a wider audience. It is also incredibly simple to put together, and looks hugely impressive, especially when you arrange the pecans attractively on top.

PREPARATION TIME **15 minutes** • COOKING TIME **1 hour 30 minutes** • **SERVES 8**

200g (7oz) **sweet shortcrust pastry**

plain flour, for dusting

150ml (5fl oz) **maple syrup**

60g (2oz) **unsalted butter**

175g (6oz) **light soft brown sugar**

½ tsp **vanilla extract**

pinch of **salt**

3 **eggs**

200g (7oz) **shelled pecan nuts**

1 Roll the pastry out on a lightly floured surface, then use it to line a 23cm (9in) loose-bottomed tart tin. Trim around the top edge of the tin, and prick the base all over with a fork. Chill for at least 30 minutes.

2 Preheat the oven to 200°C (400°F/Gas 6). Line the pastry case with greaseproof paper, and fill with baking beans. Blind bake for 10 minutes. Remove the paper and beans, and return to the oven for another 10 minutes, or until pale golden. Remove the pastry case from the oven temperature and reduce the temperature to 180°C (350°F/Gas 4).

3 Pour the maple syrup into a saucepan, and add the butter, sugar, vanilla extract, and salt. Place the pan over a low heat, and stir constantly until the butter has melted, and the sugar

dissolved. Remove the pan from the heat, and leave the mixture to cool until it feels just tepid, then beat in the eggs, one at a time. Stir in most of the pecan nuts, then pour the mixture into the pastry case. Arrange the reserved nuts on the surface of the mixure as desired.

4 Bake for 40–50 minutes, or until just set. Cover with a sheet of foil if it is browning too quickly.

5 Remove the pie from the oven, transfer it to a wire rack and leave to cool for 15–20 minutes. Remove from the tin and either serve it warm or leave it on the wire rack to cool completely.

DOUGH, PASTRY, AND CAKE KNOW-HOW: *See* Sweet shortcrust pastry **p457**
DOUGH, PASTRY, AND CAKE KNOW-HOW: *See* Blind bake **p462**

Banoffee pie

It's worth boiling two cans of condensed milk at the same time, then keeping one chilled in the fridge for ready-made dulce de leche.

PREPARATION TIME **20 minutes, plus milk boiling and chilling** • **SERVES 8**

397g can **sweetened condensed milk**

200g (7oz) **digestive biscuits**, crushed

1 tbsp **light soft brown sugar**

60g (2oz) **butter**, melted

3 **bananas**

2 tsp **lemon juice**

300ml (10fl oz) **whipping cream** or **double cream**

2 tbsp **espresso coffee**, cooled

a little grated **dark chocolate**

a few toasted chopped **nuts** (optional)

1 To make the dulce de leche, remove any label on the condensed milk. Put the unopened can in a saucepan of water. Bring to the boil, reduce the heat, part-cover with a lid and simmer gently for 3 hours, topping up with water as it evaporates. (Do not allow the water to boil dry, or the can may explode.) Remove from the pan and leave to cool.

2 Mix the biscuit crumbs with the brown sugar and melted butter in a bowl. Press into the base and up the sides of a 20cm (8in) flan dish. Chill in the refrigerator until firm.

3 Slice the bananas and toss them in the lemon juice. Spread them over the biscuit base.

4 Open the can of dulce de leche and spread it evenly over the bananas.

5 Whip the cream with the cold espresso until softly peaking, then spread over the dulce de leche. Sprinkle with a little grated chocolate and some chopped nuts, if using. Chill for at least 1 hour before serving.

FROM **Ordinary** TO **Extraordinary**

Make a **tropical vegan version** with coconut and lime flavours. For a vegan dulce de leche, bring 840ml (1½ pints) **coconut milk** with 170g (6oz) **brown sugar** to the boil with ½ tsp **salt**. Reduce the heat to low and cook for 1–2 hours, stirring regularly, until thick and deep brown. Allow to cool before using. Use **vegan digestive biscuits** and **vegan margarine** for the base, adding a finely chopped ball of **stem ginger**. Substitute the dairy cream for **coconut cream**, mixing it with the finely grated zest of 1 unwaxed **lime** instead of coffee. Sprinkle with grated **vegan dark chocolate** to serve.

EGGS AND DAIRY PRODUCTS KNOW-HOW: *See* Whip cream **p438**

Summer pudding

For a perfect finish every time, set aside a little of the fruit juice from the saucepan. When you come to serve the pudding, brush this juice over any white patches.

PREPARATION TIME **20–25 minutes, plus chilling** • COOKING TIME **5 minutes** • **SERVES 6**

12 slices of **white bread**, crusts removed

125g (4½oz) **blackcurrants**

125g (4½oz) **redcurrants**

150g (5½oz) **caster sugar**

250g (9oz) **mixed berries**, such as **strawberries, raspberries, mulberries,** and **blueberries**

1 Line a 900ml (1½ pint) pudding basin with the bread slices, beginning with a circle cut to fit the base, then overlapping slices evenly around the side. Reserve a few slices of bread to cover the fruit later.

2 Add the currants and sugar to a heavy-based saucepan, and cook over a low heat until soft and the juices have run. Stir in the mixed berries and cook for 1 minute, or until just softening.

3 Spoon some of the juices over the bread, then fill the basin with the fruit. Make sure the fruit is packed well into the basin. Cover the fruit with the reserved slices of bread, ensuring it is completely covered with an even layer.

4 Stand the basin in a dish to catch any overspill of juice. If there is any more juice remaining in the saucepan, spoon this over the top layer of bread. Cover with cling film and place a small plate on top. Put a weight on the plate and chill overnight.

5 Invert the pudding onto a serving plate to serve.

Profiteroles

Much easier to make than you might think, home-made choux buns are infinitely better – crisp and buttery – than flabby shop-bought versions.

PREPARATION TIME **30 minutes, plus chilling** • COOKING TIME **30 minutes** • **SERVES 4**

FOR THE CHOUX BUNS

60g (2oz) **plain flour**

50g (1¾oz) **unsalted butter**

2 **eggs**, lightly beaten

FOR THE FILLING AND TOPPING

400ml (14fl oz) **double cream**

200g (7oz) **dark chocolate**, broken into pieces

25g (scant 1oz) **unsalted butter**

2 tbsp **golden syrup**

1 Preheat the oven to 220°C (425°F/Gas 7). Line 2 large baking trays with baking parchment. Sift the flour onto a separate piece of baking parchment.

2 Put the butter and 150ml (5fl oz) water into a small saucepan and heat gently until melted. Bring to the boil, remove from the heat, and tip in the flour. Beat quickly with a wooden spoon until the mixture is thick, smooth, and forms a ball in the centre of the saucepan. Cool for 10 minutes.

3 Gradually add the eggs, beating well after each addition. Use enough egg to form a stiff, smooth, and shiny paste. Spoon the mixture into a piping bag fitted with a 1cm (½in) plain nozzle.

4 Pipe walnut-sized rounds, set well apart, on the prepared baking trays. Bake for 20 minutes, or until risen, golden, and crisp. Remove from the oven and make a small slit in the side

of each bun to allow the steam to escape. Return to the oven for a further 2 minutes, allow them to crisp, then transfer to a wire rack to cool completely.

5 When ready to serve, pour 100ml (3½fl oz) cream into a saucepan and whip the remainder until just peaking. Pile into a piping bag fitted with a 5mm (¼in) plain nozzle.

6 Add the chocolate, butter, and golden syrup to the saucepan with the cream and heat very gently until melted, stirring frequently. Meanwhile, pipe the whipped cream into each choux bun and pile onto a serving plate or cake stand.

7 When the sauce has melted, mix well, and pour over the choux buns. Serve immediately.

FROM **Ordinary** TO **Extraordinary**

Make a **colourful version** with red **pomegranates** and green **pistachios**. Stir 4 tbsp **ground pistachios** into the cream filling. Make a pomegranate icing instead of chocolate sauce. Sift 225g (8oz) **icing sugar** into a bowl, then gradually whisk in 2–3 tbsp **pomegranate juice** until you have a pink icing the consistency of double cream. Use this to ice each profiterole. Sprinkle with **pomegranate seeds** and **chopped pistachios** to serve.

EGGS AND DAIRY PRODUCTS KNOW-HOW: *See* Whip cream **p438**
DOUGH, PASTRY, AND CAKE KNOW-HOW: *See* Choux pastry **p457**

Tiramisu

The name of this luscious pudding means "pick-me-up" in Italian.

PREPARATION TIME 20 minutes, plus cooling and chilling • **SERVES 4**

120ml (4fl oz) cold **espresso coffee**

75ml (2½fl oz) **coffee-flavoured liqueur**

350g (12oz) **mascarpone cheese**

3 tbsp **caster sugar**

360ml (12fl oz) **double cream**

14 **sponge fingers**

cocoa powder, to decorate

coarsely grated **dark chocolate**, to decorate

1 Mix the coffee and liqueur together in a shallow, wide serving bowl and set aside.

2 Put the mascarpone cheese and sugar in a bowl, and beat for a minute or so, until the sugar dissolves. Whip the cream in another bowl until it holds its shape, then fold it into the mascarpone mixture. Put a couple of spoonfuls of the mixture in the bottom of a serving dish.

3 Dip and turn 1 sponge finger in the coffee mixture until just soaked, then place it on top of the mascarpone in the dish; repeat with 6 more sponge fingers, placing them side by side in the dish. Cover with half the remaining mascarpone mixture, then soak and layer the remaining sponge fingers. Top with the remaining mascarpone and smooth the surface. Cover the dish with cling film and chill for at least 4 hours.

4 Sprinkle the top with cocoa powder and grated chocolate just before serving.

FLAVOURINGS KNOW-HOW: *see* Prepare chocolate **p395**
EGGS AND DAIRY PRODUCTS KNOW-HOW: *see* Whip cream **p438**

Tarte Tatin

A lovely recipe that is a deserved French masterpiece. You may have to carefully prise out any apple pieces that have become stuck to the tin, and rearrange them on top to serve.

PREPARATION TIME **30 minutes, plus chilling** • COOKING TIME **35 minutes** • **SERVES 8**

FOR THE PASTRY

150g (5½oz) **unsalted butter**

50g (1¾oz) **caster sugar**

225g (8oz) **plain flour**, plus extra for dusting

1 **egg**, lightly beaten

FOR THE APPLE TOPPING

150g (5½oz) **unsalted butter**, softened

200g (7oz) **caster sugar**

6 large **dessert apples**, such as Granny Smith's, peeled and quartered

1 To make the pastry, cream the butter and sugar together until blended. Gradually mix in the flour, then stir in the egg to bind it together. Turn the mixture onto a lightly floured surface and knead until smooth. Wrap in cling film and chill for at least 1 hour.

2 Preheat the oven to 220°C (425°F/Gas 7). For the topping, melt the butter in a 30cm (12in) round ovenproof baking tin over a medium heat. When the butter has melted, add the sugar, stirring occasionally. Increase the heat slightly until the mixture begins to bubble, then continue cooking, stirring occasionally, for 5 minutes, or until it is a light, toffee colour. Remove from the heat. Alternatively, make the toffee mixture in a non-stick saucepan and transfer to a lightly greased, similar-sized flan dish.

3 Arrange the apple pieces in the tin or flan dish, rounded-side down and tightly packed together.

4 Roll out the pastry to form a circle large enough to fit over the top of the apples with room to spare. Arrange the pastry neatly on top of the fruit and tuck the edges into the pan. Bake for 30 minutes, or until the pastry is lightly browned and cooked. Allow the tart to stand for 10 minutes before carefully inverting onto a large serving plate. Serve while still warm.

FROM **Ordinary** TO **Extraordinary**

Try a **fragrant quince** version. Make as instructed, using baked quince instead of apples. Preheat the oven to 150°C (300°F/Gas 2). Put the **quince** in a covered dish with 2 tbsp each of **honey** and water and 1 **cinnamon stick**. Bake the fruit for around 3 hours, until rosy in colour and deeply aromatic. Leave to cool, then use in place of the apples.

FRUIT AND NUTS KNOW-HOW: *See* Peel and prepare apples **p422**
DOUGH, PASTRY, AND CAKE KNOW-HOW: *See* Sweet shortcrust pastry **p457**

Chocolate brownies

Unlike other cakes, brownies should be removed from the oven before they are fully baked. If you use a skewer to test for doneness, it should emerge with quite a lot of moist crumb sticking to it, or the brownie will be dry.

PREPARATION TIME **20 minutes** • COOKING TIME **1 hour 15 minutes** • **MAKES 16**

50g (1¾oz) **dark chocolate**, chopped

25g (scant 1oz) **unsalted butter**

3 **eggs**

1 tbsp **clear honey**

225g (8oz) **light soft brown sugar**

75g (2½oz) **self-raising flour**

115g (4oz) **walnuts**, roughly chopped

60g (2oz) **white chocolate**, chopped

1 Preheat the oven to 160°C (325°F/Gas 3). Grease and line a 20cm (8in) deep, square cake tin with baking parchment.

2 Put the dark chocolate and butter into a small heatproof bowl over a saucepan of simmering water until melted, stirring occasionally. Don't let the bowl touch the water. Remove the bowl from the pan and set aside to cool slightly.

3 Beat the eggs, honey, and brown sugar together, then gradually beat in the melted chocolate mixture. Sift the flour

over, add the walnut pieces and white chocolate to the bowl, and gently fold the ingredients together. Pour the mixture into the prepared tin.

4 Put the tin in the oven and bake for 30 minutes. Cover loosely with foil and bake for a further 45 minutes. The centre should be a little soft. Leave to cool completely in the tin on a wire rack.

5 When cold, cut into squares. Store in an airtight container.

FROM **Ordinary** TO **Extraordinary**

Transform these into **raspberry cheesecake brownies**. Make the brownie batter as instructed. In a bowl, mix 200g (7oz) **cream cheese**, 2 **egg yolks**, and 75g (2½oz) **caster sugar**. Spoon the brownie mixture into the tin, then add dollops of the cheesecake mixture and a handful of **raspberries**. Swirl everything together and bake as instructed.

Victoria sponge cake

The epitome of British baking. Using good butter and high-quality eggs will give a golden hue to the crumb, as well as a richness to the flavour.

PREPARATION TIME 20 minutes • COOKING TIME 20–25 minutes • SERVES 8

175g (6oz) **unsalted butter**, softened

175g (6oz) **caster sugar**

3 **eggs**, lightly beaten

1 tsp **vanilla extract**

175g (6oz) **self-raising flour**

6–8 tbsp **raspberry jam**

150ml (5fl oz) **double cream**

icing sugar, to dust

1 Preheat the oven to 190°C (375°F/Gas 5). Lightly grease 2 20cm (8in) sandwich tins and line the bottom of the tins with baking parchment.

2 Beat the butter and sugar together until pale and fluffy. It is important to beat the mixture well at this stage to incorporate as much air as possible, to help prevent the eggs from curdling.

3 Mix the eggs and vanilla in a jug and add to the mixture a little at a time, beating well after each addition. If the mixture begins to curdle, beat in 1–2 tbsp of the flour. Sift the flour, and fold into the egg mixture using a large metal spoon or spatula.

4 Divide the mixture equally between the prepared tins, and spread evenly to level the tops. Bake for 20–25 minutes, until pale golden and springy to the touch. Allow the cakes to cool in the tins for 5 minutes, before turning out onto a wire rack. Peel off the lining paper, and allow to cool completely.

5 When the cakes are cool, place one upside down on a serving plate, and spread with the raspberry jam. Lightly whip the cream, until just holding its shape, and spread over the jam. Add the remaining cake layer, and dust lightly with icing sugar before serving.

FROM **Ordinary** TO **Extraordinary**

For a **subtle spin on afternoon tea**, flavour the sponge with Earl Grey. Crush 3 tsp **Earl Grey tea leaves** with a pestle and mortar or a mini food processor, and mix it into the cake batter with the flour. Bake as instructed. Substitute **orange or lemon curd** for the raspberry jam and sprinkle the finished cake with finely grated **unwaxed orange or lemon zest**.

EGGS AND DAIRY PRODUCTS KNOW-HOW: *See* Whip cream **p438**
DOUGH, PASTRY, AND CAKE KNOW-HOW: *See* Prepare and line a cake tin **p464**

Carrot cake

This cake is super-moist, thanks to the oil used in the batter instead of butter, and the grated carrots. An all-in-one recipe, this is a good place for new bakers to start.

PREPARATION TIME **25 minutes** • COOKING TIME **30–35 minutes** • **SERVES 8**

215g (7½oz) **plain flour**

200g (7oz) **caster sugar**

1½ tsp **bicarbonate of soda**

1 tsp **baking powder**

1 tsp **ground cinnamon**

½ tsp each **ground cloves, nutmeg,** and **allspice**

salt

150ml (5fl oz) **sunflower** or **corn oil**

3 **eggs**

165g (5½oz) **carrots**, peeled and grated

125g (4½oz) **walnuts**, chopped

150g (5½oz) **sultanas**

FOR THE FROSTING

225g (8oz) **cream cheese**

75g (2½ oz) soft **unsalted butter**

2 tsp pure **vanilla extract**

450g (1lb) **icing sugar**, sifted

grated zest of 1 unwaxed **orange**

1 Preheat the oven to 180°C (350°F/Gas 4). Grease and line a traybake tin about 23 x 30cm (9 x 12in). In a large bowl, combine the flour, sugar, bicarbonate of soda, baking powder, spices, and salt.

2 Beat together the oil and eggs, then stir them into the flour mixture until just combined. Add the carrots, walnuts, and sultanas and mix well.

3 Pour the mixture into the prepared tin and spread evenly. Bake for 30–35 minutes, or until a knife inserted in the centre comes out clean. Cool in the tin.

4 To make the frosting, beat the cream cheese, butter, and vanilla together with an electric mixer until smooth. Gradually beat in the icing sugar. Fold in the orange zest with a spatula. Spread the frosting over the top of the cooled cake.

Black Forest gâteau

This classic cake has stood the test of time. Don't waste the remaining cherry juice – use it to create a syrup for a fruit salad.

PREPARATION TIME **55 minutes** • COOKING TIME **40 minutes** • **SERVES 8**

85g (3oz) **unsalted butter**, melted, plus extra for greasing

6 **eggs**

175g (6oz) **caster sugar**

125g (4½oz) **plain flour**

50g (1¾oz) **cocoa powder**

1 tsp **vanilla extract**

2 x 425g cans pitted **black cherries**

4 tbsp **Kirsch**

600ml (1 pint) **double cream**

150g (5½ oz) **dark chocolate**, grated

1 Preheat the oven to 180°C (350°F/Gas 4). Lightly grease and line a 23cm (9in) deep springform cake tin with baking parchment. Put the eggs and sugar into a large heatproof bowl, and place over a saucepan filled with simmering water. Don't let the bowl touch the water. Whisk until the mixture is pale and thick, and will hold a trail. Remove from the heat and whisk for another 5 minutes, or until cooled slightly.

2 Sift the flour and cocoa powder together, then fold into the egg mixture using a large metal spoon or a spatula. Fold in the vanilla and butter. Transfer to the prepared tin and level the surface. Bake in the oven for 40 minutes, or until risen and just shrinking away a little from the sides. Turn the cake out onto a wire rack, discard the lining paper, and cover with a clean cloth. Allow the cake to cool completely.

3 Carefully cut the cake into 3 even layers. Drain 1 can of cherries, placing 6 tbsp of the juice into a bowl with the Kirsch. Roughly chop the drained cherries. Drizzle one-third of the Kirsch and cherry syrup over each layer of sponge.

4 Whip the cream until it just holds its shape. Place 1 cake layer onto a serving plate. Spread a thin layer of cream over the top of the sponge, and scatter with half the chopped cherries. Repeat with the second layer and top with the final layer. Using a palette knife, spread a thin layer of cream around the edges of the cake to cover, and spoon the remaining cream into a piping bag fitted with a star-shaped nozzle.

5 Using a spoon or a palette knife, press the grated chocolate onto the side of the cake. Pipe swirls of cream around the top edge of the cake. Drain the second tin of cherries and use them to fill the centre of the cake. Scatter any remaining chocolate over the piped cream.

FLAVOURINGS KNOW-HOW: *See* Prepare chocolate **p395**
EGGS AND DAIRY PRODUCTS KNOW-HOW: *See* Whip cream **p438**
DOUGH, PASTRY, AND CAKE KNOW-HOW: *See* Prepare and line a cake tin **p464**

Red velvet cupcakes

An American classic, this cake batter contains a touch of cocoa, and is tinted with food colouring for the characteristic hue. Do use natural food colouring if you can.

PREPARATION TIME **15 minutes** • COOKING TIME **15 minutes** • **MAKES 12**

100g (3½oz) **self-raising flour**

15g (½oz) **cocoa powder**

½ tsp **baking powder**

115g (4oz) **unsalted butter**, softened

115g (4oz) **caster sugar**

2 **eggs**

1 tsp **red food colouring**

FOR THE FROSTING

200g (7oz) **cream cheese**

6 tbsp **icing sugar**

200ml (7fl oz) **double cream**

1 Preheat the oven to 180°C (350°F/Gas 4). Line a bun tray with 12 paper cases.

2 Sift the flour, cocoa powder, and baking powder together into a large mixing bowl. Add the softened butter, caster sugar, eggs, and food colouring. Beat with a wooden spoon, electric hand whisk, or mixer until well combined. Spoon the mixture into the cupcake cases, and bake for 15 minutes, or until well risen and the centres spring back when lightly pressed. Transfer to a wire rack to cool.

3 To make the frosting, place the cream cheese in a bowl and lightly whip with the icing sugar. Then whisk in the double cream until soft peaks form.

4 Remove a thin layer of cake from the top of each cupcake, reserving the scraps. Swirl over the frosting. Crumble the scraps into crumbs and sprinkle over the frosting to decorate.

FROM **Ordinary** TO **Extraordinary**

For **centres exploding with fruitiness**, fill each cake with a berry coulis. Bake the cakes as instructed and leave to cool. In a heavy-based saucepan over a medium heat, stir together 250g (9oz) **blackcurrants** and 60g (2oz) **caster sugar**, just until the berries give up their juices and the sugar dissolves. Leave to cool. Carefully spoon out a small hole from the centre of each cake and add 1 tsp coulis into the holes. Frost as instructed, covering the coulis, and serve.

Madeleines

You will need a shell-shaped madeleine mould to make these tender cakes.

PREPARATION TIME **15–20 minutes** • COOKING TIME **10 minutes** • MAKES **12**

60g (2oz) unsalted **butter**, melted but
not hot, plus extra for greasing

60g (2oz) **plain flour**, sifted, plus extra
for dusting

60g (2oz) **caster sugar**

2 **eggs**

1 tsp **vanilla extract**

icing sugar, for dusting

1 Preheat the oven to 180°C (350°F/Gas 4). Carefully brush the moulds with melted butter and dust with flour.

2 Put the sugar, eggs, and vanilla extract into a mixing bowl and whisk until the mixture is pale, thick, and will hold a trail. This should take 5 minutes with an electric whisk, or slightly longer if you are using a hand whisk.

3 Sift the flour over the top and pour the melted butter down the side of the mixture. Using a large metal spoon, fold them in carefully and quickly, being careful not to knock out any air.

4 Fill the moulds with the mixture and bake in the oven for 10 minutes. Remove from the oven and transfer to a wire rack to cool, before dusting with icing sugar.

Shortbread

Handle these biscuits as little as possible for the 'shortest', most crumbly, results.

PREPARATION TIME **15 minutes** • COOKING TIME **20 minutes** • MAKES **10**

175g (6oz) **unsalted butter**, softened

75g (2½oz) **caster sugar**, plus extra
for sprinkling

250g (9oz) **plain flour**, plus extra
for dusting

½ tsp **salt**

1 Preheat the oven to 180°C (350°F/Gas 4). In a large bowl, beat the butter and sugar together until soft and creamy. Add the flour and salt, and carefully mix together until well combined and the mixture forms into a firm dough.

2 Turn out onto a lightly floured surface and knead gently until smooth. Roll the dough out to a thickness of 5mm (¼in). Using a 7.5cm (3in) fluted cutter, stamp out 10 rounds.

3 Arrange the shortbread on a large baking tray, spaced slightly apart. Prick the tops with a fork and bake for 20 minutes, or until lightly golden. Sprinkle with sugar and allow them to cool on the baking tray.

▲ Madeleines

Scones

Try to cut out as many as possible before re-forming the dough, as those cut first will rise highest.

PREPARATION TIME **25 minutes** • COOKING TIME **12–15 minutes** • **MAKES 8**

225g (8oz) **self-raising flour**, plus extra for dusting

½ tsp **salt**

60g (2oz) unsalted **butter**, cubed

50g (1¾oz) **sultanas**

30g (1oz) **caster sugar**

150ml (5fl oz) **milk**, plus extra for brushing

clotted cream and **jam**, to serve

1 Preheat the oven to 220°C (425°F/Gas 7). Sift the flour and the salt into a large mixing bowl. Rub in the butter with your fingertips, until the mixture resembles coarse breadcrumbs, then mix in the sultanas and sugar. Make a well in the centre and pour in the milk, then stir together, bringing in the flour from the edges, with a knife or spoon.

2 Turn the soft, sticky dough out onto a lightly floured work surface. Knead as briefly as possible and flatten to about 2.5cm (1in) thick.

3 Dip a 6cm (2½in) biscuit cutter in flour, then use to cut rounds from the dough. Re-form the dough, as necessary, to cut sufficient scones.

4 Place the scones on a baking tray and brush the tops with a little milk. Put the tray on the top shelf of the oven and bake for 12–15 minutes, or until golden. Remove from the oven and cool on a wire rack. Serve while still warm, split and filled with clotted cream and jam.

Flapjacks

These chewy bars make a great addition to a lunch box on a day out walking.

PREPARATION TIME **15 minutes, plus cooling** • COOKING TIME **40 minutes** • **MAKES 16–20**

225g (8oz) unsalted **butter**, plus extra for greasing

225g (8oz) **light soft brown sugar**

2 tbsp **golden syrup**

350g (12oz) **rolled oats**

1 Preheat the oven to 150°C (300°F/Gas 2). Lightly grease a 25cm (10in) square cake tin.

2 Put the butter, sugar, and golden syrup in a large saucepan over a medium-low heat and cook until the butter has melted. Remove the pan from the heat and stir in the oats.

3 Transfer the mixture to the prepared tin and press down firmly. Bake for 40 minutes, or until evenly golden and just beginning to brown at the edges.

4 Leave to cool for 10 minutes, then cut into 16 squares, or 20 rectangles. Leave in the tin until completely cooled.

▲Scones

Tuile biscuits

These make excellent finishing touches to most sweet dishes. Cover the rolling pin with cling film before curving them over, or else mould them into a cling film-lined muffin mould to make bowl-shaped tuiles.

PREPARATION TIME **10 minutes** • COOKING TIME **30 minutes** • MAKES **15**

50g (1¾oz) **unsalted butter**, softened

50g (1¾oz) **icing sugar**

1 **egg**

50g (1¾oz) **plain flour**

1 Preheat the oven to 200°C (400°F/Gas 6). Place the butter and icing sugar in a bowl, and cream together until light and fluffy. Beat in the egg and gently fold in the flour.

2 Line a baking tray with baking parchment. Place 1–2 tsp of the mixture on the lined baking tray and spread it thinly to make a round 6–8cm (2½–3½in) in diameter. Make another 1 or 2 rounds on the tray. Bake for 5–8 minutes, or until they just start to turn a pale golden colour.

3 Remove the baking tray from the oven and, working quickly, slide a palette knife under the tuiles to release them, then drape them over a rolling pin so that they cool in a curved shape.

4 Repeat the baking and shaping process with the remaining tuile mixture.

MASTERCHEF RECIPES

RECIPES FROM THE
MASTERCHEF SERIES TO
TAKE YOUR COOKING
TO THE NEXT LEVEL.

Goat's cheese and red onion tart

LISA FAULKNER Celebrity champion 2010

PREPARATION TIME **25 minutes, plus chilling** • COOKING TIME **55 minutes** • **SERVES 4**

FOR THE PASTRY

small sprig of **thyme**

100g (3½oz) **plain flour**

25g (scant 1oz) **butter**

25g (scant 1oz) **lard**

FOR THE RED ONION JAM

25g (scant 1oz) **butter**

25g (scant 1oz) **soft brown sugar**

1 tbsp **balsamic vinegar**

1–2 tbsp **cassis**

salt and freshly ground **black pepper**

2 **red onions**, finely sliced

FOR THE GOAT'S CHEESE

175g (6oz) crumbly **goat's cheese**

1 **egg yolk**

1–2 tbsp **double cream**

FOR THE SALAD

handful of **rocket leaves**

2 tbsp **olive oil**

2 tsp **lemon juice**

1 To make the pastry, strip the thyme leaves into a blender or a food processor and add the flour, butter, and lard. Mix on the pulse setting to form crumbs. Gradually add enough cold water (about 2–3 tbsp) to form a soft dough. Wrap in cling film and chill for 30 minutes.

2 To make the onion jam, melt the butter in a sauté pan and add the sugar, vinegar, cassis, and some seasoning. Add the onions, bring to the boil and cook, uncovered, over a very low heat for 30 minutes.

3 Heat the oven to 200°C (400°F/Gas 6). Place a sturdy baking sheet in the oven. Divide the pastry into quarters, then roll them out, and use to line four 10cm (4in) loose-bottomed tart tins. Line with greaseproof paper and baking beans. Place on the heated baking sheet and cook for 10 minutes. Remove the beans and lining paper and return to the oven for 5 minutes. Leave to cool for a few minutes.

4 Trim away any rind on the goat's cheese and crumble the cheese into a bowl. Mix with the egg yolk and a splash of cream. Season with salt and pepper.

5 Reserve about a third of the red onion jam to use as garnish, then divide the rest between the tartlets and spoon the goat's cheese mixture on top. Return to the oven for 7–8 minutes, or until the tops are bubbling and tinged with brown.

6 For the salad, rinse the rocket leaves and pat dry. Pour the olive oil and lemon juice into a bowl, and season with plenty of salt and pepper. Add the rocket leaves and toss gently to coat.

7 To serve, place a spoonful of red onion jam on the centre of each plate. Carefully remove the tarts from their tins and sit them on top of the jam. Top with rocket salad and serve.

Wonton soup

PING COOMBES Champion 2014

PREPARATION TIME **45 minutes, plus soaking and marinating** • COOKING TIME **45 minutes** • **SERVES 4**

FOR THE DUMPLINGS

25g (scant 1oz) dried **shiitake mushrooms**

150g (5½oz) fresh **white crab meat**

150g (5½oz) **minced pork**, not lean

1 tsp **chicken stock granules**

¼ tsp freshly ground **white pepper**

1 tsp **cornflour**

½ tsp **sesame oil**

1 tsp plus 1 tbsp **light soy sauce**

1½ tsp **caster sugar**

150g (5½oz) fresh **fine egg noodles**

FOR THE MUSHROOM SOUP

100g (3½oz) dried **shiitake mushrooms**

1 **chicken carcass**

1 tbsp flavourless **vegetable oil**

100g (3½oz) **Chinese leaf stalks**, shredded

1 tsp **chicken stock granules**

1 tsp **black rice vinegar**

4–6 **Chinese leaves** (trimmed of stalk, keep the stalks for the soup), shredded

80g (2¾oz) **enoki mushrooms**

FOR THE GARLIC OIL

3 tbsp **vegetable oil**

2 **garlic cloves**, finely chopped

FOR THE PICKLED MUSHROOMS

100ml (3½fl oz) **rice vinegar**

2 tbsp **granulated sugar**

handful of **shimeji mushrooms**, broken into bite-sized pieces

TO SERVE

flavourless **vegetable oil**, for deep-frying

30g (1oz) **wonton skins**, cut into strips

2 spring **onions**, green part only, finely sliced

3–4 **pickled chillies**, finely chopped

1 Soak the dried shiitake mushrooms for both the dumplings and for the soup in 2 bowls of hot water for 30 minutes, then drain. Very finely chop the mushrooms for the dumplings, but leave the mushrooms for the soup whole.

2 Meanwhile, marinate the crab and pork with the stock granules, white pepper, cornflour, sesame oil, 1 tsp of the soy sauce, and ½ tsp of the sugar. Stir in the finely chopped mushrooms.

3 Make the garlic oil: heat up the oil in a frying pan and throw in the garlic. Fry for 3 minutes, or until the garlic turns a light shade of brown. Remove from the heat and set aside to cool, then strain to remove the garlic.

4 Blanch the noodles for 1 minute, then plunge them into cold water to stop the cooking. Drain very well, then marinate with the remaining 1 tbsp of soy sauce, 1 tsp of sugar, and 1 tsp of the garlic oil, but make sure the mixture is not too wet.

5 Make 12 small quenelles of the crab and pork mixture and carefully wrap each in noodles. Set aside.

6 Preheat the oven to 200°C (400°F/Gas 6). Cut the chicken carcass in half and roast it in the oven for 10 minutes. In a saucepan, heat the oil and sauté the soaked, drained shiitake mushrooms and Chinese leaf stalks, then add the roast carcass and pour in 1.5 litres (2¾ pints) water. Cover and boil for 10 minutes, then pass through a sieve into a clean saucepan. Reduce by half to 1 litre (1¾ pints) and add the stock granules. Remove from the heat and add the vinegar, Chinese leaves, and enoki mushrooms.

7 For the pickled mushrooms, gently heat the vinegar and sugar together, just until the sugar has dissolved. Remove from the heat, add the mushroom pieces, and leave to pickle for at least 20 minutes.

8 Set up a steamer and steam the noodle-wrapped dumplings for 10 minutes.

9 Meanwhile, heat the oil for deep-frying to 180°C (350°F). Deep-fry the wonton skins for 1–2 minutes until golden, then remove with a slotted spoon and drain on kitchen paper.

10 Divide the spring onions and pickled chillies between 4 bowls. Assemble the steamed, noodle-wrapped wontons on top and serve with the pickled shimeji mushrooms and the mushroom soup. Top with the crispy wonton skins.

Thai prawn soup with lemongrass

IWAN THOMAS Celebrity finalist 2009

PREPARATION TIME **10 minutes** • COOKING TIME **15 minutes** • **SERVES 4**

16 large raw **tiger prawns**, shells on

1 litre (1¾ pints) **chicken stock**

2 stalks fresh **lemongrass**, lightly pounded, cut into 2.5cm (1in) lengths

50g (1¾oz) fresh **galangal**, sliced

10 **kaffir lime leaves**, shredded

500g (1lb 2oz) **enoki mushrooms**

4 tbsp **nam pla** (Thai fish sauce)

3 tbsp **nam prik pao** (chilli paste in oil)

4 tbsp **lime juice**

5 fresh **Thai (bird's eye) chillies**, crushed

TO GARNISH

10g (¼oz) **coriander**, torn

1 small **red pepper**, deseeded and cut into fine ribbons

1 Wash the prawns and shell them without removing the tails.

2 Bring the chicken stock to the boil in a large saucepan. Add the lemongrass, galangal, and lime leaves.

3 Bring back to the boil, then add the enoki mushrooms, nam pla, nam prik pao, and lime juice. Add the prawns and fresh chillies.

4 As soon as the prawns turn pink (about 2 minutes), serve the soup garnished with the coriander and strips of red pepper.

Open lasagne of roasted squash and wild mushrooms with sage butter

TIM KINNAIRD Finalist 2010

PREPARATION TIME **1 hour 15 minutes** • COOKING TIME **1 hour** • **SERVES 4**

FOR THE PASTA

good pinch of **saffron strands**

150g (5½oz) **tipo "00" flour**

salt

1 large **egg**

1 **egg yolk**

FOR THE SQUASH

1 small **Crown Prince squash**, peeled and seeded, about 350g (12oz) peeled weight, and cut into bite-sized pieces

1 tbsp **extra virgin olive oil**

salt and freshly ground **black pepper**

¼–½ tsp **chilli flakes**

FOR THE MUSHROOMS

knob of **butter**

200g (7oz) mixed **wild mushrooms**, such as **girolles**, **porcini**, and **pied blue**, wiped and evenly chopped

1 **garlic clove**, finely chopped

3 tbsp **Marsala wine**

2–3 tbsp chopped **flat-leaf parsley**

100ml (3½fl oz) **double cream**

FOR THE SAGE BUTTER

75g (2½oz) **unsalted butter**

small bunch of fresh **sage**, leaves only

1 Preheat the oven to 220ºC (425ºF/Gas 7). Soak the saffron in 2 tsp warm water for 10 minutes. Make the pasta dough (see p471), adding the saffron and water to the dough with the eggs.

2 Put the squash on a baking tray, drizzle with the olive oil, and scatter over the salt, pepper, and chilli flakes. Roast for 35 minutes or until soft and tinged with brown. Shake the tin occasionally for even roasting.

3 To cook the mushrooms, melt the butter in a large sauté pan until it foams, add the mushrooms and salt and pepper, and fry over high heat for 4–5 minutes or until just turning golden. Reduce the heat to medium, add the garlic, and fry for 1 minute. Add the Marsala and bubble for a few minutes. Stir in the parsley and cream and set aside.

4 For the sage butter, melt the butter in a heavy pan and cook gently until it turns a warm nutty brown. Take care not to burn it. Set aside.

5 Divide the dough into 2 and roll into sheets.

6 Bring a pan of water to the boil. Brush off the excess flour from the pasta, place in the water, and boil for 4–5 minutes or until al dente. Drain in a colander and then cut out twelve 8cm (3in) diameter circles using an oiled round pastry cutter. Brush with olive oil and set aside.

7 Just before serving, tear up nearly all the sage leaves and add to the cooled butter. Warm gently for 1–2 minutes and also warm the mushroom mixture and squash. Stack up the pasta separated by a layer of squash and a layer of mushrooms. Spoon over the sage butter and garnish with the remaining sage.

PASTA, NOODLES, AND GNOCCHI KNOW-HOW: *See* Make pasta dough **p471**

Roast tomato arancini with a basil-yogurt dressing

LUKE OWEN Finalist 2014

PREPARATION TIME **1 hour** • COOKING TIME **1 hour** • **SERVES 4**

FOR THE ARANCINI

300g (10½oz) **piccolo tomatoes**

2 tbsp **olive oil**, plus more for roasting the tomatoes

sea salt and freshly ground **black pepper**

2 **banana shallots**, finely chopped

1 large **celery stick**, finely chopped

2 **garlic cloves**, finely chopped

150g (5½oz) **arborio rice**

100ml (3½fl oz) **white wine**

500ml (18fl oz) **tomato passata**

100g (3½oz) **plain flour**, plus extra for dusting

12 **mozzarella pearls** (mini mozzarella balls)

1 **large egg**, lightly beaten

100g (3½oz) **panko breadcrumbs**, for coating

light **olive oil**, for deep-frying

FOR THE DRESSING

large bunch of **basil**, plus extra leaves to serve

1½ tbsp **extra virgin olive oil**

300g (10oz) **Greek yogurt**

English mustard, to taste

lemon juice, to taste

TO SERVE

12 **piccolo tomatoes** (about 2 sprigs on the vine)

200g (7oz) **crème fraîche**

1 For the arancini, preheat the oven to 180°C (350°F/Gas 4). Place the tomatoes for both the arancini and for serving in 2 baking trays, keeping them separate, removing them from the vines but leaving the vines in the tray for flavour. Lightly oil and salt them, then roast for 40 minutes.

2 Pour 2 tbsp olive oil into a wide frying pan. Add the shallots, celery, and garlic and sweat over a low heat for 5 minutes with a good pinch of salt until all the ingredients are soft and translucent. Add the rice and stir so that the oil coats all the grains. Increase the temperature to medium-high and add the wine. Allow the wine to mostly disappear, then add one-quarter of the passata. Stir gently until the risotto just begins to dry out, then add another one-quarter of the passata. Repeat until it is all used. Take the roast tomatoes for the arancini, squash with a fork or potato masher, and add to the risotto.

3 Continue to cook, adding up to 200ml (7fl oz) boiling water, a ladleful at a time, until the rice is almost cooked and the risotto is thick. Taste and season. Quickly cool by plunging the base of the saucepan into a sink of ice-cold water.

4 Divide the mixture into 12 equal portions. With lightly floured hands, shape one portion of the cooled mixture into a ball around a mozzarella pearl. Repeat to make 12 risotto balls. Place the flour, egg, and panko crumbs in 3 separate shallow dishes. Coat each risotto ball in flour, then egg, then breadcrumbs. Cover the arancini and leave the coating to set in the fridge for at least 30 minutes.

5 Once set, heat the olive oil for deep-frying in a deep-fat fryer or a large saucepan to 180°C (350°F). Deep-fry the arancini over a medium-low heat for 4 minutes in batches of 4. Once crisp and golden, remove with a slotted spoon, blot off excess oil on kitchen paper, and season with salt.

6 For the dressing, reserve a few basil leaves for serving, then blend the remaining basil with the oil in a blender or food processor until as smooth as possible. Add the yogurt and season with salt, English mustard, and a touch of lemon juice.

7 To serve, drizzle the plates with the basil-yogurt dressing, Place 3 arancini on each plate and top each with a spoon of crème fraîche. Add the reserved basil leaves and roasted tomatoes to finish.

Mushroom ravioli with truffle, Pecorino, and sage

DALE WILLIAMS Finalist 2013

PREPARATION TIME **35 minutes, plus chilling** • COOKING TIME **15 minutes** • **SERVES 4**

FOR THE PASTA

100g (3½oz) '00' pasta flour, plus extra for dusting

1 egg, plus 1 egg yolk

pinch of sea salt

1 tbsp extra virgin olive oil

FOR THE FILLING

250g (9oz) chestnut mushrooms

freshly ground black pepper

1 tsp salted butter

½ shallot, finely chopped

1 garlic clove, crushed

1 tbsp finely chopped parsley leaves

1 tsp finely chopped thyme leaves

1 tsp truffle oil, plus extra to serve

40g (1½oz) good-quality cream cheese

1 tsp Dijon mustard

TO SERVE

75g (2½oz) best-quality sea salted butter

10 sage leaves

juice of ½ lemon

Pecorino shavings, to taste

truffle shavings, to taste

1 To make the pasta, place the flour on a work surface and make a well in the centre. Add the egg, egg yolk, salt, and oil. Use a fork to gently mix the flour and liquid in circular motions until it is all incorporated. Use your hands to bring the dough together and knead for 10 minutes until rich in colour, firm and elastic. Wrap in cling film and chill for 20–30 minutes.

2 For the filling, brush any dirt from the mushrooms with a firm brush. Place them in a food processor and pulse for a maximum of 10 seconds into a coarse crumb.

3 Add the mushrooms to a dry non-stick pan over a medium heat and season with salt and pepper. Cook for 6–8 minutes, stirring occasionally, or until they have shrunk to half their original size and excess water has evaporated. Push them to the side of the pan and add the butter, shallot, garlic, and herbs. Let them sizzle for 2 minutes, then stir in the mushrooms. Cook over a low heat for a further minute or so or until any liquid evaporates. Transfer to a bowl. Stir in the truffle oil, cream cheese, and mustard, mix well, then chill.

4 Remove the pasta dough from the fridge and place on a floured work surface. Roll it out to a long rectangle around 1cm (½in) thick. Clamp a pasta machine to your worktop and work the dough to around 1mm (¹⁄₃₂in) thick. Take care not to split the dough, and be patient as it is worth the effort.

5 When you have a sheet of dough around 1 metre (3ft 3in) long and 12–15cm (5–6in) wide, place it on a floured work surface. With a teaspoon, place mounds of filling 2cm (¾in) from one edge of the pasta dough, along the length of the dough. Fold the dough lengthways over the filling, encasing the ravioli, and use your hands to shape them into small domes, pressing the edges well. Using a ravioli cutter, cut out 12–16 perfectly trimmed ravioli. Place on a clean plate dusted with flour and refrigerate until needed.

6 Take the ravioli from the fridge 10–15 minutes before you plan to cook, to allow them to come to room temperature. Bring a large saucepan of lightly salted water to the boil.

7 Meanwhile, divide the butter between 2 separate large sauté pans, heat until lightly foaming, and add the sage leaves and a generous squeeze of lemon juice.

8 Gently drop the ravioli into the boiling water a few at a time, and simmer for 3–4 minutes until cooked. Remove them with a slotted spoon and divide between the pans of sage butter. Toss the ravioli in the butter, before dividing between serving plates with a bit of sage butter and crispy sage on each.

9 Dress with Pecorino and truffle shavings and finish with extra truffle oil and black pepper.

PASTA, NOODLES, AND GNOCCHI KNOW-HOW: *See* Use a pasta machine **p472**
PASTA, NOODLES, AND GNOCCHI KNOW-HOW: *See* Assemble ravioli **p474**

Lamb samosas

DAKSHA MISTRY Finalist 2006

PREPARATION TIME **50 minutes** • COOKING TIME **15 minutes** • **SERVES 4**

250g (9oz) **minced lamb**

½ **onion**, finely chopped

1 **garlic clove**, finely chopped

½ tsp **curry powder**

¼ tsp **chilli powder**

½ tsp **ground turmeric**

¼ tsp ground roasted **cumin seeds**

½ **green chilli**, deseeded and finely chopped

1 tbsp chopped **coriander**

¼ tsp grated fresh **root ginger**

½ tsp **salt**

freshly ground **black pepper**

squeeze of **lemon juice**

1 litre (1¾ pints) **sunflower oil**, for deep-frying

4 sprigs of **coriander**, to garnish

FOR THE PASTRY

115g (4oz) **plain flour**

1 tsp **salt**

1 tbsp **sunflower oil**

about 3 tbsp warm **water**

1 To make the pastry, mix the flour and salt in a bowl. Make a well in the centre and add the oil and enough water to make a firm dough. Knead the dough on a floured surface until smooth and roll into a ball. Cover in cling film and set aside at room temperature for 30 minutes.

2 For the filling, put all the ingredients except the oil and coriander sprigs into a bowl and mix thoroughly with your hands.

3 Divide the pastry into 6 equal pieces. Roll each piece into a ball and cover with cling film to stop them from drying out. Roll each ball of pastry into a 12.5cm (5in) circle and then divide into 2 equal semicircles with a knife.

4 Place a level tbsp of the mixture on one half circle of the semicircle of pastry. Then fold the other half circle across the filling to form a triangle. Dampen the edges with water and gently seal the open edges. Repeat for the other samosas.

5 Heat the oil in a large saucepan. To test when the oil is hot enough, drop a small piece of bread into it and as soon as it starts to sizzle, remove it and start frying the samosas, 4 at a time. Cook each batch for about 5 minutes, turning occasionally, or until the samosas are crisp and brown. Remove them from the pan, drain on kitchen paper, and serve 2 or 3 samosas per person while still warm, garnished with the coriander.

VEGETABLES KNOW-HOW: *see* Deseed and cut chillies **p373**

Scallops with beetroot pearls, black quinoa, and radish and fennel pickle

EMMA SPITZER Finalist 2015

PREPARATION TIME **1 hour, plus chilling and marinating** • COOKING TIME **25 minutes** • **SERVES 4**

6 scallops

1 tbsp **extra virgin olive oil**

a few drops of **black pepper oil**

a few drops of **lemon oil**

sea salt and freshly ground **black pepper**

juice of 1 **lime**

100g (3½oz) **black quinoa**

½ **cucumber**

sumac, micro-coriander and **red amaranth**, to serve

FOR THE BEETROOT PEARLS

olive oil

150ml (5fl oz) **beetroot juice**

3 tsp **agar agar flakes**

FOR THE PICKLED VEGETABLES

100ml (3½fl oz) **attika vinegar**

100g (3½oz) **granulated sugar**

1 **fennel bulb**

3 **radishes**

1 small **beetroot**

FOR THE DRESSING

1 bunch of **coriander**

1 **garlic clove**

100ml (3½fl oz) **olive oil**

1 tsp roasted and finely crushed **caraway seeds**

2 lightly bruised **cardamom pods**

½ tsp crushed **peppercorns**

1 **red chilli**, deseeded and finely chopped

juice of 1 **lemon**, plus **lemon segments** from 1 **lemon**

1 Trim the scallops of roe. Heat the extra virgin olive oil, black pepper oil, lemon oil, and a pinch of salt in a frying pan over a medium-high heat. Fry the scallops, turning once, for 1 minute each side, until golden but not overcooked. Reserve 2 scallops and finely chop the rest.

2 To make the beetroot pearls, put a tall glass of olive oil into the freezer for 1 hour. Mix the beetroot juice in a saucepan with the agar agar flakes and bring to the boil. Boil until the flakes dissolve, around 5 minutes. Let the liquid stand for another 5 minutes, or until it reaches 50°C (122°F). Put it into a syringe and add droplets to the cold oil to make the pearls. Drain the pearls from the oil and set aside.

3 For the pickled vegetables, combine the attika vinegar and sugar with 200ml (7fl oz) water in a saucepan. Gently heat the mixture until the sugar has dissolved, then set aside to cool slightly. Finely slice the fennel with a mandolin and place in a bowl. Repeat for the radishes and beetroot. Divide the slightly cooled pickling liquid between each bowl and set them aside.

4 For the dressing, trim and clean the roots of the coriander and place into a food processor. Crush the garlic with ¼ tsp salt in a mortar and pestle and add to the coriander with

2 tbsp of water. Whizz to a purée. Put the olive oil into a mixing bowl and whisk in the coriander purée. Add the caraway seeds, cardamom pods, peppercorns, chilli, lemon juice, and lemon segments. Stir together and taste for seasoning, adding more salt if needed.

5 Finely slice the 2 reserved scallops horizontally. Add some lime juice to the sliced scallops and set aside. Boil the quinoa in water for about 15 minutes until cooked but still retaining a slight bite. Drain off any excess water.

6 Peel, deseed, and very finely chop the cucumber and mix with the chopped scallops. Add some of the dressing to the mix and set aside to let the flavours infuse.

7 To serve, place a line of dressing down the centre of each plate. Sprinkle some quinoa over the top and dot the pickled vegetables down each line of dressing. Divide the beetroot pearls, the cucumber and scallop mixture, and finally the slices of scallops between the plates. Sprinkle with sumac and garnish with micro-herbs.

SHELLFISH KNOW-HOW: *see* Prepare scallops **p287**
FLAVOURINGS KNOW-HOW: *see* Prepare spices **p391**
FRUITS AND NUTS KNOW-HOW: *see* Segment citrus fruit **p424**

Smoked mackerel pâté

Inspired by **STEVEN WALLIS** Champion 2007

PREPARATION TIME **20 minutes, plus chilling** • **SERVES 4**

250g (9oz) **cold-smoked mackerel fillets**

50g (1¾oz) **crème fraîche**

25g (scant 1oz) **mascarpone cheese**

3 stems of **fennel fronds**, plus extra
to garnish

grated zest and juice of 1 **lime**

grated zest of ½ **orange**

fleur de sel

½ tsp **coriander seeds**, toasted

3 tbsp **hazelnut oil**

salt and freshly ground **black pepper**

½ tsp **sugar**

4 tsp **Muscat vinegar**

3 **chicory heads**

25g (scant 1oz) **hazelnuts**, toasted
and finely chopped

baby chervil, to garnish

pea shoot tendrils, to garnish

1 Finely pick through the smoked mackerel to remove any bones, remove the skin, and break the flesh into pieces in a food processor. Add the crème fraîche, mascarpone cheese, fennel fronds, lime and orange zest, and the lime juice. Season with the fleur de sel and blend to a smooth pâté consistency. Chill for 30 minutes.

2 To prepare the vinaigrette, mix together the coriander seeds and hazelnut oil, season with salt and pepper, and add the sugar. Then add the Muscat vinegar, whisk well, and set aside.

3 To serve, trim the chicory leaves by cutting a good third of the leaves from the end. Allow 3 leaves per person. Spoon in a neat quenelle of pâté onto the cut end of each leaf. Drizzle over the vinaigrette, and scatter over the chopped hazelnuts. Finish with a pinch of fleur de sel and baby chervil leaves, fennel fronds, and pea shoot tendrils.

Smoked haddock timbale with poached quail's egg

CHRISTINE HAMILTON Celebrity finalist 2010

PREPARATION TIME **15 minutes** • COOKING TIME **30 minutes** • SERVES 4

4 **baby beetroots** (or 1 mature beetroot, peeled and quartered)

salt and freshly ground **black pepper**

splash of **olive oil**

2–3 sprigs of **thyme** (optional)

butter, for greasing

150g (5½oz) **smoked haddock fillet**, skin removed

400ml (14fl oz) **double cream**

4 **egg yolks**

2 tbsp **chopped dill**

2 tbsp **chopped chives**

4 **quail's eggs**

FOR THE SALAD DRESSING

1 tbsp **lemon juice**

½ tbsp **olive oil**

½ tbsp **walnut oil**

½ tbsp **wholegrain mustard**

1 tbsp **caster sugar**

ground **black pepper**

TO SERVE

small bag of **rocket** and **watercress**

50g (1¾oz) **walnut pieces**

1 Preheat the oven to 170°C (340°F/Gas 3–4). Season the whole baby beetroots or mature beetroot quarters with salt and pepper and wrap tightly in kitchen foil with olive oil and thyme (if using). Roast in a corner of the oven for 30 minutes.

2 Butter 4 timbale moulds. Poach the haddock lightly for 2–3 minutes in 200ml (7fl oz) of cream. Drain and reserve the cream.

3 In a bowl, whisk together the reserved and remaining cream, egg yolks, dill, chives, and a good pinch of black pepper.

4 Break the haddock into pieces with a fork and divide between the timbale moulds. Pour the cream mixture into each mould.

5 Place the moulds in a deep roasting tray or oven dish. Add 3–4cm (1¼–1½ in) of water to the tray or dish before placing it in the preheated oven on a high shelf. Bake for 20 minutes, or until the timbales are set and do not wobble when moved.

6 Meanwhile, poach the quail's eggs by breaking each gently into a pan of just-simmering water and poaching for 30 seconds. When cooked, plunge into iced water.

7 In a small bowl, whisk together all the ingredients for the lemon and walnut dressing.

8 Remove the timbales from the oven and allow to cool before unmoulding. Arrange the dressed salad leaves on each plate, with the beetroot, and sprinkle over the finely chopped walnut. Position a timbale in the centre and place a poached quail's egg on top.

Crispy squid with green peppercorn and chilli dressing

SUSIE CARTER Quarter-finalist 2006

PREPARATION TIME **15 minutes** • COOKING TIME **5 minutes** • **SERVES 4**

4 medium **squid**, cleaned

juice of 1 **lime**

salt and freshly ground **black pepper**

groundnut oil, for deep-frying

3 tbsp **cornflour**

FOR THE DRESSING

2 tbsp fresh **green peppercorns**

1 **red chilli**, deseeded and finely chopped

3cm (1¼in) piece fresh **root ginger**, finely grated

2 **garlic cloves**, crushed

3 tbsp **nam pla** (Thai fish sauce)

3 tbsp **rice vinegar**

75g (2½oz) **caster sugar**

2 tsp **soy sauce**

juice of 1 **lime**

TO SERVE

4 slices of **lime**

coriander leaves

1 To make the dressing, put all the ingredients in a small pan and simmer, stirring, until the sugar has dissolved and the mixture has thickened. Leave to cool.

2 Open out the body sac of the squid and cut each one into about 8 rectangles. With the inside facing up, score a diamond pattern with a sharp knife, taking care not to cut all the way through. Douse with lime juice, season well with salt and pepper, and leave to cure for 2 minutes.

3 Heat plenty of groundnut oil in a large saucepan or deep fat fryer to 180°C (350°F).

4 Dry the squid thoroughly on kitchen paper then toss with the cornflour. Shake off the excess and deep fry in batches for 2 minutes until golden and crisp. Drain on kitchen paper then quickly toss with a few spoonfuls of the dressing and serve immediately with a slice of lime on the side and coriander to garnish.

SHELLFISH KNOW-HOW: *See* Clean squid **p289**

Sea bass with sweet potato, porcini, Parma ham, and figs

TONY RODD Finalist 2015

PREPARATION TIME **45 minutes** • COOKING TIME **30 minutes** • SERVES 4

50g (1¾oz) dried **porcini mushrooms**

a little **unsalted butter**

olive oil

2–4 **figs**, quartered

50g (1¾oz) **Parma ham**, chopped

micro red amaranth

FOR THE FIG JUS

sea bass bones, or other **fish bones**

50g (1¾oz) **unsalted butter**

1 **banana shallot**, chopped

3 **lemon thyme** sprigs

100ml (3½fl oz) **chicken stock**

2 **figs**, halved

FOR THE SWEET POTATO PURÉE

1 large **sweet potato**

100g (3½oz) **unsalted butter**

150ml (5fl oz) **double cream**

FOR THE SEA BASS

2 x 100g (3½oz) **sea bass fillets**

sea salt and freshly ground **black pepper**

dash of **vegetable oil**

25g (scant 1oz) **unsalted butter**

juice of ½ **lemon**

1 Soak the mushrooms in just-boiled water for 30 minutes, then rinse well to remove any grit.

2 Meanwhile, prepare the fig jus: cook the fish bones in a little of the butter and add the shallot. Add water to cover and simmer over a low heat for 20 minutes (no longer, or the stock will start to take on a bitter taste). Pass through a sieve, then reduce the stock in a saucepan with the lemon thyme. Add the chicken stock and halved figs and reduce further. Pass through a sieve and add the remaining butter to finish.

3 For the sweet potato purée, cut the sweet potato into cubes and soften in a saucepan with a little of the butter. Add the cream and simmer for 20 minutes. Blend and pass through a fine sieve. Season and add the remaining butter.

4 Cut the soaked mushrooms into small pieces and fry in a saucepan in a little butter over a medium heat. Heat a little oil in another saucepan and fry the fig quarters, flesh-side down, until cooked.

5 To prepare the sea bass, cut each fillet in half and season with salt and pepper. Heat the vegetable oil in a hot pan and place the fish skin-side down in the pan. Add the butter to the pan and baste. Flip the fillets, cook for 1–2 minutes, then remove from the pan. Squeeze some lemon juice on top.

6 To serve, divide the sweet potato purée between 4 plates. Add a fish fillet to each plate, then garnish with the porcini, ham, herbs, and fried fig quarters. Spoon on the fig jus, or serve it on the side.

Winkles, cockles, and mussels on toast, langoustines, and saffron mayonnaise

JANE DEVONSHIRE Champion 2016

PREPARATION TIME **1 hour** • COOKING TIME **55 minutes** • **SERVES 6**

500g (1lb 2oz) **cockles**

500g (1lb 2oz) **mussels**

2 tbsp **plain flour**

500g (1lb 2oz) **winkles**, preferably live

1 tbsp **olive oil**, plus extra for the dressing

3 **garlic cloves**, finely chopped

250ml (9fl oz) **dry white wine**

big bunch of **flat-leaf parsley**, reserving a few finely chopped leaves to serve

lemon juice, for the dressing

sea salt, to taste

FOR THE MAYONNAISE

1 **garlic bulb**

250ml (9fl oz) **flavourless oil**, plus extra to drizzle; I use **sunflower oil**

5–6 **saffron threads**

2 **large egg yolks**

1 tbsp **lemon juice**, or to taste

FOR THE TEMPURA

6 **langoustines**

50g (1¾oz) **cornflour**

75g (2½oz) **plain flour**

1 tsp **baking powder**

100ml (3½fl oz) **ice-cold sparkling water** or **soda water**

vegetable oil, for deep-frying

6 **caperberries**

TO SERVE

loaf of good-quality **white bread**

micro garlic chives (optional)

micro red amaranth (optional)

1 Put the cockles and mussels in a large bowl of water with 1 tbsp of flour and leave in a cool place for at least 2 hours to flush out the grit. Repeat for the winkles, using a separate bowl.

2 Preheat the oven to 200°C (400°F/Gas 6). To make the mayonnaise, slice the top from the garlic bulb to reveal the tops of each clove. Place on a sheet of foil and drizzle with oil. Seal the foil loosely, then bake for 40 minutes, or until the garlic is soft. Squeeze the roasted garlic from the skins. Meanwhile, put the saffron in a small bowl with a little warm water and leave for 20 minutes.

3 Put the egg yolks into the bowl and whisk until the mixture is light, fluffy, and paler. Very carefully whisk in half the oil. Once the mixture is thickening, mix in 1 tbsp warm saffron water; you will see the mixture loosening. Slowly add the remaining oil, followed by lemon juice and salt to taste. Mix in one-quarter of the roast garlic, or to taste, and the saffron. If it is a little thick, use the remaining saffron water to loosen it.

4 Rinse the cockles and mussels well. Discard any that are cracked, or do not shut when tapped sharply. Put the olive oil into a sauté pan, add the garlic and cook for up to 1 minute, or until aromatic but without colour. Add the wine and cook for 2–3 minutes, or until boiling and the strong alcohol smell has gone. Add the cockles, mussels, and half the parsley. Cover and cook for 2–3 minutes or until the shellfish open (discard any that do not open). Strain, reserving the cooking liquor. Remove the cockles and mussels from their shells and dress with olive oil, a little lemon juice, and chopped parsley.

5 Boil the winkles in salted water for 3–4 minutes. Plunge into iced water, then remove from their shells: put a large pin under the "foot" (the hard bit) and twist so the meat comes out in one piece. Remove the foot and place the winkles into a bowl.

6 Put the reserved cockle and mussel liquor into a saucepan to boil. Add the remaining parsley sprigs until wilted, then remove and plunge into iced water to retain their colour. Finely chop half the wilted parsley and add to the winkles. Put the remaining wilted parsley in a blender and, using a little of the cooking liquor, blend to a purée. Mix into the winkles.

7 To make the tempura, remove the langoustines from their shells: twist off the heads and use a pair of scissors to cut either side of the sharp shell, leaving all the meat undamaged. Whisk together the flours, baking powder, and sparkling water to make a batter that coats a finger. Bring the oil for deep-frying to 180°C (350°F). If you do not have a thermometer, test with a little batter: if it sinks, then rises golden and crisp, it is ready.

8 Toast the bread and cut into 12 "soldiers". Pile mussels and cockles on half of the toasts, divide between 6 plates, and dress with micro garlic chives, if using. Pile the winkles onto the other 6 toasts and divide them between the plates, too. Smear a little mayonnaise on each plate and sprinkle with amaranth, if using.

9 Coat the langoustines in batter and drop into the oil. Leave to turn deep golden, then remove with a slotted spoon and place on kitchen paper to blot off excess oil. Repeat with the caperberries. Add to the plates and serve.

Spinach and ricotta ravioli with walnut pesto and a cream and basil sauce

CHRIS GATES Finalist 2009

PREPARATION TIME **1 hour 15 minutes** • COOKING TIME **1 hour** • **SERVES 4**

FOR THE PASTA

150g (5½oz) **tipo "00" flour**, plus extra to dust

350g (12oz) **semolina flour**

2 large **eggs**

10 **egg yolks**

FOR THE FILLING

20g (¾ oz) **butter**

200g (7oz) **spinach**

salt and freshly ground **black pepper**

350g (12oz) **ricotta** or **soft goat's cheese**

grated zest of 1 **lemon**

FOR THE PESTO

30g (1oz) **walnuts**

1 bunch of **basil**

1 **garlic clove**, chopped

25g (scant 1oz) **Parmesan cheese**, freshly grated

olive oil

FOR THE SAUCE

1 **shallot**, finely chopped

1 tbsp **olive oil**

500ml (16fl oz) **double cream**

juice of 1 **lemon**

1 To make the pasta, blitz all of the ingredients in a food processor until you have a mixture the consistency of breadcrumbs. Empty onto a floured surface and knead into a silky dough. Wrap in cling film and leave to rest in the refrigerator for about 1 hour.

2 Meanwhile, make the filling. Melt the butter in a large pan and wilt the spinach. Season with salt and pepper. Squeeze out any water and place in a bowl. Add the ricotta and lemon zest and season to taste.

3 For the pesto, toast the walnuts in a dry pan until golden. Using a pestle and mortar, break them up with the garlic and basil leaves, reserving the stalks. Add the Parmesan, loosen with oil, and season.

4 For the cream sauce, sauté the chopped shallot in a pan with the oil until softened. Add the reserved basil stalks and soften for 3–4 minutes. Add the cream and allow to reduce slightly. Season with salt and pepper and add the lemon juice.

5 Using a pasta machine, roll out the pasta to the thinnest setting. Make 2 rectangular dough sheets. Place scoops of the filling on top of the first dough sheet at intervals about 5cm (2in) apart. Brush round the filling with a little water and top with the second sheet of dough. Using your fingers, press round the filling to remove any air. Cut out the ravioli, using a fluted pastry cutter about 5cm (2in) in diameter.

6 Cook the ravioli in boiling salted water for about 5 minutes. Drain and serve on warm plates with the cream sauce and pesto spooned over and a scattering of basil leaves as a garnish.

PASTA, NOODLES, AND GNOCCHI KNOW-HOW: *See* Use a pasta machine **p474**
PASTA, NOODLES, AND GNOCCHI KNOW-HOW: *See* Assemble ravioli **p476**

Scallop and langoustine tortellini with a prawn bisque sauce and crackling

LUKE OWEN Finalist 2014

PREPARATION TIME **1 hour** • COOKING TIME **1 hour** • SERVES 4

FOR THE CRACKLING
200g (7oz) **pork skin**, from the belly

a little **olive oil**

sea salt and freshly ground **black pepper**

FOR THE WHITE TORTELLINI
100g (3½oz) **'00' flour**, plus extra for dusting

1 **egg**

¼ tsp **fennel seeds**

50ml (1¾fl oz) **white wine**

50g (1¾oz) **Gruyère cheese**

pinch of **English mustard powder**

handful of **curly parsley**, finely chopped

1 tsp **plain flour**

juice of ½ **lemon**, or to taste

FOR THE BLACK TORTELLINI
105g (3½oz) **'00' flour**

1 **egg**

4g packet **squid ink**

12 **queen scallops**, trimmed of roe

25ml (scant 1oz) **double cream**

FOR THE BISQUE SAUCE
12 **king prawns** with shells

200ml (7fl oz) **olive oil**

4 **shallots**, roughly chopped

2 **carrots**, roughly chopped

2 **fennel bulbs**, roughly chopped

2 **garlic cloves**, roughly chopped

bunch of **tarragon**

1 tbsp **paprika**

large pinch of **cayenne pepper**

2 tbsp **tomato purée**

½ tsp **harissa paste**

100ml (3½fl oz) **brandy**

100ml (3½fl oz) **white wine**

500ml (18fl oz) **fish stock**

500ml (18fl oz) **chicken stock**

Tabasco sauce, to taste

juice of ½ **lemon**, to taste

75ml (2½fl oz) **double cream**

TO SERVE
8 **scallops**, with roe

a little **olive oil**

knob of **unsalted butter**

fennel fronds

1 Preheat the oven to 220°C (425°F/Gas 7). Score the pork skin, brush with oil, salt generously, then put on a trivet in a roasting tin and roast for 40–50 minutes until golden and crisp. Set aside.

2 Meanwhile, for the white tortellini dough, put the '00' flour and egg in a food processor and blend until it comes together as a dough. Dust with flour, wrap in cling film, and chill for at least 1 hour. Lightly toast the fennel seeds in a dry saucepan over a medium-high heat. Add the wine and reduce by half, then gradually add the Gruyère over a low heat, constantly stirring to prevent the mix from splitting. Once it is glossy, stir in the mustard powder, parsley, flour, and lemon juice to taste. Chill.

3 Make the black tortellini dough as for the white tortellini dough, adding the squid ink to the mixture, then chill. For the filling, dry the scallops on kitchen paper and place in a cold food processor. Add the cream, salt and pepper, blend until smooth, then chill.

4 Roll out the white tortellini dough using a pasta machine (see p472). Lay out the strip of pasta and cut into 16 squares. Place 1 tsp of the filling in the centre of 1 square. With a point facing you, dab the 2 sides furthest from you with water, then fold the corner facing you to meet the furthest corner. Use your fingers to seal 1 side first, then push the air out before sealing the other side. On the side now facing you, take the right hand corner and

pull across to the opposite corner, dab the left corner with water and pull it, too, across, then stick them together. Repeat for the remaining white tortellini, then repeat the whole process with the black tortellini dough.

5 For the sauce, shell the prawns and fry the shells in the oil with the shallots, carrots, fennel, garlic, tarragon, paprika, cayenne, tomato purée, and harissa. Allow to soften, letting them catch slightly, then increase the heat, add the brandy and wine, and boil for 10 minutes. Add the stocks and reduce by half. Using a stick blender or food processor, blend until smooth, then press through a fine sieve. Take your time here, as the better you press, the smoother the bisque will be. Return to a saucepan and reduce by half again. Add Tabasco and lemon juice to taste. Just before serving, add the cream and season, then add the prawns to cook through.

6 To serve, trim the scallops and pat dry. Lightly oil and salt them. Fry in a hot pan for 1 minute each side, add the butter, and remove from the heat, leaving them in the pan for 3–5 minutes. Cook the tortellini for 3 minutes in boiling, salted water. Drain. Make a pool of sauce on each plate and add the black and white tortellini, alternating the colours. Place 2 scallops per plate among the tortellini, then add the prawns. Finally, add fennel fronds and shards of the pork crackling.

Nasi lemak

PING COOMBES Champion 2014

PREPARATION TIME **45 minutes, plus soaking and marinating**   •   COOKING TIME **25 minutes, plus standing**   •   **SERVES 6**

FOR THE SAMBAL IKAN BILIS

12 **dried chillies**

50g (1¾oz) good-quality **ikan bilis** (dried anchovies)

7 **red chillies**, trimmed

10 small round **shallots**, chopped

2 **garlic cloves**, peeled

2 **lemongrass stalks**, trimmed and chopped

½ tbsp **shrimp paste**

150ml (5fl oz) **vegetable oil**

3–4 tbsp **tamarind paste**

¾ tbsp **caster sugar**

1 tsp **soy sauce**

FOR THE TURMERIC FRIED CHICKEN

6 **chicken wings** (winglets only, not the drumettes)

1 tbsp **ground turmeric**

1 tsp **salt**

½ tbsp **ground coriander**

1 tbsp **vegetable oil**, plus extra for deep-frying

2 **eggs**, lightly beaten

25g (scant 1oz) **salted crisps**, smashed

FOR THE SAMBAL PRAWNS

6 **dried chillies**

2 **lemongrass stalks**, trimmed and chopped

2 **candlenuts**

1 **garlic clove**, peeled

1 tsp **shrimp paste**

5–7 **shallots**, peeled and chopped

6 large **tiger prawns**, tails on

100ml (3½fl oz) **vegetable oil**

½ tbsp **caster sugar**

1 tbsp **tamarind paste**

1 tsp **salt**

FOR THE COCONUT RICE

300g (10oz) **jasmine rice**

250ml (9fl oz) **coconut milk**

1 fresh **pandan leaf**

1cm (½in) slice of **fresh root ginger**

large pinch of **salt**

TO SERVE

50g (1¾oz) **ikan bilis**

6 **quail's eggs**

1 **cucumber**

handful of salted roasted **peanuts**

edible pansies (optional)

1 Bring some water to the boil in a small saucepan, add the dried chillies for the sambal ikan bilis and the sambal prawns, and simmer for 5 minutes. Remove from the heat and leave to sit for 15 minutes, then drain.

2 For the sambal ikan bilis, soak the ikan bilis in hot water for 15 minutes, then drain. Blend with the fresh chillies, shallots, garlic, lemongrass, shrimp paste, and the 12 soaked chillies until smooth. Heat the oil in a wok, then fry the paste until the oil separates. Add the remaining ingredients and leave to cool.

3 For the chicken, push the flesh down along the bones and remove the bigger bone of the wing. Shape the meat into a neat ball. Rub it with the turmeric, salt, coriander, and 1 tbsp oil, cover, and leave for at least 30 minutes at room temperature (the longer the better). Heat the oil for deep-frying to 180°C (350°F). Dip the chicken in the beaten egg, coat it in the smashed crisps, then deep-fry for about 4 minutes, until golden and cooked.

4 To make the sambal prawns, blend the 6 soaked chillies, lemongrass, candlenuts, garlic, shrimp paste, and shallots to make a paste. Coat the prawns in 2 tbsp of the paste and marinate for 30 minutes. Heat the oil, then fry the remaining

sambal paste until fragrant and the oil separates. Add the sugar, tamarind, and salt. Taste: it should have a good balance of spicy, sweet and tangy flavours. In a frying pan, fry the prawns until just cooked. Top with the sambal paste.

5 Put the rice, coconut milk, and 200ml (7fl oz) water in a saucepan and stir. Knot the pandan leaf, then push it into the rice with the ginger and salt. Bring to a gentle simmer (but do not stir), until the liquid evaporates and the surface of the rice has bubbles forming on top. Turn off the heat and cover. Leave for 30 minutes, then fluff up the rice with a fork.

6 Now prepare the garnishes. Dry-fry the ikan bilis for a few seconds in the oil you used for the chicken, scooping them out as they turn light brown. Boil the quail's eggs for 2 minutes, plunge into cold water to stop the cooking, and peel (or fry the eggs, if you prefer). Peel the cucumber and scoop out balls with a melon baller, or just cut it into 2cm (¾in) chunks.

7 Serve a scoop of rice on each plate. Add the chicken, prawns, and a spoonful of sambal. Serve the remaining sambal on the side. Add the halved quail's eggs and fried ikan bilis, then scatter with cucumber pieces, peanuts, and pansies (if using).

Spiced battered fish and chips

DHRUV BAKER Champion 2010

PREPARATION TIME **15 minutes** • COOKING TIME **1 hour 15 minutes** • SERVES 4

4 John Dory fillets, or other white fish, approx. 150g (5½oz) each

handful of coriander, roughly chopped, to garnish

FOR THE MUSHY PEAS

250g (9oz) dried split green or yellow peas

2 onions, chopped

2 bay leaves

salt and freshly ground black pepper

handful of coriander, chopped

1–2 red chillies, deseeded and chopped

1–2 green chillies, deseeded and chopped

juice of 2–3 limes

300g (10oz) frozen or fresh peas

FOR THE BROWN SAUCE

2 tbsp tamarind paste

4 tsp caster sugar

juice of 2 limes

pinch of chilli powder

FOR THE CHIPS

4–6 large Maris Piper potatoes, peeled and cut into chips

groundnut oil, for deep frying

FOR THE BATTER

150g (5½oz) plain flour

2 tsp baking powder

½ tsp fennel seeds

¼ tsp turmeric

¼ tsp chilli powder

¼ tsp ground coriander

¼ tsp ground cumin

¼ tsp brown mustard seeds

½ tsp ginger paste, or freshly grated root ginger

½ tsp garlic paste, or 1 garlic clove, finely crushed

1 Put the dried peas in a saucepan with 1 litre (1¾ pints) of water, the onions, bay leaves, and some black pepper. Boil for 1¼ hours or until the peas are tender and mushy, adding more water if necessary. Add the coriander, chillies, and lime juice. In another pan, boil the frozen or fresh peas for 4–5 minutes or until just tender, then drain and crush, using a fork. Stir into the split peas and season with salt.

2 For the sauce, put the tamarind paste in a small pan with the sugar, lime juice, and 4 tbsp of water. Add the chilli powder. Boil over medium-high heat for 5 minutes or until reduced to a sticky sauce.

3 Parboil the chips in a pan of boiling water for 5 minutes, then drain. Preheat a deep-fat fryer or deep saucepan two-thirds filled with oil to 160°C (325°F). Cook the chips

in batches for 5–6 minutes, then drain on kitchen paper. Increase the temperature of the oil to 180°C (350°F) and return the chips to the pan to crisp and turn golden. Toss in salt.

4 For the batter, mix the flour, baking powder, spices, ginger, and garlic with 150–170ml (5–6fl oz) iced water until smooth. Dip 2 pieces of fish in batter and deep fry for 7–8 minutes, turning once or twice. Drain and set aside to keep warm, then repeat with the remaining fish.

5 Serve the battered fish with the chips and mushy peas alongside. Drizzle a little brown sauce over and garnish the plates with coriander.

VEGETABLES KNOW-HOW *see* Deseed and cut chillies **p373**
VEGETABLES KNOW-HOW *see* Make chips **p375**

Mauritian lobster curry with spiced peas

SHELINA PERMALLOO Champion 2012

PREPARATION TIME **1 hour** • COOKING TIME **1 hour** • SERVES 6

FOR THE STOCK

sea salt and freshly ground **black pepper**

3 **lobsters**

50g (1¾oz) **coriander stalks**

2 **banana shallots**, finely chopped

1 **garlic** bulb, halved, skins on

1 thumb of **fresh root ginger**, peeled and finely chopped

FOR THE SAUCE

1 tbsp **vegetable oil**

2 **banana shallots**, finely chopped

4 **garlic cloves**, finely chopped

thumb of fresh root **ginger**, peeled and finely chopped

1 **red chilli**, finely chopped

12 **curry leaves**

2 tbsp mild Madras **curry powder**

1 tsp **ground cumin**

1 tsp **ground coriander**

1 tsp **ground turmeric**

4 **vine tomatoes**, chopped

400ml can **coconut milk**, extra to serve

75g (2½oz) finely chopped **coriander leaves** and stalks

FOR THE PEAS

drizzle of **olive oil**

400g (14oz) frozen **petits pois**

2 tsp **cumin seeds**

1 tsp **garam masala**

1 tsp **hot chilli powder**

finely grated zest of 1 unwaxed **lemon** and juice of ½ **lemon**

FOR THE POTATO BAJA

vegetable oil, for deep-frying

2 King Edward **potatoes**, 450g (1lb) in total, peeled and grated

80g (2¾oz) **gram flour**

1 tsp **chilli powder**

3 tsp chopped **coriander leaves**

2 tsp chopped **mint leaves**

2 **garlic cloves**, finely chopped

FOR THE LOBSTER

dash of **vegetable oil**

knob of **unsalted butter**

juice of ½ **lemon**

2 **garlic cloves**, finely chopped

1 tsp finely grated fresh root **ginger**

micro coriander (optional)

1 For the stock, heat a large pan of salted water to a rolling boil, weigh the lobsters, add them, and cook for 10 minutes per 450g (1lb). Place the cooked lobsters in ice-cold water, reserving the cooking water. Remove all the meat and set aside. Return the shells to the cooking water with the remaining stock ingredients. Bring to the boil and cook for 20 minutes. Strain and leave to cool.

2 To make the curry sauce, heat the oil in a large saucepan and fry the shallots, garlic, ginger, chilli, and curry leaves in the oil with some salt for 3–4 minutes. Add the spices and tomatoes and cook for 5 minutes. Pour in the coconut milk and 500ml (18fl oz) of the lobster stock and cook for a further 20 minutes. Scatter with the coriander leaves and stalks, season with salt, then pour into a food processor and process until smooth. Pass through a fine-mesh sieve. Set aside.

3 For the peas, sauté everything in a pan over a medium heat for 5 minutes, splashing in some water if it gets dry. Crush slightly with the back of fork. Set aside, covering to keep warm.

4 To make the potato baja, preheat the oil in a deep-fat fryer or large saucepan to 180°C (350°F). Combine all of the ingredients in a large bowl. Place large tablespoons of the mixture into the oil and deep-fry for around 3 minutes, until golden brown. Fry about 3 at a time, but do not overcrowd the pan. Drain on kitchen paper.

5 Melt the oil and butter for the lobster in a sauté pan. Sear the reserved lobster meat in the oil and butter, lemon juice, garlic, ginger, and salt and pepper for less than 1 minute, just to warm it through and add a flash of flavour.

6 To serve, place a ring of the spiced peas in the centre of each plate. Top this with the lobster, followed by a potato baja, then pour the curry sauce around. Drizzle some extra coconut milk into the curry sauce to create a lovely marbled effect, then dress the plate with micro coriander, if using.

SHELLFISH KNOW-HOW: *see* **Extract the meat from a cooked lobster p284**

Seared tuna with an Asian glaze

ANGELA KENNY Semi-finalist 2009

PREPARATION TIME **20 minutes** • COOKING TIME **8 minutes** • **SERVES 4**

4 **carrots**

4 **courgettes**

8 tbsp **dark soy sauce**

4 **limes**

6 tbsp **demerara sugar**

12–16 **Charlotte potatoes**, peeled and sliced into discs

60ml (2fl oz) **white miso paste**

60ml (2fl oz) **mirin**

90ml (3½ fl oz) **dry sake**

2 tbsp **rice wine vinegar**

1 tbsp **oil**

4 **tuna steaks**, 175–200g (6–7oz) each

salt and freshly ground **black pepper**

1 With a potato peeler, shave the carrots and courgettes into long strips. Place in a mixing bowl with 3 tbsp soy sauce, the juice and zest of 1½ limes, and 4 tbsp sugar.

2 Put the potatoes in a large pan with boiling water to cover and the white miso paste. Cook for about 10 minutes until the potatoes are tender and then drain.

3 Place the mirin, sake, remaining sugar and soy sauce, rice wine vinegar, and the juice and zest of the remaining limes in a frying pan over a medium heat and reduce to a syrup consistency – about 10 minutes.

4 Season the tuna with salt and pepper. Heat another frying pan until hot, add the tuna, and sear on both sides for about 3 minutes.

5 Once the tuna is cooked, transfer it to the frying pan containing the glaze and turn to coat it. Heat the ribbon vegetables in the glaze for 2 minutes, then serve with the tuna and potatoes.

Pan-fried chicken breast with sesame seeds and a mango hollandaise

JAYE WAKELIN Quarter-finalist 2007

PREPARATION TIME **15 minutes** • COOKING TIME **20 minutes** • SERVES 4

4 **chicken breasts**, skinned

2 large **egg yolks**

salt and freshly ground **black pepper**

1 tbsp **lemon juice**

1 tbsp **white wine vinegar**

125g (4½oz) **salted butter**

1 ripe **mango**, peeled, stoned, and chopped

2 tbsp **sesame seeds**

1 tbsp **groundnut oil**

25g (scant 1oz) **butter**

400g (14oz) **purple sprouting broccoli**

1 Remove the chicken from the refrigerator at least 30 minutes before preparation.

2 To make the hollandaise, place the egg yolks in a blender with salt and pepper to taste and blend thoroughly. Heat the lemon juice and vinegar to simmering point in a small saucepan, then remove the pan from the heat. Switch on the blender again and pour the hot lemon liquid through the vent in the top of it in a steady stream. Switch off the blender.

3 In the same saucepan, melt the butter over a low heat. With the blender running as before, add the butter to the egg mixture in a steady stream. The mixture should now look like runny mayonnaise. Pour it out into a clean bowl.

4 Add the chopped mango to the blender and blitz until smooth and puréed. Stir into the hollandaise, cover with cling film, and set aside.

5 Spread the sesame seeds over a plate and press the chicken breasts onto them, coating each one evenly. Melt the oil and butter in a frying pan over a medium heat, taking care that the butter doesn't brown. Add the chicken breasts and fry gently on both sides until cooked through – about 5–8 minutes on each side. At this point the butter in the pan will look brown but will not have burnt. Meanwhile, steam the broccoli until tender – about 8 minutes.

6 Return the mango hollandaise to a clean saucepan and reheat gently, taking care not to let it bubble and separate. Put the sliced chicken breasts on plates and serve with the hollandaise spooned over. This dish goes well with any stir-fried Chinese greens or purple sprouting broccoli with a little soy sauce.

FRUITS AND NUTS KNOW-HOW: *see* Prepare a mango **p425**

Roast Moroccan lamb with couscous and harissa sauce

HELEN GILMOUR Quarter-finalist 2007

PREPARATION TIME **1 hour, plus marinating** • COOKING TIME **30 minutes** • **SERVES 4**

2 cannons of **lamb**, about 350g (12oz) each

FOR THE MARINADE

200ml (7fl oz) **olive oil**

juice of ½ **lemon**

1 **onion**, finely chopped

3 tbsp chopped **flat-leaf parsley**

3 tbsp chopped **mint**

5 tbsp chopped **coriander**

1½ tsp ground **cumin**

1 tsp **paprika**

1 tsp **sea salt** and freshly ground **black pepper**

FOR THE COUSCOUS

100g (3½oz) **medium grain couscous**

6 **dried apricots**, chopped

50g (1¾oz) **golden sultanas**

25g (scant 1oz) **salted butter**

200ml (7fl oz) **chicken stock**

25g (scant 1oz) flaked **almonds**

20g (¾oz) **mint**, finely chopped

20g (¾oz) **coriander**, finely chopped

200g (7oz) can **chickpeas**

25g (scant 1oz) nibbed **pistachios**

½ tsp ground **cinnamon**

3 tbsp **olive oil** (optional)

FOR THE HARISSA SAUCE

3 tbsp **rose harissa paste**

2 tbsp **plain yogurt**

1 Combine all the marinade ingredients, pour over the lamb, and set aside to marinate for a minimum of 2 hours, or overnight if you can.

2 Prepare the couscous. Place the couscous, apricots, and sultanas in a bowl. Add the butter, and pour over the chicken stock so there is just enough to cover the grains. Cover with cling film and set aside for 10 minutes to allow the stock to be absorbed.

3 Toast the almonds in a dry pan until golden and set aside in a bowl. Add the mint and coriander.

4 Fluff the couscous with a fork and add half the chickpeas and stir through. Add the almonds and herbs, and then the pistachios and mix thoroughly. Finally, add the cinnamon and season with salt and pepper, and add some olive oil, if required.

5 For the harissa sauce, mix the harissa paste with the yogurt and warm it in a small saucepan over a low heat, but do not overheat as it may split.

6 Heat a frying pan until hot and cook the lamb for 8–10 minutes. Remove from the pan, cover with foil, and leave to rest for 5 minutes.

7 To assemble, divide the couscous between 4 plates and place slices of lamb and a spoonful of the harissa sauce alongside. A spoonful of cacïk is the perfect accompaniment.

RICE, GRAINS, AND PULSES KNOW-HOW: *see* Rehydrate instant couscous **p448**

Loin of venison with celeriac purée, braised cabbage, and redcurrant jus

ALEX RUSHMER Finalist 2010

PREPARATION TIME **20 minutes** • COOKING TIME **1 hour 30 minutes** • **SERVES 4**

700g (1lb 9oz) **loin of venison**

1 tbsp **olive oil**

knob of **butter**

100g (3½oz) **porcini** or **wild mushrooms**, cut into thick slices

FOR THE CABBAGE

knob of **butter**

1 small **shallot**, diced

300g (10oz) **red cabbage**, quartered, cored, and sliced

1 **apple**, cored, peeled, and sliced

1 tbsp **clear honey**

3 tbsp **red wine vinegar**

100ml (3½fl oz) **red wine**

200ml (7fl oz) **chicken stock**

salt and freshly ground **black pepper**

FOR THE CELERIAC

1 **celeriac**, approx. 800g (1¾lb)

juice of 1 **lemon**

3 tbsp **double cream**

25g (scant 1oz) **butter**

500ml (16fl oz) **vegetable oil**

FOR THE JUS

knob of **butter**

1 **shallot**, diced

8 **juniper berries**

50g (1¾oz) **redcurrants**

150ml (5fl oz) **port**

150ml (5fl oz) **veal stock**

2 tsp **redcurrant jelly**

1 For the cabbage, melt the butter in a large heavy saucepan. Add the shallot and cook for about 5 minutes to soften. Add the remaining ingredients and season. Cover with greaseproof paper and a lid, and braise over a very low heat for 1½ hours, stirring occasionally.

2 Peel the celeriac and shave off 4 strips to make crisps. Put in a bowl of iced lemon water and set aside. Dice the rest. Put in a pan with water to cover, salt, and lemon juice and bring to the boil. Simmer for 15–20 minutes or until soft. Drain and transfer to a blender or food processor. Add the cream, butter, and seasoning and purée. Keep warm.

3 For the jus, melt the butter in a pan. Cook the shallot for 3 minutes to soften. Add the berries and redcurrants and

cook for 1 minute, then stir in the port and reduce by half. Pour in the stock and reduce again. Stir in the jelly and pass through a sieve into a pan to keep warm.

4 Season the venison and fry in the oil for 10–15 minutes, turning once. Cook longer if you prefer your meat less pink. Remove the venison from the pan, leave to rest, and then slice. Add the butter and mushrooms to the pan and fry for about 2 minutes to cook through.

5 Just before serving, drain and dry the celeriac shavings. Deep-fry in the vegetable oil for 2–3 minutes until crisp. Drain on kitchen paper. Spoon the purée and cabbage onto 4 plates and top with the venison and mushrooms. Drizzle over the sauce and garnish with the crisps.

VEGETABLES KNOW-HOW: *see* Core and shred cabbage **p369**

Thai beef massaman curry with jasmine rice

ALIX CARWOOD Quarter-finalist 2008

PREPARATION TIME **25 minutes** • COOKING TIME **55 minutes** • SERVES 4

500g (1lb 2oz) **lean rump steak**, cut into bite-sized chunks

5 **cloves**

10 **cardamom pods**

3 tbsp **vegetable oil**

400ml can **coconut milk**

2 tbsp **nam pla** (Thai fish sauce)

175ml (6fl oz) **beef stock**

60g (2oz) unsalted **peanuts**, skinned

1 large **Maris Piper potato**, peeled and cut into chunks

1.5cm (½in) piece fresh **root ginger**

1–2 tbsp **palm sugar**

1–2 tbsp **tamarind paste**

FOR THE CURRY PASTE

1 **red chilli**

1 stalk of **lemongrass**

1cm (½in) **galangal** or 1 tsp **galangal in sunflower oil**

5 **cloves**

1 **cinnamon stick**

10 **cardamom pods**

3 **garlic cloves**

3 **shallots**

large handful of **coriander**

3 tbsp **olive oil**

TO SERVE

300g (10oz) **jasmine rice**

unsalted **peanuts**, skinned

coriander leaves, to garnish

1 To make the curry paste, put all the ingredients in a food processor with a little olive oil and blend until they form a paste.

2 For the beef curry, put the cloves and cardamom in a frying pan and dry fry to release the fragrance. Remove and set aside.

3 Put a little of the vegetable oil in the pan and fry 5 tbsp of the curry paste over a medium heat for 5 minutes until the fragrance is released. Add the beef and fry until browned.

Then add the remaining ingredients to the pan and bring to the boil. Reduce to a simmer and cook for about 45 minutes until the beef is tender and the sauce is reduced.

4 Bring a pan of water to the boil. Add a pinch of salt and then the jasmine rice. Reduce the heat and leave to simmer for about 10 minutes until the rice is cooked through.

5 Serve the curry in a bowl, sprinkled with peanuts, with the jasmine rice to one side, garnished with coriander.

SAVOURY SAUCES AND STOCKS KNOW-HOW: *see* Make beef stock **p485**

Beef Wellington with mash, creamed Savoy cabbage, and an oxtail jus

LIZ MCCLARNON Celebrity champion 2008

PREPARATION TIME **40 minutes** • COOKING TIME **1 hour** • SERVES **4**

4 fillets of **beef**, about 175g (6oz) each

3 **Maris Piper potatoes**, peeled and chopped

4 large stoneless **prunes**

4 tsp **mango chutney**

2 **streaky bacon rashers**, cut in half

250g (9oz) ready-made **puff pastry**

200g (7oz) **chestnut mushrooms**, chopped

75g (2½oz) **salted butter**

salt and freshly ground **black pepper**

2 tsp **truffle oil**

½ **Savoy cabbage**, shredded

400ml (14fl oz) **double cream**

1 tbsp **olive oil**

3 sprigs of **thyme**

2 sprigs of **rosemary**

FOR THE OXTAIL JUS

2 **garlic cloves**, chopped

1 **shallot**, chopped

1 tbsp **olive oil**

3 sprigs of **flat-leaf parsley**, chopped

300ml (10fl oz) **port**

200ml (7fl oz) **oxtail stock**, plus 4 tbsp

1 Preheat the oven to 200°C (400°F/Gas 6). Bring a large saucepan of salted water to the boil, add the potatoes and simmer for 20 minutes, or until cooked. Drain and keep warm.

2 For the oxtail jus, put the garlic cloves and shallot in a frying pan with the oil and parsley. Add the port, bring to the boil, and reduce by three-quarters. Then add the stock and reduce by half. Keep warm.

3 Fill the hole in each prune with the chutney and roll in a piece of streaky bacon. Pierce with a cocktail stick and cook on a baking tray in the oven for 7 minutes. Remove from the oven and keep warm.

4 Roll out the pastry and cut out four 8cm (3¼in) diameter circles. Put them on a floured baking sheet, glaze with a little milk, then cook in the oven for 12 minutes, until golden. Remove and keep warm.

5 Meanwhile, cook the mushrooms in 25g (scant 1oz) of the butter in a saucepan, add seasoning and the truffle oil. Keep warm.

6 Put the cabbage in 300ml (10fl oz) of the double cream in a saucepan, and add seasoning. Cook for 10–12 minutes until tender.

7 Mash the potatoes with the rest of the double cream and butter.

8 Cover the beef in the olive oil and salt and pepper. Heat a frying pan and when hot, seal the beef for a few seconds on each side. Transfer to a roasting tin, add the thyme and rosemary, and spoon the extra stock over the top. Put in the oven for 6 minutes.

9 To assemble, place a puff pastry circle on each plate. Score a circle in the top, push it down, and fill with mushrooms. Add some creamed cabbage, a prune in bacon, and quenelles of mash. Place a fillet of beef on top, add the jus, and serve.

DOUGH, PASTRY, AND CAKES KNOW-HOW: *see* Roll out puff pastry **p459**

Raspberry-blackberry parfait with chocolate mousse

TONY RODD Finalist 2015

PREPARATION TIME **1 hour, plus chilling** • COOKING TIME **40 minutes** • SERVES 4

FOR THE PARFAIT

4 tsp **water**

50g (1¾oz) **caster sugar**

3 **egg yolks**

150ml (5fl oz) **double cream**

150ml (5fl oz) **raspberry purée**

juice of ½ **lemon**

150ml (5fl oz) **blackberry purée**

FOR THE SORBET

100ml (3½fl oz) **water**

80g (2¾oz) **granulated sugar**

200g (7oz) **raspberries**

juice of ½ **lemon**

FOR THE MOUSSE

100g (3½oz) **dark chocolate**, chopped

30g (1oz) **unsalted butter**

3 **eggs**, separated

25g (scant 1oz) **caster sugar**

FOR THE CHOCOLATE SHARD

100g (3½oz) **dark chocolate**, chopped

FOR THE CHOCOLATE GANACHE

3½ tbsp **double cream**

(3½oz) **dark chocolate**, chopped

FOR THE BLACKBERRY COULIS

100g (3½oz) **blackberries**

4 tsp **caster sugar**

¼ **gelatine sheet**

TO SERVE

edible pansies (optional)

1 For the parfait, heat the water and sugar in a saucepan over a medium heat, stirring until the sugar dissolves. Whisk the yolks in a separate bowl until pale, then pour over the sugar water, whisking all the time. Whip the cream to soft peaks and combine this with the egg mixture. Separate into 2 bowls. Add the blackberry purée and half of the lemon juice to the first bowl and the raspberry purée and remaining lemon juice to the second.

2 Divide half of the blackberry mixture between 4 x 8cm (3in) ring or cylindrical moulds and freeze for 20 minutes, until just set. Then pour over all the raspberry mixture and freeze again. Finally, divide the remaining blackberry mixture between the moulds and, once again, freeze until just set.

3 Now make the sorbet. Heat the water and sugar in a saucepan over a medium heat, stirring until the sugar dissolves. Purée the raspberries and add to the saucepan with the lemon juice. Chill, then churn in an ice cream machine until frozen.

4 For the mousse, put the chocolate and butter in a heatproof bowl and place over a saucepan of simmering water until melted (make sure the bowl does not touch the water). Whisk the egg yolks and sugar together until pale, then mix with the chocolate. Whisk the egg whites to soft peaks, fold into the mousse, cover, and chill.

5 To make the chocolate shard, melt the chocolate and pour on to a baking sheet lined with silicone paper. Leave to set, then cut into shards with a sharp knife. Chill until set.

6 For the ganache, heat the cream to boiling point and pour it over the chopped chocolate in a bowl. Leave for 30 seconds, then stir until the chocolate melts and the mixture is smooth.

7 To make the coulis, purée the blackberries and mix with the caster sugar in a saucepan over a medium heat, stirring until the sugar dissolves. Soak the gelatine in 1 tsp boiling water for 5 minutes, then squeeze out the water and add to the blackberry mixture. Remove the saucepan from the heat and stir until dissolved.

8 Place a parfait on a serving plate with a quenelle of raspberry sorbet and some chocolate ganache. Add a smear of coulis and place a quenelle of mousse on top. Decorate with ganache, a chocolate shard, and the pansies (if using).

Rice crispie cake with chocolate mousse, cherry sorbet, and cherries in Kirsch

DAVID COULSON Professionals finalist 2010

PREPARATION TIME **50 minutes, plus freezing** • **SERVES 4**

FOR THE SORBET

100g (3½oz) caster sugar

400g (14oz) jar of **griotines**
or **black cherries in Kirsch**

FOR THE CAKE

50g (1¾oz) **dark chocolate**
(68% cocoa solids)

30g (1oz) **rice crispies**

1 tbsp **golden syrup**

100g (3½oz) **condensed milk**

1 packet of **popping candy**

FOR THE MOUSSE

75g (2½oz) **dark chocolate**
(68% cocoa solids)

2 **eggs**, separated

100ml (3½fl oz) **double cream**

FOR THE POACHING SYRUP

150ml (5fl oz) reserved **Kirsch syrup**
from the jar of cherries

1 tbsp **caster sugar**

1 **star anise**

1 **cinnamon stick**

1 To make the sorbet, put the sugar in a saucepan with 100ml (3½fl oz) of water. Gently heat to dissolve the sugar, then boil for 1 minute to make a stock syrup. Drain the jar of cherries. Set aside 4 cherries and reserve the Kirsch syrup for poaching them.

2 Add the remaining cherries to the stock syrup and blend in a liquidizer or food processor until smooth. Pour into an ice-cream maker and churn. Transfer to a suitable container and freeze.

3 To make the cake, melt the chocolate in a glass bowl set over a pan of simmering water. Stir in the rice crispies, syrup, and condensed milk and add the popping candy. Divide the crispie cake between 4 glass dessert dishes and set aside, but not in the refrigerator.

4 For the mousse, melt the chocolate and stir in the egg yolks. Softly whip the cream and fold into the chocolate mix. Beat the egg whites until stiff, then fold into the mix until well combined. Spoon the mousse into the glasses on top of the crispie mixture.

5 Put the reserved Kirsch in a pan and stir in the sugar. Add the reserved cherries, the star anise, and the cinnamon stick. Simmer for 5 minutes. Remove the cherries and spices with a slotted spoon and reduce the sauce to a syrup. Reserve the cherries and discard the spices.

6 To finish, use a melonball scoop to put a small scoop of the sorbet on top of the mousse and decorate with a poached cherry. Serve immediately with the syrup in a jug alongside.

EGGS AND DAIRY PRODUCTS KNOW-HOW: *see* Separate yolks and whites **p430**

Exploding lemon macarons

TIM KINNAIRD Finalist 2010

PREPARATION TIME **55 minutes, plus standing and chilling** • COOKING TIME **25 minutes** • **SERVES 4**

FOR THE MACARONS

180g (6oz) **caster sugar**

3 tbsp **water**

4 **egg whites**, near their sell-by date

180g (6oz) ground **almonds**

180g (6oz) **icing sugar**

1 tsp **yellow food colouring**

FOR THE LEMON CURD

4 **egg yolks**

grated zest and juice of 6 **lemons**

70g (2¼fl oz) **caster sugar**

70g (2¼fl oz) **salted butter**

TO SERVE

popping candy (optional)

1 Preheat the oven to 150°C (300°F/Gas 2) and line 2–3 baking sheets with baking parchment.

2 To make the macarons, dissolve the sugar in 3 tbsp of water over low heat for about 8 minutes, stirring occasionally. Increase the heat and allow the sugar to boil for about 10 minutes, without stirring, until it reaches 118°C (244°F) – "soft boil" temperature.

3 Whisk the egg whites in a free-standing mixer until they start to foam. Still mixing, gradually add the sugar syrup in a steady stream until the sugar is incorporated and the egg whites form stiff peaks.

4 In a separate bowl, mix together the ground almonds, icing sugar, 165g (5½oz) of the egg whites, and the food colouring. Mix together until the meringue flows like lava.

5 Pipe 5cm (2in) circles of the meringue mixture onto the baking parchment with at least 2cm (¾in) gaps between each circle. Leave for 45 minutes for the shells to dry a little and a crust to form.

6 Bake in the oven for about 15 minutes. Remove from the oven to cool and then gently remove from the paper.

7 While the biscuits are resting, make the lemon curd. Put the egg yolks, lemon zest and juice, and caster sugar into a saucepan and heat gently with half the butter for about 10 minutes until the curd thickens.

8 Strain the lemon curd into a bowl to remove the zest and whisk in the remaining butter. Chill in the refrigerator until the curd is firm and the biscuits are cool.

9 Sandwich pairs of macarons with lemon curd and put them back in the refrigerator to chill, preferably overnight.

10 Remove the macarons from the refrigerator an hour before serving. Slightly moisten them by lightly brushing them with a moistened pastry brush and sprinkle with popping candy (if using).

EGGS AND DAIRY PRODUCTS KNOW-HOW: *see* Separate yolks and whites **p430**
EGGS AND DAIRY PRODUCTS KNOW-HOW: *see* Whisk egg whites **p431**
EGGS AND DAIRY PRODUCTS KNOW-HOW: *see* Shape meringues **p437**

Strawberries with sablé biscuits and orange and lemon syllabub

JAMES NATHAN Champion 2008

PREPARATION TIME **40 minutes** • COOKING TIME **8 minutes** • SERVES 4

FOR THE SABLÉ BISCUITS

100g (3½oz) **plain flour**

75g (2½oz) **unsalted butter**

100g (3½oz) **golden caster sugar**

grated zest of 1 **lemon**

2 **egg yolks**

FOR THE SYLLABUB

50g (1¾oz) **caster sugar**

grated zest and juice of 1 **orange**

grated zest and juice of 1 **lemon**

300ml (10fl oz) **double cream**

FOR THE STRAWBERRY COULIS

350g (12oz) **strawberries** (English if possible)

50g (1¾oz) **icing sugar**

3 tbsp **Grand Marnier**

TO DECORATE

icing sugar, for sprinkling

mint leaves

1 Preheat the oven to 200°C (400°F/Gas 6). To make the biscuits, mix the flour, butter, sugar, lemon zest, and egg yolks together in a food processor until a soft ball of dough is formed. Rest in the refrigerator for about 30 minutes. Roll out thinly. Cut out 8 biscuits with a 7–8cm (2¾–3¼in) biscuit cutter and bake in the oven on a greased baking tray until golden, about 6–8 minutes.

2 To make the coulis, hull 200g (7oz) of the strawberries. Purée with the icing sugar and Grand Marnier in a food processor. Check for sweetness and adjust if necessary. Pass through a fine sieve and chill the mixture until required.

3 For the syllabub, combine the sugar and zest and juice from the orange and lemon. Whisk the cream until it forms soft peaks. Add the citrus mixture and whisk to firm peaks. Chill until required.

4 To serve, put a swirl of the coulis on each plate. Set a biscuit alongside it. Put a few spoonfuls of syllabub in the centre of the biscuit and surround with the remaining strawberries, halved lengthways to make pillars. Top with another biscuit. Sprinkle with icing sugar and add some mint leaves to finish.

Lavender mousse with honeycomb and a blackberry sauce

MAT FOLLAS Champion 2009

PREPARATION TIME **50 minutes** • **SERVES 4**

FOR THE BLACKBERRY SAUCE

300g (10oz) **blackberries**

200g (7oz) **caster sugar**

FOR THE LAVENDER MOUSSE

13g (½oz) **gelatine leaves**, cut into pieces

500ml (16fl oz) **whole milk**

5 **egg yolks**

40g (1½oz) **caster sugar**

500ml (16fl oz) **whipping cream**

20g (¾oz) **lavender flower heads**

12 drops **lavender essence**

FOR THE HONEYCOMB

75g (2½oz) **caster sugar**

2 tbsp **golden syrup**

1 tsp **bicarbonate of soda**

1 Set aside 12 blackberries of different sizes for decoration. Then put the remaining blackberries in a pan with the caster sugar and add 100ml (3½fl oz) cold water, stir and heat gently until the sugar has dissolved. Bring the sauce to the boil, reduce the heat, and simmer for 5 minutes or until the sauce has reduced by half and thickened. Pass through a sieve, discard the blackberry pulp, and leave to cool.

2 Transfer the sauce into a jug and pour a little into 4 freezerproof glasses, which the mousse will be served in. Put the glasses in the freezer and set the rest of the sauce aside in the refrigerator.

3 For the lavender mousse, put the gelatine in iced water for about 10 minutes to soften. Pour the milk into a saucepan and bring it to the boil. Place the egg yolks and sugar into a bowl and mix. Stir in the milk. Return to the pan, stirring and warming gently for 5 minutes or until the sauce coats the back of a spoon, making a crème anglaise. Drain any excess water from the gelatine and add to the pan and stir until dissolved. Set aside to cool.

4 Whip the cream until stiff peaks are formed. Add the lavender heads and combine. Stir in the lavender essence, a drop at a time, until the flavour is to your taste. Gently fold the cream into the crème anglaise.

5 Remove the glasses from the freezer and pour the mixture over the frozen berry sauce. Return to the freezer for 20 minutes.

6 To make the honeycomb, heat the sugar and golden syrup slowly in a saucepan, stirring constantly for 3 minutes or until the sugar is dissolved. Stir in the bicarbonate of soda and then pour onto a silicone sheet and leave to cool. Put into a plastic bag and gently smash it.

7 To serve, make a line of blackberry sauce on each plate and top with the reserved blackberries. Add the frozen mousses and put a piece of broken honeycomb in the top of each one and add a small pile of honeycomb crumbs alongside.

FLAVOURINGS KNOW-HOW: *See* Use gelatine **p393**

EGGS AND DAIRY PRODUCTS KNOW-HOW: *See* Whip cream **p438**

Pears belle Hélène

STEVEN WALLIS Champion 2007

PREPARATION TIME **20 minutes, plus freezing** • COOKING TIME **20 minutes** • **SERVES 4**

FOR THE PEARS

1 tbsp **caster sugar**

4 **bay leaves**

3 **cardamom pods**

2 **vanilla pods**

2 **Comice pears**, with stalks

FOR THE ICE CREAM

300ml (10fl oz) **double cream**

200ml (7fl oz) **whole milk**

2 **vanilla pods**, slit, seeds scraped out but reserved

4 **egg yolks**

85–100g (3–3½oz) **caster sugar**

FOR THE CHOCOLATE SAUCE

1 tsp **caster sugar**

300ml (10fl oz) **double cream**

2 x 100g (3½oz) bars **dark chocolate** (70% cocoa solids)

1 First make the ice cream. Pour the cream and milk into a saucepan. Add the vanilla pods and seeds to the pan and heat gently until steaming but not boiling. Leave to infuse for 5 minutes.

2 Whisk the egg yolks and sugar together until pale and foamy. Remove the vanilla pods and gradually whisk the warm cream into the egg yolk mixture. Return to the pan and cook, stirring, over low heat until a custard thick enough to coat the back of a wooden spoon is formed. Transfer to an ice-cream maker and churn.

3 To cook the pears, pour 300ml (10fl oz) boiling water into a saucepan, add the sugar, and stir to dissolve. Add the bay leaves and cardamom and vanilla pods. Heat gently to boiling point. Peel and core the pears, leaving the stalk intact. Add to the syrup, cover with a lid, and poach gently for 20 minutes or until tender.

4 For the chocolate sauce, put the sugar in a pan with 1 tbsp boiling water and stir until the sugar is dissolved. Set aside. Warm the cream in a heavy pan, add the chocolate piece by piece, and stir very briefly to melt. Remove from the heat and stir in the sugar syrup. Keep warm.

5 To serve, slice the pears in half lengthways, then make vertical cuts about 5mm (¼in) apart. For each diner, scoop out a ball of ice cream the size of a small orange and place in a chilled deep dessert bowl. Carefully lift the pear on top and mould it around the ice cream. Set the bowl on a plate and serve the chocolate sauce on the side.

EGG AND DAIRY PRODUCTS KNOW-HOW: *see* Whip cream **p438**

Lemon posset with limoncello crumb, lime air, and burnt grapefruit

SIMON WOOD Champion 2015

PREPARATION TIME **1 hour, plus chilling** • COOKING TIME **20 minutes** • SERVES **4**

FOR THE LEMON POSSET
300ml (10fl oz) **double cream**

100g (3½oz) **golden caster sugar**

finely grated zest and juice of
2 unwaxed **lemons**

FOR THE LIME TUILE
1 **egg white**

40g (1¼oz) **caster sugar**

40g (1¼oz) **plain flour**

finely grated zest of 1 **unwaxed lime**

22g (¾oz) **unsalted butter**, melted,
plus extra for the baking tray

FOR THE LIMONCELLO CRUMB
100g (3½oz) **caster sugar**

2 tsp **limoncello**

55g (2oz) shelled **unsalted pistachios**

unsalted butter, for the baking tray

FOR THE LIME AIR
150ml (5fl oz) **lime juice**

50ml (1¾fl oz) **water**

1g (about ¼ tsp) **soy lecithin**

FOR THE BURNT GRAPEFRUIT
1 pink **grapefruit**

1 white **grapefruit**

TO SERVE
edible **pansies** (optional)

1 Heat the cream and sugar together over a gentle heat, stirring until the sugar dissolves. Turn off the heat and add the lemon zest and juice. Divide between 4 serving dishes or glasses and chill for at least 3 hours, or up to 24 hours.

2 Preheat the oven to 180°C (350°F/Gas 4). Make the tuile: whisk the egg white lightly, then whisk in the sugar. Sift in the flour and mix to a smooth paste, then stir in the lime zest and melted butter. Butter a baking tray, then place 4 spoonfuls of the mixture on it, spaced well apart. Bake for 10 minutes, until golden brown. Remove carefully from the tray with a palette knife and curl over a cling film-lined rolling pin, for curved tuiles, or roll them tighter, for tuile "cigars".

3 For the limoncello crumb, heat the caster sugar in a small saucepan with the limoncello over a medium heat, until the sugar dissolves and turns to a light caramel. Take off the heat,

stir in the pistachios, pour on to a buttered baking tray, spread out, and allow to cool. Break into pieces, then pulse to crumbs in a food processor.

4 To make the lime air, mix all the ingredients in a bowl and use a hand-held blender to whisk until bubbles form.

5 Segment both the grapefruits and char the segments on both sides with a blowtorch.

6 To serve, sprinkle the possets with the pistachio crumb, add the burnt grapefruit segments, spoon on the lime air. Decorate with pansies (if using), and serve with a lime tuile.

FRUITS AND NUTS KNOW-HOW: *see* Segment citrus fruit **p424**

Almond panna cotta with poached tamarillos and berries

TIM KINNAIRD Finalist 2010

PREPARATION TIME **30 minutes, plus chilling** • COOKING TIME **40 minutes** • **SERVES 4**

4 leaves of **gelatine**

250ml (8fl oz) **whole milk**

250ml (8fl oz) **double cream**

1 **vanilla pod**

50g (1¾ oz) **caster sugar**

few drops of **almond extract**

FOR THE TAMARILLOS

100g (3½oz) **caster sugar**

1 **vanilla pod**

1 **cinnamon stick**

1 **bay leaf**

4 **tamarillos**, halved lengthways

FOR THE BERRIES

50g (1¾oz) **caster sugar**

60ml (2fl oz) **cassis**

50g (1¾oz) **raspberries**

50g (1¾oz) **blueberries**

1 To make the panna cotta, first soak the gelatine in cold water for 10 minutes to soften. Pour the milk and cream into a saucepan, split the vanilla pod, and add to the pan. Bring to the boil, remove from the heat, and allow to infuse for few minutes. Shake off excess water from the gelatine and stir into the pan. Add the sugar, then continue to stir over low heat until completely melted. Take out the vanilla pod and stir in the almond extract.

2 Lightly oil 4 individual pudding basins that will hold 135ml (4½fl oz) of panna cotta then set them on a tray. Pour the mixture into each. Chill for at least 2 hours, or until completely set.

3 For the tamarillos, pour 200ml (7fl oz) water into a saucepan and add the sugar, vanilla, cinnamon, and bay leaf. Cook over low heat until the sugar has dissolved.

Increase the heat and, when simmering, add the tamarillos and poach for about 5–10 minutes. Remove from the heat and leave to cool in the syrup.

4 For the berries, pour 100ml (3½fl oz) water into a saucepan, add the sugar and cassis, and bring to the boil. Add the berries and cook slowly for about 30 minutes, stirring occasionally. The mixture should appear syrupy.

5 Dip the pudding basins in hot water for a couple of seconds, then turn out onto the centre of each serving plate. Top with a berry and serve alongside 2 halves of a tamarillo and a spoonful of the poached berries.

FLAVOURINGS KNOW-HOW: *see* Use gelatine **p393**
EGGS AND DAIRY PRODUCTS KNOW-HOW: *see* Whip cream **p438**

Hazelnut and raspberry meringue

NADIA SAWALHA Celebrity champion 2007

PREPARATION TIME **20 minutes** • COOKING TIME **40 minutes** • **SERVES 4**

115g (4oz) whole shelled **hazelnuts**

4 large **egg whites**

250g (9oz) **caster sugar**

1 tsp **vanilla extract**

1 tbsp **raspberry vinegar**

300ml (10fl oz) **double cream**

200g (7oz) fresh **raspberries**

icing sugar, to dust

1 Preheat the oven to 160°C (325°F/Gas 3). Butter a 20cm (8in) sandwich tin and line with baking parchment.

2 Halve and dry fry the hazelnuts until lightly toasted, reserving a few.

3 Whisk the egg whites until stiff. Add the sugar 1 tbsp at a time and continue beating until the mixture is very stiff and stands in peaks. Whisk in the vanilla extract and vinegar, then fold in the hazelnuts.

4 Transfer to the sandwich tin. Alternatively, make individual portions by placing dollops of the meringue mix straight on to baking parchment, forming a slight hollow for the filling. Bake in the oven for 20–30 minutes, or until lightly browned and holding its shape. Leave to cool in the tin for 10 minutes then transfer to a serving dish.

5 Whip the cream and pile onto the centre of the meringue when it is completely cold. Place the raspberries. Finely chop the reserved hazelnuts and sprinkle over. Dust with icing sugar just before serving.

EGGS AND DAIRY PRODUCTS KNOW-HOW: *see* **Whisk egg whites p431**
EGGS AND DAIRY PRODUCTS KNOW-HOW: *see* **Whip cream p438**

Pear and butterscotch frangipane tart

SUSIE CARTER Quarter-finalist 2006

PREPARATION TIME **45 minutes** • COOKING TIME **40 minutes** • SERVES 4

50g (1¾oz) caster sugar

clotted cream, to serve

FOR THE BUTTERSCOTCH SAUCE

50g (1¾oz) unsalted butter

50g (1¾oz) light muscovado sugar

2 tbsp golden syrup

2 tbsp double cream

FOR THE PASTRY

200g (7oz) plain flour

100g (3½oz) butter

1 egg, beaten

FOR THE TART FILLING

50g (1¾oz) ground almonds

50g (1¾oz) caster sugar

50g (1¾oz) butter

1 egg

few drops of almond extract

2 pears, with stalks, to serve

1 To make the butterscotch sauce, put the butter, sugar, and golden syrup into a small saucepan and bring slowly to the boil, stirring. Reduce the heat and simmer for 3 minutes or until thick. Stir in the cream, then remove from the heat and set aside to cool.

2 Make the pastry by rubbing the butter into the flour, then adding enough cold water to bind into a pliable dough. Rest in the refrigerator for 30 minutes, then roll out on a floured surface and use to line 4 tartlet cases about 10cm (4in) in diameter. Trim the excess with scissors, allowing a little to overhang, and prick all over the base with a fork.

3 Preheat the oven to 180°C (350°F/Gas 4). Line each pastry case with baking parchment and bake blind for 10 minutes. Remove the baking parchment and beans, brush the pastry with beaten egg, and return to the oven for 5–10 minutes or until crisp.

4 Spoon 2 tbsp butterscotch sauce into each pastry case and reserve the rest to serve with the finished tarts. To make the frangipane, whisk together all the tart filling ingredients except the pears until light and spoon into the pastry cases to come halfway up the sides.

5 Peel the pears and cut in half through the stalk. Carefully remove the core, then slice along the length like a fan, without cutting all the way through at the stalk end. Use half a pear to top each tartlet, snuggling it down. Bake for 20 minutes or until the pear and frangipane are both cooked. Leave to cool a little.

6 Heat the caster sugar in a small pan, shaking occasionally until it has liquefied and turned light brown. Pour onto a non-stick baking mat in a thin layer and leave to cool for a few minutes. When set, break into shards. Serve the tartlets with a pool of butterscotch sauce, a quenelle of clotted cream, and a caramel shard.

Acorn panna cotta with toffee popcorn and pear-hazelnut millefeuille

ANDREW KOJIMA Finalist 2012

PREPARATION TIME **1 hour, plus infusing and soaking** • COOKING TIME **1 hour** • SERVES 6

FOR THE ACORN PANNACOTTA

30g (1oz) **acorns** or **hazelnuts**, shelled

300ml (½ pint) **double cream**

100ml (3½fl oz) **milk**

50g (1¾oz) **caster sugar**

1 **gelatine leaf**

oil spray, or a little **unsalted butter**, for greasing

FOR THE MOCHA TUILE

2 tbsp **liquid glucose**

120g (4½oz) **caster sugar**

15g (½oz) **Valhrona cocoa powder**

15g (½oz) **espresso powder**

FOR THE TOFFEE POPCORN

25g (scant 1oz) **popping corn**

50g (1¾oz) **caster sugar**

50g (1¾oz) **muscovado sugar**

30g (1oz) **unsalted butter**

sea salt

FOR THE PEAR MILLEFEUILLE

4 x 16g (½oz) sheets of **filo pastry**

50g (1¾oz) **unsalted butter**, melted

25g (scant 1oz) **icing sugar**, plus extra for dusting and sweetening

250ml (9fl oz) **perry (pear cider)**

125g (4½oz) **caster sugar**

1 **vanilla pod**

1 **cinnamon stick**

1 ripe **Williams pear**

juice of ½ **lemon**

25g (scant 1oz) very good-quality **milk chocolate**, chopped

25g (scant 1oz) **blanched hazelnuts**

150ml (5fl oz) **double cream**

1–2 tbsp **milk**, if needed

1 For the panna cotta, preheat the oven to 180°C (350°F/Gas 4). Roast the acorns for 10 minutes until they are deep brown. Grind coarsely in a food processor, then put in a saucepan with the cream, milk, and sugar. Place over a medium heat and bring to the boil, then leave to infuse for 30 minutes.

2 In a small bowl, soak the gelatine in 1 tbsp iced water for 3 minutes, or until soft. Return the acorn infusion to the boil. Whisk in the gelatine, then strain through a sieve into a jug. Grease 6 silicone dariole or pudding moulds with oil spray or butter. Pour in the mixture, cover, and chill until set.

3 For the tuile, preheat the oven to 180°C (350°F/Gas 4). Heat the glucose and sugar in a saucepan until it reaches 127°C (261°F) on a sugar thermometer. Stir in the cocoa and espresso, then pour on to a silicone mat, put another on top and roll into a sheet using a rolling pin. Leave to harden for 15 minutes. Blitz to a powder in a food processor. Sprinkle over a silicone-lined baking tray and bake for 4–5 minutes to melt it into a thin, glass-like sheet. Cool, then break into shards.

4 For the toffee popcorn, pop the corn in the microwave, according to the packet instructions. Heat the caster sugar in a heavy-based saucepan until it melts and turns caramel in colour. Add the muscovado sugar, whisk in the butter, and

season with sea salt. Allow all the ingredients to melt. Reserve half the toffee. Coat the popcorn in the remaining toffee and pour on to a silicone mat to set.

5 For the millefeuille, preheat the oven to 180°C (350°F/Gas 4). Brush the filo with butter and dust with icing sugar. Place each between 2 sheets of baking parchment and sandwich between 2 baking sheets. Bake for 10 minutes, until dark golden. Cool on a wire rack, then cut into 12 rectangles using a sharp knife.

6 Bring the perry to a simmer with the caster sugar, vanilla, and cinnamon, stirring to dissolve. Peel the pear and carve out balls with a melon baller (or cut into neat pieces). Coat with lemon juice. Add to the perry and leave to cool. Drain.

7 Melt the chocolate over a bain-marie and cool slightly. Blitz the hazelnuts in a food processor. Whip the cream to soft peaks, then fold in the nuts and chocolate, with milk to loosen, if needed. Taste and add icing sugar, if required.

8 To serve, place a panna cotta on a plate and top with a tuile shard. Assemble the millefeuille: coat 1 filo piece with hazelnut cream, spoon over the pears, and top with another filo piece. Drizzle the plate with the reserved toffee, then scatter over the popcorn.

White chocolate mousse with raspberry and elderflower jelly

CLAIRE LARA Professionals champion 2010

PREPARATION TIME 1 hour, plus chilling • **COOKING TIME** 30 minutes • **SERVES 4**

5 leaves of **gelatine**

200ml (7fl oz) **double cream**

150g (5½oz) **Valrhona white chocolate**

400g (14oz) **raspberries**

150g (5½oz) **caster sugar**, plus extra for scattering over the filo sheets

3 tbsp **elderflower cordial**

4 sheets of **filo pastry**

50g (1¾oz) **butter**, melted

2 tsp chopped freeze-dried **raspberries**

1 Soak 2 of the leaves of gelatine in cold water for at least 10 minutes to soften. Whip the cream until soft peaks form.

2 Melt the chocolate in a bowl set over a pan of barely simmering water, making sure the bowl is clear of the water. Remove the bowl from the pan. While the chocolate is still warm (not hot), squeeze the excess water from the gelatine and stir the gelatine into the chocolate. Whisk the chocolate into the whipped cream and transfer to a piping bag with a plain nozzle. Place in the refrigerator for 20 minutes to set.

3 Meanwhile, place the remaining leaves of gelatine in cold water to soften. Reserving 12 raspberries, whizz the rest of the raspberries to a purée with the sugar in food processor, then pass through a sieve.

4 Place the raspberry purée and elderflower cordial in a pan and heat gently, then stir in the gelatine. Warm over low heat until the gelatine is dissolved. Pour into mini muffin tins, sit a raspberry on top of each, and put in the refrigerator to set.

5 Preheat the oven to 200°C (400°F/Gas 6). Cut each sheet of filo pastry into 4 rectangles. Brush with melted butter and sugar and bake in the oven for 3 minutes until crispy, then remove and cool. Scatter with freeze-dried raspberries.

6 To serve, on each plate pipe 3–4 lines of mousse on top of a filo rectangle and top with another piece of filo. Repeat twice, finishing with a piece of filo pastry. Serve with the jellies alongside.

FLAVOURINGS KNOW-HOW: *see* Use gelatine **p393**

Pear tarte Tatin and candied walnuts with gorgonzola ice cream

JACK LUCAS Finalist 2014

PREPARATION TIME **1 hour, plus chilling time** • COOKING TIME **50 minutes** • SERVES 4

FOR THE GORGONZOLA ICE CREAM

225ml (8fl oz) **milk**

150ml (5fl oz) **whipping cream**

75g (2½oz) **egg yolk**

75g (2½oz) **caster sugar**

90g (3oz) **mild gorgonzola dolce**

FOR THE TARTE TATIN

75g (2½oz) **sugar**

25g (scant 1oz) **unsalted butter**

2 very ripe **pears**, peeled, cored, and sliced

200g (7oz) **all-butter puff pastry sheet**

FOR THE POACHED PEAR

2 **pears**

50g (1¾oz) **granulated sugar**

100ml (3½fl oz) **water**

5 tsp **Poire William liqueur**

FOR THE CANDIED WALNUTS

50g (1¾oz) **walnut halves**

100g (3½oz) **granulated sugar**

flavourless **vegetable oil**, for deep-frying

TO SERVE

red amaranth (optional)

1 For the ice cream, put the milk and cream in a saucepan and bring to the boil. In a separate bowl, beat the egg yolk and sugar until pale and fluffy. Add the milk mixture, whisking constantly, then return to the pan and heat, stirring constantly, until the mixture starts to thicken. Crumble in the gorgonzola and stir until smooth. Cover and chill, then churn in an ice cream machine.

2 To bake the tarte, preheat the oven to 220°C (425°F/Gas 7). Melt the sugar and butter in a saucepan until the mixture becomes dark and caramelized. Add the pears and cook, turning, until softened and coated in the thick caramel. Line 4 x 9cm (3½in) ramekins with the pears and caramel. Pierce the puff pastry all over with a fork, then cut out 12cm (4½in) circles and place over the pears. Bake for 20–30 minutes until the pastry is crisp.

3 Meanwhile, make the poached pears. Peel, quarter, and core the pears, place in a sauté pan with the sugar, water, and liqueur and cook until tender. Strain and reserve the liquid. Keep 1 pear for garnish, and purée the other with 1–2 tbsp of the liquid.

4 To make the candied walnuts, preheat the oven to 190°C (375°F/Gas 5). Lightly toast the nuts in the oven before adding to the reserved pear syrup, adding the 100g (3½oz) sugar. Stir to dissolve the sugar, then bring to the boil, simmering until the syrup coats the nuts. Drain the nuts. Bring the oil to 180°C (350°F) in a large saucepan or a deep-fat fryer. Add the nuts for just 5 seconds; any longer and they burn to a crisp. Remove with a slotted spoon and drain on greaseproof paper.

5 To serve, turn the tartes out onto 4 serving plates. Place a swipe of pear purée on each plate, then add a poached pear quarter and a scoop ice cream on top. Sprinkle with candied walnuts and red amaranth (if using).

Rhubarb crumble tart with syllabub and rhubarb syrup

DICK STRAWBRIDGE Celebrity finalist 2010

PREPARATION TIME **45 minutes, plus chilling** • COOKING TIME **1 hour** • SERVES 4

225g (8oz) **sugar**, plus 3 tbsp

450g (1lb) **rhubarb**, cut into 1cm (½in) pieces

2 pieces of **stem ginger**, finely diced

FOR THE NUT CRUST

50g (1¾oz) blanched **hazelnuts**, toasted

25g (scant 1oz) **icing sugar**

100g (3½ oz) **plain flour**

50g (1¾ oz) **butter**

½ tsp **vanilla extract**

1 small **egg**, beaten

FOR THE CRUMBLE TOPPING

100g (3½oz) **plain flour**

50g (1¾oz) **butter**

25g (scant 1oz) **demerara sugar**

finely grated zest of 1 **lemon**

FOR THE SYLLABUB

300ml (10fl oz) **double cream**

1–2 tbsp **ginger wine** or **brandy**

2 tbsp **ginger syrup** from the stem ginger jar

1 piece of **stem ginger**, finely sliced

1 First make a syrup by dissolving 225g (8oz) of the sugar in a saucepan with 300ml (10fl oz) of boiling water. Preheat the oven to 180°C (350°F/Gas 4). Add half the rhubarb to the syrup, bring to the boil, then leave until completely cold. Put the remaining rhubarb in an ovenproof dish and sprinkle over 3 tbsp of sugar. Bake in the oven for about 20 minutes or until softened. Allow to cool, then drain and mix with the slices of stem ginger, reserving 8 slices for decoration. Strain the cold rhubarb syrup into a jug and chill.

2 For the nut crust, put the nuts and sugar in a food processor and mix briefly to combine. Add the remaining ingredients except the egg and mix on the pulse setting. With the machine running, gradually pour in the egg and mix to form a ball. Wrap in cling film and chill for 30 minutes. Divide into 4 equal pieces and press into the base of four 10cm (4in) tart tins. Chill for 10 minutes.

3 Increase the oven heat to 190°C (375°G/Gas 5). Cook the tarts for about 8–10 minutes or until pale golden. Meanwhile, make the crumble. Put all the ingredients in a food processor and mix briefly to form crumbs. Spread out on a baking sheet and cook for 8–10 minutes or until pale golden. Give the crumble a stir halfway through cooking.

4 Divide the rhubarb between tart cases and top with the crumble. Bake for 10 minutes or until heated through.

5 For the syllabub, put the cream, wine, and ginger syrup into a bowl and whisk to form soft peaks. Chill for 10 minutes.

6 Serve the tarts warm with the syllabub, decorating the syllabub with slices of stem ginger. Place a cup of pink rhubarb syrup alongside.

Rhubarb tarte Tatin served with mascarpone

MARIANNE LUMB Professionals finalist 2009

PREPARATION TIME **15 minutes** • COOKING TIME **30 minutes** • **SERVES 4**

200g (7oz) ready-made **puff pastry**

6 sticks **rhubarb**

150g (5½oz) **unsalted butter**, softened

125g (4½oz) granulated **sugar**

grated zest of 1 **orange**

2 **vanilla pods**, each split and cut into 4 pieces

200g (7oz) **mascarpone cheese**

1 Preheat the oven to 190°C (375°F/Gas 5) and get out 4 heatproof blini pans. Roll the puff pastry to about 3mm (⅛in) thick and cut into 4 discs with a diameter slightly larger than the pans. Prick each disc and leave to chill in the refrigerator.

2 Choose the thicker pieces of rhubarb and cut to fit the 4 pans perfectly in 2 layers. Cover the base of each pan with the butter and then sprinkle over the sugar, orange zest, and a piece of vanilla pod, and then add the rhubarb pieces.

3 Cook the rhubarb on a very high heat on the hob for about 10 minutes to reach a good, bitter caramelization. Check by carefully lifting up the rhubarb with a palette knife, but do not be tempted to stir the rhubarb.

4 Cover each pan carefully with a disc of puff pastry, allowing the pastry to tuck just inside the pans. Place the pans on a baking sheet and cook for 20–30 minutes, or until the puff pastry is perfectly cooked and the tartes have a good caramelization. Remove from the oven and allow to rest for a few minutes.

5 Carefully invert each pan onto a plate, letting the tarte drop gently down. Serve immediately, each topped with a scoop of mascarpone cheese and a remaining piece of vanilla pod, to decorate.

DOUGH, PASTRY, AND CAKES KNOW-HOW: *see* Roll out puff pastry **p459**

Coconut ice cream, almond dacquoise, and coffee caramel with Thai basil

LARKIN CEN Finalist 2013

PREPARATION TIME **1 hour, plus chilling and infusing** • COOKING TIME **1 hour** • **SERVES 6**

FOR THE COCONUT ICE CREAM

300ml (10fl oz) **double cream**

150ml (5fl oz) **coconut milk**

½ **vanilla pod**, seeds scraped out

3 **egg yolks**

60g (2oz) **caster sugar**

30g (1oz) **desiccated coconut**

FOR THE THAI BASIL GEL

100g (3½oz) **Thai basil**, 10 leaves reserved

65g (2¼oz) **caster sugar**

2½ tsp **agar agar**

FOR THE COCONUT CONSOMMÉ

250g (9oz) **coconut milk**

30g (1oz) **caster sugar**

¼ tsp **salt**

FOR THE ALMOND DACQUOISE

100g (3½oz) **skin-on almonds**

4 drops of **French almond oil**

140g (5oz) **caster sugar**

3 **egg whites**

pinch of **salt**

FOR THE COFFEE CARAMEL

250ml (9fl oz) **double cream**

2 tsp instant **coffee powder**

1 **vanilla pod**, seeds scraped out

200g (7oz) **white granulated sugar**

TO GARNISH

spriglets of **Thai basil**, or basil flowers in season (optional)

1 First, make the ice cream. Combine the cream, coconut milk, and vanilla seeds in a saucepan, bring to the boil, then strain and leave to cool. Whisk the egg yolks and sugar until pale, then gradually whisk in the warm coconut mixture. Return to the saucepan and stir over a low heat until the mixture coats the back of a spoon. Allow to cool, stir in the desiccated coconut, then churn in an ice-cream machine until smooth and frozen.

2 For the Thai basil gel, pour 1 litre (1¾ pints) water into a saucepan and bring to the boil. Remove from the heat. Place the basil in a sieve and dunk into the water for 40 seconds. Remove and plunge the sieve straight into ice-cold water to stop the cooking process and set the bright green colour. Drain very well. Put in a food processor with 100ml (3½fl oz) ice-cold water and blend finely. Strain the basil water through muslin or a fine sieve.

3 Boil the sugar, agar agar, and 160ml (5¾fl oz) in a saucepan, stirring until dissolved. Let it cool. When it is setting, slowly add 120ml (4fl oz) of the basil water, blitzing with a hand-held blender until smooth. Cover and chill.

4 For the coconut consommé, put all the ingredients into a saucepan with the 10 reserved Thai basil leaves. Bring to the boil, then leave to infuse for 4 hours. Strain everything through muslin, pressing all the flavour through.

5 To make the dacquoise, preheat the oven to 130°C (250°F/Gas ½) and line 3 baking sheets with baking parchment. Put the almonds and almond oil in a food processor with 100g (3½oz) sugar and grind to a powder. Meanwhile, whisk the egg whites, salt, and remaining 40g (1½oz) sugar to soft peaks. Gently fold in the almond mixture, spoon into a piping bag and pipe 6 small circles on to the prepared baking sheets. Bake for 50 minutes, until crisp and golden, then allow to cool.

6 Now make the coffee caramel. Combine the cream, coffee, and vanilla seeds and pod in a saucepan. Bring to just below the boil, then remove from the heat and allow to infuse for 30 minutes.

7 Meanwhile, put the sugar in a heavy-based saucepan with 4 tbsp water and place over a medium heat. Do not stir. Wait until the sugar has dissolved and become golden brown, swirling the pan occasionally. Beat the caramel into the coffee cream and mix until smooth and shiny. Strain the mixture, let it cool, then decant into a squeezy bottle.

8 To serve, spoon a little coconut consommé into soup plates. Add scoops of ice cream. Stir the basil gel to loosen it, then add drops of it on to the plates with drops of the coffee caramel. Place an almond dacquoise on the side, or break it up first, if you prefer, and scatter with basil spriglets or flowers (if using).

Chocolate-pistachio salted caramel tart, cinnamon pear, and Kirsch cream

EMMA SPITZER Finalist 2015

PREPARATION TIME **1 hour, plus chilling** • COOKING TIME **35 minutes** • **SERVES 6**

FOR THE TART BASE

200g (7oz) **shelled unsalted pistachios**, plus extra,crushed, for sprinkling

120g (4½oz) **unsalted butter**

100g (3½oz) **cocoa powder**

150g (5½oz) **caster sugar**

FOR THE FILLING

100g (3½oz) **light muscovado sugar**

4 tbsp **golden syrup**

1½ tsp **sea salt**

100ml (3½fl oz) **double cream**

1 tsp of **vanilla extract**

6 tbsp **pistachio paste**

FOR THE GANACHE

200g (7oz) **dark chocolate** (70% cocoa solids), chopped, or preferably in buttons

100g (3½oz) **unsalted butter**, chopped

300ml (½ pint) **double cream**

4 tbsp light **muscovado sugar**

4 **egg yolks**

splash of **vanilla extract**

FOR THE CARAMELIZED PEAR

2 tbsp **golden caster sugar**

1 tsp **ground cinnamon**

2 ripe **William pears**, peeled, cored, and sliced

FOR THE SOUR CHERRY SYRUP

100g (3½oz) **sour cherries**

1 **cinnamon stick**

100ml (3½fl oz) **maple syrup**

FOR THE MERINGUE

2 **egg whites**

pinch of **sea salt**

50g (1¾oz) **caster sugar**

1 tsp **cornflour**

FOR THE KIRSCH CHANTILLY CREAM

150ml (5fl oz) **double cream**

1 tsp **vanilla extract**

1 tbsp **icing sugar**

1½ tbsp **Kirsch**

1 For the tart base, whizz the pistachios in a food processor until finely ground. Add the butter, cocoa powder, and sugar, and pulse to a smooth, sticky dough. Wrap in cling film and freeze for 15 minutes. Preheat the oven to 160°C (325°F/Gas 3). Roll out the dough between 2 sheets of cling film until large enough to line a 32 x 15cm (13 x 6in) tart tin. Trim off any excess, prick the base, and freeze for another 15 minutes, then bake for 10–12 minutes.

2 For the filling, combine the muscovado sugar, syrup, and salt in a small saucepan and stir over a low heat until the sugar dissolves. Increase the heat and add the cream, vanilla extract, and pistachio paste. Reduce the heat and stir for a few minutes. Remove from the heat, beat until smooth, then leave to cool. Pour it into the tart base, smooth out, and chill in the fridge.

3 Put the chocolate and butter for the ganache into a bowl. Combine the cream and sugar in a saucepan and bring to the boil, stirring all the time. Pour over the chocolate mixture evenly and leave for 1 minute, before stirring gently to melt. Whisk in the egg yolks and vanilla. Pour over the tart and return to the fridge to set. Once set, sprinkle a line of crushed pistachios down either side of the tart.

4 For the caramelized pear, combine the sugar and cinnamon in a bowl. Coat the pears in this mixture, then place in a dry pan over a medium heat. Fry, turning as needed, until golden.

5 For the syrup, put the sour cherries in a small saucepan with 100ml (3½fl oz) water and the cinnamon stick. Bring to the boil and simmer for 3 minutes. Stir in the maple syrup. Remove and reserve a few nice-looking cherries, discard the cinnamon stick, then blend the remaining mixture.

6 For the meringue, dissolve the sugar and cornflour in 2 tbsp water over a low heat to 121°C (248°F). Whisk the egg whites and salt to form stiff peaks, then gradually add the hot sugar syrup, whisking continuously. Whisk until the mixture is cold, then put into a piping bag.For the Kirsch cream, combine all the ingredients in a bowl and whisk to soft peaks.

7 To serve, pipe meringue on to a plate, then blowtorch until golden. Add a rectangular slice of tart, pear slices, and a drizzle of sour cherry syrup. Serve with a quenelle of the cream, then sprinkle with the remaining crushed pistachios and the reserved cherries.

EGGS AND DAIRY PRODUCTS KNOW-HOW: *See* Make Italian meringue **p436**

Banana soufflé with blueberry coulis

NATALIE BRENNER Quarter-finalist 2010

PREPARATION TIME **30 minutes** • COOKING TIME **25 minutes** • **SERVES 4**

FOR THE COULIS

150g (5½oz) **blueberries**

50g (1¾oz) **sugar**

FOR THE SOUFFLÉS

15g (½oz) **unsalted butter**

4 tsp **sugar**

1 large, ripe **banana**, roughly chopped

1 tbsp **clear honey**

2 large **eggs**, whites only

1 tbsp **caster sugar**

TO SERVE

icing sugar

1 tbsp **double cream**

1 For the coulis, place the blueberries and sugar in a saucepan with 100ml (3½fl oz) water and bring to the boil. Take off the heat and allow to cool, then blend, using a hand-held blender or by transferring to a food processor, and pass through a sieve. Put back on the heat, bring to the boil, and reduce until syrupy. Set aside to cool.

2 Preheat the oven to 200°C (400°F/Gas 6) and place a baking sheet in the oven to heat. Evenly grease 4 ramekins with the butter, then coat the inside with a layer of sugar.

3 Place the banana in a food processor, add the honey, and blend until smooth.

4 Place the egg whites in a clean, dry bowl and whisk until the whites form soft peaks. Gradually add the caster sugar, whisking all the time, until soft peaks are formed.

5 Using a spatula, fold one-third of the egg whites into the banana mixture relatively vigorously, then very gently fold in the remainder. Spoon the soufflé mix into the ramekins, tap on the work surface to expel any air, and run a finger around the rim to create a "top hat" effect.

6 Put the soufflés on the preheated baking sheet and place in the oven and bake them for 10–12 minutes until risen.

7 To serve, put the coulis in a small jug on each plate. Place the soufflés in the ramekins on the plate, and sprinkle icing sugar on them just before serving.

EGGS AND DAIRY PRODUCTS KNOW-HOW: *see* **Whisk egg whites p431**
EGGS AND DAIRY PRODUCTS KNOW-HOW: *see* Bake a soufflé **p434**

Sticky toffee pudding

WENDI PETERS Celebrity finalist 2009

PREPARATION TIME **20 minutes** • COOKING TIME **35 minutes** • **SERVES 4**

85g (3oz) sugared, stoned **dates**, chopped

85g (3oz) **light soft brown sugar**

45g (1½oz) **unsalted butter**, softened

1 **egg**

115g (4oz) **plain flour**

1 tsp **bicarbonate of soda**

1 tbsp **vanilla extract**

FOR THE TOFFEE SAUCE

150g (5½oz) **demerara sugar**

85g (3oz) **unsalted butter**, softened

4 tbsp **double cream**

1 Preheat the oven to 180°C (350°F/Gas 4). Butter a 16 x 12cm (6½ x 5in) ovenproof dish.

2 Put the dates into a bowl and pour over just enough boiling water to cover them.

3 In a separate bowl, cream together the soft brown sugar and the butter. Beat the egg into the creamed mixture with some of the flour before adding the rest of the flour.

4 Add the bicarbonate of soda and vanilla extract to the dates and then stir into the creamed mixture until well mixed. Pour into the ovenproof dish and bake in the oven for 30–35 minutes or until well risen and a cake skewer when inserted comes out clean.

5 Just before the pudding is cooked, make the toffee sauce. Preheat the grill to hot. Put the demerara sugar, butter, and cream into a saucepan and heat gently. Let simmer for 3 minutes. Remove the pudding from the oven, pour over half the sauce, and place under the grill until it bubbles.

6 Serve the pudding while hot with the remaining sauce poured over the top or alongside as an accompaniment.

Dark chocolate and almond torte with amaretto cream, raspberries, and passion fruit

DHRUV BAKER Champion 2010

PREPARATION TIME **30 minutes** • COOKING TIME **30 minutes** • **MAKES 8 SLICES**

150g (5½oz) **dark chocolate** (70% cocoa solids)

125g (4½oz) **unsalted butter**

5 **eggs**, separated

175g (6oz) **light soft brown sugar**

175g (6oz) ground **almonds**

100ml (3½fl oz) **amaretto**, plus 1 tbsp for amaretto cream

100ml (3½fl oz) **double cream**

1 punnet **raspberries**

2 **passion fruit**, peeled, cut in half, and seeds scooped out

icing sugar, to taste

1 Preheat the oven to 150°C (300°F/Gas 2). Line the base of a 23cm (9in) diameter springform baking tin with baking parchment and butter the sides.

2 Melt the chocolate and butter in a large bowl placed over a saucepan of simmering water. Once melted, remove from heat and leave to cool slightly.

3 In a separate bowl, whisk the egg whites with a whisk until they form peaks.

4 Mix the sugar and almonds in the chocolate mixture, then stir in the egg yolks and the 100ml (3½fl oz) of amaretto.

5 Finally, fold the egg whites into the chocolate mixture using a metal spoon. Pour the mixture into the prepared tin and bake for about 30 minutes or until firm on top and a skewer comes out clean. Remove the torte from the oven and allow to cool for a few minutes.

6 Whip the cream with a whisk and pour in the remaining amaretto.

7 Put the passion fruit flesh into a blender or food processor and blend to a pulp. Push through a sieve and add icing sugar to taste.

8 To serve, place a slice of the torte on each plate. Drizzle over some passion fruit coulis and add a spoonful of the cream and a few raspberries.

EGGS AND DAIRY PRODUCTS KNOW-HOW: *see* Whisk egg whites **p431**
EGGS AND DAIRY PRODUCTS KNOW-HOW: *see* Whip cream **p438**

Baked lime cheesecake with rum cream

DENNICE RUSSELL Semi-finalist 2009

PREPARATION TIME **25 minutes** • COOKING TIME **25 minutes** • **SERVES 4**

8 **digestive biscuits**, crushed

50g (1¾oz) **unsalted butter**, melted

300g (10oz) **mascarpone cheese**

100g (3½oz) **ricotta cheese**

1 tbsp **plain flour**

100g (3½oz) **caster sugar**

40g (1½oz) **desiccated coconut**

grated zest and juice of 3 **limes**, plus strands of lime zest, to decorate

2 **eggs**

1 **vanilla pod**, scraped

FOR THE RUM CREAM

200ml (7fl oz) **double cream**

1 tbsp **icing sugar**

4 tbsp **dark rum**

1 Preheat the oven to 180°C (350°F/Gas 4). Mix the biscuits into the melted butter. Place four 10cm (4in) chef's rings on a baking sheet and press in the biscuit mix.

2 Put the cheeses, flour, sugar, coconut, lime juice and zest, eggs, and the seeds of the vanilla pod into a bowl and whisk until blended.

3 Pour onto the biscuit base and bake for 20 minutes, until golden. It should be slightly wobbly in the centre when ready. Leave to cool in the oven.

4 To make the rum cream, put the cream, icing sugar, and rum into a bowl and whisk to form soft peaks.

5 Put the cooled cheesecakes onto serving plates and top with quenelles of rum cream and strands of lime.

MASTERCHEF KNOW-HOW

ESSENTIAL TOOLS, SKILLS, AND INGREDIENTS FOR THE HOME COOK.

Kitchen knives

QUALITY KNIVES ARE A MUST for every cook. Choose the best you can afford that feel right for you. They should be well-balanced, made of high carbon stainless steel (inferior metal will not give a true, sharp edge), with solid handles that feel comfortable in your hand. Buy from a shop where you can touch and feel them, preferably with an expert on hand to advise you. Here is a selection of the most important ones you will need. Well-chosen knives make food preparation a pleasure.

FILLETING KNIFE

USE FOR FILLETING AND BONING. A slightly flexible knife with a narrow blade for sliding under and round bones, and skin of meat, poultry, and fish.

PARING KNIFE

USE FOR PEELING AND SMALL CUTTING TASKS. It has a short blade for easy manoeuvrability, and a sharp point for removing blemishes.

CARVING KNIFE

USE FOR CARVING SLICES OF MEAT AND POULTRY. It is thinner and longer than a chef's knife for precision cutting of thin slices.

SERRATED UTILITY KNIFE

USE FOR PREPARING TENDER FRUIT AND VEGETABLES. The sharp, serrated edge cuts through soft skin and flesh without damaging it.

CHEF'S KNIFE

SMALL CHEF'S KNIFE

USE FOR CHOPPING AND SLICING. Particularly useful for preparing small amounts of meat, vegetables, or fruit.

ALL-PURPOSE KNIFE

USE FOR GENERAL LIGHT CUTTING. Also known as a utility knife. If not buying a whole range, this is a must-have, multi-purpose utensil.

BREAD KNIFE

USE FOR CUTTING BREAD AND SIMILAR FOODS. The long blade and widely serrated edge make it easy to cut thick or thin, even slices.

SANTOKU KNIFE

USE FOR PRECISION SLICING. The Japanese chef's knife is cleverly constructed to slice delicate meats, fish, and vegetables very thinly.

USE FOR A WHOLE RANGE OF TASKS. The tip is for fine chopping or mincing, the middle for general knife jobs, the heel for heavy-duty work.

Pots and pans

ESSENTIAL KIT FOR EVERY COOK. Choose pans that are right for you and for your cooker. The look and feel of them are matters of personal preference, but each pan needs particular qualities. Here is some general advice on what to look for.

CHOOSE A FRYING PAN with flared, not straight, sides. It should have a handle that is comfortable to hold. It needs a thick base, for even distribution of heat, so meat and poultry brown quickly and efficiently, but not too heavy so you can shake and toss food in the pan easily. Choose one with a lid for covering food when you want to finish dishes in the oven, or stew them in their own juices on the hob.

FRYING PAN

YOUR STEAMER INSET should be made of stainless steel, with a wide area of tiny holes in the base to allow maximum steam to surround the food. It should be large enough to fit your biggest pan but with graduated sides so it also fits a smaller one. You can buy one as part of a pan set so the lid of the large saucepan also fits the steamer. If not, choose one with a tight-fitting lid to prevent steam escaping, and make sure it will fit snugly over your own pots.

STEAMER INSET

USE YOUR SAUTÉ PAN for frying tender meat, poultry, game, fish, seafood, vegetables, or fruit quickly in just enough oil or butter (or a mixture of both) to coat the base of the pan. Choose a pan with straight sides and a solid base so it conducts and retains the heat well to maintain a high temperature. Move the food by either jerking the pan itself or turning the food with a spatula. Don't toss as often as for stir-frying, though, or the temperature will reduce too much. If you put a lid on the pan you can also use it for braising food.

SAUTÉ PAN

A DEEP CASSEROLE is an important piece of equipment for serious cooks. Use for soups, stews, braises, and boiling joints or puddings. It should be flameproof and ovenproof so foods can be browned in it on the hob, the liquid added, brought to the boil, then the whole thing put in the oven (or finished on the hob) according to the recipe. Choose the correct sized pot for the amount of food you are cooking. It is no good putting ingredients for 1 or 2 people in a huge, family-sized one. They will dry out as there won't be sufficient liquid to cover them, and there will be much wasted heat in the empty pot.

CASSEROLE

249

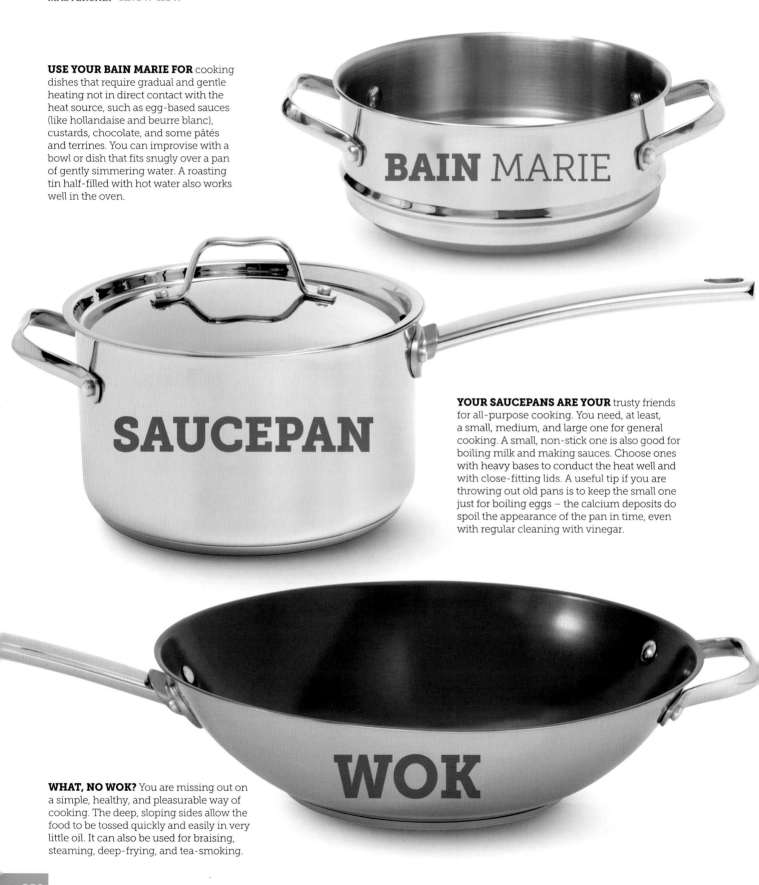

USE YOUR BAIN MARIE FOR cooking dishes that require gradual and gentle heating not in direct contact with the heat source, such as egg-based sauces (like hollandaise and beurre blanc), custards, chocolate, and some pâtés and terrines. You can improvise with a bowl or dish that fits snugly over a pan of gently simmering water. A roasting tin half-filled with hot water also works well in the oven.

BAIN MARIE

SAUCEPAN

YOUR SAUCEPANS ARE YOUR trusty friends for all-purpose cooking. You need, at least, a small, medium, and large one for general cooking. A small, non-stick one is also good for boiling milk and making sauces. Choose ones with heavy bases to conduct the heat well and with close-fitting lids. A useful tip if you are throwing out old pans is to keep the small one just for boiling eggs – the calcium deposits do spoil the appearance of the pan in time, even with regular cleaning with vinegar.

WOK

WHAT, NO WOK? You are missing out on a simple, healthy, and pleasurable way of cooking. The deep, sloping sides allow the food to be tossed quickly and easily in very little oil. It can also be used for braising, steaming, deep-frying, and tea-smoking.

Additional equipment

Choose best-quality equipment to hold you in good stead for years. Some items are considered essential, while others are useful to have if you enjoy particular types of cooking – and have lots of storage space!

THE MUST-HAVES

APPLE CORER Choose one with a sharp bottom edge to cut easily into the fruit flesh.

BAKING TINS Buy as you need them. Shallow, rectangular and deep square for different tray bakes, and a loaf tin are useful to start.

BLENDER Your food processor or mixer may have one as an attachment, alternatively buy a hand blender.

BUN TIN A 12-section one is a must for individual cakes, pies, muffins, and Yorkshire puddings.

CAKE TINS A range of sizes are useful: deep round, and/or square, with loose bottoms. You need 2 sandwich tins, too.

CARVING FORK It should have 2 long tines to steady the meat whilst carving, and a protective guard.

GRATER Choose a multi-sided one with different-sized slots and a comfortable handle. A Parmesan grater is also worth having.

ELECTRIC HAND WHISK For whisking cream, and egg whites, or instead of a balloon whisk when whisking egg mixtures over a bain marie.

FISH SLICE It should be flexible enough to slide under foods without causing damage, and have a heat-proof handle.

FOOD PROCESSOR OR ELECTRIC MIXER Useful attachments include a whisk, chopper, shredder, and blender.

GRIDDLE PAN A cast-iron, ridged one for chargrilling. You can also buy a flat one for making Scotch pancakes and oat cakes but a heavy skillet would also do this instead.

MIXING BOWLS Have several of different sizes. A copper one is best for whisking egg whites.

PASTRY BRUSH Bristle ones are traditional, silicone is more practical for all-purpose brushing.

PASTRY CUTTERS Both fluted and plain ones in graduated sizes are useful.

PIE DISH Choose a fairly deep one for top crust pies. It should have a lip all around for the pastry to adhere to.

PIPING (PASTRY) BAG WITH NOZZLES For piping and/or filling, choux buns, meringues, and other mixtures.

POTATO PEELER For preparing vegetables, and shaving cheese and chocolate.

PUDDING BASINS Choose varying sizes to suit your needs.

RAMEKINS Plain white are the most practical for oven-to-table use.

ROASTING TIN Have at least 2, one for roasting vegetables, one for meat. They should be heavy-duty so that it can be heated on the hob when necessary.

SLOTTED SPOON For removing foods from oil or other liquid.

RUBBER OR PLASTIC SPATULA For scraping out; wooden for stirring and turning food.

STRAINER/STRAINER INSERT Use with a stockpot or casserole for making chicken stock or cooking pasta.

SWISS ROLL TIN Use for Swiss rolls and roulades. Also useful as a shallow baking tin.

TART/FLAN TIN Good to have one loose-bottomed one for easy removal, and one deep ceramic one for oven-to-table.

WIRE RACK A large rectangular one is the most practical.

THE MIGHT-NEEDS

BAMBOO STEAMER Use to steam vegetables, meat, and fish.

CHEESECLOTH (MUSLIN) A new disposable dish cloth can also work.

KUGELHOPF MOULD Use any similar sized receptacle instead.

LOBSTER CRACKER/SMALL HAMMER Nut crackers will also do.

MADELEINE TIN Can also use an ordinary bun tin.

MANDOLIN The best way to slice vegetables thinly, but a sharp knife will do instead.

MEZZALUNA Really useful for chopping herbs.

OMELETTE PAN Choose a heavy-based, non-stick one. A frying pan can be used instead. Use for crêpes too.

OYSTER KNIFE Any small, sharp-pointed knife will also do.

PESTLE AND MORTAR White porcelain ones are good all-rounders for looks and efficiency.

PIE PLATE Handy for making double-crust pies.

POULTRY SHEARS The best way to joint poultry or feathered game, but a sharp cook's knife will also do.

SEAFOOD FORK/LOBSTER PICK A small cocktail fork or fine skewer will also do.

SPRINGFORM CAKE TIN Good for more delicate cakes that need careful handling.

SUGAR THERMOMETER The best way to test sugar stages.

TWEEZERS Useful for pulling out bones when filleting fish, or for placing intricate garnishes or decorations in place.

Round white sea fish

BUY Some species are dwindling so only buy those that are sustainably fished. Choose the freshest, best-looking specimens. Look for bright eyes and smooth, glistening skin. If fresh, fish should either have no smell at all, or should smell pleasantly of the sea, with no underlying offensive odour. **STORE** Ideally, fish should be eaten on the day it's bought, but it can be stored for up to 24 hours well-wrapped in the coldest part of the refrigerator. Freeze fish in double-layered freezer bags, with as much air extracted as possible, for up to 3 months.

▲ Coley

EAT Cuts: fillets. Good, cheap alternative to cod. Deep-fry, pan-fry in batter or breadcrumbs, bake, steam, poach, in fish pie, fish cakes, and soup. Also available hot-smoked (undyed and dyed), dried, or salted. **FLAVOUR PAIRINGS** Butter, milk, beer batter, parsley, chives, bacon, Cheddar cheese. **IN SEASON** April–December

▲ Hake

EAT Cuts: fillets, steaks. Some stocks very depleted. Coley or pollock can be used instead. Pan-fry, roast, poach, sauté, grill. Also available salted or smoked. **FLAVOUR PAIRINGS** Olive oil, smoked paprika, butter, lemon, onions, garlic, tomatoes. **IN SEASON** August–January

Ling ▶

EAT Cuts: whole, fillets, steaks. Buy line-caught from inshore. Steam, pan-fry, grill, or bake. Also available salted or dried. **FLAVOUR PAIRINGS** Onions, garlic, potatoes, leeks, bacon, coriander leaf, parsley, sage, Cheddar cheese. **IN SEASON** August–February

▲ Cod

EAT Cuts: fillets, steaks, loins, fresh and pressed roe. Some successfully farmed. Deep-fry or pan-fry in batter or breadcrumbs, bake, poach, cook in soup or chowder, grill. Also available cold-smoked (undyed and dyed), salted, or dried. **FLAVOUR PAIRINGS** Dill, parsley, bay leaf, lemon, olive oil, tomatoes, olives, capers, garlic, breadcrumbs, butter, cheese sauce, cider, white wine. **IN SEASON** May–January

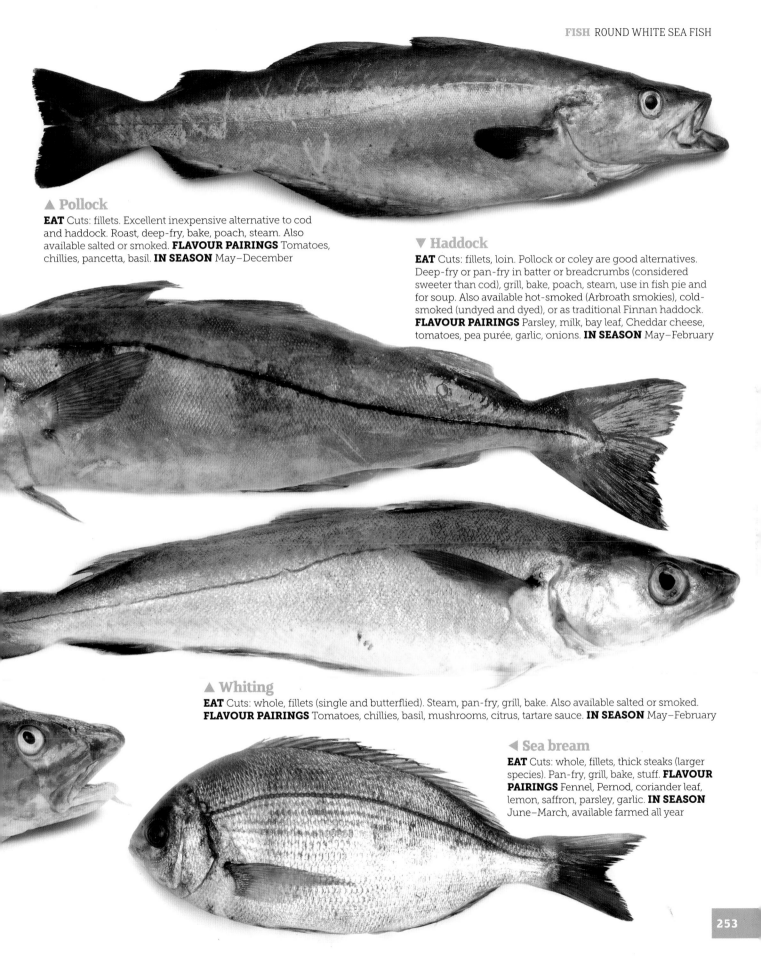

▲ Pollock

EAT Cuts: fillets. Excellent inexpensive alternative to cod and haddock. Roast, deep-fry, bake, poach, steam. Also available salted or smoked. **FLAVOUR PAIRINGS** Tomatoes, chillies, pancetta, basil. **IN SEASON** May–December

▼ Haddock

EAT Cuts: fillets, loin. Pollock or coley are good alternatives. Deep-fry or pan-fry in batter or breadcrumbs (considered sweeter than cod), grill, bake, poach, steam, use in fish pie and for soup. Also available hot-smoked (Arbroath smokies), cold-smoked (undyed and dyed), or as traditional Finnan haddock. **FLAVOUR PAIRINGS** Parsley, milk, bay leaf, Cheddar cheese, tomatoes, pea purée, garlic, onions. **IN SEASON** May–February

▲ Whiting

EAT Cuts: whole, fillets (single and butterflied). Steam, pan-fry, grill, bake. Also available salted or smoked. **FLAVOUR PAIRINGS** Tomatoes, chillies, basil, mushrooms, citrus, tartare sauce. **IN SEASON** May–February

◄ Sea bream

EAT Cuts: whole, fillets, thick steaks (larger species). Pan-fry, grill, bake, stuff. **FLAVOUR PAIRINGS** Fennel, Pernod, coriander leaf, lemon, saffron, parsley, garlic. **IN SEASON** June–March, available farmed all year

253

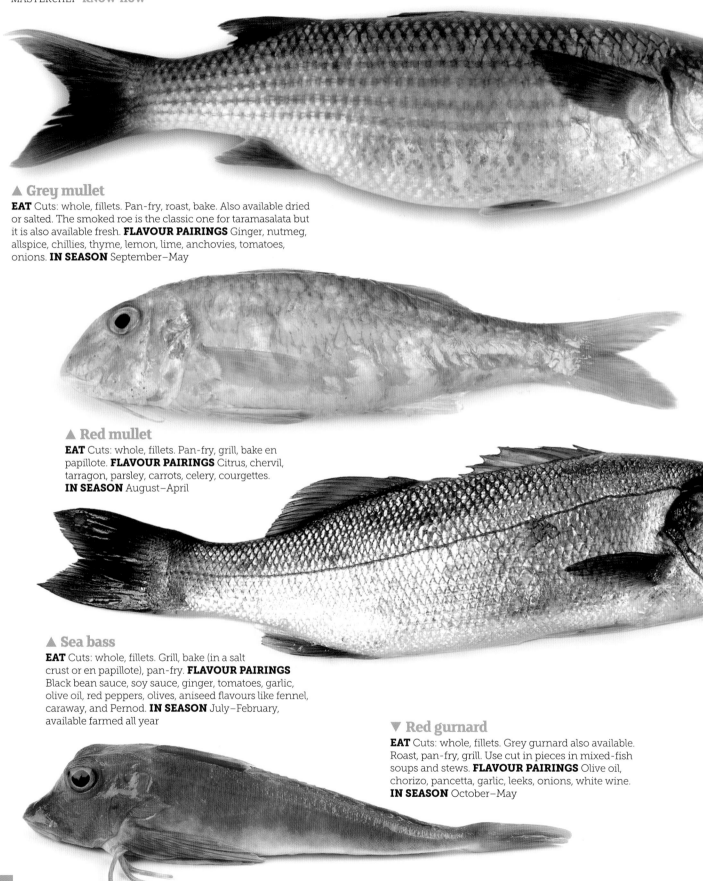

▲ Grey mullet

EAT Cuts: whole, fillets. Pan-fry, roast, bake. Also available dried or salted. The smoked roe is the classic one for taramasalata but it is also available fresh. **FLAVOUR PAIRINGS** Ginger, nutmeg, allspice, chillies, thyme, lemon, lime, anchovies, tomatoes, onions. **IN SEASON** September–May

▲ Red mullet

EAT Cuts: whole, fillets. Pan-fry, grill, bake en papillote. **FLAVOUR PAIRINGS** Citrus, chervil, tarragon, parsley, carrots, celery, courgettes. **IN SEASON** August–April

▲ Sea bass

EAT Cuts: whole, fillets. Grill, bake (in a salt crust or en papillote), pan-fry. **FLAVOUR PAIRINGS** Black bean sauce, soy sauce, ginger, tomatoes, garlic, olive oil, red peppers, olives, aniseed flavours like fennel, caraway, and Pernod. **IN SEASON** July–February, available farmed all year

▼ Red gurnard

EAT Cuts: whole, fillets. Grey gurnard also available. Roast, pan-fry, grill. Use cut in pieces in mixed-fish soups and stews. **FLAVOUR PAIRINGS** Olive oil, chorizo, pancetta, garlic, leeks, onions, white wine. **IN SEASON** October–May

▲ John Dory

EAT Cuts: whole, fillets. Pan-fry, grill, steam, bake, stew. **FLAVOUR PAIRINGS** Garlic, white wine, cream sauces, mushrooms, sage, capers, lemon, crème fraîche. **IN SEASON** September–May

◄ Monkfish

EAT Cuts: tail, fillets, steaks, cheeks, shoulder flaps. The liver is considered a delicacy. Pan-fry, roast, grill (fillets or kebabs), stir-fry. **FLAVOUR PAIRINGS** Chorizo, prosciutto crudo, bacon, sage, rosemary, butter, olive oil, lemon, lime, chillies, capers, mushrooms. **IN SEASON** August–January

255

Oily sea fish

BUY Choose line- or net-caught fish from sustainable sources. They should have slippery, shiny, bright-coloured skin and firm flesh. For whole fish the eyes should be bright and the gills prominent, red, and clean. They should have a mild, pleasantly fishy smell. **STORE** Best eaten fresh. Store, well-wrapped, in the coldest part of the refrigerator for up to 24 hours. If not previously frozen, they can be frozen like round white fish for up to 3 months.

Skipjack tuna

Yellowfin tuna

▲ Tuna

EAT Cuts: Steaks, whole loins. Grill, pan-fry, stir-fry. Avoid plain grilling as the flesh pales to an unattractive dull brown. Don't overcook – it should be pink in the middle. Can be eaten raw, if very fresh, as sushi or carpaccio. Also available dried, smoked, salted, or canned.
FLAVOUR PAIRINGS Sesame seeds and oil, teriyaki, rice wine vinegar, wasabi, pickled ginger, tandoori spices, tomatoes, garlic, olives, capers. **IN SEASON** All year

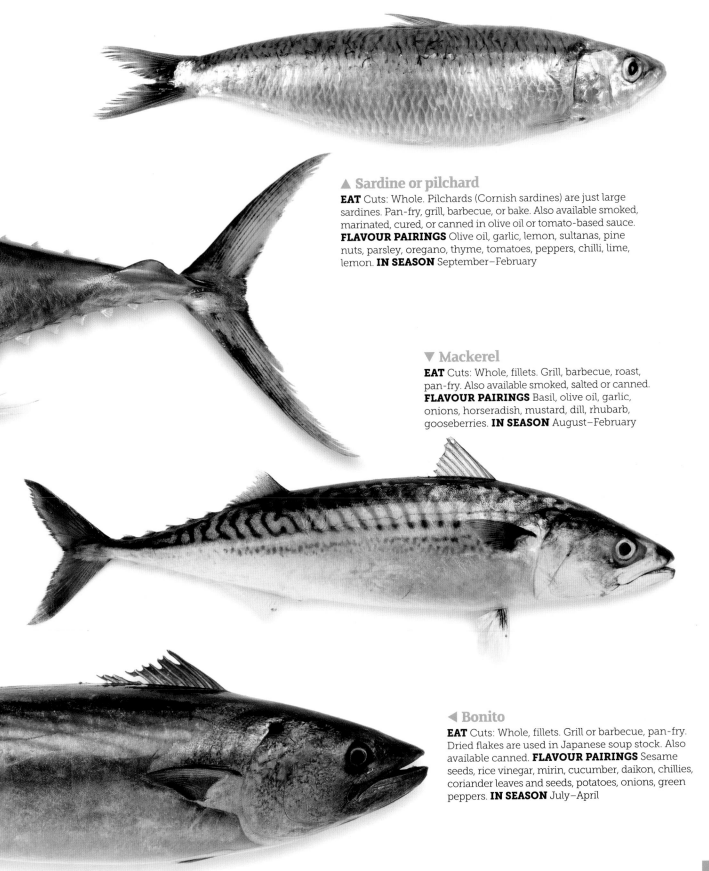

▲ Sardine or pilchard

EAT Cuts: Whole. Pilchards (Cornish sardines) are just large sardines. Pan-fry, grill, barbecue, or bake. Also available smoked, marinated, cured, or canned in olive oil or tomato-based sauce.
FLAVOUR PAIRINGS Olive oil, garlic, lemon, sultanas, pine nuts, parsley, oregano, thyme, tomatoes, peppers, chilli, lime, lemon. **IN SEASON** September–February

▼ Mackerel

EAT Cuts: Whole, fillets. Grill, barbecue, roast, pan-fry. Also available smoked, salted or canned.
FLAVOUR PAIRINGS Basil, olive oil, garlic, onions, horseradish, mustard, dill, rhubarb, gooseberries. **IN SEASON** August–February

◄ Bonito

EAT Cuts: Whole, fillets. Grill or barbecue, pan-fry. Dried flakes are used in Japanese soup stock. Also available canned. **FLAVOUR PAIRINGS** Sesame seeds, rice vinegar, mirin, cucumber, daikon, chillies, coriander leaves and seeds, potatoes, onions, green peppers. **IN SEASON** July–April

◀ Anchovy

EAT Cuts: Whole fresh, or preserved marinated, or in salt, brine or oil, in jars or cans, also as paste or essence. Buy sustainably sourced. Pan-fry whole fresh fish. Add preserved to everything from salade niçoise to pizzas, pasta sauces and bagna cauda dip, where they are "melted" in olive oil with spices and butter.
FLAVOUR PAIRINGS Sherry vinegar, white wine vinegar, shallots, tomatoes, marjoram, oregano, sage, thyme, parsley, olive oil. **IN SEASON** All year

▲ Scad (horse mackerel)

EAT Cuts: Whole, fillets. Grill or barbecue, pan-fry. **FLAVOUR PAIRINGS** Chilli, ginger, soy sauce, Chinese five-spice powder, coconut milk, tomatoes, peppers.
IN SEASON September–May

Salmon ▶

EAT Cuts: Whole, fillets, steaks. It is recommended not to buy wild salmon as it is becoming rare. Choose good quality farmed salmon from an MSC-rated source instead. Pan-fry, poach, grill, bake. Also available smoked, and the salted roe as red keta, a caviar substitute.
FLAVOUR PAIRINGS Lemon, butter, hollandaise sauce, dill, samphire, tarragon, ginger, harissa paste, soy, sesame, chillies, coriander leaves.
IN SEASON Farmed all year

▲ Sprat

EAT Cuts: Whole. Either gut it yourself or cook ungutted and hold in your fingers to eat off the bone. Pan-fry, grill, or barbecue. Also available smoked, canned, or salted. **FLAVOUR PAIRINGS** Beetroot, red and white wine vinegar, flat-leaf parsley, coriander leaf and seeds, lemon. **IN SEASON** September–February

▲ Herring

EAT Cuts: Whole, fillets, soft and hard roes. Pan-fry, grill or barbecue, bake, souse or pickle. Tiny immature herrings (and often other fish) are sold as whitebait but are overexploited so best avoided. Also available smoked (kippers, bloaters, buckling), marinated, or canned. **FLAVOUR PAIRINGS** Soured cream, dill, onions, oatmeal, bacon, horseradish, mustard, lemon, capers, parsley. **IN SEASON** All year

▼ Sea trout

EAT Cuts: Whole, fillets, steaks. Also known as salmon trout. It is the migratory form of the brown river trout. Poach, steam, grill, pan-fry, bake. **FLAVOUR PAIRINGS** Mayonnaise, watercress, hollandaise sauce, lemon, dill, parsley. **IN SEASON** Wild April–October, available farmed all year

Flat fish

BUY Like other fish, they are not all sustainable. Real skate, sadly, is very rare, and wild Atlantic halibut is endangered, so it is now farmed. Many flat fish, however, are thriving but may have minimum size fishing requirements so avoid if small. Choose fish with firm flesh, moist, not slimy skin, and a fresh smell. **STORE** Eat fresh or store, well-wrapped, for up to 24 hours in the coldest part of the refrigerator. Freeze whole or fillets (unless previously frozen) for up to 3 months.

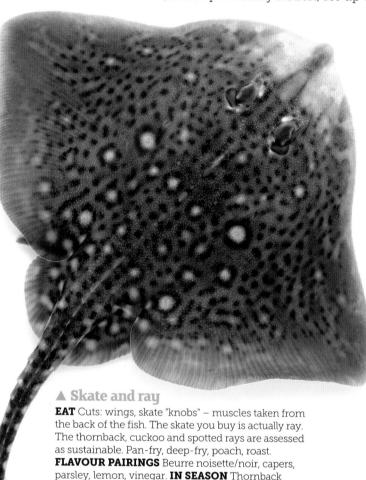

▲ Plaice

EAT Cuts: whole, fillets. Pan-fry, poach, deep-fry, steam, bake.
FLAVOUR PAIRINGS Butter, lemon, parsley, sage, thyme, breadcrumb- or rice-based stuffing, chestnut mushrooms, grapes, white wine, potatoes. **IN SEASON** April–December

Dab ▶

EAT Cuts: whole. Pan-fry, grill. Also available dried, salted, or smoked. **FLAVOUR PAIRINGS** Shallots, prawns, mushrooms, parsley, tarragon, lemon, lime, capers, gherkins, anchovy butter. **IN SEASON** July–March

▲ Skate and ray

EAT Cuts: wings, skate "knobs" – muscles taken from the back of the fish. The skate you buy is actually ray. The thornback, cuckoo and spotted rays are assessed as sustainable. Pan-fry, deep-fry, poach, roast.
FLAVOUR PAIRINGS Beurre noisette/noir, capers, parsley, lemon, vinegar. **IN SEASON** Thornback September–February, Cuckoo June–November, Spotted August–March

Dover sole ▶

EAT Cuts: whole, fillets. A 450g (1lb) fish will serve 1 person generously. Grill, pan-fry. **FLAVOUR PAIRINGS** Butter, lemon, parsley, tarragon, cucumber, mint, shiitake mushrooms, truffle oil, white grapes.
IN SEASON July–March

◄ **Halibut**

EAT Cuts: fillets, steaks. Pan-fry, steam, grill, poach, bake. Also available dried, salted, or cold-smoked. **FLAVOUR PAIRINGS** Butter, beurre blanc, nutmeg, gherkins, capers, lemon, bacon, spicy sausages, charcuterie. **IN SEASON** Farmed all year

Turbot ▶

EAT Cuts: fillets, steaks. Steam, pan-fry, bake with a crust, roast, grill. **FLAVOUR PAIRINGS** Wild mushrooms, Champagne, cream, butter, shellfish stock, lemon, prawns, Gruyère cheese, Parmesan. **IN SEASON** Wild September–March, available farmed all year

▲ **Brill**

EAT Cuts: fillets, steaks. Excellent and underrated. Pan-fry, poach, steam, bake with a crust, roast, grill. **FLAVOUR PAIRINGS** Bacon, shallots, wild mushrooms, white wine, garlic, tomatoes, lemon, crab or prawn sauce. **IN SEASON** October–February

◄ **Lemon sole**

EAT Cuts: whole, fillets. Pan-fry, grill, poach. **FLAVOUR PAIRINGS** Béchamel sauce, parsley, chives, lemon, butter, cider. **IN SEASON** September–March

261

Freshwater fish

BUY One tends to think of fish being from the sea but, of course, there are many delicious species that grace British and foreign rivers and lakes. Several are now farmed, increasing their sustainability. The skin should be shiny and slippery or even slimy, the flesh firm and moist, not wet. On whole fish, the eyes should be prominent and bright. **STORE** Unless frozen, eat on day or purchase, or store well-wrapped in the bottom of the refrigerator for up to 24 hours. Fresh caught fish can be frozen, gutted, whole or in fillets, for up to 2 months.

◀ Tilapia

EAT Cuts: whole, fillets. Also available salted or dried. Pan-fry, deep-fry, steam, bake, barbecue, or grill.
FLAVOUR PAIRINGS Chilli, palm sugar, nam pla (Thai fish sauce), shrimp paste, coriander leaves, coconut, galangal. **IN SEASON** Farmed all year

Barramundi ▶

EAT Cuts: whole, fillets, steaks, the pearl (cheek) is a speciality. Pan-fry, grill, barbecue, poach, steam. **FLAVOUR PAIRINGS** Pak choi, lime, chilli, fresh herbs, white wine.
IN SEASON Wild April–August, available farmed all year

▲ Catfish

EAT Cuts: whole, fillets. Also available smoked, dried, or salted. Pan-fry, deep-fry, grill, bake, poach.
FLAVOUR PAIRINGS Cornmeal, sesame seeds, soured cream, mushrooms, spring onions, parsley, bay leaf, thyme. **IN SEASON** Farmed all year

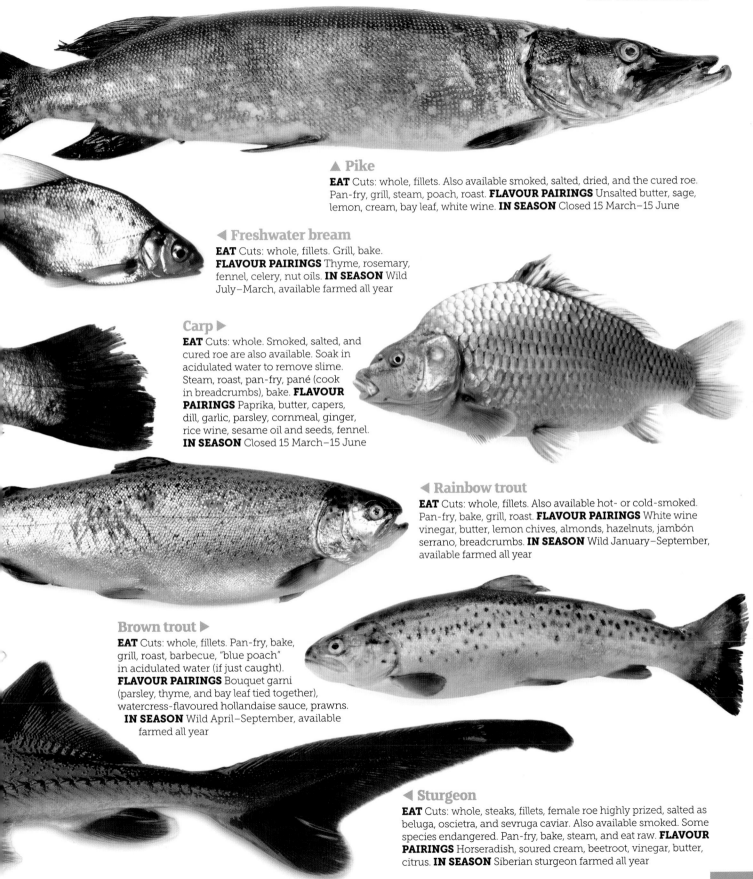

▲ Pike
EAT Cuts: whole, fillets. Also available smoked, salted, dried, and the cured roe. Pan-fry, grill, steam, poach, roast. **FLAVOUR PAIRINGS** Unsalted butter, sage, lemon, cream, bay leaf, white wine. **IN SEASON** Closed 15 March–15 June

◄ Freshwater bream
EAT Cuts: whole, fillets. Grill, bake. **FLAVOUR PAIRINGS** Thyme, rosemary, fennel, celery, nut oils. **IN SEASON** Wild July–March, available farmed all year

Carp ▶
EAT Cuts: whole. Smoked, salted, and cured roe are also available. Soak in acidulated water to remove slime. Steam, roast, pan-fry, pané (cook in breadcrumbs), bake. **FLAVOUR PAIRINGS** Paprika, butter, capers, dill, garlic, parsley, cornmeal, ginger, rice wine, sesame oil and seeds, fennel. **IN SEASON** Closed 15 March–15 June

◄ Rainbow trout
EAT Cuts: whole, fillets. Also available hot- or cold-smoked. Pan-fry, bake, grill, roast. **FLAVOUR PAIRINGS** White wine vinegar, butter, lemon chives, almonds, hazelnuts, jambón serrano, breadcrumbs. **IN SEASON** Wild January–September, available farmed all year

Brown trout ▶
EAT Cuts: whole, fillets. Pan-fry, bake, grill, roast, barbecue, "blue poach" in acidulated water (if just caught). **FLAVOUR PAIRINGS** Bouquet garni (parsley, thyme, and bay leaf tied together), watercress-flavoured hollandaise sauce, prawns. **IN SEASON** Wild April–September, available farmed all year

◄ Sturgeon
EAT Cuts: whole, steaks, fillets, female roe highly prized, salted as beluga, oscietra, and sevruga caviar. Also available smoked. Some species endangered. Pan-fry, bake, steam, and eat raw. **FLAVOUR PAIRINGS** Horseradish, soured cream, beetroot, vinegar, butter, citrus. **IN SEASON** Siberian sturgeon farmed all year

263

Smoked, salted, and dried fish

BUY Choose hot-smoked fish that is moist but not slimy and has a strong, pleasant aroma. Pick cold-smoked fish that is dry, glossy, and smells smoked but not too strong. Some salted and dried fish has a pungent smell that is not an indication of poor quality. **STORE** Keep smoked fish well-wrapped in the fridge. Best eaten within 24 hours; vacuum-packed hot-smoked will keep longer. Freeze for up to 2 months. Salted and dried fish can be kept for many months, well wrapped, in a cool, dark place. **IN SEASON** Available all year.

HOT-SMOKED the fish is cooked during smoking in a kiln, after brining or salting

Mackerel
fillets

**▲ Kiln-smoked
salmon**

EAT Cuts: sides, fillets, ready-flaked.
Serve cold or add to quiches, pasta, or scrambled eggs.
Make sure it is piping hot before serving, but do not
overheat or it will toughen and change in texture.
FLAVOUR PAIRINGS Eggs, rocket, beetroot, soured
cream, horseradish, cream, olive oil, lemon, dill.

▲ ▶ Mackerel

EAT Cuts: whole, fillets (plain or encrusted with
pepper and other toppings). Serve cold or as pâté.
Can be flaked and added to other dishes (see kiln-
smoked salmon). **FLAVOUR PAIRINGS** Horseradish,
mustard, cream and crème fraîche, cream cheese,
honey, sesame oil, dill, coriander leaves, beetroot,
celeriac, waxy potatoes.

Whole mackerel

Trout fillet

Whole trout

◀ ▲ Trout

EAT Cuts: whole, fillets. Best eaten cold or as pâté,
but can be flaked and used like kiln-smoked salmon.
FLAVOUR PAIRINGS Lemon, horseradish, waxy
potatoes, rocket, watercress, dill, chives, cream
cheese, crème fraîche.

COLD-SMOKED the fish remains raw after being heavily brined and slow-smoked at a low temperature

◀ Salmon

EAT Cuts: whole sides, slices, trimmings. Smoked salmon and other more artisanal products (such as smoked swordfish and tuna) can be simply sliced and served with a squeeze of lemon juice and a good grinding of black pepper, or added to more complex dishes. **FLAVOUR PAIRINGS** Citrus, horseradish, dill, parsley, scrambled eggs.

Undyed haddock

◀▲ Haddock

EAT Cuts: fillets, whole (Arbroath smokies, Finnan haddock). Poach in milk to remove saltiness. The classic fish for kedgeree. **FLAVOUR PAIRINGS** Spinach, rice, eggs, mild curry powder, tomatoes, parsley, cheese sauce, poached eggs.

Dyed haddock

SALTED AND DRIED

▲ Salt cod

EAT Cuts: fillets, steaks. Soak 36–48 hours in several changes of cold water before use. Poach, bake, casserole, stew. **FLAVOUR PAIRINGS** Olive oil, garlic, parsley, basil, olives, tomatoes, potatoes, citrus, capers, red peppers, chorizo.

▲ Anchovies

EAT Cuts: whole, fillets. Soak in milk briefly to remove some of the saltiness, soften, and round the flavour. Use on pizzas or to garnish Mediterranean dishes like salade niçoise or pissaladière. **FLAVOUR PAIRINGS** Garlic, onions, tomatoes, chillies, olives, cheese, spinach, pine nuts, butter, olive oil.

Gut a fish through the stomach

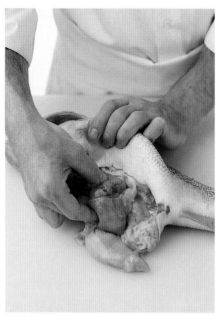

1 Place the fish on its side. Holding it firmly, make a shallow incision in the underside from just before the fin to the head.

2 Remove the guts using your hands, and cut off the gills, taking care not to cut yourself on them, as they can be very sharp.

3 Rinse the cavity with cold running water to remove any remaining blood or guts. Pat dry with kitchen paper. The fish can now be scaled.

Gut a fish through the gills

1 Hook a finger under the gills to lift them from the base of the head. Using sharp kitchen scissors or a knife, cut off the gills and discard.

2 Hold the fish steady with one hand while you put your fingers through the hole formed by the removed gills and pull out the guts.

3 Make a small slit in the stomach at the ventral (anal) opening and use your fingers to pull out any remaining guts. Rinse under cold water.

Scale and trim fish

1 Lay the fish on paper on a work surface. Holding the fish by the tail, use a fish scaler or the blunt side of a chef's knife to scrape the scales off, using strokes towards the head. Turn the fish over and repeat.

2 Using a pair of kitchen scissors, and taking care with any sharp spines, remove the dorsal (back) fin. Then cut off the belly fins, and the two on either side of the head.

Skin a dover sole

1 Lay the fish dark-side up on a board. Hold the end of the tail, and with a sharp knife, make a small incision through the dark skin at the tail end, cutting at an angle but not all the way through.

2 Using a clean tea towel to give you some grip on the slimy skin, take hold of the flap of skin where you made your incision, and slowly pull the skin away, while holding the tail down with the other hand.

Bone a flat fish

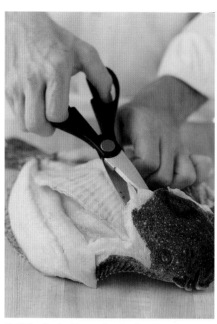

1 With the fish dark-side up, cut to (not through) the backbone (in the centre) from head to tail. Cut away the flesh one half at a time, to expose the backbone.

2 Slide the knife under the backbone to cut away the flesh. Use scissors to snip each end of the backbone, then cut it through the middle.

3 Lift the backbone pieces from the flesh and discard. Before stuffing, be sure to check for, and remove, any remaining bones.

Bone a round fish through the stomach

1 Open the fish by making an incision from the tail to the head. Using the blade of your knife, loosen the backbone (transverse bones) on the top side, then turn the fish over to loosen the other side.

2 Using kitchen scissors, snip the backbone from the head and tail ends. Starting at the tail, peel the bones away from the flesh and discard. Check for, and remove, any remaining bones left in the flesh.

Bone a round fish from the back

1 Cut down the back of the fish, cutting along one side of the backbone from head to tail. Continue cutting into the fish, keeping the knife close on top of the bones. When you reach the belly, don't cut through the skin.

2 Turn the fish over and cut down the back from tail to head, along the other side of the backbone. Continue cutting as before, to cut away the flesh from that side of the backbone too.

3 Using kitchen scissors, snip the backbone at the head and tail ends, then remove it. Pull out the guts (known as the viscera) and discard. Rinse the cavity under cold running water and pat dry.

4 Gently open out the stomach cavity and remove any pin bones (the line of tiny bones down each side of the fish) using large tweezers or small needle-nose pliers.

Fillet a flat fish

1 Start with a whole fish, skinned, trimmed, and gutted; a Dover sole is shown here. Slice all the way across the base of the head, down to the backbone, to separate the fillet from the head.

2 Starting at the head end, cut along one side of the fish, a short distance from the edge, slicing just above the bone and keeping the knife almost flat. Make the same cut along the outer edge of the other side.

3 Returning to the first side, insert the knife and cut all the way across the fish, with a long stroking action. Release the fillet at the backbone and continue cutting to the other side, until the whole fillet is released.

4 Lift off the fillet in a single piece and then turn the fish over to repeat the process. Smaller types of flat fish, such as Dover sole, are commonly cut into whole fillets and a single fish will be enough for two people.

Fillet a small round fish

1 If you are leaving the skin on the fillets, first scale the fish. Then, with a long, sharp filleting knife, cut into the fish at the head end, behind the gills, cutting at an angle until the blade reaches the backbone.

2 Beginning just behind the head, and near the gills, insert the knife, and keeping it flat, cut the fish along the length of the back, cutting along the top side of the backbone.

3 Then starting again just behind the head, continue cutting over the bone, keeping the blade as flat as possible, and folding the fillet back as you go. Once you have reached the tail end, remove the fillet.

4 Set the first fillet aside and turn the fish over. Repeat the process to remove the second fillet, but this time make an incision just before the tail and cut towards the head.

Prepare flat fish

1 Place the fish on a board, dark-side down. Cut along the stomach with a sharp knife and pull out the guts and any roe.

2 Cut off the fins on both sides of the fish with sharp kitchen scissors, taking care not to cut into the body.

3 Put some greaseproof paper underneath the fish and scrape off the scales with a fish scaler or the back of a chef's knife.

4 Use your finger to hook the gills away from the body, and then cut them off with scissors. Rinse the fish under cold running water.

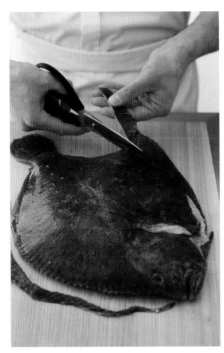

5 To skin the flat fish, place it dark-side up on a board, then using scissors, cut off the fins about 5mm (¼in) from the body.

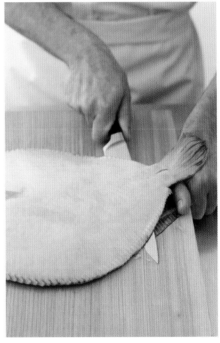

6 Turn the fish over and slide a sharp knife just under the skin at the tail end, while you pull the dark skin away with your other hand.

Cut fish steaks

1 Gut the fish through the stomach, then scale it and trim off the fins. Rinse the fish inside and out under cold running water and pat dry with kitchen paper. Cut off the head at a point just behind the gills.

2 Holding the cleaned, dried fish firmly on its side with one hand, use a sharp chef's knife to cut across the body to slice away steaks of the required thickness.

Skin a fillet

1 Place the fillet skin-side down. Using a long, sharp knife, make an incision near the tail end, tilting the blade at a slight angle. Carefully cut through the flesh just to, but not through, the skin.

2 Angle the blade of the knife until it is almost flat, and with your other hand, firmly grasp the end of the skin. Keep the knife as close to the skin as possible as you cut, and slowly pull the skin away from the fillet.

Serve whole cooked fish

1 Carefully cut along the top of the fish from head to tail, then starting from the top, gently pull away the skin, working towards the stomach. Remove any dark flesh and scrape away the tiny bones along the back.

2 Using the edge of a spoon, cut down the centre of the fish and carefully lift away the top 2 fillets, one at a time. Break the backbone at the head and tail ends and remove. Replace the top fillets on the fish.

Serve whole flat fish

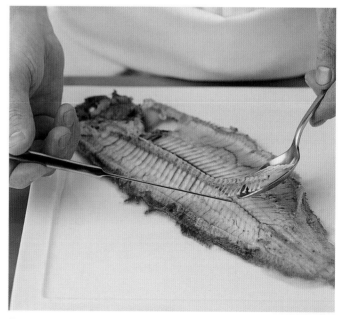

1 Place the fish on a warmed plate. Using a knife and spoon, push away the tiny fin bones from both sides of the fish. Cut along both sides of the backbone with the spoon, just through the flesh as far as the bone.

2 Lift off the top 2 fillets, one at a time and set aside. Lift out the backbone and discard. Check for any stray bones and remove them, then replace the top fillets on the fish.

Bake fish in foil

1 Use this technique for baking a whole fish. If your chosen recipe includes a stuffing, spoon it into the cavity, then secure in place with 1 or 2 wooden cocktail sticks.

2 Wrap the fish in lightly oiled or buttered foil to make a well-sealed parcel. Bake in a preheated oven at 180°C (350°F/Gas 4) for 25 minutes for small fish, or 35–40 minutes for large fish, or until the flesh along the back is opaque.

Steam fish

1 To use a bamboo steamer, pour water into a wok to just below where the steamer fits (make sure it doesn't touch the water). Add any flavourings, then bring the water to a simmer. Put the basket in the wok.

2 Put the fish in the steamer and sprinkle over any extra flavourings. Cover tightly, and steam fillets for 3–4 minutes, whole fish up to 350g (12oz) for 6–8 mins, and up to 900g (2lb) for 12–15 minutes.

Grill fish

1 Brush a grill rack with oil. Add the fish, brush the surface with oil, and season to taste with salt and pepper. Position the grill rack 10cm (4in) from the heat and grill for half the time specified in the recipe.

2 Using a pair of tongs, carefully lift the fish from the rack and turn over. Continue grilling for the remaining time specified, or until the flesh flakes easily when tested with a fork.

Pan-fry fish

1 Heat equal amounts of oil and butter in a heavy frying pan over a medium-high heat until foaming. Season the fish, then add it to the pan, skin-side down, and fry for half the time specified in the recipe.

2 Use a spatula or fish slice to turn the pieces over, then continue frying the fish for the remaining cooking time, or until it is light golden brown and the flesh flakes easily when tested with a fork.

Batter and fry fish

1 Mix the batter by combining 150g (5½oz) plain flour, 2 tsp dried yeast, 1 tbsp sunflower oil, and 180ml (6fl oz) beer, and leave to stand for 30 minutes. Put 2 tbsp seasoned flour in a dish and coat the pieces of fish.

2 Beat the egg white in a medium bowl until stiff peaks form when the whisk is lifted. Gently fold the whisked egg white into the batter, using a wooden spoon, until combined.

3 Using a 2-pronged fork, dip a piece of fish in the batter, turning to coat thoroughly. Lift out the fish and hold it over the bowl for 5 seconds so excess batter can drip off.

4 Heat enough groundnut or other oil for deep frying to 190°C (375°F). Carefully lower the fish, 1 or 2 pieces at a time into the oil and deep-fry, turning once, for 6–8 minutes, or until golden brown and crisp.

Shellfish, other seafood, and specialities

BUY Shellfish, seafood, and other creatures should look fresh, shells should be unbroken, and bivalves shut (or will close when tapped sharply). There should be signs of life in all live creatures. Crabs and lobsters should feel heavy for their size. All seafood should smell pleasantly of the sea. **STORE** Unless frozen, eat on day of purchase. Live crustaceans and molluscs can be stored briefly below 3°C (37°F) in a lightly covered bowl towards the bottom of the refrigerator. Cover live lobsters or crabs with a damp tea towel or seaweed to prevent dehydration.

▼ Lobster

EAT Available live whole, or cooked, whole and tail meat, fresh or frozen. For live, freeze for 2 hours to stun, then boil 10 minutes per 450g (1lb), split and grill, bake, or eat cold. **FLAVOUR PAIRINGS** Mayonnaise, brandy, white wine, sherry, citrus, Parmesan, cream, chilli, tarragon, parsley, chives, salad leaves, shallots. **IN SEASON** October–June

▲ Brown crab

EAT Available occasionally live, mostly cooked whole and claws, ready dressed in shell, white crabmeat, frozen and canned. Toss into salads, reheat in pasta and rice dishes, sauté, in soups and sandwiches. **FLAVOUR PAIRINGS** Mayonnaise, chilli, lemon, parsley, dill, potatoes, butter, Worcestershire sauce, anchovies. **IN SEASON** July–March

▲ Fresh water crayfish

EAT Available whole, live or cooked, or frozen cooked, and tails. Native white ones (pictured) are endangered. Buy farmed signal crayfish. For live, freeze for 45 minutes to stun, then boil for 5 minutes, or sauté. **FLAVOUR PAIRINGS** Melted butter, salad leaves, mayonnaise, citrus. **IN SEASON** Farmed all year

▲ Langoustine (Dublin Bay prawn)

EAT Available whole, live, or cooked, shelled tails, breaded scampi, fresh or frozen. Boil, pan-fry, poach, deep-fry (breaded scampi). **FLAVOUR PAIRINGS** Mayonnaise, citrus, tomatoes, garlic, butter, tarragon, lovage, parsley, chives, tartare sauce. **IN SEASON** December–August

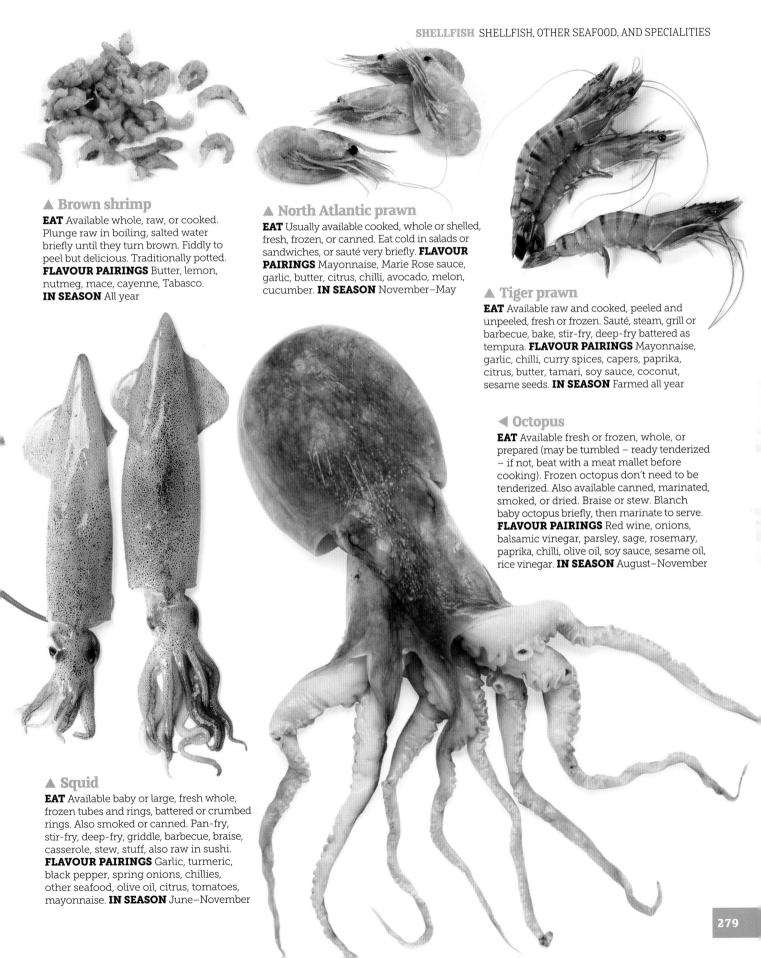

▲ Brown shrimp

EAT Available whole, raw, or cooked. Plunge raw in boiling, salted water briefly until they turn brown. Fiddly to peel but delicious. Traditionally potted. **FLAVOUR PAIRINGS** Butter, lemon, nutmeg, mace, cayenne, Tabasco. **IN SEASON** All year

▲ North Atlantic prawn

EAT Usually available cooked, whole or shelled, fresh, frozen, or canned. Eat cold in salads or sandwiches, or sauté very briefly. **FLAVOUR PAIRINGS** Mayonnaise, Marie Rose sauce, garlic, butter, citrus, chilli, avocado, melon, cucumber. **IN SEASON** November–May

▲ Tiger prawn

EAT Available raw and cooked, peeled and unpeeled, fresh or frozen. Sauté, steam, grill or barbecue, bake, stir-fry, deep-fry battered as tempura. **FLAVOUR PAIRINGS** Mayonnaise, garlic, chilli, curry spices, capers, paprika, citrus, butter, tamari, soy sauce, coconut, sesame seeds. **IN SEASON** Farmed all year

◄ Octopus

EAT Available fresh or frozen, whole, or prepared (may be tumbled – ready tenderized – if not, beat with a meat mallet before cooking). Frozen octopus don't need to be tenderized. Also available canned, marinated, smoked, or dried. Braise or stew. Blanch baby octopus briefly, then marinate to serve. **FLAVOUR PAIRINGS** Red wine, onions, balsamic vinegar, parsley, sage, rosemary, paprika, chilli, olive oil, soy sauce, sesame oil, rice vinegar. **IN SEASON** August–November

▲ Squid

EAT Available baby or large, fresh whole, frozen tubes and rings, battered or crumbed rings. Also smoked or canned. Pan-fry, stir-fry, deep-fry, griddle, barbecue, braise, casserole, stew, stuff, also raw in sushi. **FLAVOUR PAIRINGS** Garlic, turmeric, black pepper, spring onions, chillies, other seafood, olive oil, citrus, tomatoes, mayonnaise. **IN SEASON** June–November

▲ Periwinkle

EAT Available live or cooked in the shell, shucked fresh, and pickled in vinegar. Rinse live ones in salt water before boiling for 3–5 minutes. Pick off the sucker, then extract the meat with a winkle picker or pin. **FLAVOUR PAIRINGS** Chilli vinegar, malt vinegar, lemon juice, garlic butter, watercress. **IN SEASON** July–January

▲ Whelk

EAT Available live and cooked in the shell. Rinse live ones in salted water before boiling for 10–12 minutes. Pick off sucker and extract the meat with a pin or small fork. Eat, or crumb-coat and fry first. **FLAVOUR PAIRINGS** Malt vinegar, garlic butter, parsley, tarragon, chives. **IN SEASON** January–September

▲ Cockle

EAT Available live in the shell, or cooked and shucked, frozen, in jars in brine or vinegar. **FLAVOUR PAIRINGS** Malt vinegar, parsley, capers, gherkins, cucumber. **IN SEASON** September–February

▲ Razor clam

EAT Available live in the shell. Best lightly steamed or grilled (the flesh toughens if overcooked). Good served in their shells with flavoured butter or a sauce. **FLAVOUR PAIRINGS** Garlic, butter, parsley, coriander leaves, white wine, shallots, cream, chilli. **IN SEASON** October–April

▲ Clam

EAT Available live in the shell, or shucked frozen, canned, or as clam juice. There are several species (surf clams pictured). Chop large clams or cook in chowder, shuck smaller specimens and enjoy them raw, or steam open to add to soups, pasta, or rice. **FLAVOUR PAIRINGS** Cream, onions, garlic, white wine, chives, parsley, oregano, thyme, bay leaf, tomatoes. **IN SEASON** October–April

Common mussels

Green-lipped mussels

◄ ▲ Mussels

EAT Available live in the shell, cooked fresh, frozen, canned, in vinegar, or smoked. Green-lipped usually sold cooked on half shell, or frozen. Steam, bake, grill, stuff. Remove the shell if adding to soups or stews. **FLAVOUR PAIRINGS** White wine, cider, Pernod, butter, garlic, cream, shallots, chillies, fennel, ginger, lemongrass, parsley, coriander leaves, dill, rosemary. **IN SEASON** Wild October–March, available farmed all year

King scallop

Queen scallop

▲ Sea urchin

EAT Available whole, live. Also fermented to make sea urchin paste. Eat raw, bake with eggs, or add to creamy fish sauces. **FLAVOUR PAIRINGS** Lemon, black pepper, eggs, cream. **IN SEASON** Available all year (best September–April)

◄ ▲ Scallops

EAT Available in the shell, prepared on half shell, prepared and trimmed (processed). Also frozen (with or without coral), canned, smoked, or dried. Pan-fry (fresh and smoked), steam, poach, grill, or barbecue. **FLAVOUR PAIRINGS** Bacon, chorizo, black pudding, red peppers, red onion, olive oil, sesame oil, black beans, spring onions, chillies, ginger, cream, bay leaf, parsley. **IN SEASON** King October–March; Queen June–September

Pacific oysters

◄ ▲ Oysters

EAT Available live in the shell, smoked, and canned. Shuck and serve raw with their juice in the half shell, deep-fry, pan-fry, poach, grill, bake. **FLAVOUR PAIRINGS** (Raw) red wine vinegar, shallots, Tabasco, lemon juice; (cooked) anchovy essence, butter, spinach, cream, Parmesan cheese. **IN SEASON** Native September–April, Pacific farmed all year

Native oysters

▲ Abalone

EAT Available fresh in the shell, frozen meat/steaks ready tenderized, canned, dried, salted. Tenderize fresh by pounding before cooking. Sauté or pan-fry briefly. Add dried to soup and simmer a long time to add flavour. **FLAVOUR PAIRINGS** Shiitake mushrooms, sesame, soy sauce, ginger, garlic, butter, parsley, oyster sauce. **IN SEASON** Restricted wild harvest, available farmed all year

Snails ▲

EAT Available live in the shell but often bought ready-cooked vacuum-packed with their shells, or canned with shells separately. If live, they need purging for several days before boiling. Once cooked, bake in garlic butter, or add shucked ones to tarts or terrines. **FLAVOUR PAIRINGS** Garlic butter with lemon or rosemary, olive oil with red wine vinegar and black pepper. **IN SEASON** Available farmed all year

▲ Frogs' legs

EAT Available fresh or frozen. Avoid wild, buy farmed. Pan-fry, add to soup. **FLAVOUR PAIRINGS** Butter, lemon, garlic, black pepper, Calvados, cream, apple, mixed herbs. **IN SEASON** Available farmed all year (best April–October)

Clean a live lobster

1 Keep the the claws closed with rubber bands. Hold the lobster firmly on a board. Push the tip of a heavy chef's knife into the head and quickly bring the blade down towards the board, splitting the lobster in two.

2 Hold the lobster's body with one hand, while you remove the claws with the other. Do this either by twisting the claws off, or if that is not possible, by cutting them off with the chef's knife.

3 Now separate the main sections of the lobster by firmly holding the body with one hand, and the head the other. Then twist them in opposite directions and pull apart.

4 Using a spoon, remove the tomalley (the green coloured liver) and any coral (the black roe) from the head and tail sections, and set aside to use in a sauce or stuffing. You can now cook the tail section and claws.

Clean a live crab

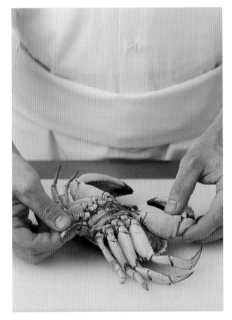

1 Hold the crab on its back, insert the tip of a chef's knife directly behind the eyes, and quickly bring the blade down. Pull and twist off the tail.

2 Holding down the central part of the body and the leg section with one hand, pull off the top shell with the other.

3 Using kitchen scissors, cut off the gills and remove the spongy bag behind the eyes. Cut the crab in half, or into quarters.

Clean a live soft-shell crab

1 Hold the crab firmly, then using sharp kitchen scissors, make a cut across the front of the crab to remove the eyes and mouth.

2 Now pull the top shell away slightly, so that you can cut away and discard the gills from both sides of the body.

3 Turn the crab onto its back. Unfold the tail flap (the apron) and pull it off. This procedure also removes the guts (viscera).

283

Extract the meat from a cooked lobster

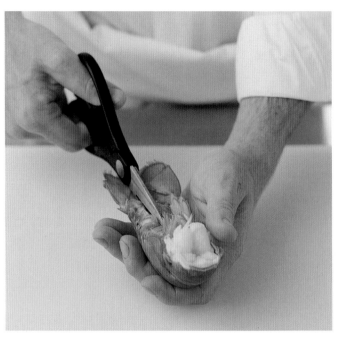

1 Rinse the lobster under cold running water and pat dry with kitchen paper, then place on a cutting board. Take hold of the tail and twist it sharply away from the body to detach it.

2 Set the lobster's body aside and turn the tail over with the shell-side down. Using a pair of sharp kitchen scissors, and beginning at the far end of the tail, cut down the centre towards the thickest part.

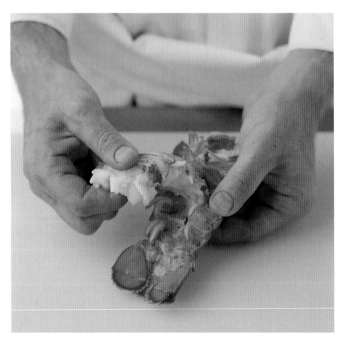

3 Using your thumbs, pull the shell apart along the line where you cut it with scissors, and fold the shell back. You should now be able to extract the meat in one piece.

4 To remove the meat from the claws, crack them open with a lobster cracker or a small hammer. Once the shell has been opened, extract the meat inside carefully, and discard any attached membrane.

Dress a cooked crab

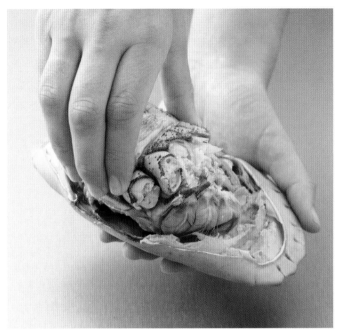

1 Pull away the claws and legs and set aside, then twist off the tail flap and discard. To separate the body from the carapace, crack it under the tail, then prise the two sections apart, pulling the body from the tail end.

2 Remove the gills (dead man's fingers) attached to the main body, and check for stray gills left in the carapace. Remove the stomach sac as well, which will either be attached to the body or in the carapace.

3 Cut the body of the crab into quarters and pick out the white meat, using a seafood fork or lobster pick. Remove any pieces of shell or membrane. Scoop out the brown meat from the carapace with a spoon.

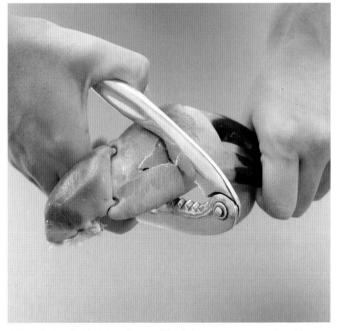

4 Break the shell of the claws with a lobster, or nut cracker. Extract the meat, and remove the cartilage, then check for any shell or membrane. Crack the legs across their narrowest part, then pick the meat with a fork.

Clean mussels

1 As mussels are cooked and often served in their shells, they must be thoroughly cleaned. Scrub the mussels under cold running water to brush away any grit, and scrape off barnacles with a small knife.

2 Live mussels usually have a fibrous attachment called a "beard" which needs to be removed. Pinch the stringy thread between your finger and thumb and firmly jerk it away from the mussel shell.

Prepare prawns

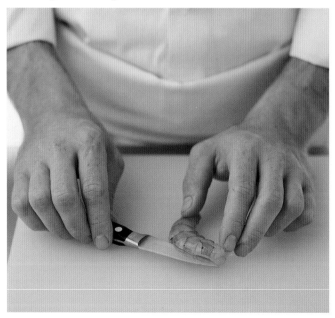

1 To remove the intestinal vein, cut lightly along the back of the prawn with a paring knife. Remove the vein with your fingers or the knife tip, and rinse the prawn under cold running water.

2 To butterfly a prawn, cut along the deveined back and splay it open, but take care not to cut all the way through. Rinse under cold running water and pat dry with kitchen paper.

Prepare scallops

1 Scrub the shell under cold running water before you open the scallop. Slide a knife between the top and bottom shell to open it, then carefully detach the scallop from the bottom shell with the knife.

2 Pull away and discard the viscera and frilled membrane. You can leave the cream and orange coral (roe) attached to the scallop, or remove it too if you wish. Gently rinse the scallop under cold running water.

Pick cooked crayfish

1 Crayfish should be cooked in a large pan of boiling water or flavoured broth for 5–7 minutes and then removed to cool. When they are cool enough to handle, simply break off the head section.

2 Now hold the tail between your thumb and forefinger, and gently squeeze the tail until you hear the shell crack. Remove the meat in one piece by carefully pulling away the sides of the shell.

Open oysters

1 Hold the oyster flat in a towel, and insert the tip of an oyster knife into the hinge to open the shell. Keep the blade close to the top of the shell so the oyster is not damaged. Cut the muscle, and lift off the top shell.

2 Detach the oyster from the bottom shell by carefully sliding the blade of your knife beneath the oyster. Oysters can be served raw on the half shell (scrub the shells thoroughly before opening), or removed and cooked.

Open clams

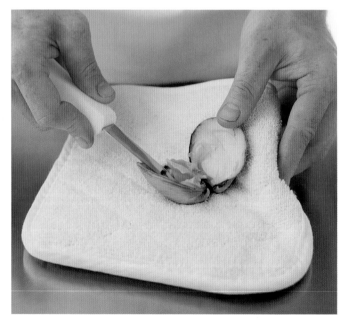

1 Clean the clams under cold running water and discard any open ones. Place the clam in a towel to protect your fingers, then insert the tip of a long sharp knife and twist to force the shells apart.

2 Using the tip of your knife, sever the muscle that attaches the clam to the shell, and release the clam. If using soft-shell clams, remove and discard the dark membrane before serving.

Clean squid

1 First pull the mantle (the body) and tentacles apart. The head, viscera, and ink sac will come away with the tentacles. The black "ink" can be used to flavour and colour sauces, pasta, and rice.

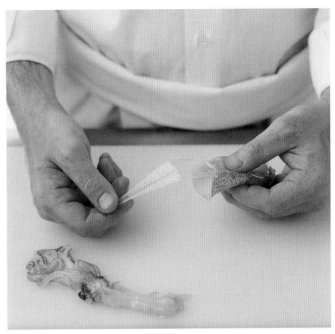

2 Next, push a forefinger into the body cavity, to extract the transparent, plastic-like quill (the inner lining). Hook your finger around it, pull it out, and discard.

3 Separate the tentacles from the head, cutting above the eye. Discard the head and viscera, but retain the ink sac if required by your chosen recipe. (Be sure to use it immediately though, or discard.)

4 Open the tentacles to pull out the ball-shaped beak and discard it. Rinse the tentacles and mantle under cold running water, then pat dry with kitchen paper. The squid is ready to be cooked.

Poultry

BUY Intensively farmed poultry is cheaper than organic or free-range birds but doesn't have the same flavour or texture. Buy poultry from a quality source, and check that the meat is plump and not dry. The bird should have a clean fresh smell, and the skin should have no tears or bruising. If corn-fed it will be yellow; if not, the flesh should be pale pink with whitish skin. Also available frozen and smoked. **STORE** Put in a sealed container in the bottom of the fridge, so that it can't touch or drip on other foods. If the bird has giblets, remove and store separately. Cook within 2 days. Freeze fresh poultry for up to 12 months (3 months for giblets). Thaw completely before cooking.

Whole chicken ▶

EAT Roast, pot-roast, poach. Stuff the neck end, if liked, or, when roasting, put a whole onion and/or fresh herbs/lemon in the body cavity for added flavour. **FLAVOUR PAIRINGS** Sage and onion or parsley and thyme stuffing, lemon, honey, barbecue sauce, Cajun spices, Tandoori spices, paprika, bread sauce, redcurrant jelly, cider, white wine.

▲ Chicken leg quarter

EAT The drumstick and thigh together. Stew, casserole, or marinate or add a spicy rub, then barbecue or grill. **FLAVOUR PAIRINGS** Cajun or curry spices, thyme, tarragon, chives, garlic, lardons, red or white wine, cider, mushrooms, tomatoes.

◀ Chicken breast quarter

EAT The whole breast with the wing and part of the rib cage and backbone attached. Use in the same way as the leg quarter; particularly good stewed with cider, or dipped in milk then flavoured breadcrumbs and oven-fried in sizzling oil. **FLAVOUR PAIRINGS** As for leg quarter, but also bananas, bacon, sweetcorn, soured cream, chives.

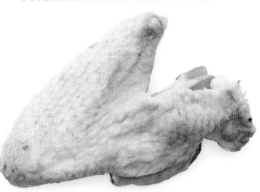

▲ Chicken drumstick

EAT The end of the leg, excellent finger food. Roast, grill, or barbecue plain, marinated, or basted with sauce. **FLAVOUR PAIRINGS** Butter, olive oil, garlic, barbecue sauce, sweet and sour sauce, cumin, garam masala, curry paste, harissa paste, chilli, Worcestershire sauce, honey, lemon.

▲ Chicken thigh

EAT Cheaper than breasts, sold with or without skin, boned or whole. Roast plain (boned can be stuffed first), casserole, curry, braise. **FLAVOUR PAIRINGS** Curry spices, pesto, olive oil, chopped fresh herbs, garlic.

▲ Chicken wing

EAT Popular barbecued as buffalo wings and for making stock. **FLAVOUR PAIRINGS** Chinese five-spice powder, soy sauce, barbecue sauce, jerk seasoning, Cajun spices, garam masala.

▲ Chicken breast

EAT One of the most popular cuts, being tender and easy to cook. Available with or without skin. Can be cooked whole, cut in strips or cubes, or beaten flat as escalopes. Stir-fry, pan-fry, grill (with skin or wrapped in bacon), stew, or casserole. **FLAVOUR PAIRINGS** Thai green curry paste, coconut, nam pla, ginger, oyster sauce, black bean sauce, bacon/pancetta, chorizo, prawns.

▲ Chicken supreme

EAT The breast with part of the wing bone attached. Sold with or without skin. Good for stuffing before cooking (like chicken Kiev), then coat in egg and crumbs, pan-fry, bake. **FLAVOUR PAIRINGS** Butter, fresh herbs, garlic, cream, white wine, brandy, white grapes, mushrooms.

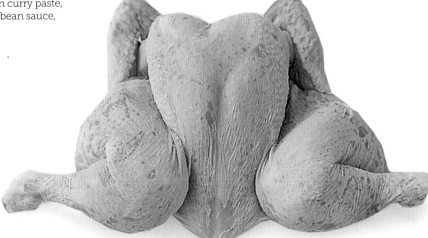

▲ Poultry liver

EAT Fresh or frozen. Trim, chop, and sauté until cooked but soft. Serve on bruschetta or salad leaves, with pasta or rice, or in pâtés and terrines. Slice fresh foie gras and quickly fry, or, if preserved, serve chilled. **FLAVOUR PAIRINGS** Butter, garlic, shallots, woody herbs, bacon, eggs, truffles, figs, prunes, Sauternes, sherry.

▲ Poussin

EAT The French name for young chicken. Sold 4–6 weeks old. Roast, bake, or simmer whole or stuffed birds; grill, fry, or barbecue spatchcocked ones. **FLAVOUR PAIRINGS** Bacon, garlic, shallots, tomatoes, citrus, mushrooms, saffron, lemongrass, kaffir lime, rosemary, thyme, tarragon, bay leaf, pesto, soy sauce, white wine, barbecue sauce.

◀ Whole duck

EAT Roast or pot-roast whole, or cut in portions. Prick with a fork and rest on a trivet in a roasting tin to allow fat to drain away. **FLAVOUR PAIRINGS** Sage, onion, garlic, spring onions, apples, oranges, turnips, ginger, cherries, soy sauce, hoisin sauce, honey, vinegar, wine, peas, baby white onions, lettuce. **IN SEASON** All year

▲ Duck breast

EAT Sold with or without skin and in goujons. If cooking with skin, score or prick it, then pan-fry skin-side down or grill skin-side up to melt and release fat. Use a little oil or butter if cooking without skin. Good in warm salads. Stir-fry goujons. **FLAVOUR PAIRINGS** Berries, currants, pomegranate, baby leaves, cherry tomatoes, cucumber, red onion, olives, fruit vinegar, olive oil, pomegranate syrup.

▲ Duck crown

EAT A convenient joint for carving – it is the breast (the choicest part) with wings, no legs. Best roasted but can be braised. **FLAVOUR PAIRINGS** The same as for the whole bird, but try rubbing with smoked sea salt before cooking.

▲ Duck leg portion

EAT Grill, fry, roast, casserole, or use to make confit. Prick the skin before cooking to release the fat. **FLAVOUR PAIRINGS** All the above plus juniper berries, coriander seeds, thyme for confit.

Whole goose ▶

EAT Stuff neck end only. Roast. Goose leg confit is also available. Can be jointed and braised, or casseroled. **FLAVOUR PAIRINGS** Apples, onions, red cabbage, tomatoes, white beans, spicy sausages, ginger, sage, oatmeal, almonds, apricots, prunes, soy sauce, red wine. **IN SEASON** September–December (some for Michaelmas in September but most bred for Christmas)

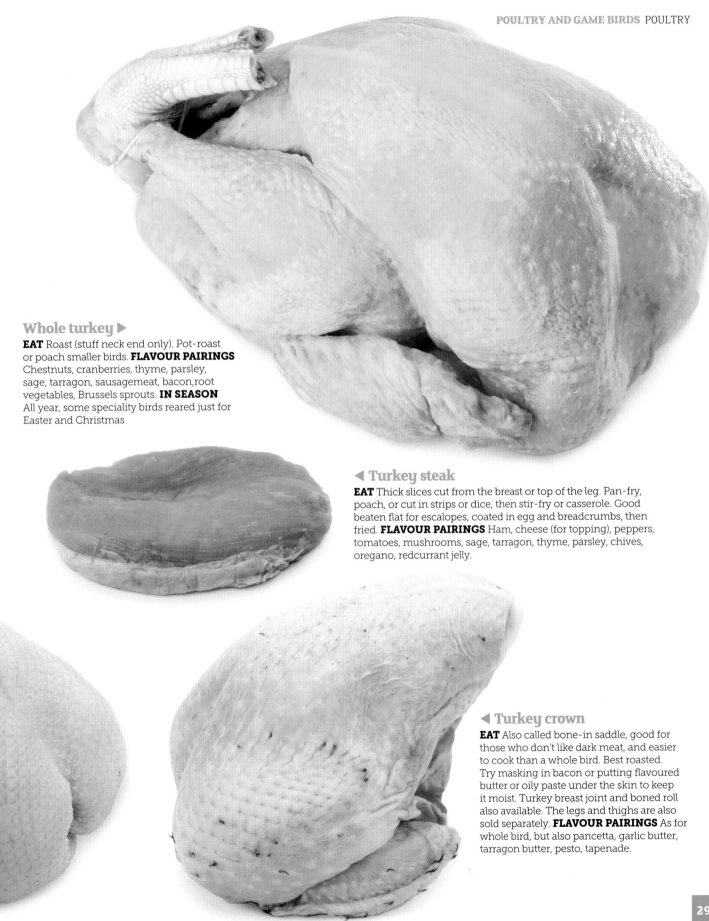

Whole turkey ▶

EAT Roast (stuff neck end only). Pot-roast or poach smaller birds. **FLAVOUR PAIRINGS** Chestnuts, cranberries, thyme, parsley, sage, tarragon, sausagemeat, bacon, root vegetables, Brussels sprouts. **IN SEASON** All year, some speciality birds reared just for Easter and Christmas

◀ Turkey steak

EAT Thick slices cut from the breast or top of the leg. Pan-fry, poach, or cut in strips or dice, then stir-fry or casserole. Good beaten flat for escalopes, coated in egg and breadcrumbs, then fried. **FLAVOUR PAIRINGS** Ham, cheese (for topping), peppers, tomatoes, mushrooms, sage, tarragon, thyme, parsley, chives, oregano, redcurrant jelly.

◀ Turkey crown

EAT Also called bone-in saddle, good for those who don't like dark meat, and easier to cook than a whole bird. Best roasted. Try masking in bacon or putting flavoured butter or oily paste under the skin to keep it moist. Turkey breast joint and boned roll also available. The legs and thighs are also sold separately. **FLAVOUR PAIRINGS** As for whole bird, but also pancetta, garlic butter, tarragon butter, pesto, tapenade.

Game birds

BUY Wild game should only be bought in season. Buy from reliable sources and don't accept any illegally shot birds. Quail are farmed. Game birds may have a strong smell but shouldn't be rancid. The flesh should be firm and the skin taut. Avoid if bruised or those with badly shot breasts. Guinea fowl (not shown as not, technically, game birds) should be cooked like chicken. **STORE** Remove all giblets and store separately. Wrap well and store on a plate at the bottom of the fridge for 2–3 days. Birds can be frozen for 6 months, giblets for 3 months.

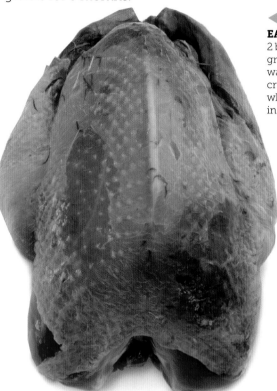

◀ Grouse

EAT Available whole or as boned breasts. Allow 1 whole bird or 2 breasts per person. Bard (cover) with bacon and roast whole, pan-fry, grill, or braise. **FLAVOUR PAIRINGS** Bacon, ham, celery, shallots, watercress, wild mushrooms, game chips, bread sauce, buttered crumbs, orange, honey, juniper berries, redcurrants, cranberries, whisky, wine. **IN SEASON** 12 August–10 December (30 November in Northern Ireland)

▲ Partridge

EAT Sold whole. Roast (bard with bacon first), pan-fry, grill, braise. Allow 1 bird per person. **FLAVOUR PAIRINGS** Bacon, cream, cabbage, watercress, lentils, shallots, wild mushrooms, grapes, lemon, pears, quinces, redcurrants, chestnuts, walnuts, turnips, kohl rabi, juniper berries, sage, chocolate, wine. **IN SEASON** 1 September–1 February (31 January in Northern Ireland)

▲ Woodcock

EAT Available whole. Roast boned and stuffed, or whole; spatchcock to grill or pan-fry. It is traditionally roasted undrawn, with the beaked head pushed into the body to truss it, usually served on a fried or toasted croûte. Allow 1 bird per person. **FLAVOUR PAIRINGS** Butter, bacon, cream, shallots, garlic, watercress, ginger, bay leaf, parsley, thyme, nutmeg, lemon, apples, grapes, soy sauce, Madeira. **IN SEASON** 1 October–31 January

▲ Quail

EAT Available whole. Bard with bacon and roast, halve or spatchcock to grill, pan-fry, or braise. Allow 1 or 2 birds per person. **FLAVOUR PAIRINGS** Bacon, butter, cream, peppers, mushrooms, truffle, quinces, grapes, cherries, prunes, almonds, honey, cumin, cinnamon, brandy, white and red wine. **IN SEASON** Farmed all year

◄ Pheasant

EAT Traditionally sold as a brace (cock and hen). Available whole, and boned breasts sold separately. Roast whole (bard with bacon first), braise, or casserole. Pan-fry or grill breasts. Allow 1 bird for 2–3 people, or 1 breast per person. **FLAVOUR PAIRINGS** Bacon, cream, celery, onions, cabbage, apples, quinces, bitter oranges, prunes, walnuts, beetroot, Jerusalem artichokes, game chips, bread sauce, buttered crumbs, Calvados, brandy, red wine, port, cider. **IN SEASON** 1 October–1 February (31 January in Northern Ireland)

Teal ▶

EAT The smallest wild duck. One bird will only give a small portion but the flavour is worth it. Roast quickly (serve slightly pink), braise, or casserole. **FLAVOUR PAIRINGS** Apples, bitter oranges, sage, thyme, white wine, peas, onions and lettuce (for braising), cider, spring onions, hoisin and plum sauce, soy sauce, ginger, garlic. **IN SEASON** 1 September–31 January

▲ Wood pigeon

EAT Pigeons and squabs (farmed birds) are sold whole, as crowns, or as boned breasts. Allow 1 bird or 2–3 breasts per person. Stew, casserole, or cook in pies. Quickly roast young birds. Pan-fry or grill breasts (serve pink). **FLAVOUR PAIRINGS** Bacon, cream, red cabbage, mushrooms, spinach, chilli, garlic, orange, redcurrants, blueberries, juniper berries, chocolate, honey, soy sauce, red wine. **IN SEASON** All year (best February–May)

▲ Mallard

EAT Sold whole or as pairs of breasts. Grill or fry breasts (cook rare), and thinly slice to serve. Roast whole young birds. Braise, stew, or casserole older ones. Allow 1 breast or 1 bird between 2–3 people. **FLAVOUR PAIRINGS** Ginger, garlic, mushrooms, onions, coriander leaf, parsley, sage, apples, bitter oranges, plums, cherries, redcurrants, cider, red wine, soy sauce. **IN SEASON** 1 September–31 January

Joint a chicken

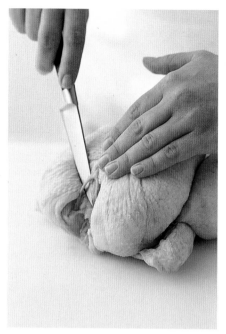

1 To remove the wishbone, scrape the flesh away from it, using a sharp knife, then twist it with your fingers and discard.

2 With the chicken breast-side up on a board, use a sharp knife to cut through the thigh joint and separate the leg from the rest of the bird.

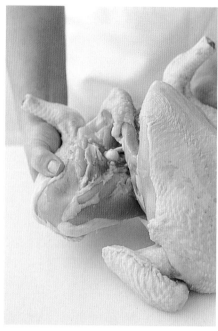

3 Now pull the leg back to dislocate the leg joint. You should hear a distinct popping sound when the ball separates from the socket.

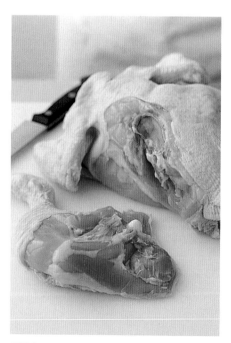

4 If there is any skin or meat still attached to the bird's body, use your knife to free it. Repeat steps 2 and 3 to remove the other leg.

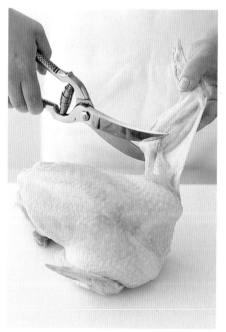

5 Pull the wing straight, then cut through the middle joint with poultry shears to remove the winglet. Repeat for the other winglet.

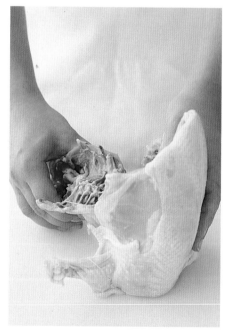

6 Now grasp the backbone with your hands and firmly pull it away from the upper part of the body (the 2 breasts and wings).

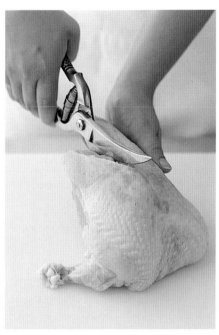

7 To remove the lower end of the backbone, use poultry shears to cut it away from the remaining body.

8 Starting at the neck, use poultry shears to cut all the way through the backbone to separate the breasts.

9 The chicken is now cut into 4 pieces. Any leftover bones (such as the backbone) can be used to make chicken stock.

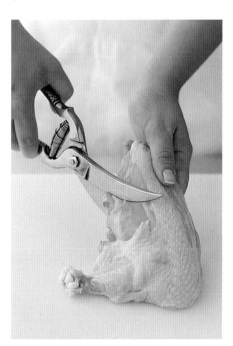

10 Use poultry shears to cut each breast in half diagonally, producing one wing and one breast. Repeat to separate the other breast.

11 Cut each leg through the knee joint (above the drumstick) that connects to the thigh, and cut through to separate.

12 Now, there are two drumsticks, 2 thighs, 2 wings, and 2 breasts. The chicken is divided into 8 pieces.

Bone a chicken breast

1 Working from the widest end of the breast (the wing), use sharp poultry shears to cut away the backbone and ribs.

2 Now use a sharp knife to cut the meat away from the bone. To create a neat fillet, carefully follow the shape of the breastbone.

3 There will be a small inner fillet on the underside of the breast. To remove it, cut away any connecting membrane.

Bone a leg

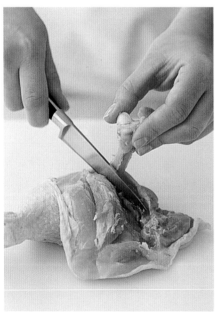

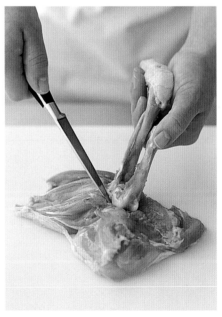

1 Place the leg skin-side down on a board. Using a sharp knife, cut the flesh away from the start of the thigh bone and work down.

2 Using the same technique, start from the knuckle and cut all the way down the length of the drumstick.

3 Lift the bones up from the central knuckle joint. Then using short strokes with the tip of your knife, remove the 2 bones from the flesh.

Bone a thigh

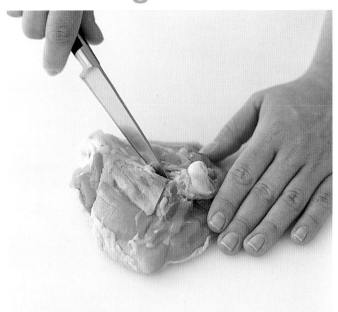

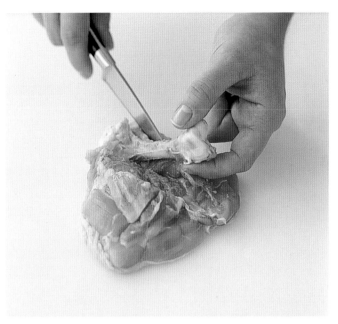

1 Place the thigh skin-side down on a cutting board. Using a small, sharp knife, pierce the flesh at one end of the thigh bone and carefully cut away the flesh to expose it.

2 Make another small incision through the flesh, following the contour of the exposed bone. Cut around the bone to cut it completely free from the flesh and discard, or use for stock.

Bone a drumstick

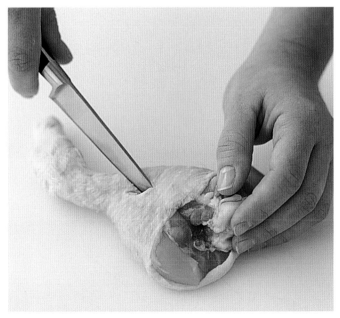

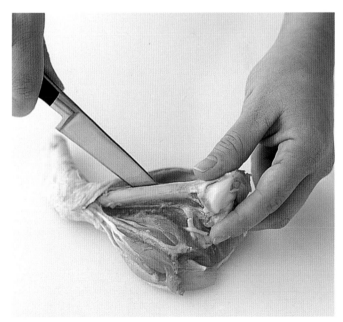

1 Holding the drumstick steady, and starting in the middle of the drumstick, insert the tip of your knife until you locate the bone. Slice along the bone in both directions to expose it fully.

2 Open the flesh out and using short strokes to minimize tearing, neatly cut around the bone to free it completely from the flesh and discard, or use for stock.

Spatchcock a bird for grilling

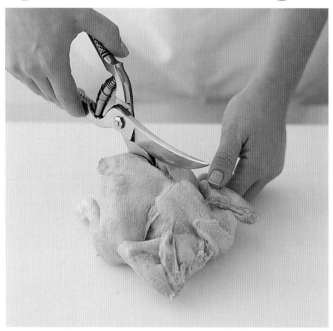

1 Place the bird upside down. Cut along one side of the backbone using sharp poultry shears, then do the same along the other side, and take out the backbone. Open out the two halves and turn the bird over.

2 Press down on the bird with both hands to flatten it out to a more uniform thickness. This will help both to tenderize the meat and make sure that it cooks more evenly.

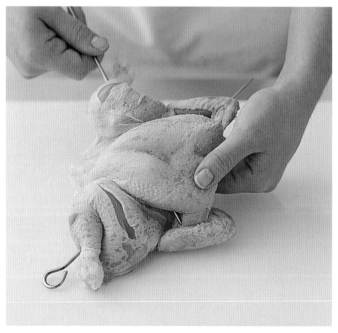

3 Once flattened out, use a sharp knife to cut a few slashes into the legs and thighs. This will help the heat to penetrate the dense flesh of the thigh and leg meat more thoroughly.

4 Push a metal skewer through the right leg to the left wing, and another one through the left leg to the right wing, to form an "X" shape. The spatchcocked bird can now be marinated before being grilled or roasted.

Deep-fry chicken

1 Cream butter and herbs or other flavourings according to your chosen recipe. Shape into a block, wrap in foil and freeze.

2 Flatten the chicken breasts by placing each one between 2 sheets of cling film before flattening out gently with a rolling pin.

3 Divide the butter into 4 pieces and put one in the centre of each flattened chicken breast. Roll the escalope tightly around the butter.

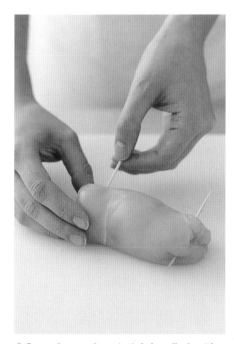

4 Once the escalope is tightly rolled, with no butter mixture showing, secure it at each end with a cocktail stick.

5 Coat the chicken in lightly beaten egg, then roll the meat in breadcrumbs and leave the coated parcels to set in the refrigerator.

6 In a deep-frying pan, heat some sunflower or vegetable oil to 190°C (375°F). Fry the chicken for about 10 minutes, until golden.

Stuff a chicken breast

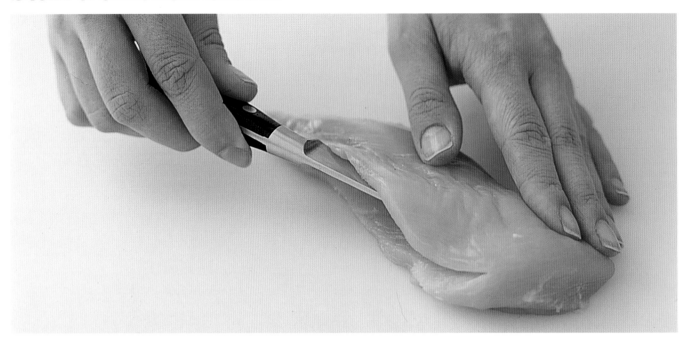

1 With one hand lightly pressing on the chicken breast to keep it in place, use a sharp knife to cut a pocket about 4cm (1½in) deep in the side of the breast fillet. Take care not to pierce the flesh all the way through to the other side.

2 Holding back one side of the chicken breast, press the stuffing from your chosen recipe into the pocket. Do this firmly, but take care not to overfill, then roll the flesh back so that it closes over the stuffing neatly.

Bread and fry poultry or meat escalopes

1 Place each fillet between 2 pieces of cling film, then pound them with a rolling pin (without too much pressure on any one point) until the fillets have increased in area and reached an even thickness.

2 Remove the cling film and season the fillets to taste with salt, pepper, and freshly chopped herbs. Dip the seasoned fillets into beaten egg, coating each side evenly.

3 Turn the fillets in breadcrumbs, pressing an even coat to both sides. Repeat the process with the remaining fillets and cook immediately, or cover, and leave to set in the refrigerator for 10–15 minutes.

4 Heat 1cm (½in) of oil in a frying pan until hot and fry the fillets for 4–5 minutes on each side until cooked through (test with a sharp knife to ensure that there are no pink juices). Drain on kitchen paper.

Marinate chicken

1 Mix the marinade ingredients in a bowl. In another bowl large enough to hold the chicken in a single layer, coat the chicken with the marinade. Cover the bowl and chill in the refrigerator for a minimum of 1 hour.

2 Dry-marinating, which involves no liquid, is an extension of the process of seasoning poultry. The mixture should be left on the bird for at least 1 hour for it to penetrate the meat more than just skin-deep.

Rest, carve, and portion

1 Allow the cooked chicken to rest in a warm place for 15 minutes, covered with foil. This allows the juices to flow throughout the bird and helps to keep the meat moist.

2 Transfer the bird to a cutting board, breast-side up. Remove the legs by cutting the skin between the leg and the body and pushing the blade down to where the leg bone joins the body.

3 Work the blade from side to side a little to loosen the joint, then with a slight sawing motion, push the blade through the joint, cutting the leg free. Transfer the leg to a warmed plate and repeat with the other leg.

4 Remove a breast by cutting as if you are dividing the bird in half, just to one side of the breastbone. As the blade hits the bone, cut along the bone to remove all the meat. Repeat on the other side.

5 Place one breast cut-side down on the cutting board. Using horizontal strokes, slice the breast into as many pieces as possible, leaving the wing with a section of breast meat attached.

6 Carve each leg by cutting it in half through the joint at the midway point. You shouldn't need to cut through any bone. As you reach the joint, work the blade into the joint to separate the pieces.

Beef

BUY Best-quality beef indicates its origin and breed. Dark red meat will have been matured (3–4 weeks) so should be more tender with good flavour. Muscle meat that is marbled with fat cooks and tastes best, but avoid excessive fat round the edge. **STORE** Keep on the bottom shelf of the refrigerator, well-wrapped on a plate to catch any drips, joints and steaks up to 3 days, and mince and offal for no more than 2 days. Freeze joints and steaks for up to 12 months, stewing or braising meat 8 months, mince 3 months. **IN SEASON** All year.

Sirloin joint ▶

EAT The finest joint, when sold on the bone, it can include the eye of the fillet the other side of the bone (like T-bone steak). Also sold boned and rolled. Roast. **FLAVOUR PAIRINGS** English mustard, horseradish, Yorkshire puddings, parsnips and other root vegetables.

▲ Fillet steak

EAT Very lean and tender, but less flavour than sirloin or rump. Roast whole, wrap in pastry (Beef Wellington), or slice into thick steaks and grill or pan-fry. Serve raw as carpaccio and steak tartare. **FLAVOUR PAIRINGS** Any of the other steak flavourings, liver pâté, oysters (stuff with before grilling), port sauce, soy sauce, oyster sauce, ginger, Cajun spices, garlic.

▲ Sirloin steak

EAT Tender, well-flavoured, marbled with fat, and best well matured. Grill or pan-fry. **FLAVOUR PAIRINGS** Peppers, onions, olives, savoury butters (see T-bone), green or black peppercorn sauce, béarnaise sauce.

◀ T-bone steak

EAT Thick slice of sirloin cut down through the bone, hence the "T" shape, with sirloin one side and fillet the other. Grill or pan-fry. **FLAVOUR PAIRINGS** Savoury butters – anchovy, parsley, mixed herb and garlic, oregano, chilli.

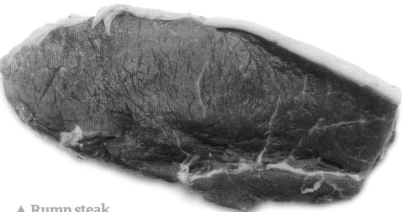

▲ Rump steak

EAT Best well matured to tenderize. Excellent flavour, thick and juicy. Try marinating in red wine and herbs. **FLAVOUR PAIRINGS** Fried onions, potato chips, mushrooms, French mustard, red wine sauce.

▲ Chuck or shoulder

EAT Can be sold as a joint but usually diced as stewing steak, or minced. Stew, curry, casserole, braise. Cook ox liver or heart in the same way. **FLAVOUR PAIRINGS** Onions, garlic, tomatoes, mushrooms, aubergines, carrots, celery, Indian curry spices, Thai red curry paste, star anise, chilli, cinnamon, ginger.

▲ Silverside

EAT Less expensive joint. Roast, pot-roast, or stew with carrots (boiled beef and carrots). Also sold salted. **FLAVOUR PAIRINGS** Mustard, carrots, parsnips, onion, red wine, cinnamon, olives, tomatoes.

▲ Brisket

EAT Inexpensive joint, full of flavour, that needs long slow cooking. Trim excess fat before cooking. Also sold salted. **FLAVOUR PAIRINGS** Mustard, root vegetables, mushrooms, bay leaf, bouquet garni, rosemary, thyme, parsley.

◄ Oxtail

EAT Cook long and slow until meltingly tender for soups or stews. Best cooled quickly, chilled overnight, then fat removed before re-heating. Look out for other beef offal; ox heart, liver, tripe, tongue, and kidney. **FLAVOUR PAIRINGS** Bacon, celery, parsnip, carrot, swede, onions, nutmeg, cumin, allspice, mustard, red wine, brown ale, soy sauce.

Lamb and mutton

BUY Lambs are animals up to 1 year old. Hoggets are 1–2 year old sheep. Older animals are known as mutton. Native lamb increases in size through the year; imported meat, which arrives fresh or frozen, can be any size. Lamb should have just a thin covering of hard white fat. Trim the excess before cooking. Young lamb is the most tender, mutton has the best flavour. **STORE** Keep wrapped, on a plate to catch any drips, in the bottom of the fridge for up to 3 days. Freeze joints and chops up to 12 months, diced meat 8 months, mince 3 months. **IN SEASON** May–September, imported all year.

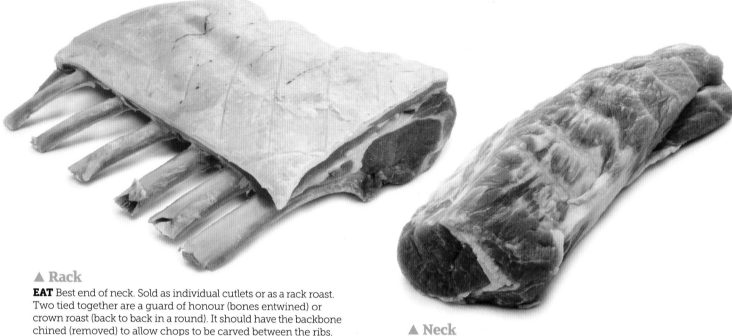

▲ Rack

EAT Best end of neck. Sold as individual cutlets or as a rack roast. Two tied together are a guard of honour (bones entwined) or crown roast (back to back in a round). It should have the backbone chined (removed) to allow chops to be carved between the ribs. Allow 2–3 chops per person (depending on size). Roast with or without a crust (try breadcrumbs, olives, and herbs); serve pink. **FLAVOUR PAIRINGS** Garlic, rosemary, mint, honey, olives, harissa paste, aubergines, yogurt, baby spring vegetables.

▲ Neck

EAT Trim sinews before cooking. Quickly roast whole, or cut in slices and pan-fry very quickly. **FLAVOUR PAIRINGS** Mint, oregano, garlic, cinnamon, star anise, dried fruit, haricot beans, spring onions, dill, lemon.

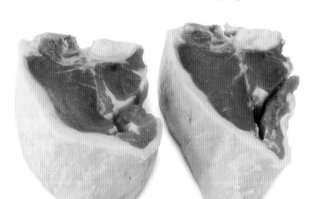

▲ Loin chops

EAT Double loin chops (pictured) have fillet one side of the bone and loin the other (like T-bone steak). Pan-fry, grill, braise, or roast. **FLAVOUR PAIRINGS** Mint jelly, tomatoes, onions, garlic, oregano.

▲ Noisettes

EAT Boned and tied loin chops are very tender. Grill, pan-fry, or roast. **FLAVOUR PAIRINGS** Red wine, port, redcurrants, rosemary, lemon, garlic.

Leg ▶

EAT Whole or half. Roast or slow-roast. Try rubbing with paprika, dried oregano, garlic, and seasoning before cooking. Also available as steaks to grill or pan-fry.
FLAVOUR PAIRINGS Garlic, oregano and potatoes (Greek-style slow-roast), mint sauce/jelly, redcurrant jelly, roast onions or leeks, onion sauce, celery, carrots, paprika, flageolet beans.

▲ Kidney

EAT Remove outer membrane, halve, snip out white core with scissors. Sauté or grill and serve in a sauce (don't overcook), braise or add to hotpots. Slice liver and cook the same way. **FLAVOUR PAIRINGS** Cream, shallots, mushrooms, lemon, brandy, sherry, mustard, Worcestershire sauce, tomatoes, sausages, bacon.

Shank ▶

EAT Shanks need long slow cooking, so braise or casserole. Lamb's hearts can be cooked the same way.
FLAVOUR PAIRINGS Turnips, carrots, celery, leeks, tomato purée, redcurrant or mint jelly, white, red, or rosé wine.

◀ Mutton shoulder

EAT Mutton shoulder is usually simmered (known as boiled), or diced for curries, stews, and casseroles. Lamb shoulder is roasted, or diced or minced and used the same way.
FLAVOUR PAIRINGS Caper or onion sauce (boiled mutton), turnips, carrots, leeks, yogurt, aubergines, cinnamon, apricots, prunes, raisins, curry spices, oregano, mint, rosemary, pearl barley.

Pork

BUY Choose outdoor-reared pork for best flavour and on welfare grounds. All pork should be pink (pale or more deeply coloured, depending on the cut), not grey or red. The fat should be soft and white. The whole animal commercially roasted – hog roast – is now popular for parties and festivals. **STORE** Keep wrapped, on a plate to catch any drips, in the bottom of the refrigerator, for up to 3 days. Freeze joints, chops, and steaks up to 9 months, diced meat and belly slices 4 months, mince 3 months.

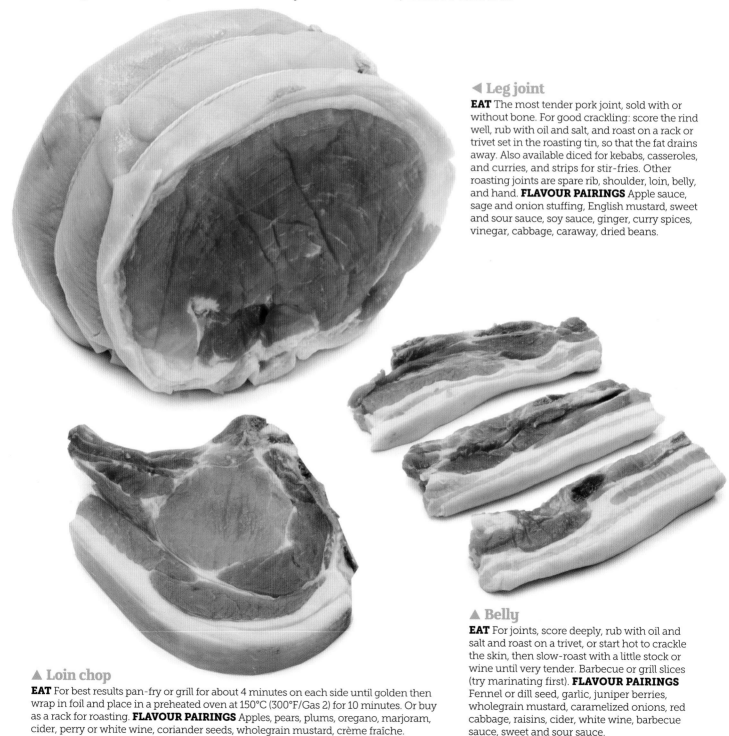

◄ Leg joint

EAT The most tender pork joint, sold with or without bone. For good crackling: score the rind well, rub with oil and salt, and roast on a rack or trivet set in the roasting tin, so that the fat drains away. Also available diced for kebabs, casseroles, and curries, and strips for stir-fries. Other roasting joints are spare rib, shoulder, loin, belly, and hand. **FLAVOUR PAIRINGS** Apple sauce, sage and onion stuffing, English mustard, sweet and sour sauce, soy sauce, ginger, curry spices, vinegar, cabbage, caraway, dried beans.

▲ Belly

EAT For joints, score deeply, rub with oil and salt and roast on a trivet, or start hot to crackle the skin, then slow-roast with a little stock or wine until very tender. Barbecue or grill slices (try marinating first). **FLAVOUR PAIRINGS** Fennel or dill seed, garlic, juniper berries, wholegrain mustard, caramelized onions, red cabbage, raisins, cider, white wine, barbecue sauce, sweet and sour sauce.

▲ Loin chop

EAT For best results pan-fry or grill for about 4 minutes on each side until golden then wrap in foil and place in a preheated oven at 150°C (300°F/Gas 2) for 10 minutes. Or buy as a rack for roasting. **FLAVOUR PAIRINGS** Apples, pears, plums, oregano, marjoram, cider, perry or white wine, coriander seeds, wholegrain mustard, crème fraîche.

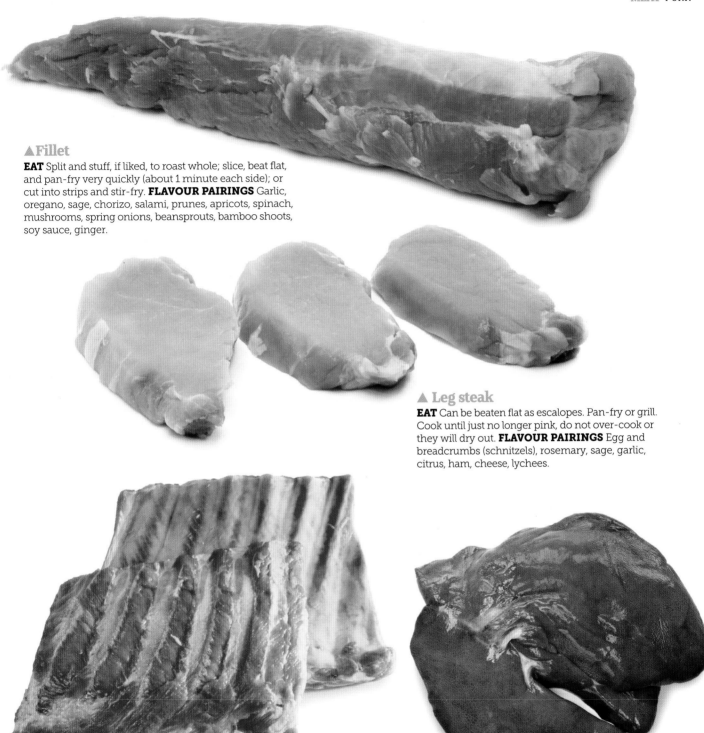

▲Fillet

EAT Split and stuff, if liked, to roast whole; slice, beat flat, and pan-fry very quickly (about 1 minute each side); or cut into strips and stir-fry. **FLAVOUR PAIRINGS** Garlic, oregano, sage, chorizo, salami, prunes, apricots, spinach, mushrooms, spring onions, beansprouts, bamboo shoots, soy sauce, ginger.

▲ Leg steak

EAT Can be beaten flat as escalopes. Pan-fry or grill. Cook until just no longer pink, do not over-cook or they will dry out. **FLAVOUR PAIRINGS** Egg and breadcrumbs (schnitzels), rosemary, sage, garlic, citrus, ham, cheese, lychees.

▲ Ribs

EAT Chinese ribs are the trimmed ribs, sold as a rack or individually cut. Do not confuse with spare rib joints or chops. **FLAVOUR PAIRINGS** Barbecue sauce, chilli, soy sauce, honey, citrus, pineapple, Worcestershire sauce, tomatoes, Chinese five-spice powder.

▲ Liver

EAT Soak in milk to remove its strong taste before frying. Braise, casserole, use in pâtés and terrines. Look out for kidneys, cheeks, ears, and trotters to braise, too. **FLAVOUR PAIRINGS** Sage, onions, bacon, juniper berries, hazelnuts, watercress, brandy, mushrooms, red wine, cider, root vegetables.

Goat, rabbit, venison, and veal

BUY All these meats are lower in fat than the others. Rose veal is from calves reared with their mothers, with access to grass and grain. Avoid white veal; these calves are reared solely on milk, a practice which is now highly frowned upon. Either should be lean, pale-coloured, and firm. Goat is interchangeable with lamb. Young goat is called kid. Venison is farmed all year, but several species are shot in the wild during the hunting season (the dates are different in each country of the UK, by species and for bucks or does). Rabbit is also farmed but wild rabbit is becoming widely available too. **STORE** Keep wrapped, on a plate to catch any drips, at the bottom of the refrigerator. Use within 2–3 days. Freeze veal, goat, or venison joints up to 12 months, steaks, chops, or diced meat up to 8 months, rabbit for up to 6 months and mince up to 3 months. **IN SEASON** All year, except wild venison (available July–April) and wild rabbit (July–December).

GOAT

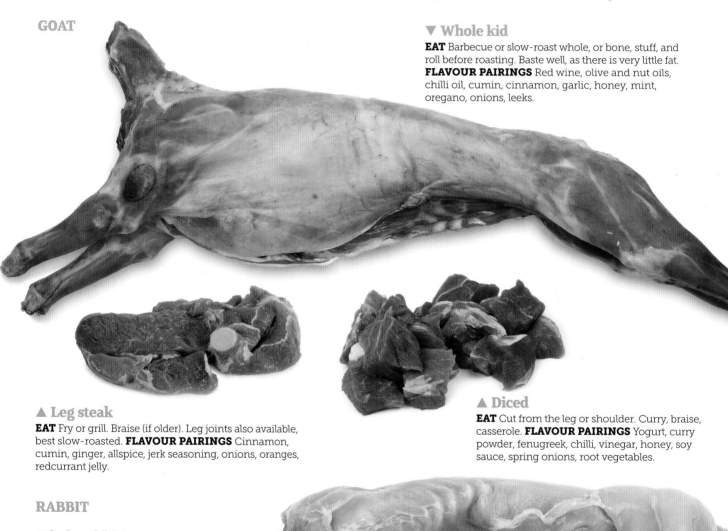

▼ Whole kid

EAT Barbecue or slow-roast whole, or bone, stuff, and roll before roasting. Baste well, as there is very little fat. **FLAVOUR PAIRINGS** Red wine, olive and nut oils, chilli oil, cumin, cinnamon, garlic, honey, mint, oregano, onions, leeks.

▲ Leg steak

EAT Fry or grill. Braise (if older). Leg joints also available, best slow-roasted. **FLAVOUR PAIRINGS** Cinnamon, cumin, ginger, allspice, jerk seasoning, onions, oranges, redcurrant jelly.

▲ Diced

EAT Cut from the leg or shoulder. Curry, braise, casserole. **FLAVOUR PAIRINGS** Yogurt, curry powder, fenugreek, chilli, vinegar, honey, soy sauce, spring onions, root vegetables.

RABBIT

Whole rabbit ▶

EAT Usually jointed into 5 or 6 pieces before cooking. The saddle and legs are the best parts. Grill, roast, braise, stew, cook in a pie. **FLAVOUR PAIRINGS** Bacon, carrots, fennel, celery, sweetcorn, mushrooms, tomatoes, olives, coriander leaf, parsley, rosemary, thyme, lemon, prunes, mustard, soy sauce, cider, white wine.

VENISON

▲ Rolled haunch

EAT Haunches from smaller deer may be roasted whole, or boned, or sliced into steaks. Large haunches can be left on the bone but are usually parted into individual muscles, rolled, and tied. Roast (cook pink), braise. **FLAVOUR PAIRINGS** Guinness, red wine, port, redcurrant jelly, prunes, juniper berries, bay leaf, thyme, cream, chanterelle mushrooms.

▲ Fillet or tenderloin

EAT The boned out saddle (back) yields the fillet and the loin. They are often confused, but the loin is thicker so takes longer to cook. Roast or braise whole. Pan-fry, grill, or barbecue steaks. **FLAVOUR PAIRINGS** Bacon, pears, cream, fennel, red cabbage, pomegranate, berries, pine nuts, red wine, vermouth.

VEAL

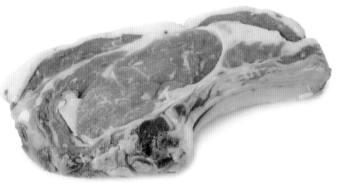

▲ Osso buco

EAT Thick slices of shin/shank become meltingly tender when slow-cooked. The marrow from the bone enriches the sauce, or is eaten with a teaspoon. **FLAVOUR PAIRINGS** Tomatoes, white wine, gremolata (chopped parsley, garlic, anchovy fillets, and lemon zest), Risotto alla milanese.

▲ Loin chop

EAT Similar to a T-bone steak and still a large chop. Grill or fry. **FLAVOUR PAIRINGS** Tarragon or parsley butter, garlic, rosemary, sage, white wine, cream, brandy, lemon, shallots.

◀ Escalope

EAT This leg cut is beaten flat and either rolled round a filling before frying or braising, or coated in egg and breadcrumbs (wiener schnitzel) and pan-fried. The leg (and shoulder) can also be diced. **FLAVOUR PAIRINGS** Egg and breadcrumbs, Parmesan, melting cheeses, ham, cream, mushrooms, sorrel, spinach, gherkins, capers, tomato sauce, potato salad.

Veal, venison, and rabbit essentials

Use this chart to identify the best way to cook the most popular cuts of veal, venison, and rabbit.

Meat cooking chart

VEAL	DESCRIPTION	GRILL/BARBECUE
Sirloin/Loin	Also called fillet or chump end. Prime roasting joint, bone-in, or boneless. Loin chops are a popular veal cut.	Preheat grill or barbecue. Chops: brush with melted butter or oil. Grill or barbecue 2–3 minutes each side for pink, 5–6 minutes for well-done.
Leg	Topside (cushion) is a prime roasting joint. Thick steaks are cut from the topside or rump. Thin slices, beaten flat, are escalopes. Tender, lean, diced leg is good for kebabs or quick casseroles.	Preheat grill or barbecue. Leg steaks: grill or barbecue as loin chops. Escalopes: brush with oil, season, grill or barbecue 2 minutes each side. Diced leg: marinate first, if liked. Thread on kebab skewers, grill, or barbecue 6–8 minutes, turning frequently.
Fillet	Lean and very tender cooked whole or in steaks.	Grill or barbecue fillet steak as loin chop.
VENISON		
Haunch (back leg)	From small deer it may be the whole leg. From larger ones, usually cut in smaller joints and rolled, or cut in pavés or steaks, or diced.	From young deer only. Preheat grill or barbecue. Steaks: brush with oil or melted butter. Brown both sides quickly. Grill 1½ minutes on each side (rare), 2 minutes on each side (medium). Wrap in foil and leave in a warm place to rest for 5 minutes. Do not overcook or will become tough. Diced meat: marinate first. Thread on skewers. Grill 3–4 minutes, turning occasionally.
Fillet or Tenderloin/ Loin	Whole or steaks.	Grill or barbecue loin steaks as for haunch steaks.
Saddle	Highly prized back joint of fillets and loins jointed by backbone.	Not recommended.
Mince	Lean trimmings with fat and sinew removed before mincing.	Preheat grill or barbecue. Press well-seasoned mince on oiled skewers, or form burgers. Brush with oil, grill or barbecue 8–10 minutes, turning once or twice until no longer pink.
RABBIT		
Whole, Jointed	Wild rabbits usually sold whole. Females and small males make best eating. Farmed also sold jointed.	Joints from young wild, or farmed rabbits. Marinate first. Preheat grill or barbecue. Cook for 8–10 minutes, turning occasionally.

FRY	ROAST	BRAISE/STEW/CASSEROLE
Fry in butter (or butter and oil) for 2–3 minutes each side for pink, 5–6 minutes for well-done.	Brush with oil. Season with pepper. Roast at 200°C (400°F/Gas 6) for 20 minutes per 450g (1lb) plus 20 minutes for pink, 30 minutes per lb plus 30 minutes for well done. Rest 10–15 minutes.	Chops: brown on both sides. Add browned vegetables, liquid, and flavourings. Cover and cook at 180°C (350°F/Gas 4) for 1½–2 hours, joints for the same.
Escalopes: egg and crumb, stuff and roll, sandwich in pairs with filling, or coat in batter. Fry in oil (or butter and oil) for 3 minutes each side. If uncoated, fry 2 minutes each side. Diced meat: fry 5 minutes, stirring and turning.	Cook as loin for 20 minutes per 450g (1lb) plus 20 minutes for pink, 30 minutes per lb plus 30 minutes for well done. Rest 10–15 minutes.	Cook thick steaks, cubes, or whole joints as for sirloin/loin. Steaks: cook for 1 hour. Diced leg: cook for 1–1½ hours. Joints: cook for 1½–2 hours.
Fry fillet steak as loin chop.	Roast whole fillet as loin but for 15 minutes per 450g (1lb) plus 15 minutes for pink, 25 minutes per 450g (1lb) plus 25 minutes for well-done.	Braise fillet steaks as leg steaks; whole fillets as diced leg.
From young deer only. Steaks: fry quickly in butter (or butter and oil) 1 minute each side (rare), 2 minutes each side (medium) then wrap in foil and finish in a low oven 150°C (300°F/Gas 2) for 10 minutes. Diced meat: fry quickly in butter (or butter and oil) for 3 minutes, stirring. Remove and make sauce.	From young deer only. For pink meat: measure diameter of rolled haunch. Preheat oven to 230°C (450°F/Gas 8). Brown 2½ minutes per 1cm (½in) then reduce heat to 110°C (225°F/Gas ¼). Roast for 3 minutes per 1cm (½in) then rest for 3 minutes per 1cm (½in).	Bone-in and boneless joints (young deer): brown meat, add vegetables, liquid, and flavourings. Cook at 190°C/375°F/Gas 5 for 1½–2 hours. Steaks: cook as joints for 1½ hours. Diced meat: cook at 160°C (325°F/Gas 3) for 1½ hours. Joints and steaks (older deer): cook at 180°C (350°F/Gas 4) for 2–3 hours.
Fry steaks as for haunch.	Roast loin joint as for haunch joint.	Cook as for haunch joint from young deer.
Not recommended.	Roast as haunch joint.	Cook as haunch from young deer.
Fry meatballs or burgers in hot oil (or butter and oil) for 8–10 minutes, until cooked through, turning once or twice.	Not recommended.	Brown mince and vegetables. Add liquid and flavourings. Cover and cook at 160°C (325°F/Gas 3) for 1½–2 hours.
Not recommended.	Joints from young wild, or farmed rabbits. Marinate first. Roast in a preheated oven at 200°C (400°F/Gas 6) for 25–30 minutes, basting occasionally.	Young wild or farmed rabbits: brown all over in hot oil or butter and oil. Add vegetables, liquid, and flavourings. Cook at 160°C (325°F/Gas 3) for 1–1½ hours. Older wild rabbits: cook at 150°C (300°F/Gas 2) for 2 hours until tender.

Cured and air-dried meats

BUY There are hundreds of cured and air-dried meats, made using a wide variety of cuts and techniques: these are the most common ones used in cooking. Sold by weight, from delicatessens, butchers, and supermarkets, most are also available pre-packed. **STORE** Unopened packs will keep several weeks (check sell-by date) in the refrigerator; unpackaged or opened packs should be eaten within a week.

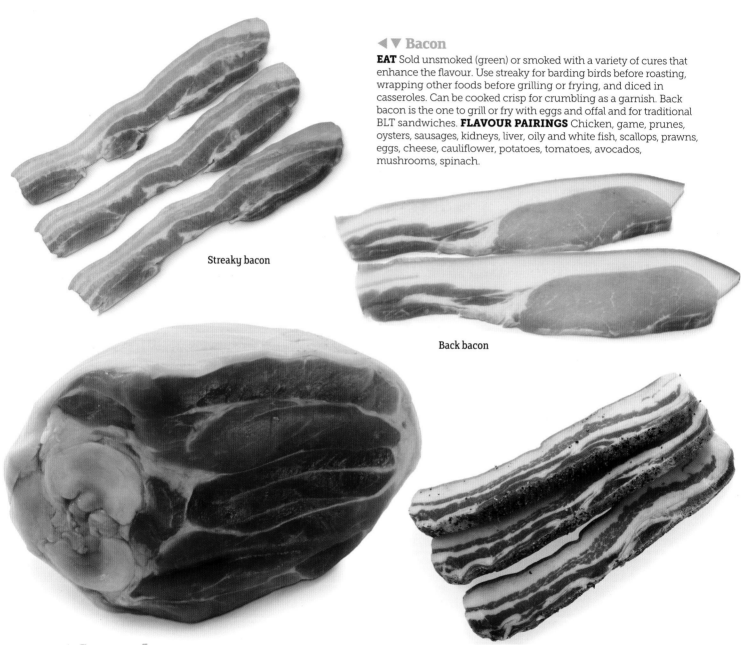

◄▼ Bacon

EAT Sold unsmoked (green) or smoked with a variety of cures that enhance the flavour. Use streaky for barding birds before roasting, wrapping other foods before grilling or frying, and diced in casseroles. Can be cooked crisp for crumbling as a garnish. Back bacon is the one to grill or fry with eggs and offal and for traditional BLT sandwiches. **FLAVOUR PAIRINGS** Chicken, game, prunes, oysters, sausages, kidneys, liver, oily and white fish, scallops, prawns, eggs, cheese, cauliflower, potatoes, tomatoes, avocados, mushrooms, spinach.

Streaky bacon

Back bacon

▲ Gammon/ham

EAT Available smoked or unsmoked, raw as steaks, or thick rashers to fry or grill, or as joints (with or without the bone) to boil or roast. Heavily salted joints should be soaked in several changes of cold water before cooking. It is also sold cooked ready to eat, hot or cold. **FLAVOUR PAIRINGS** Pineapple, dried fruits, mustard, cloves, honey, onion, bay leaf, parsley sauce, butter beans, carrots, tomatoes, eggs, cheeses.

▲ Pancetta

EAT Use in pasta sauces, casseroles, risottos, and soups, to top pizzas, and to wrap fish and poultry before grilling or pan-frying. Thinly sliced rolled pancetta can be served as an antipasto. **FLAVOUR PAIRINGS** Cheeses, asparagus, tomatoes, chillies, sweet peppers, bacon, chicken, game birds, meaty white fish, onions, garlic, eggs, cream, white beans.

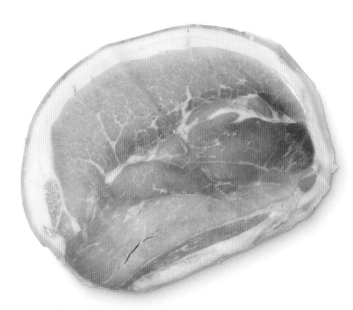

▲ Jambon de Paris

EAT Also known as jambon blanc, the common French brine-cured boneless ham is usually sold already boiled. It is the favourite cooked ham in France for quick meals and sandwiches. **FLAVOUR PAIRINGS** French and wholegrain mustards, Gruyère, chips, buckwheat crêpes, eggs, tomatoes.

▲ Prosciutto crudo

EAT The most widely known of the dry-cured hams. There are many regional cures, including the famous Parma, considered to be the best, and San Daniele from Friuli. Usually sold very thinly sliced. Serve as an antipasto, in sandwiches, salads or added at the last minute to cooked dishes. Use to wrap fish or meat before grilling, pan-frying, or baking. **FLAVOUR PAIRINGS** Parmesan, mozzarella, gherkins, figs, melon, asparagus, tomatoes, olives.

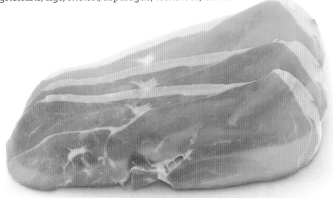

▲ Jamón serrano

EAT Meaning "mountain ham" in Spanish, these salted and air-cured hams have many regional variations. They have a sweet, rich flavour and chewy texture. Eat in tapas or like prosciutto crudo. **FLAVOUR PAIRINGS** Olives, gherkins, Manchego cheese, figs, rustic bread, nutmeg, eggs, red wine.

▲ Bresaola

EAT To make this well-known antipasto, boned beef from the hind leg is salted and flavoured with juniper berries and herbs for a few days, then air-dried. Valtellina in the Italian Alps is the centre of production. **FLAVOUR PAIRINGS** Olive oil, tomatoes, Parmesan, gherkins, olives, celeriac remoulade, rocket, mozzarella, rustic bread.

▲ Jamón ibérico

EAT A highly esteemed Spanish ham from black Iberian pigs, it is salted then air-dried for 1–2 years. The best comes from pigs grazed in the native oak forests, to produce wonderfully flavoured meat. Best enjoyed raw. **FLAVOUR PAIRINGS** Fino sherry (chilled), rustic bread, asparagus, scrambled eggs, baby broad beans, melon, figs, tomato and garlic bread (pan con tomate).

Sausages

BUY There are hundreds of sausages made in the world, some fresh, some cooked, and some semi-dried. Here is a selection, readily available and popular with chefs. Fresh are usually bought whole. Cooked and dried, or semi-dried are available whole or sliced. Fresh and cooked should be moist and smell pleasant. Dried may have a strong but not unpleasant smell, and the white powder on the exterior improves the flavour.
STORE Wrap or leave in the packaging in the refrigerator. Use fresh within a few days, and cooked within a week. Dried and semi-dried will keep a long time (whole sausages don't need refrigerating; they can be hung in a cool, dry place). Fresh and cooked sausages can be frozen for up to 2 months.

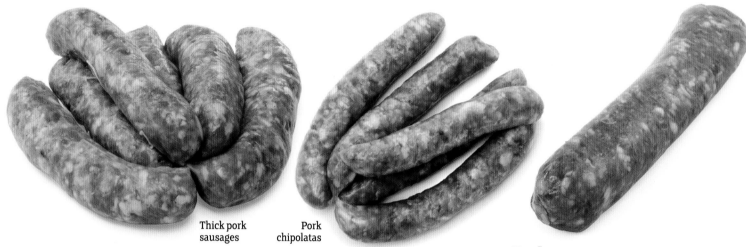

Thick pork sausages

Pork chipolatas

▲ Pork sausage

EAT The traditional British banger available plain, well-seasoned, with herbs, spices, or other flavourings, as either thick sausages or thinner chipolatas. They must contain at least 42 per cent pork but the higher the meat content, the better quality the sausage. They can be made of other meats, such as lamb or venison. Dry-fry, grill, barbecue, bake, casserole. **FLAVOUR PAIRINGS** Potatoes, white beans, onions, apples, sage, mustard, tomato ketchup, cider, cabbage, tomatoes, mushrooms, Yorkshire pudding.

▲ Toulouse sausage

EAT Made from pork shoulder and belly, this coarse-textured sausage is one of the classic ingredients of cassoulet. Casserole, grill, fry. **FLAVOUR PAIRINGS** White beans, belly pork, duck confit, celery, onions, tomatoes, garlic, cloves, bay leaf, flat leaf parsley.

▲ Cumberland sausage

EAT Sold in a continuous coil, Cumberland sausage has a high chopped pork content, which gives it a firm, dense, meaty texture. Fry, grill, or barbecue. **FLAVOUR PAIRINGS** Mustards, tomato sauce, barbecue sauce, chilli sauce, shallots, rosemary, red wine, white beans.

▲ Beef sausage

EAT Generally leaner than pork sausages with a drier texture. They may need extra fat when frying, so drain well before serving. Also popular in casseroles. **FLAVOUR PAIRINGS** Onions, root vegetables, tomatoes, peppers, red beans, oregano, paprika, chilli, cumin, coriander seed and leaf, brown ale, mustard, Worcestershire sauce, barbecue sauce.

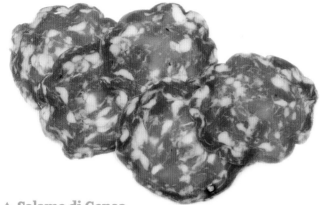

▲ Salame di Genoa

EAT Made from pork and veal, moistened with red wine, this garlicky, peppery air-dried sausage has a high fat content. The casing is usually pulled off before eating. Slice thinly for appetizers, in salads, scatter over pizzas, use to flavour sauces, rice dishes, stews, and pastries. **FLAVOUR PAIRINGS** Parmesan, mozzarella, rocket, spinach, tomatoes, olives, gherkins, rustic bread.

▲ Chorizo

EAT Semi-dried and dried Spanish chorizo are generally made from pork and pork fat, spiced with smoked paprika to give either spicy (picante) or mild, sweet (dulce) flavours. The semi-dried are sliced or diced and sautéed, then often added to other dishes; the fatter, dried ones are sliced and eaten cold. **FLAVOUR PAIRINGS** Chicken, seafood, pork, mushrooms, peppers, aubergines, courgettes, pasta, white beans, chickpeas, rice, chimichurri sauce (parsley, sherry vinegar, oregano, chilli, olive oil).

▲ Black pudding

EAT Made from pig's blood, oatmeal or breadcrumbs, pork fat, onions and other flavourings, black pudding is a favourite with chefs in many dishes. It is also fried as part of a British breakfast. **FLAVOUR PAIRINGS** Bacon, eggs, scallops, halibut, turbot, lamb, pork, venison, rabbit, raisins, red wine, chickpeas, white beans, lentils, potatoes.

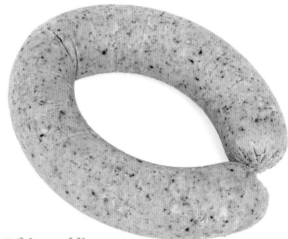

▲ White pudding

EAT Made of highly seasoned pork fat and oatmeal, white pudding usually contains no meat. In Scotland it is called mealie pudding and, when scooped out of the casing, skirlie. Slice or leave whole and pan-fry, or deep-fry in batter. **FLAVOUR PAIRINGS** Black pudding, tomatoes, eggs, bacon, toasted or fried bread, white beans, scallops, halibut, or other meaty fish.

▲ Boudin noir

EAT The French version of black pudding contains little or no cereal but usually has diced pork fat and sometimes meat as well as apple, onion, chestnut, or other ingredients. Usually served sliced and fried. **FLAVOUR PAIRINGS** Walnuts, pears, apples, oranges, chestnuts, cabbage, white wine, red wine, Dijon and wholegrain mustards.

◀ Boudin blanc

EAT Made from a mixture of pork, chicken, veal, and rabbit, enriched with cream and eggs, they are sold ready-poached, but are still, usually, fried or grilled. **FLAVOUR PAIRINGS** Caramelized onions, leeks, red wine, brandy, port, tomatoes, wild mushrooms, spinach, black truffles, cream.

319

Butterfly a leg of lamb

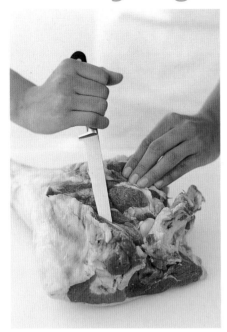

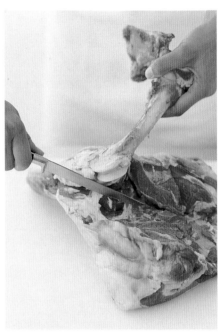

1 Place the lamb fleshiest-side down. Locate the pelvis and hold firmly, while using a sharp, long-bladed knife to cut around the leg bone.

2 Cut from the pelvis to the bottom of the leg. Using short strokes (to prevent tearing), work the knife around the bone to release it.

3 Keeping close to the bone, continue using short strokes, then cut away the flesh from around the ball and socket joint and the shank.

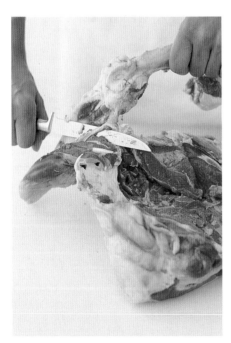

4 Cut through the sinew and tendons. All 3 bones (the pelvis, thigh, and shank) should come away in one piece.

5 Open out the leg so that the meat lies flat on the board. With short strokes, cut through the thick meaty pieces on either side.

6 Open out the flesh of the butterflied leg. Cut thin fillets from thicker areas and fold them over thinner parts to ensure more even cooking.

Bone a saddle of lamb

1 Using a sharp knife, cut away the membrane covering the fatty side of the saddle, then turn it over. Working from the centre, cut 2 fillets from either side of the backbone and reserve to cook alongside the saddle.

2 Loosen the outside edge of one side of the backbone using short, slicing strokes. Working from the side edge towards the centre, release the side of the backbone. Repeat with the other side.

3 Starting at one end, use short, slicing strokes to cut under and around the backbone. As the bone is gradually released from the flesh, lift it away, and cut beneath it.

4 Work from the centre outwards, to cut away the meat and fat from the outer flaps. When the flaps are clean, square off the edges. Turn the saddle over, score through the fat on the other side, and cook as desired.

French trim a rack of lamb

1 Remove the blade bone by cutting under the skin along the edge of the cut. Then, slice horizontally from the skin, tight against the backbone, down to the ribs. Turn the cut vertically and chop the backbone away.

2 Now trim off the elastin and any flank meat. To form the "rack", expose about 5cm (2in) of the bone at the thin end of the ribs. Make a horizontal cut down to the ribs all the way across, and slice away the meat above.

3 Remove the meat between the ribs by cutting down the length of the exposed portion of rib, getting the knife tight against the bone, then cut across and slice up along the edge of the next rib.

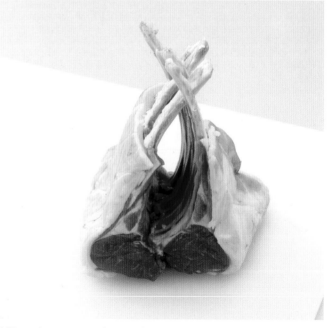

4 If serving two people, a traditional method is to form a "guard of honour" by chopping the rack in two and intersecting the bones. For four people, tie two racks of lamb together, skin-side in, to form a "crown".

Tunnel bone a leg of lamb

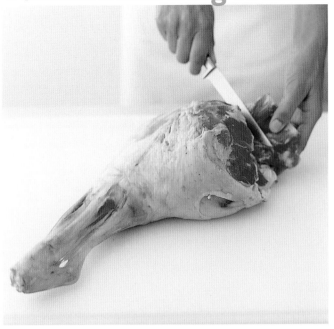

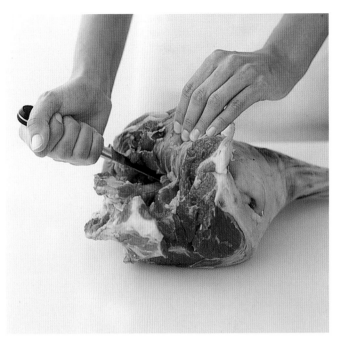

1 With the fleshiest side down, place the lamb on a board. At the top of the leg, find the pelvic bone and hold it firmly while you work around it. Use the tip of your knife close to the bone and expose it with small cuts.

2 Once the pelvic bone is exposed, work your way inside the leg, cutting all the way down the thighbone to the bottom. Keep readjusting your hold, and turning the meat to ensure that your knife stays close to the bone.

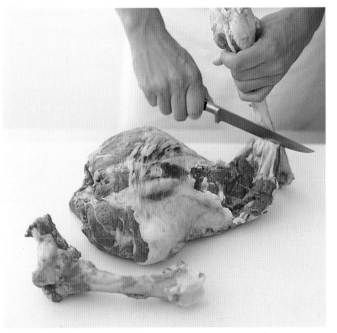

3 When you reach the base of the thighbone at the ball and socket joint, firmly grip the thighbone. Cut through the ball and socket joint, and pull the thighbone to work it free. Repeat the process with the shank bone.

4 Pull the shank bone through to the outside of the leg so that you can access it more easily. Continue working around the bone with your knife until it comes away and the leg is entirely free of bones.

Cook steaks to perfection

For a very rare steak, cook the meat for 2–3 minutes, until just seared on both sides. The steak should feel very soft when pressed, and the interior should be reddish purple when the meat is sliced.

To cook a rare steak, look for the point where drops of blood come to the surface, then turn the steak over and cook for a total of 6–8 minutes. It should feel soft and spongy, and the interior should be red.

For a medium-rare steak, cook for a total of 8–10 minutes, but turn the meat when drops of juice are first visible. The steak should offer resistance when pressed, and be pink in the centre.

A well-done steak needs to be cooked for 12–14 minutes in total. Turn the meat when drops of juice are clearly visible. The steak should feel firm and be uniformly brown throughout.

1 Heat the grill pan (alternatively a grill or a barbecue) over a high heat. Brush both sides of the steaks with oil, and season with salt and freshly ground black pepper.

2 When the pan is very hot, place the steaks diagonally across the ridges. Cook for half the desired time, (turning 45 degrees to create the diamond pattern) then turn the steaks over. Remove them and allow to rest.

Carve roast beef

1 Place the roast on a cutting board with the ends of the ribs facing up. Holding the meat steady with a carving fork, use a sawing action to cut downwards against the sides of the bones.

2 Remove the bones and position the meat fat-side up on the board. With a sawing action, cut downwards, across the grain of the meat, into slices of your desired thickness. Reserve the pan juices to make a gravy.

Cabbages

BUY There are winter, spring, summer, and autumn varieties. Look for solid heads with a clean, fresh smell, and no yellowing leaves. The cut end should be moist not dry. **STORE** Keep whole heads for several weeks in plastic bags in the vegetable drawer of the refrigerator. Once cut, they deteriorate and lose nutrients. Shred, blanch, and freeze for up to 12 months.

▼ Savoy cabbage

EAT The blanched outer leaves are excellent stuffed and braised. Steam, boil, braise, stir-fry.
FLAVOUR PAIRINGS Bacon, celery, butter, onions, garlic, tomatoes, walnuts, hazelnuts.
IN SEASON September–February (best December–February)

▲ Round green cabbage

EAT Steam or boil, but best braised or finely shredded and stir-fried. **FLAVOUR PAIRINGS** Carrots, onions, celery, soy sauce, ginger, garlic, potatoes. **IN SEASON** August–May (best December–March)

▲ Kohlrabi

EAT Available green (white), or purple. Peel and cook like turnips in soups and stews, steam, or boil. **FLAVOUR PAIRINGS** Parsley sauce, star anise, ginger, garlic, tomatoes, lamb, beef, game birds. **IN SEASON** July–November

▲ White cabbage

EAT Stir-fry, sauté, braise, shred raw for salads. Also available as coleslaw and fermented as sauerkraut. **FLAVOUR PAIRINGS** Mayonnaise, wine vinegar, mustard, caraway seeds, smoked sausages, pork, ham, carrots, onions, nuts, apples, celery. **IN SEASON** November–June (best December–February)

▲ Red cabbage

EAT Braise with an acid like vinegar, wine, or lemon juice to give a vibrant colour. Pickle and shred raw for winter salads.
FLAVOUR PAIRINGS Vinegars, red wine, brown sugars, apples, pears, raisins, onions, celery, fennel seeds, bacon, ham, pork, liver. **IN SEASON** November–May (best December–February)

▲ Brussels sprouts

EAT Steam or lightly boil whole, shred, and stir-fry, or use in salads. **FLAVOUR PAIRINGS** Melted butter, chestnuts, walnuts, hazelnuts, toasted pine nuts, sausages, crispy bacon. **IN SEASON** November–March

Flowering greens

BUY Choose tight heads with a uniform colour. Avoid any that are discoloured, damaged, or have yellowing leaves. Avoid purple sprouting broccoli with tiny yellow flowers or woody stems. **STORE** Best eaten fresh, but can be stored loosely wrapped in the vegetable drawer of the fridge for 3–4 days. Blanch and freeze florets or broccoli stems for up to 12 months.

▲ Common cauliflower

EAT Separate into tiny florets to eat raw for salads and crudités, or blitz into "rice". Boil or steam whole or in florets, roast, add to soup, cook, then bake in a sauce, or deep-fry in batter. **FLAVOUR PAIRINGS** Brown butter, Gruyère, blue or Cheddar cheese (crumbled or in sauce), garlic, olive oil, parsley, lemon. **IN SEASON** All year (best in autumn)

▼ Purple cauliflower

EAT Also look out for orange heads. Cut in florets, best steamed to keep its colour. **FLAVOUR PAIRINGS** Béchamel sauce, tomatoes, Parmesan (or other cheeses), bacon. **IN SEASON** All year (best in autumn)

▲ Chinese broccoli

EAT Also called gai lan, this sometimes has small white flowers. Stir-fry or braise. **FLAVOUR PAIRINGS** Oyster sauce, soy sauce, ginger, garlic, cashew nuts. **IN SEASON** Autumn and spring

▲ Calabrese

EAT Blanch tiny florets, or add raw, to salads. For larger florets, boil, steam, or cook, then bake in a sauce. Pare stalks and cut in batonettes to cook and eat, too. **FLAVOUR PAIRINGS** Bacon, anchovies, pesto, chillies, cheese, béchamel sauce, pine nuts, lemon, garlic, olive oil. **IN SEASON** July–November, imported all year

▲ Romanesco

EAT Tastes like mild cauliflower. Cook in the same way. **FLAVOUR PAIRINGS** Olive oil and toasted flaked almonds (to dress), Italian hard cheeses, cherry tomatoes, olives, cream. **IN SEASON** September–November

▲ Purple sprouting broccoli

EAT White also available. Steam, lightly boil, stir-fry. **FLAVOUR PAIRINGS** Tomatoes, leeks, chillies, butter, olive oil, garlic, Parmesan cheese, spring onions, citrus, hollandaise sauce. **IN SEASON** January–April, imported in winter

Leafy greens

BUY All have a sweetish flavour with varying hints of bitterness. Choose firm stalks with fresh green leaves.
STORE Eat fresh or store, wrapped in moist paper in a plastic bag in the vegetable drawer of the refrigerator, for 2–3 days. Shred large leaves, separate stalks from leaves of chard, blanch, and freeze up to 6 months.

▲ White Swiss chard

EAT Add young leaves to salads. Steam, braise or stir-fry larger leaves and stalks separately. The leaves can also be used as wrappers; serve the stalks like asparagus. **FLAVOUR PAIRINGS** Ham, garlic, onion, chillies, olive oil, butter, hollandaise sauce (stalks).
IN SEASON July–November

▲ Rainbow chard

EAT Use baby leaves in salads. Stir-fry, steam, or boil larger ones like spinach. **FLAVOUR PAIRINGS** Nutmeg, spring onions, toasted almonds and pine nuts, butter, olive oil. **IN SEASON** July–November

▲ Spinach

EAT Throw baby leaves in salads or scatter over pizzas. Spinach shrinks a great deal when cooked. Steam or wilt with no extra water, or in hot butter, stir-fry. **FLAVOUR PAIRINGS** Bacon, fish, anchovies, eggs, cheeses, yogurt, cream, butter, olive oil, garlic, onions, avocados, mushrooms, lemon, nutmeg, curry spices. **IN SEASON** All year

▲ Cavolo nero

EAT Widely used in Tuscan cooking. Good in braises, soups and casseroles. Lightly steam or sauté. **FLAVOUR PAIRINGS** Garlic, onions, chillies, peppers, white beans, spicy sausages, pancetta, potatoes, tomatoes, olive oil. **IN SEASON** September–March

▲ Kale

EAT Red kale is softer than green, curly kale. Blanch young leaves to add to winter salads. Boil, steam, braise, stir-fry, add to soups and stews. **FLAVOUR PAIRINGS** Bacon, ham, venison, sausages, oily fish, clams, eggs, citrus, tomatoes. **IN SEASON** September–March

▲ Spring greens

EAT Boil, steam, braise, stir-fry, add to soups and stews, finely shred and deep-fry for crispy "seaweed". **FLAVOUR PAIRINGS** Bacon, ham, lemon, onions, potatoes, salt pork, garlic, Chinese five-spice powder. **IN SEASON** February–April

◀ Mustard greens

EAT Baby leaves add a distinctive, peppery taste to salads. Steam, stir-fry, stew, braise. **FLAVOUR PAIRINGS** Fish, seafood, ham, pork, chicken, butter, garlic, soy sauce, rice vinegar, ginger, chillies. **IN SEASON** September–March

▲ Pak choi (bok choy)

EAT Steam or braise baby ones whole. Chop larger ones and stir-fry or add to soup. Blanch whole leaves and use as wrappers. **FLAVOUR PAIRINGS** Prawns, pork, chicken, spring onions, water chestnuts, mangetout, cashew nuts, soy sauce, oyster sauce, coriander leaves. **IN SEASON** September–March, imported all year

▲ Chinese spinach

EAT Similar to European spinach, eat raw when young, steam or stir-fry older leaves. **FLAVOUR PAIRINGS** Toasted sesame seeds, star anise, mushrooms, eggs, rice, prawns, coriander leaf, chillies, ginger, garlic. **IN SEASON** June–October

▲ Chinese leaves (napa cabbage)

EAT Shred raw for salads or cut in larger chunks and stir-fry, braise or ferment as kimchi, a spicy Korean pickle. **FLAVOUR PAIRINGS** Spring onions, ginger, sambal oelek, garlic, sesame seeds, rice vinegar. **IN SEASON** September–December, imported all year

329

Root vegetables

BUY All roots should be dry and fresh-smelling. Avoid any that are wet (usually over-chilled). If bought with leaves intact, they should be fresh, not wilted or discoloured. Twist them off before storing or the roots go limp. **STORE** If unwashed, no need to refrigerate (except salsify, scorzonera, and water chestnut). Store in a cool, dark place for up to a week if small, 2–3 weeks if large. If washed (and salsify, scorzonera and water chestnut), store in a paper bag in the vegetable drawer in the refrigerator for up to 1 week.

▼ Carrots

EAT Peel maincrop, but only wash and scrub, or scrape, if necessary, young ones. Cut in batonettes for crudités, grate or shave in ribbons for salads. Steam, boil, roast, braise, sauté or stir-fry, add to soups, stews, and casseroles. Also good for cakes and muffins. **FLAVOUR PAIRINGS** Beef, citrus, ginger, celery, chervil, fennel, thyme, parsley, coriander leaf, watercress, peas, pine nuts, cumin, cinnamon, mixed spice, other roots, particularly beetroot, honey. **IN SEASON** Early young carrots, March–September; maincrop, September–February, imported all year

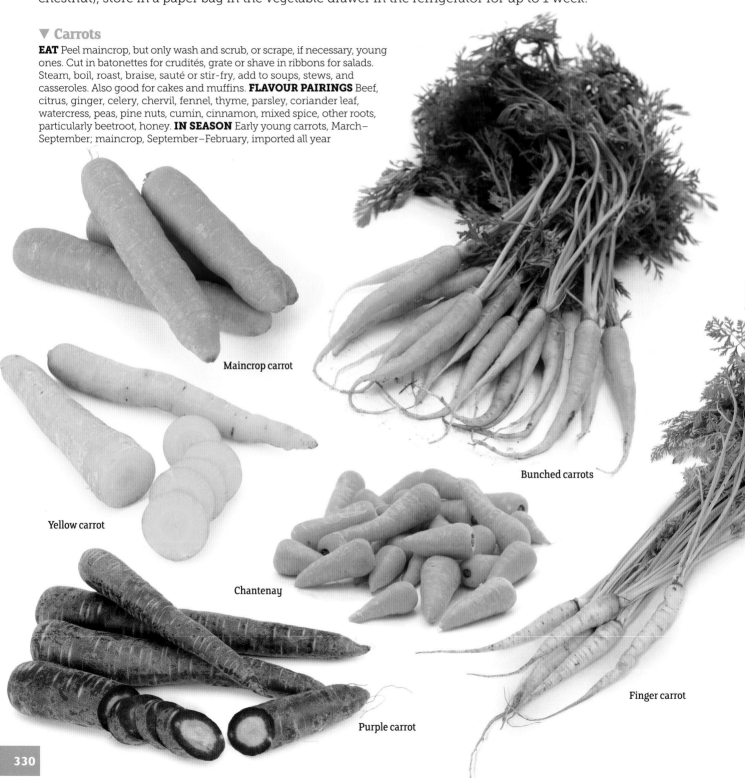

Maincrop carrot

Yellow carrot

Bunched carrots

Chantenay

Finger carrot

Purple carrot

Purple swede

▲ Swede

EAT Cut in batonettes for crudités or grate in salads. Boil, steam, bake, roast, deep-fry as chips. Add to soups, stews, and casseroles. Good alternative mash (on own or with potato) for topping minced meat and fish pies.
FLAVOUR PAIRINGS Bacon, liver, onions, carrots, cream, butter, lemon, black pepper, nutmeg, thyme.
IN SEASON October–March, imported all year

Yellow swede

White turnip

▲ Turnip

EAT Scrub and cook whole if baby, or peel and cut in pieces if larger. Cut in batonettes for crudités and grate in salads. Boil, steam, roast, sauté, or stir-fry, add to soups, stews and casseroles. Good mashed with potatoes. Leaves can be cooked like other greens. **FLAVOUR PAIRINGS** Lamb, bacon, duck, goose, game, cheeses, apples, mushrooms, potatoes, sherry.
IN SEASON Winter crop, all year; baby turnips, June–July

Purple turnip

▲ Parsnip

EAT Peel thinly, remove any woody core from large ones. Cut in batonettes for crudités, steam, or boil, mash, deep-fry as chips or crisps, griddle slices, roast, bake, braise or sauté. Add to soups, stews, and casseroles. Good in cakes. **FLAVOUR PAIRINGS** Butter, curry powder, nutmeg, garlic, parsley, thyme, tarragon, potatoes, beef, walnuts. **IN SEASON** October–March, imported all year

▲ Water chestnut

EAT Blanch for 5 minutes then peel and slice raw in savoury and fruit salads and for crudités, stir-fry or steam in oriental dishes and, also, add to beef stews and casseroles for added crunch. Also available canned. **FLAVOUR PAIRINGS** Prawns, beef, chicken, pork, pak choi, oyster sauce, soy sauce, ginger, garlic, sesame oil. **IN SEASON** Imported all year

◀ Salsify

EAT Known as oyster plant because of its flavour. Peel and drop in acidulated water to prevent discolouration. Grate and use in salads. Boil (add a tablespoon of flour to the water to retain the white colour), steam, bake, roast, sauté, deep-fry, or add to soups, stews, and casseroles. **FLAVOUR PAIRINGS** Italian hard cheeses, béchamel sauce, onions, shallots, olive oil, lemon, nutmeg, bacon. **IN SEASON** November–February, also imported

▼ Scorzonera

EAT Known as black salsify, but is a different species. Softer and more delicate than salsify. It becomes sticky when cut, so either wear gloves or boil whole then strip off the skin (good sautéed in butter) or use as salsify. **FLAVOUR PAIRINGS** White wine, hard cheeses, cream, breadcrumbs, parsley, Parma ham. **IN SEASON** November–March (also imported)

▲ Lotus root

EAT Peel, remove the fibrous sections between the links then slice or cut in chunks. Blanch, then use in salads, or boil, steam, braise, add to soups, stews, and stir-fries. Blanched slices and seeds are also candied and can be pickled. **FLAVOUR PAIRINGS** Citrus, garlic, onion, coriander leaves, chervil, star anise. **IN SEASON** Imported all year

▲ Celeriac

EAT Cut in batonettes for crudités, or shred for salads and rémoulade. Put in acidulated water when preparing, to prevent discolouration. Steam, boil, braise, mash (good with potatoes), roast, deep-fry, or bake. Add to soups, stews, and casseroles. **FLAVOUR PAIRINGS** Bacon, beef, oily fish, cheeses, garlic, potatoes, parsley, dill, olive oil, mustard, tomatoes. **IN SEASON** September–March

▲ Parsley root

EAT Grate in salads, or slice for crudités. Bake, roast, braise, boil, steam, pan-fry or stir-fry, add to soups, stews, and root vegetable mixtures. **FLAVOUR PAIRINGS** Chicken, fish, game, eggs, mushrooms, carrots, potatoes, turnips. **IN SEASON** August–April, some imported

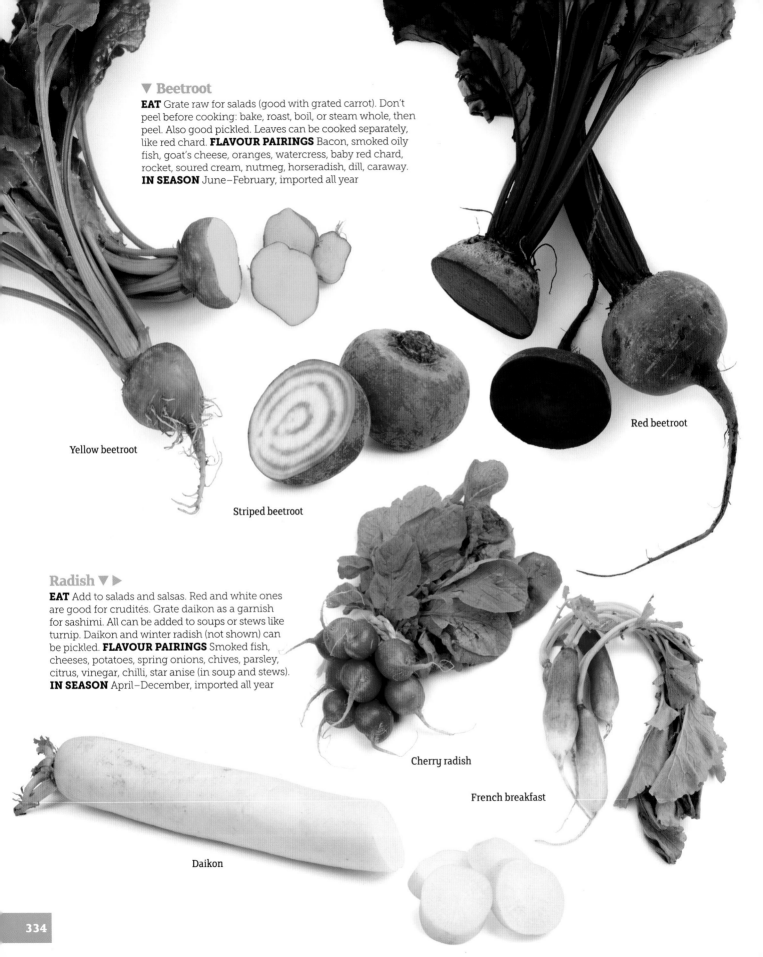

▼ Beetroot

EAT Grate raw for salads (good with grated carrot). Don't peel before cooking: bake, roast, boil, or steam whole, then peel. Also good pickled. Leaves can be cooked separately, like red chard. **FLAVOUR PAIRINGS** Bacon, smoked oily fish, goat's cheese, oranges, watercress, baby red chard, rocket, soured cream, nutmeg, horseradish, dill, caraway.
IN SEASON June–February, imported all year

Yellow beetroot

Striped beetroot

Red beetroot

Radish ▼ ▶

EAT Add to salads and salsas. Red and white ones are good for crudités. Grate daikon as a garnish for sashimi. All can be added to soups or stews like turnip. Daikon and winter radish (not shown) can be pickled. **FLAVOUR PAIRINGS** Smoked fish, cheeses, potatoes, spring onions, chives, parsley, citrus, vinegar, chilli, star anise (in soup and stews).
IN SEASON April–December, imported all year

Cherry radish

French breakfast

Daikon

Tubers

BUY All tubers should feel heavy for their size, and be firm with no broken skin or evidence of soft spots. Avoid any potatoes with green patches or signs of sprouting. They should all smell earthy and fresh. Choose Jerusalem artichokes with the fewest little knobs as they are easier to clean (and peel, if required).
STORE Keep in a paper bag or closed basket in a cool (but not cold) dark place. Best used within a week.

▲ King Edward potatoes

EAT A famous British floury potato. Mash, bake, use for gnocchi or in soup, roast, purée or chip. **FLAVOUR PAIRINGS** Butter, milk, chives, rosemary, celeriac, leeks, onions, spring onions, garlic, olive oil, lemon, hard cheeses. **IN SEASON** September–October, available stored all year

▲ Maris Piper potatoes

EAT A popular British fairly floury potato. Best for chips but also a good all-rounder. **FLAVOUR PAIRINGS** Butter, chives, parsley, curry spices, mayonnaise, tomato ketchup, malt vinegar, sea salt. **IN SEASON** September–October, available stored all year

▲ Nicola potatoes

EAT A German variety with good, waxy flesh, and a buttery flavour. Good sliced and baked in gratins, and to top meat and fish dishes. Also good for salads. **FLAVOUR PAIRINGS** Cream, crème fraîche, yogurt, garlic, nutmeg, Gruyère, Cheddar and blue cheeses, French dressing, mayonnaise, shallots, ham, bacon, pickled, salted and smoked fish. **IN SEASON** July–October, available stored all year

▲ Desirée potatoes

EAT A Dutch all-purpose variety. Bake, roast, mash, boil, add to soups and stews, deep-fry, or sauté. **FLAVOUR PAIRINGS** Cumin, Cajun spices, nutmeg, and seeds (to coat wedges), eggs, onions, mushrooms, butter, olive and nut oils. **IN SEASON** September–October, available stored all year

▲ Anya potatoes

EAT Long, waxy speciality salad potato, a cross between Pink Fir Apple and Desirée. Best boiled or steamed in the skin, but can be sautéed or roasted whole. **FLAVOUR PAIRINGS** Melted butter, pesto, parsley, thyme, mint, chives, olive oil, mustard, wine vinegar, shallots, grated citrus zest. **IN SEASON** May–October, imported most of the year

▲ Charlotte potatoes

EAT A high-quality French waxy speciality salad potato. Often available ready-washed. Best boiled or steamed in the skin. Good cold. **FLAVOUR PAIRINGS** Melted butter, mint, chives, parsley, mayonnaise, yogurt, olive oil, anchovies, citrus. **IN SEASON** May–October, imported most of the year

▲ Jersey Royal potatoes

EAT Famous heritage variety from the Channel Islands, eagerly awaited in the UK every spring for their distinctive rich, earthy flavour. **FLAVOUR PAIRINGS** Melted butter, mint, parsley, chives, thyme, spring onions. **IN SEASON** April–June

▲ Sweet potatoes

EAT Cook in their skins or peel first. Boil, steam, mash, bake, roast, sauté, deep-fry as chips or tempura. Also used in cakes, pastries and candied as sweetmeats. **FLAVOUR PAIRINGS** Apples, brown sugars, molasses, ginger, maple syrup, honey, citrus, chilli, nutmeg, Cajun spices, thyme. **IN SEASON** Imported all year

▲ Taro

EAT Steam, boil, sauté, deep-fry, or cook, then purée as a base for soufflés or croquettes. **FLAVOUR PAIRINGS** Sweet potatoes, chilli, star anise, cinnamon, cardamom, toasted sesame oil. **IN SEASON** Imported all year

▼ Yam

EAT Never eat raw. Peel before use (wear gloves as some types irritate the skin). Boil, steam, bake, roast, sauté or deep-fry as chips, add to meat stews.
FLAVOUR PAIRINGS Eggs, cheese, cream, curry powder, coconut, lime.
IN SEASON Imported all year

▲ Cassava

EAT Never eat raw. Peel then bake, boil, roast, use in stews, stir-fries or deep fry as crisps. Cassava flour is a thickening agent and made into tapioca. **FLAVOUR PAIRINGS** Butter, garlic, citrus, coriander seeds and leaves, chilli.
IN SEASON Imported all year

▲ Jicama

EAT Can be difficult to digest, so introduce slowly to the diet. Grate, dice, or julienne to add to savoury and fruit salads (try the Mexican way of sprinkling with lime juice and chilli powder), steam, boil, bake, stir-fry, sauté, braise, or pickle.
FLAVOUR PAIRINGS Chilli, lime, avocado, mango, onions, tomatoes, coriander leaves. **IN SEASON** Imported all year (best autumn to spring)

◀ Jerusalem artichoke

EAT Can be difficult for some to digest. Slice raw as crudités, grate or chop in salads (toss in lemon juice to prevent discolouration). Boil, steam, purée, use for gratins, roast, stir-fry, sauté, or deep-fry for crisps or chips. **FLAVOUR PAIRINGS** Béchamel or hollandaise sauce, butter, cream, ginger, nutmeg, lovage, parsley, lemon, spring onions, crispy bacon, pheasant and other game. **IN SEASON** October–March (best November–February)

Vegetable essentials

Choosing vegetables at their peak, storing them well, and cooking them carefully will maximize their flavour and bring out the best in them.

Buy

Vegetables are the foundation of a healthy diet, and they are at their freshest, tastiest, and most nutritious when they are in season and locally grown by sustainable methods. In season, vegetables reach their flavour peak, and this is also when they are most abundant and most economical. Local farmers are likely to grow the most flavourful varieties, including heritage types that have been selected by generations of farmers and gardeners for their superior qualities. Local growers are often organic or sustainable, too, choosing farming methods that protect the environment and preserve the soil's natural fertility without the use of chemicals.

Good colour Buy vegetables that have bright, vibrant colours with no yellowing – especially in cauliflowers and leafy greens. There should be no bruising, discolouration, blemishes, soft spots, cuts, or pits, and no suggestion of mould growth.
Firmness The vegetable should feel firm and heavy in the hand; lighter vegetables may be drying out.
Tight skin Loose skin also indicates that the vegetable is drying out, so look for taut, firm skin.
Fresh ends To ensure freshness and the quality it implies, check the cut ends of vegetables that have been harvested from a root or mother plant. The cut should look fresh and moist, not dried out, and leaves should be glossy and mid-ribs turgid.
Smell The vegetable should have a clean, fresh smell.

Store

Different vegetables store for varying lengths of time, depending on their type. See individual ingredients for storage times.

Delicate leafy vegetables store best wrapped loosely in moist kitchen paper inside a closed plastic bag or refrigerator-storage container.
Root vegetables such as carrots and parsnips keep well in an open, plastic bag in the salad drawer of the fridge.
Vegetables such as bell peppers and cabbage store well in paper bags rolled shut and placed in the salad drawer.
Potatoes store best at room temperature in the dark.
Onions are best stored in a basket at room temperature.
Tomatoes should be kept at room temperature and will continue to ripen when placed on a windowsill.
Hard vegetables such as carrots, beans, broccoli, peas, and sweetcorn, can all be frozen. Freeze cut and prepared vegetables on the day you buy them to retain all their flavours, textures, and nutrients.

Vegetable cooking chart

| VEGETABLE | BOILING | | | STEAMING |
	TIMES (IN MINUTES)	COLD/BOILING START	COOK COVERED?	TIMES (IN MINUTES)
Artichoke bottoms	20–30	cold start	no	15–20
Artichoke, whole	20–40	cold start	no	25–35
Artichoke, baby	15–18	cold start	no	15–20
Asparagus	3–4	boiling start	no	4–10
Beans, green	2–8	boiling start	no	5–12
Beetroot, whole	30–60	cold start	yes	30–60
Broccoli florets	2–3	boiling start	no	5–10
Brussels sprouts	5–12	boiling start	no	10–15
Cabbage, quartered	5–15	boiling start	no	6–15
Carrots, baby	3–4	boiling start	yes	10
Carrots, sliced/diced	5–10	boiling start	yes	8–10
Cauliflower florets	2–3	boiling start	no	5–8
Celeriac, cubed/wedges	8–10	cold start	no	8–10
Corn-on-the-cob	3–4	boiling start	no	6–10
Greens, hearty, sliced	5–7	boiling start	no	10–12
Leeks, whole/halved	10–15	boiling start	no	12–15
Mangetout	2–3	boiling start	no	5–10
Peas, fresh	3–5	boiling start	no	5–10
Potatoes, boiling/new	10–25	cold start	no	15–35
Potatoes, floury, cubed	15–20	cold start	no	15–35
Spinach	1–2	boiling start	no	3–4
Squashes, summer, sliced	5–8	boiling start	no	5–10
Squashes, winter, pieces	12–15	boiling start	yes	15–30
Swede, thickly sliced	8–12	cold start	yes	10–15
Sweet potatoes, cubed	15–35	cold start	yes	30–45
Turnip, thickly sliced/cubed	8–12	cold start	yes	10–15

Stems, shoots, and flowers

BUY Stems should be firm and plump; asparagus buds and artichoke leaves should be tight shut. Cut ends should look fresh with no dry spots. Avoid any that are wilting, damaged, or discoloured. **STORE** All are best eaten fresh but can be stored in a plastic or paper bag in the vegetable box in the refrigerator; asparagus, artichokes, and cardoons up to 3 days; celery and fennel up to 2 weeks. Blanch and freeze asparagus and artichokes up to 12 months; celery and cardoons 9 months; fennel 6 months.

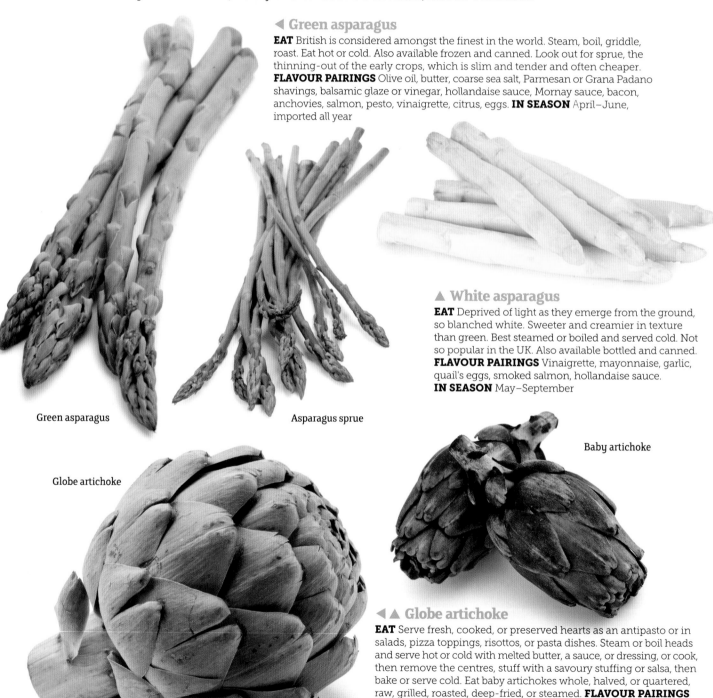

◄ Green asparagus

EAT British is considered amongst the finest in the world. Steam, boil, griddle, roast. Eat hot or cold. Also available frozen and canned. Look out for sprue, the thinning-out of the early crops, which is slim and tender and often cheaper.
FLAVOUR PAIRINGS Olive oil, butter, coarse sea salt, Parmesan or Grana Padano shavings, balsamic glaze or vinegar, hollandaise sauce, Mornay sauce, bacon, anchovies, salmon, pesto, vinaigrette, citrus, eggs. **IN SEASON** April–June, imported all year

▲ White asparagus

EAT Deprived of light as they emerge from the ground, so blanched white. Sweeter and creamier in texture than green. Best steamed or boiled and served cold. Not so popular in the UK. Also available bottled and canned.
FLAVOUR PAIRINGS Vinaigrette, mayonnaise, garlic, quail's eggs, smoked salmon, hollandaise sauce.
IN SEASON May–September

Green asparagus

Asparagus sprue

Baby artichoke

Globe artichoke

◄ ▲ Globe artichoke

EAT Serve fresh, cooked, or preserved hearts as an antipasto or in salads, pizza toppings, risottos, or pasta dishes. Steam or boil heads and serve hot or cold with melted butter, a sauce, or dressing, or cook, then remove the centres, stuff with a savoury stuffing or salsa, then bake or serve cold. Eat baby artichokes whole, halved, or quartered, raw, grilled, roasted, deep-fried, or steamed. **FLAVOUR PAIRINGS** Vinaigrette, butter, hollandaise sauce, herbs, cured and dried meats, anchovies, shellfish, tomatoes, chillies, mushrooms, cheeses, cream, garlic, lemon, white truffles. **IN SEASON** June–October

◀ Celery

EAT Serve batonettes for crudités. Stuff pieces with soft cheese or pastes. Dice in sandwiches, salads, stuffings, soups, stews, and casseroles. Steam, braise, or bake hearts. **FLAVOUR PAIRINGS** Béchamel or hollandaise sauces, cheeses, onions, cabbage, lemon, walnuts, apples, pears. **IN SEASON** September–February, imported all year

Hearts of palm ▶

EAT Available fresh or canned. Cut in thin slices for salads and platters. Steam, stir-fry, grill, sauté, or stew. **FLAVOUR PAIRINGS** Cured and dried meats, shellfish, lime, vinaigrette, tomatoes, baby salad leaves, soy sauce, wasabi, sesame oil, ginger, avocados, tropical fruits. **IN SEASON** Imported all year

▲ Florence fennel

EAT Slice or shred for salads. Cut in batonettes for crudités. Boil, steam, roast, braise, or griddle in quarters or thick slices. Cook baby fennel whole. **FLAVOUR PAIRINGS** Cheeses, fish and seafood, veal, chicken, dried and cured meats, citrus, preserved lemon (roasted with), Pernod, Puy lentils, herbs, mayonnaise. **IN SEASON** July–October, imported most of the year

▲ Cardoons

EAT Use a potato peeler to pare stalks to remove strings (do the same for outer celery stalks). Cut in batonettes for crudités (good with bagna cauda). Boil, steam, braise, stew, sauté, or use for soup. **FLAVOUR PAIRINGS** Veal, anchovies, olive oil, hard cheeses, butter, cream, lemon, almonds. **IN SEASON** June–September

341

Peas, beans, and other pods

BUY Those with edible pods should be bright green and snap easily. Those for shelling should be plump but not over-full. Swollen beans and peas will be tough and mealy textured. Choose corn cobs with moist, bright green husks and creamy yellow kernels rather than deep gold, or the sugar will already have turned to starch. **STORE** Best eaten fresh but can be kept for 1–2 days in a plastic bag in the vegetable drawer in the refrigerator. Blanch, then freeze for up to 12 months.

▲ Mangetout

EAT Steam or use these sweet, crisp, flat pods as crudités, in salads or stir-fries. **FLAVOUR PAIRINGS** Almonds, chicken, mushrooms, soy sauce, garlic, ginger, sherry, rice wine, Chinese five-spice powder. **IN SEASON** June–October, imported all year

▲ Sugar snap peas

EAT Crunchy and sweet, use whole, or thickly slice for crudités and warm salads, or stir-fry or steam. **FLAVOUR PAIRINGS** Toasted sesame seeds, chillies, sesame oil, ginger, soy sauce, soft cheeses, oyster mushrooms, radishes, mint. **IN SEASON** June–October, imported all year

▲ Garden peas

EAT Raw in salads or cooked as a vegetable. Boil or steam until just tender, purée, or use for soup. Also available frozen (and canned but they lose their colour and texture). Look for pea shoots, the tender tops of the plants, to add to salads, too. **FLAVOUR PAIRINGS** Bacon, ham, fish, duck, baby onions, lettuce, mint, thyme, chervil, mushrooms. **IN SEASON** June–October

▲ Baby corn

EAT Whole or halve as crudités, stir-fry, boil, steam, braise, slice and add to soups, stews, and casseroles. **FLAVOUR PAIRINGS** Baby vegetables, sesame oil, soy sauce, chicken, fish, duck, gammon, garlic, butter, olive oil. **IN SEASON** August–September, imported all year

▲ Sweetcorn

EAT Roast whole in the husk, or shuck first, then boil, roast, grill or barbecue. Boil, braise, bake, or sauté kernels, or add to soups and stews. Also available as kernels, frozen, or in cans. **FLAVOUR PAIRINGS** Bacon, potatoes, butter, cheese, cream, chillies, citrus. **IN SEASON** August–September, imported all year

▲ Runner beans

EAT String and thinly slice diagonally. Boil, steam, use for pickles and chutneys. Available frozen. **FLAVOUR PAIRINGS** Bacon, mushrooms, onions, tomatoes, red wine vinegar, honey, olive oil, cashew nuts. **IN SEASON** July–October, imported most of the year

▲ Helda beans

EAT No need to string. Top and tail, and cut in chunks or diagonal slices. Boil, steam, stir-fry. **FLAVOUR PAIRINGS** Citrus, melted butter, walnuts, nut oils, toasted sesame seeds, tomatoes. **IN SEASON** June–October, imported all year

▲ Broad beans

EAT Shell, then boil or steam, purée, or make into soup. Pop beans out of their skins before eating, if preferred. Available frozen and canned. **FLAVOUR PAIRINGS** Bacon, ham, fish, lamb, chicken, game, spinach, onions, cream, béchamel sauce. **IN SEASON** May–August

▲ French beans

EAT Top and tail. Cook whole or cut in short lengths. Blanch for salads, steam, or boil. Available frozen and canned. **FLAVOUR PAIRINGS** Eggs, shallots, red wine vinegar, olive oil, tomatoes, garlic, olives, oily fish, new potatoes. **IN SEASON** June–October, imported all year

▲ Edamame beans

EAT Raw (if young), steam or boil, or squeeze out the fresh soya beans. Also available frozen, shelled, or whole. **FLAVOUR PAIRINGS** Coarse sea salt, harissa paste, lamb, chicken, fish, soy sauce, ginger, garlic, chillies. **IN SEASON** June–September

▲ Yellow wax beans

EAT Rich buttery flavour. Top and tail, then steam or boil. **FLAVOUR PAIRINGS** Tomatoes, garlic, onions, olive oil, chorizo, mushrooms. **IN SEASON** June–November

▲ Okra

EAT Can eat raw but usually steam, stew, or bake in a sauce, coat in batter or cornmeal, and deep-fry or stir-fry. They have a mucilaginous quality when cooked. Can be pickled. Available frozen and canned. **FLAVOUR PAIRINGS** Butter, garlic, chillies, curry spices, coconut, green peppers, tomatoes. **IN SEASON** December–March, imported all year

Squashes, cucumbers, and chayote

BUY All these members of the gourd family should be firm, feel heavy for their size, and have unblemished skins. Choose small summer squashes – like courgettes – for best texture and flavour. The skin of winter squashes should be hard (if a thumb nail can pierce it, it won't be sweet and ripe). **STORE** Keep winter squashes in a cool dark place for up to 3 months. Keep the rest in the vegetable drawer of the refrigerator. Remove any plastic film on cucumbers first, store for up to 1 week; summer squashes up to 5 days. Wrap chayote tightly in a paper bag first, to keep for several weeks.

▲ Marrow

EAT An overgrown courgette, stuff and bake whole or in slices, roast in chunks, or steam. **FLAVOUR PAIRINGS** Sausage, mince or rice and herbs for stuffing, tomatoes, melted butter, Cheddar and Parmesan cheeses, béchamel sauce, thyme, oregano, sage, parsley. **IN SEASON** August–October

▲ Pumpkin

EAT Peel large ones before cooking. Steam or boil then purée for soups and pumpkin pie, sauté, roast or bake (small halves, seeds removed). Also available canned. **FLAVOUR PAIRINGS** Blue and Cheddar cheeses, butter, walnuts, sage, rosemary, thyme, ginger, nutmeg, cinnamon, cumin, tomatoes. **IN SEASON** September–November

◄ Spaghetti marrow

EAT Best pricked, boiled whole then split, the fibres scooped out and dressed like spaghetti. **FLAVOUR PAIRINGS** Fresh tomato sauce, bolognese sauce, olive oil, melted butter, Parmesan cheese, anchovies, mushrooms. **IN SEASON** August–October

▲ Red onion squash

EAT Flavour reminiscent of chestnuts. Roast, add to soups or sweet dishes. **FLAVOUR PAIRINGS** Red onions, chestnuts, garlic, olive oil, butter, nigella seeds, cinnamon, nutmeg, cloves. **IN SEASON** September–December

▲ Bottle gourd

EAT Peel and slice, or cut in chunks. This winter squash holds its shape well in curries and stir-fries. **FLAVOUR PAIRINGS** Coconut milk, tamarind, mustard seeds, curry leaves, cumin, coriander seed and leaf, ginger, chilli, star anise, tomatoes, onions, garlic, lentils. **IN SEASON** Imported all year

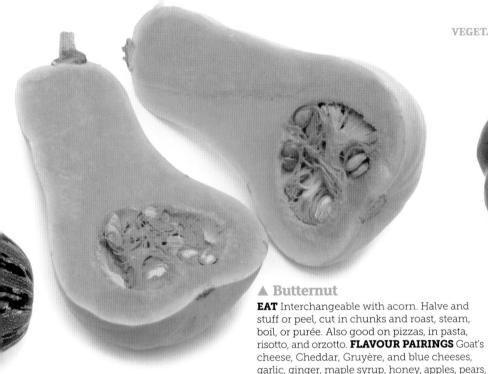

▲ Butternut

EAT Interchangeable with acorn. Halve and stuff or peel, cut in chunks and roast, steam, boil, or purée. Also good on pizzas, in pasta, risotto, and orzotto. **FLAVOUR PAIRINGS** Goat's cheese, Cheddar, Gruyère, and blue cheeses, garlic, ginger, maple syrup, honey, apples, pears, sage, thyme, rosemary, beetroot. **IN SEASON** September–December, imported all year

▲ Acorn

EAT Alternative to butternut. Halve and stuff, then bake, or peel, cut in chunks and roast, steam, boil, or purée. Try baking, filled with a herby cheese custard. **FLAVOUR PAIRINGS** Soft white cheeses, Parmesan cheese, eggs, garlic, maple syrup, honey, parsley, sage, thyme, apples, pears, quinces. **IN SEASON** September–December

▲ Bitter melon

EAT Scoop out the seeds, blanch, then salt, and leave 30 minutes before rinsing and cooking to remove bitterness. Braise, steam or stir-fry. Also available canned. **FLAVOUR PAIRINGS** Pork, fish and shellfish, soy sauce, ginger, garlic, spring onions, black bean sauce, oyster sauce. **IN SEASON** Imported all year

▲ Turk's turban

EAT Large cavity so good eaten whole. Cut slice off top and scoop out seeds. Oil outside, wrap in foil, roast, then scoop out some flesh, mix with stuffing, stuff back in and bake. Also roast in wedges. **FLAVOUR PAIRINGS** Butter, olive oil, Cheddar and goat's cheeses, breadcrumbs, rice, onions, sage, thyme, cream, bacon, ham. **IN SEASON** September–December

◀ Crown prince

EAT Roast, then purée for soups and cakes, or as a ravioli filling. **FLAVOUR PAIRINGS** Butter, eggs, nutmeg, mixed spice, cinnamon, muscovado sugar, sage, onions, ricotta cheese. **IN SEASON** September–December

◀ Courgettes

EAT Available as green and yellow. Flowers can be stuffed, or dipped in batter and fried. Grate or shave in ribbons for salads, cook baby ones whole, halve and stuff, then bake, or slice or cut in batonettes and steam, boil, braise, dip in batter and deep-fry, stir-fry, griddle or sauté. **FLAVOUR PAIRINGS** Olive oil, coarse sea salt, sweet peppers, aubergines, onions, garlic, tomatoes, curry spices, basil, parsley. **IN SEASON** May–October (flowers May–September), imported all year

Green courgette

Yellow courgette

▲ Patty pan

EAT Bake whole (with or without stuffing), slice and steam, sauté or stir-fry. **FLAVOUR PAIRINGS** Melted butter, olive oil, garlic, cumin, coriander, thyme, basil, parsley, bacon, breadcrumbs, chickpeas, hard cheeses. **IN SEASON** July–September

▼ Crookneck

EAT Has sweeter flesh than ordinary courgettes. Cook as for courgettes. **FLAVOUR PAIRINGS** Olive oil, butter, cream, Cheddar, Gruyère, and Parmesan cheeses, bacon, white beans, tomatoes. **IN SEASON** July–September

▲ Round squash

EAT Steam or stir-fry small ones whole, or halve and stuff larger ones before baking. **FLAVOUR PAIRINGS** As for courgettes, or try prawns or crab and rice stuffing with dill, parsley and lemon zest. **IN SEASON** May–October

▲ Ridge cucumbers

EAT Peel, cut in batonettes for crudités, or slice or dice for salads. Steam, braise, stir-fry, or halve and stuff then bake. **FLAVOUR PAIRINGS** Malt, balsamic or red wine vinegar, black pepper, fish, shellfish, cheese sauce, soy sauce, garlic, ginger, cream cheese, root vegetables, spring onions. **IN SEASON** June–October (best August–September)

▲ Gherkins (cornichons)

EAT From the same species as cucumbers, usually sold ready-pickled, often flavoured with dill. Key ingredient in tartare sauce. Serve with pâtés, terrines and fish; as a nibble with drinks, and as a garnish. **FLAVOUR PAIRINGS** Capers and caperberries, mayonnaise, parsley, thyme, tarragon, chervil, chicken, poultry and pig's livers, pork, salt beef, most fish.

▲ Common greenhouse cucumber

EAT Pare off evenly spaced strips of skin for an attractive finish when slicing. Best for salads, sandwiches and salsas but good grated for chilled soup. **FLAVOUR PAIRINGS** Vinegars, yogurt, dill, purslane, garlic, anchovies, cream cheese, feta cheese, fennel, mint, mayonnaise, tomatoes, chillies, avocados, tropical fruits. **IN SEASON** June–October, imported all year

▲ Burpless slicing cucumber

EAT Reputed not to cause digestive problems, so no need to peel. Good sliced, diced or grated in salads, dips and sandwiches. **FLAVOUR PAIRINGS** Yogurt, mint, coriander leaf and seeds, toasted cumin seeds, garlic, spring onions, watercress, mayonnaise. **IN SEASON** July–October

▲ Pickling cucumber

EAT Small, solid and crisp to keep their texture when pickled. Also good eaten raw, lightly dressed with French dressing or just balsamic vinegar. **FLAVOUR PAIRINGS** Rock salt, malt, white wine, and cider vinegars, coriander seeds, yellow mustard seeds, dried chillies, allspice, ginger, black peppercorns, bay leaf, dill, white onions. **IN SEASON** July–October

▲ Chayote

EAT The skin is edible on small, tender chayote, peel if larger. Steam, sauté, stir-fry, or bake (with or without stuffing), or grate for salads and salsas. **FLAVOUR PAIRINGS** Fish, shellfish, rice, garlic, onion, soft and hard cheeses, chillies. **IN SEASON** Imported all year

Onions, shallots, leeks, and garlic

BUY Choose firm onions and shallots with the outer papery skin intact and dry. Avoid if wet, stained, or smelling unpleasant. Leeks and spring onions should be crisp with white bases and bright green tops. Leeks should give a little when squeezed; if fat and hard, they will be tough. **STORE** Onions and shallots keep best in a vegetable rack or string bag in a cool dark place. Keep leeks and spring or salad onions in a sealed plastic bag in the vegetable drawer in the refrigerator for up to 5 days.

Brown onions ▶

EAT The workhorse of the kitchen. Use raw, fry, braise, stew, boil or roast. **FLAVOUR PAIRINGS** Bacon, liver, sausages, steak, lamb, pork, game, fish, curry spices, fresh herbs, tomatoes, all vegetables, cheeses. **IN SEASON** June–March (best June–September), imported all year

◀ White onions

EAT Sweet mild flavour. Good for dishes where onions not fried first, like white stews, risottos, and sauces. Ideal for batter-dipped fried onion rings, too. **FLAVOUR PAIRINGS** Tempura batter, beer batter, veal, chicken, lamb, sage, parsley, thyme, risotto rice, white beans, white wine, spinach, tomatoes. **IN SEASON** June–March (best June –September), imported all year

Red onions ▶

EAT Sweet mild flavour. Use in salads and salsas, roast, or caramelize for marmalade. **FLAVOUR PAIRINGS** Fresh and sun-dried tomatoes, peppers, aubergines, squashes, avocados, bacon, lentils, chickpeas, cheeses, oily fish, basil, thyme, bay leaf. **IN SEASON** June–March (best June–September), imported all year

▲ Banana shallot

EAT Grate or finely chop to add a sweet, subtle flavour to stews, casseroles, braises and soups, or halve and roast. **FLAVOUR PAIRINGS** Butter, balsamic vinegar, white balsamic condiment, red wine, white wine, cream, wild mushrooms, sorrel, thyme, parsley, fish. mussels and other seafood, chicken. **IN SEASON** September–March

▲ White salad onions

EAT Mild and sweet, slice or chop for salads, trim and use whole, cooked, or pickled. Use the green tops for garnish. **FLAVOUR PAIRINGS** Cream cheese, cottage cheese, soured cream, crème fraîche, yogurt, radishes, cherry tomatoes, chicken, fish, shellfish. **IN SEASON** March–September (best April–August)

▲ Pickling/pearl onions

EAT Mild sweet flavour best for pickling, but also to cook whole in white sauce, and in classic casseroles and stews. **FLAVOUR PAIRINGS** Malt, white or balsamic vinegars, coriander seeds, yellow mustard seeds, dried chillies, black peppercorns, bay leaf, milk, cream, red and white wine, beef, lardons, chicken, pork, lamb, game, fish, peas, cheese, ham. **IN SEASON** June–March (best June–September)

▲ Spring onions

EAT Chop or slice in salads, salsas, omelettes, stir-fries, and Thai curries. Finely chop and add to mashed potato. **FLAVOUR PAIRINGS** Thai red and green curry pastes, galangal, lemongrass, nam pla, eggs, potatoes, meat, chicken, fish, most cheeses. **IN SEASON** March–September (best April–August), imported all year

Round shallot ▶

EAT Use as banana or grey shallots, or can be pickled. Try them finely chopped or sliced with cheese and sage in toasted sandwiches. **FLAVOUR PAIRINGS** Malt or balsamic vinegars, coriander seeds, yellow mustard seeds, black peppercorns, cinnamon sticks, chillies, bay leaf. **IN SEASON** September–March

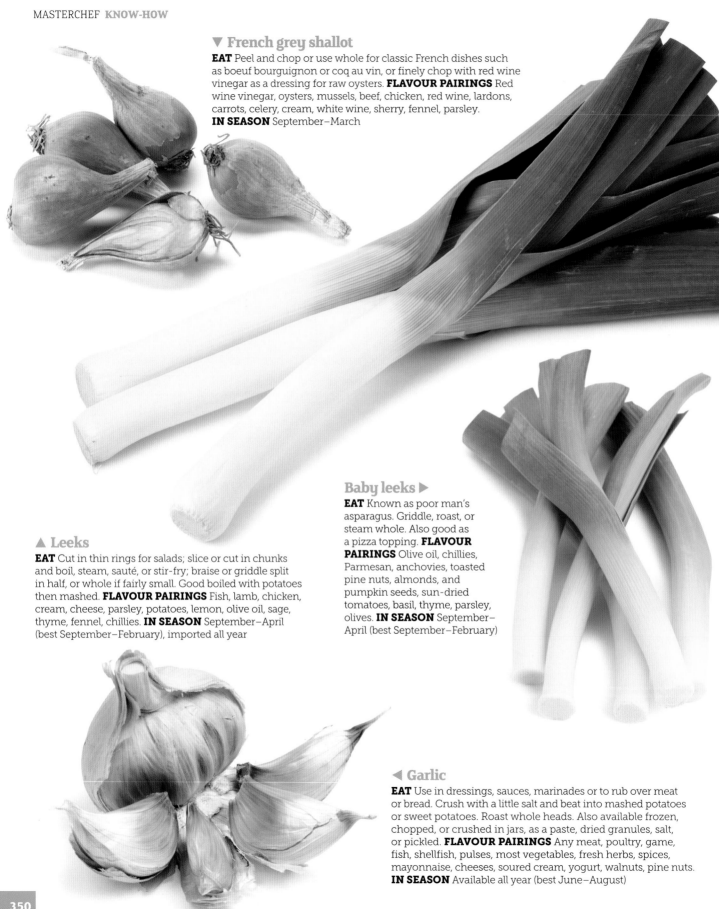

▼ French grey shallot

EAT Peel and chop or use whole for classic French dishes such as boeuf bourguignon or coq au vin, or finely chop with red wine vinegar as a dressing for raw oysters. **FLAVOUR PAIRINGS** Red wine vinegar, oysters, mussels, beef, chicken, red wine, lardons, carrots, celery, cream, white wine, sherry, fennel, parsley.
IN SEASON September–March

▲ Leeks

EAT Cut in thin rings for salads; slice or cut in chunks and boil, steam, sauté, or stir-fry; braise or griddle split in half, or whole if fairly small. Good boiled with potatoes then mashed. **FLAVOUR PAIRINGS** Fish, lamb, chicken, cream, cheese, parsley, potatoes, lemon, olive oil, sage, thyme, fennel, chillies. **IN SEASON** September–April (best September–February), imported all year

Baby leeks ▶

EAT Known as poor man's asparagus. Griddle, roast, or steam whole. Also good as a pizza topping. **FLAVOUR PAIRINGS** Olive oil, chillies, Parmesan, anchovies, toasted pine nuts, almonds, and pumpkin seeds, sun-dried tomatoes, basil, thyme, parsley, olives. **IN SEASON** September–April (best September–February)

◀ Garlic

EAT Use in dressings, sauces, marinades or to rub over meat or bread. Crush with a little salt and beat into mashed potatoes or sweet potatoes. Roast whole heads. Also available frozen, chopped, or crushed in jars, as a paste, dried granules, salt, or pickled. **FLAVOUR PAIRINGS** Any meat, poultry, game, fish, shellfish, pulses, most vegetables, fresh herbs, spices, mayonnaise, cheeses, soured cream, yogurt, walnuts, pine nuts.
IN SEASON Available all year (best June–August)

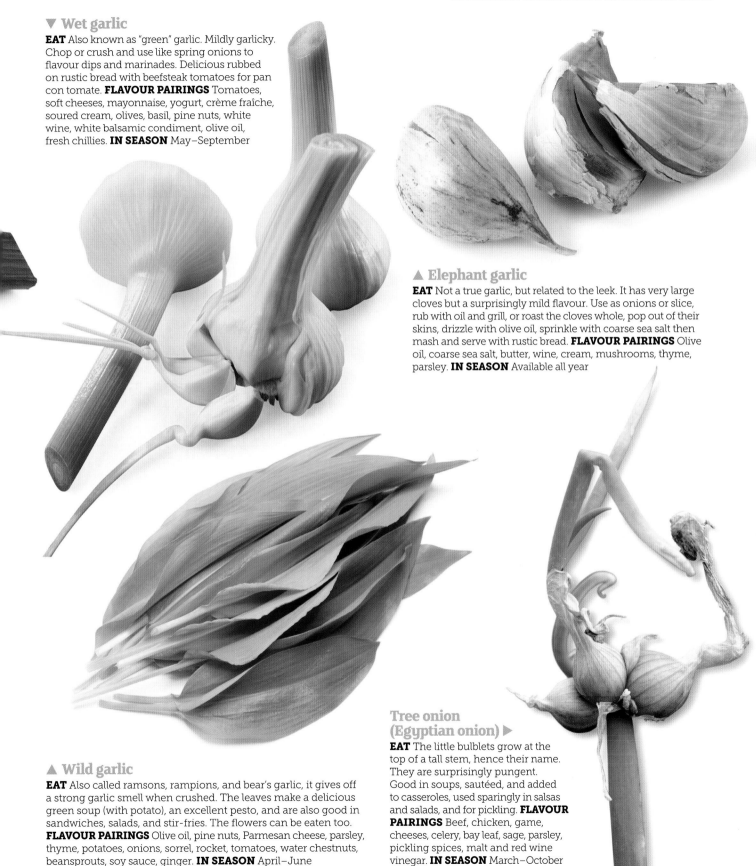

▼ Wet garlic

EAT Also known as "green" garlic. Mildly garlicky. Chop or crush and use like spring onions to flavour dips and marinades. Delicious rubbed on rustic bread with beefsteak tomatoes for pan con tomate. **FLAVOUR PAIRINGS** Tomatoes, soft cheeses, mayonnaise, yogurt, crème fraîche, soured cream, olives, basil, pine nuts, white wine, white balsamic condiment, olive oil, fresh chillies. **IN SEASON** May–September

▲ Elephant garlic

EAT Not a true garlic, but related to the leek. It has very large cloves but a surprisingly mild flavour. Use as onions or slice, rub with oil and grill, or roast the cloves whole, pop out of their skins, drizzle with olive oil, sprinkle with coarse sea salt then mash and serve with rustic bread. **FLAVOUR PAIRINGS** Olive oil, coarse sea salt, butter, wine, cream, mushrooms, thyme, parsley. **IN SEASON** Available all year

▲ Wild garlic

EAT Also called ramsons, rampions, and bear's garlic, it gives off a strong garlic smell when crushed. The leaves make a delicious green soup (with potato), an excellent pesto, and are also good in sandwiches, salads, and stir-fries. The flowers can be eaten too. **FLAVOUR PAIRINGS** Olive oil, pine nuts, Parmesan cheese, parsley, thyme, potatoes, onions, sorrel, rocket, tomatoes, water chestnuts, beansprouts, soy sauce, ginger. **IN SEASON** April–June

Tree onion (Egyptian onion) ▶

EAT The little bulblets grow at the top of a tall stem, hence their name. They are surprisingly pungent. Good in soups, sautéed, and added to casseroles, used sparingly in salsas and salads, and for pickling. **FLAVOUR PAIRINGS** Beef, chicken, game, cheeses, celery, bay leaf, sage, parsley, pickling spices, malt and red wine vinegar. **IN SEASON** March–October

Vegetable fruits

BUY Choose unblemished fruits with glossy, firm skin. Avocados should give slightly when gently squeezed in the palm of the hand. **STORE** Aubergines are best eaten fresh but can be stored in a cool dark place for 1–2 days. Ripen green breadfruit in a cool, dark place for 7–10 days. Leave unripe avocados on the windowsill to soften, then store in the fridge for 2–3 days. Tomatoes should be kept in a fruit bowl, not the refrigerator, unless overripe. Peppers and chillies will keep in a paper bag in the refrigerator for up to 2 weeks.

◄ Cherry tomatoes

EAT Whole or halved in salads, or as a snack, or lightly crush, stew in olive oil and use as a pizza topping. Also available bottled and semi-dried. **FLAVOUR PAIRINGS** Salad leaves, cucumber, celery, olives, pumpkin and sunflower seeds, red onions, basil, oregano, olive oil, balsamic vinegar, goat's cheese, mozzarella balls, rocket. **IN SEASON** July–October, imported all year

▲ Standard globe tomatoes

EAT Classic fruit that come in green and yellow as well as red varieties. Grill, fry, bake, poach, add to soups, stews and curries, or quarter or slice for salads. Also available dried, as ketchup and sauce. **FLAVOUR PAIRINGS** Bacon, eggs, fish, mushrooms, cheese, parsley, thyme, oregano, sage, cinnamon, garlic, onions, chillies, Thai red curry paste, coconut milk. **IN SEASON** July–October, imported all year

▲ Plum tomatoes

EAT Best tomato for sauces and soup, but also keeps its shape well when sliced for grilling or roasting. Use baby ones with pasta. **FLAVOUR PAIRINGS** Basil, oregano, bay, chervil, onions, garlic, bacon, olive oil, orange, celery salt. **IN SEASON** July–October, imported all year

Beefsteak tomatoes ▶

EAT Slicing tomatoes, but also good to roast, bake (with or without stuffing), sauté, or stew. Also rub on rustic bread with green garlic for the classic Pan con Tomate. **FLAVOUR PAIRINGS** Mozzarella, Parmesan, eggs (bake inside), olives, anchovies, pesto, pine nuts, almonds, rustic bread, green garlic, peppers, courgettes, aubergines, avocados, basil, oregano, marjoram, chervil. **IN SEASON** July–October, imported all year

Hass avocado

Fuerte avocado

▲ ▶ Avocado

EAT Hass has black skin when ripe and creamy flesh for mashing on toast. Green Fuerte is better for slicing. Best eaten raw but can be made into soup or baked. Slice for sandwiches, mash for guacamole, mix with sugar and cream to make ice cream. Add acid like lemon or lime juice to prevent discolouration. **FLAVOUR PAIRINGS** Parma ham, mozzarella, bacon, prawns, tomatoes, spinach, grapefruit, lime, mango, lemon, pineapple, sugar, balsamic vinegar, chillies. **IN SEASON** Imported all year

Italian long
white aubergine

Italian round
aubergine

Oval deep purple
aubergine

◀ ▲ Aubergine

EAT The most common are large purple ones, but there are also white, stripy and round Italian ones. Slice large ones and griddle, or dip in batter and deep-fry. Dice and pan-fry or stew, or roast whole then purée with spices. Baby purple ones also available to cook whole or split – ideal for curries. **FLAVOUR PAIRINGS** Ham, lamb, beef, mozzarella, feta, hard cheeses, garlic, mushrooms, tomatoes, sweet peppers, lemon, oregano, mint, thyme, chillies, olive oil, cinnamon, curry spices.
IN SEASON June–October, imported all year

Italian striped
aubergine

353

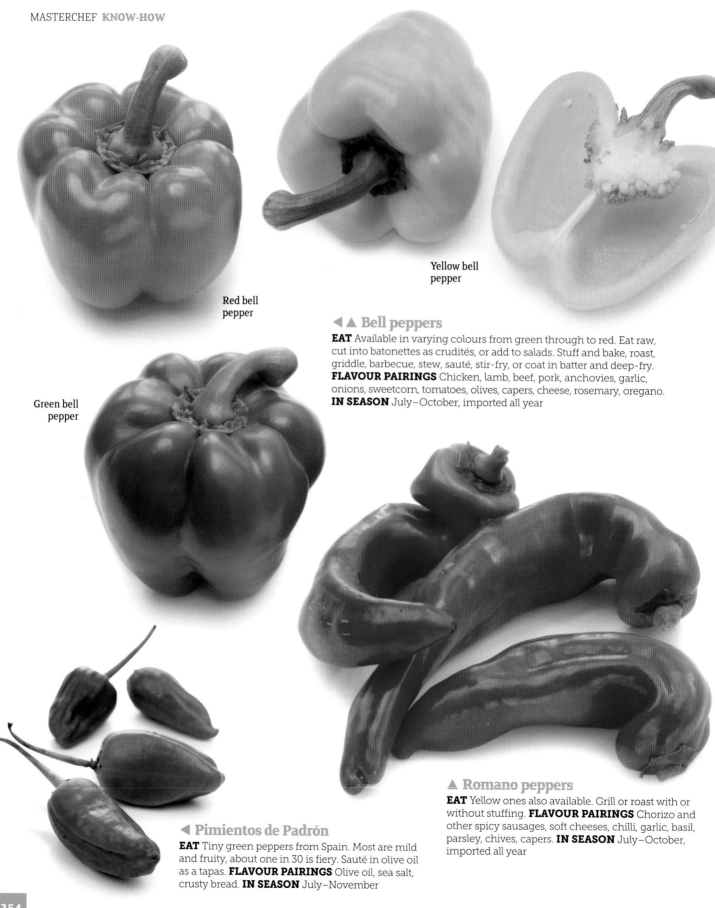

Red bell
pepper

Yellow bell
pepper

Green bell
pepper

◄ ▲ Bell peppers

EAT Available in varying colours from green through to red. Eat raw,
cut into batonettes as crudités, or add to salads. Stuff and bake, roast,
griddle, barbecue, stew, sauté, stir-fry, or coat in batter and deep-fry.
FLAVOUR PAIRINGS Chicken, lamb, beef, pork, anchovies, garlic,
onions, sweetcorn, tomatoes, olives, capers, cheese, rosemary, oregano.
IN SEASON July–October, imported all year

◄ Pimientos de Padrón

EAT Tiny green peppers from Spain. Most are mild
and fruity, about one in 30 is fiery. Sauté in olive oil
as a tapas. **FLAVOUR PAIRINGS** Olive oil, sea salt,
crusty bread. **IN SEASON** July–November

▲ Romano peppers

EAT Yellow ones also available. Grill or roast with or
without stuffing. **FLAVOUR PAIRINGS** Chorizo and
other spicy sausages, soft cheeses, chilli, garlic, basil,
parsley, chives, capers. **IN SEASON** July–October,
imported all year

◄ Scotch Bonnet chilli

EAT Crinkly, rounded chillies in a variety of colours. Extremely hot. Used in many Caribbean hot sauces and jerk seasoning.
FLAVOUR PAIRINGS Chicken, beef, pumpkin and other squashes, potatoes, sweet potatoes, yam, spring onions, garlic, spinach, allspice, bay, coconut milk, lime. **IN SEASON** July–November, imported all year

Jalapeño chilli ►

EAT Often sliced and used as a condiment or a pizza topping. Also available pickled. can be stuffed. Moderately hot.
FLAVOUR PAIRINGS Beef, spicy sausages, noodles, sweet peppers, courgettes, aubergines, peanuts, cashews, tomatoes, mozzarella, cream cheese, sheep's cheese.
IN SEASON July–November, imported all year

◄ Thai (bird's eye) chillies

EAT Used fresh and dried, these thin little chillies are red or green. Add to curries and stir-fries or chop for pastes and dips. Very hot.
FLAVOUR PAIRINGS Most spices, coriander leaf, bay leaf, coconut milk, lime, nam pla, palm sugar, galangal, spring onions, chicken, beef, pork, lamb, fish. **IN SEASON** July–November, imported all year

▲ Hungarian hot wax chilli

EAT Fleshy long chilli that can be chopped, sliced or stuffed. Use in salads, stir-fries, braises and pickles. Moderately hot.
FLAVOUR PAIRINGS Beef, pork, lamb, chicken, seafood, cream cheese, hard cheese, thyme, sage, tomatoes.
IN SEASON July–November, imported all year

▲ Serrano chilli

EAT Mexican chilli that can be stuffed but is often sliced or chopped and used in salsas and soups along with dried chillies. Moderately hot. **FLAVOUR PAIRINGS** Sweet peppers, potatoes, onions, garlic, dried chipotle chillies, avocado, tomatoes, coriander leaf, prawns, steak. **IN SEASON** July–November, imported all year

Mushrooms and truffles

BUY The mushroom season lasts from late summer to early winter, but some varieties, such as morel, appear in spring. Many species are now cultivated. If foraging for wild mushrooms, do not eat any unless you are sure they are edible – they can be delicious or deadly! All mushrooms should be fresh and dry, not damaged or slimy. They should smell earthy and sweet. **STORE** Keep in the refrigerator in a closed paper bag (never plastic) for up to a week. They dry well and can then be stored for months. Reconstitute by soaking in warm water. Some also available frozen.

▲ Cultivated white button

EAT Buttons become closed cup mushrooms as they grow. Use raw in salads and as crudités. Chop, slice, halve, or quarter to add to soups, stews, casseroles, sauces, pasta, and rice dishes. Also available sliced, dried, and frozen. **FLAVOUR PAIRINGS** Onions, garlic, tomatoes, coriander seeds and leaf, parsley, oregano, lemon, cream, crème fraîche, yogurt, white wine, sherry, steaks, chicken. **IN SEASON** Cultivated all year

▲ Chestnut or brown crimini

EAT Young portobello mushrooms. Meaty, with nutty flavour. Slice raw for salads, sauté, or stir-fry. **FLAVOUR PAIRINGS** Oregano, parsley, marjoram, chives, parsley, coriander leaf and seeds, curry spices, Thai spices, red wine, garlic, bacon, onions. **IN SEASON** Cultivated all year

▲ Enoki

EAT Cultivated in clumps, they have a crisp texture and mild flavour. Good in soups and stir-fries, or raw in salads and sandwiches. **FLAVOUR PAIRINGS** Chicken, prawns, crab, chicken and fish broth, cucumber, celery, carrot, soy sauce, garlic, beansprouts, peppers. **IN SEASON** Cultivated all year

▲ Open cup or flat

EAT Full-grown button mushrooms. They have a firm texture and earthy flavour. Grill, pan-fry, stuff, or bake. **FLAVOUR PAIRINGS** Garlic, cream, white wine, herb stuffings, cheese, pâté, bacon, eggs, parsley. **IN SEASON** Cultivated all year

▲ Portobello

EAT Large, flat, meaty mushrooms. Cook whole, chopped, or sliced. Fry, bake (with or without stuffing), or grill. **FLAVOUR PAIRINGS** Butter, garlic, cream, fresh herbs, white or rosé wine, halloumi and soft cheeses, cider, tomatoes, spring onions. **IN SEASON** Cultivated all year

▲ Morel

EAT One of the most sought after wild mushrooms. Never eat raw. Often sold dried. Best sautéed. **FLAVOUR PAIRINGS** Butter, olive oil, garlic, asparagus, leeks, cream, white wine, brandy, eggs, chicken, beef, veal, halibut, turbot, monkfish. **IN SEASON** April–May

▲ Chanterelle/girolle

EAT Highly acclaimed with a nutty, fruity flavour. Best sautéed. Good in sauces. Also available dried. **FLAVOUR PAIRINGS** Other mushrooms, beef, chicken, fish, seafood, shallots, red wine, sherry, brandy, tomatoes, cheese, ginger, soy sauce, peppers. **IN SEASON** June–January

▲ Cep/porcini

EAT Highly revered by chefs. Slice and sauté or add to risottos and pasta dishes. Also available dried. **FLAVOUR PAIRINGS** Risotto rice, pasta, cream, brandy, white wine, leeks, onions, garlic, Parma ham, Parmesan, truffle oil, beef, chicken, game, scallops. **IN SEASON** September–November

▲ Oyster

EAT Young ones are tender and mild with a slight aniseed flavour. Use in stir-fries and soups. **FLAVOUR PAIRINGS** Eggs, chicken, fish or vegetable broth, noodles, beef, chicken, pork, prawns, crab, spring onions, Chinese five-spice powder, soy sauce, rice wine vinegar. **IN SEASON** Cultivated all year

▲ Shiitake

EAT Originally from Japan, with a chewy, meaty texture and good flavour. Stir-fry or add to soups, stews and casseroles. Also available dried. **FLAVOUR PAIRINGS** Pork, chicken, beef, prawns, noodles, rice, soy sauce, ginger, garlic, spring onions, bamboo shoots, water chestnuts, beansprouts, chillies, rice wine, oyster sauce. **IN SEASON** Cultivated all year

▲ Wood blewit (pied bleu)

EAT Faint aniseed smell. Do not eat raw. Good with other mushrooms in soups, stroganoff, risottos, tarts and with pasta. **FLAVOUR PAIRINGS** Cream, crème fraîche, brandy, white wine, rice, pearl barley, lasagne, Italian hard cheeses, thyme, parsley, marjoram. **IN SEASON** September–November, cultivated all year

▲ Field

EAT The most common wild mushroom with excellent flavour, especially when mature. Fry or grill. **FLAVOUR PAIRINGS** Bacon, eggs, sausages, steak, venison, risotto rice, cream, crème fraîche. **IN SEASON** September–November

▲ White (Alba) truffle

EAT The best are from Piedmont, Italy, with complex earthy aromas and flavours. Grate or shave over hot foods. Also available dried and as flavoured oil. **FLAVOUR PAIRINGS** Eggs, risotto rice, pasta, game birds, scallops, halibut, monkfish, foie gras, potatoes, olive oil, garlic, Parmesan cheese. **IN SEASON** November–February

▲ Black (Périgord) truffle

EAT Delicate fragrance of woodland and chocolate. Shave or grate over hot foods. Also available dried, and as flavoured oil. **FLAVOUR PAIRINGS** Spaghetti, chicken, rabbit, game birds, celeriac, meaty white fish, shellfish, pancetta. **IN SEASON** November–March

Salad leaves

BUY There are an astounding variety of tasty leaves available with overlapping seasons, so there is always a supply of one kind or another to enjoy. Choose fresh-looking leaves with firm hearts, if relevant. Avoid if wilting or bruised. **STORE** Whole heads will keep in the vegetable box in the fridge for a week or more, unwashed leaves will keep in a plastic bag for several days but ready-washed deteriorate more quickly.

Chicory ▶

EAT Cut a cone shape out of base with a pointed knife to remove bitter core. Add raw to salads or use whole leaves as crudités or vessels for pastes, salsas, nut butters or cream cheese. Stir-fry, grill, braise or bake in gratins. **FLAVOUR PAIRINGS** Bacon, ham, prosciutto crudo, blue and Cheddar cheeses, nuts, garlic, watercress, olive oil, tomato salsa. **IN SEASON** October–April, imported all year

◀ Radicchio

EAT A variety of chicory. Tear the leaves and add to salads, braise, grill, or add to risottos or pasta dishes. **FLAVOUR PAIRINGS** Pancetta, hazelnuts, walnuts, pine nuts, pumpkin seeds, Italian hard cheeses, ricotta or feta cheeses, balsamic vinegar, preserved lemons, anchovies. **IN SEASON** September–March

▲ Curly endive (frisée)

EAT The classic for bistro salad. Tear, rather than cut in pieces. Can be stir-fried too. **FLAVOUR PAIRINGS** Olive oil, croûtons, smoked lardons, red onions, parsley, coriander leaf, chillies, Worcestershire sauce, poached or soft-boiled eggs. **IN SEASON** June–September

▲ Escarole (Batavia)

EAT Less bitter than curly endive, usually served in salads. **FLAVOUR PAIRINGS** Balsamic vinegar, fruit vinegars, olive oil, toasted nut and seed oils, mustard, croûtons, eggs, anchovies, avocado, pomegranate, raisins. **IN SEASON** June–September

◀ Butterhead lettuce

EAT Use leaves as soft wrappers for cold mixtures of seafood or avocado. Braise, steam or shred and cook with other vegetables like peas and onions. Tear, don't cut, leaves for salad. **FLAVOUR PAIRINGS** Peas, baby onions, anchovies, cheese, mayonnaise, olive oil, lemon juice, mustard, garlic. **IN SEASON** All year

Cos (Romaine) ▶

EAT Succulent leaves ideal for burgers, salads, sandwiches and wraps. The classic lettuce for Caesar salad. **FLAVOUR PAIRINGS** Anchovies, eggs, croutons, garlic, Parmesan, chicken, onions, citrus, herbs, honey, mustard. **IN SEASON** June–September, imported all year

◀ Red oak

EAT Thin soft leaves and crunchy stalks used in typical mesclun mix of leaves and shoots. **FLAVOUR PAIRINGS** Rocket, chicory, chervil, dandelion, purslane, olives, tomatoes, red onions, artichokes, avocado, beetroot, carrots, olive oil, citrus, fruit and wine vinegars. **IN SEASON** April–September

Iceberg ▶

EAT Crisp but bland. Shred for sandwiches or add to burgers. Braise or blanch, and stuff with meat, fish, chicken or vegetable mixtures, then steam. Use leaves as vessels for mayonnaise-dressed salad mixes. **FLAVOUR PAIRINGS** Seafood, Russian salad, rice or pasta salads, minced chicken, pork, veal or liver, soy sauce, ginger, garlic. **IN SEASON** June–September, imported all year

▲ Little Gem

EAT Sweet baby cos variety, excellent in salads and sandwiches, or halve or quarter, then braise or steam. Use whole leaves as vessels. **FLAVOUR PAIRINGS** Mushrooms, spring onions, garlic, peas, bacon, Italian hard cheeses, tabbouleh, walnuts. **IN SEASON** April–September, imported all year

▲ Lollo Rosso

EAT Good for adding contrasting texture and colour to mixed salads. **FLAVOUR PAIRINGS** Pears, apples, pomegranate, blueberries, green salad leaves, cheese, walnuts, toasted pine nuts, pumpkin seeds, olive oil, toasted nut oils, citrus, wine, sherry and cider vinegars, chorizo, salami. **IN SEASON** April–September

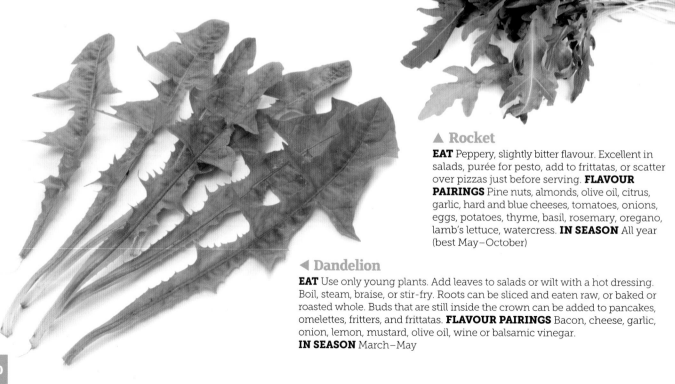

▲ Rocket

EAT Peppery, slightly bitter flavour. Excellent in salads, purée for pesto, add to frittatas, or scatter over pizzas just before serving. **FLAVOUR PAIRINGS** Pine nuts, almonds, olive oil, citrus, garlic, hard and blue cheeses, tomatoes, onions, eggs, potatoes, thyme, basil, rosemary, oregano, lamb's lettuce, watercress. **IN SEASON** All year (best May–October)

◄ Dandelion

EAT Use only young plants. Add leaves to salads or wilt with a hot dressing. Boil, steam, braise, or stir-fry. Roots can be sliced and eaten raw, or baked or roasted whole. Buds that are still inside the crown can be added to pancakes, omelettes, fritters, and frittatas. **FLAVOUR PAIRINGS** Bacon, cheese, garlic, onion, lemon, mustard, olive oil, wine or balsamic vinegar. **IN SEASON** March–May

◀ Mizuna

EAT Often mixed with other salad leaves, good in sandwiches, as a bed for seafood, with sautéed meats or chicken livers, and as a garnish. Steam or stir-fry briefly, then toss in noodle dishes. **FLAVOUR PAIRINGS** Pork, chicken livers, fish, shellfish, ginger, lemon, sesame oil, olive oil, toasted seeds, tamari. **IN SEASON** All year (best September–May)

Lamb's lettuce (corn salad) ▶

EAT Excellent in warm or cold mixed salads or thrown into sautés at the last minute so it just wilts. **FLAVOUR PAIRINGS** Onions, croûtons, sweetcorn, honey, mustard, cherry tomatoes, toasted seeds, pears, avocados, lardons. **IN SEASON** May–November

Purslane ▶

EAT The fleshy leaves are slightly mucilaginous and can be used to thicken soups and stews in the same way as okra. Add leaves to salads, stir-fries, soups, and stews. Pickle in salt and white wine vinegar. The flowers are good in salads and for garnishing. **FLAVOUR PAIRINGS** Beetroot, broad beans, cucumber, spinach, potatoes, tomatoes, eggs, feta cheese, yogurt. **IN SEASON** May–October

▲ Watercress

EAT Use in salads, sandwiches, and as a garnish. Stir-fry or use for soups and sauces. **FLAVOUR PAIRINGS** Cucumber, beetroot, goat's cheese, eggs, salmon, other oily fish, chicken, duck, oranges, potatoes. **IN SEASON** All year

Salad cress ▶

EAT The sprouting leaves of cress seeds. Add to salads, sandwiches, and use as a garnish. **FLAVOUR PAIRINGS** Eggs, salmon, sardines, tuna, Cheddar cheese, cream cheese, tomatoes, cucumber. **IN SEASON** All year

▲ Nori

EAT Wrap these crispy toasted seaweed sheets around warm vinegared sushi rice and vegetable or fish fillings, to make Japanese sushi rolls or Korean gimbap, or crumble into Asian-style salads. **FLAVOUR PAIRINGS** Sesame, sugar, rice, rice vinegar, salt, fish, noodles, avocado, cucumber, daikon, carrot, chilli, kimchi.

Peel and dice an onion

1 Using a sharp chef's knife, hold the onion firmly in one hand, then cut the bulb lengthways in half and peel off the skin, leaving the root intact to hold the layers together.

2 Lay one half cut-side down on the board. Hold it in place while you make a few slices into the onion horizontally, making sure that you cut up to, but not through, the root.

3 Hold the horizontally sliced onion firmly, then with the forward tip of your knife, slice down through the layers vertically, cutting as close to the root as possible. Repeat, slicing at regular intervals.

4 Now, cut across the vertical slices that you have just made, to produce an even dice. Use the root to hold the onion steady, then discard this part when the rest of the onion has been diced.

Wash and cut leeks julienne

1 With a sharp knife, trim off the root end and some of the dark, green leaf top. Cut the leek in half lengthways and spread the layers apart.

2 Rinse the leek under cold running water to remove the soil that tends to collect between the layers, then pat it dry with kitchen paper.

3 Lay the halved leek flat-side down on the chopping board and slice it into thick or thin strips, according to the recipe.

Peel and chop garlic

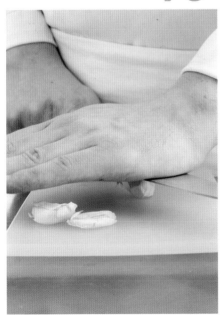

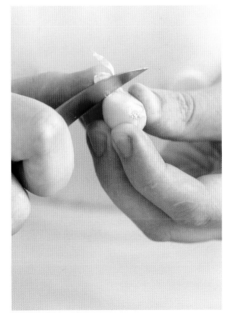

1 Place each garlic clove on a cutting board. Cover with the flat side of a large knife and pound with the palm of your hand.

2 Pushing down on the cloves should make it easier to peel away the papery skin. Discard this, then cut off the ends of each clove.

3 Slice the clove into slivers lengthways, then cut across into tiny chunks. Collect the pieces into a pile and chop again for finer pieces.

Skin and deseed tomatoes

1 Hold the tomato steady in one hand, while you use a sharp knife to score an "X" through its skin at the base.

2 Completely immerse the tomato in boiling water for around 20 seconds, or until you can see the skin begin to split.

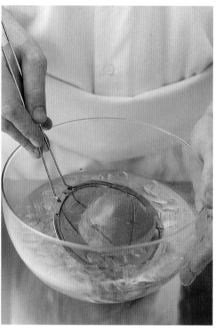

3 Remove the tomato from the boiling water with a slotted spoon and immediately plunge it into iced water to cool it.

4 When the tomato is cool enough to handle, use a paring knife to peel off the skin, starting at the base where you made the "X".

5 Slice the tomato in half, then gently squeeze it in your hand to force the seeds out over a bowl and discard them.

6 Place the now seedless tomato on a board and hold it firmly with one hand while you slice it first into strips and then into dice.

Peel and cut into julienne

1 Hold the vegetable firmly in one hand while you peel it thinly using a vegetable peeler or small paring knife. If you are peeling beetroot, you may wish to wear rubber gloves to prevent staining your hands.

2 Place the peeled vegetable on a clean board and hold it steady while you use a chef's knife to trim the sides. Do this as evenly as possible, to form a square shape.

3 Holding the trimmed block gently but firmly, cut it into equal slices of the thickness of 3mm (⅛in) for julienne vegetables, and 5mm (¼in) if you are preparing batonettes.

4 Stack the vegetable slices, just a few at a time to avoid them sliding about, and cut each batch into neat, square-edged batonettes that are the same thickness as the slices.

365

Cut courgette batonettes

1 Place the courgette on a board and cut off both ends. Cut it in half lengthways, then hold the courgette firmly on its side and cut each half again to make slices 5mm (¼in) thick.

2 Now put each slice of courgette flat on the board and cut across it with a sharp chef's knife to make equal-sized batonettes: sticks with an approximate width of 5mm (¼in).

Cut carrot batonettes

1 Cut each carrot in half crossways. Set a mandolin blade to a 5mm (¼in) thickness and hold it steady. Press the carrot with the other hand (keeping your fingers clear). Slice up and down until the slices are uniform.

2 Stack the carrot slices and neaten them by by cutting the rounded sides away with a sharp knife to achieve a rectangular shape. Then cut the stacked carrot slices lengthways to make strips of equal width.

Prepare asparagus

1 With a sharp chef's knife, cut the hard ends from the asparagus spears. If the ends are woody, bend them with your finger until they snap off (they will break at the point where they become more fibrous).

2 To ensure that the asparagus is really tender, hold the tip of the spear very carefully so that you do not bruise it, then use a vegetable peeler to peel off a thin layer of skin from all sides of the stalk.

Remove sweetcorn kernels

1 Remove the husks and all the silk thread from the corn-on-the-cob. Rinse the husked corn under cold running water.

2 Place the blunt end on the cutting board. Use a sharp chef's knife and slice straight down the cob. Rotate the cob and repeat.

3 To extract the "milk", hold the cob upright in a bowl and use your knife to scrape down the side. Turn the corn and repeat.

Turn vegetables

1 If necessary, peel the vegetables first, then using a sharp knife, cut them into pieces that are 5cm (2in) long.

2 Now, holding a vegetable piece between your thumb and forefinger, begin slicing off the sides to create a curve.

3 Keep turning the vegetable piece in your hand as you cut. The aim is to create a rugby ball shape with 7 curved sides.

Prepare a mirepoix

1 For stocks and some braised dishes, cut an onion lengthways into quarters, and celery, carrots, and leeks into 5cm (2in) chunks.

2 Braised dishes and stews require smaller chunks, so cut the onion, celery, carrots, and leeks into a 2cm (¾in) dice.

3 For dishes with a short cooking time, cut the celery, carrot, and leek into a 5mm (¼in) dice. Dice the onion using the crosshatch method.

Core and shred cabbage

1 Hold the head of the cabbage firmly on the cutting board and use a sharp knife to cut it in half, straight through the stalk end.

2 Cut the halves again through the stalk lengthways, and slice out the core (which will be tough) from each quarter.

3 Working with each quarter at a time, place the wedge cut-side down. Cut across the cabbage, creating broad or fine shreds.

Trim, wash, and dry salad leaves

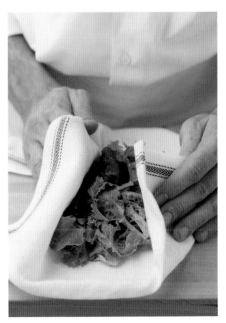

1 Trim the ends of the leaves and discard any discoloured ones. If any of the leaves are tough, cut out the stalk from each one.

2 Place the salad leaves in a colander and rinse under running water or immerse in cool water. Shake them gently to loosen any dirt.

3 Drain the leaves, then gently pat dry with a clean tea towel or kitchen paper. Alternatively, use a salad spinner to remove excess water.

Stone and remove avocado flesh

1 Hold the avocado firmly in one hand, then with a chef's knife, slice straight into the avocado, cutting all the way around the stone.

2 Once the avocado has been cut all the way around, gently twist the two halves in opposite directions and separate.

3 Strike the cutting edge of your knife into the stone and lift the knife (wiggling it if necessary) to remove it from the avocado.

4 To release the avocado stone from your knife, use a wooden spoon to carefully prise it away, then discard the stone.

5 Quarter the avocado and hold it very gently to avoid damaging the flesh, then use a paring knife to peel away and discard the skin.

6 To dice an avocado, cut it into neat slices lengthways, then repeat the cuts crossways to the desired size.

Prepare whole artichokes

1 Hold the artichoke firmly by the stalk, then with a pair of strong kitchen scissors, snip off the tough tips of the leaves.

2 Now cut through the stalk at the base of the artichoke. Take care to hold the artichoke firmly while you do this.

3 Pull out any tough, darker green leaves and discard. Then cut through the pointed tip. The artichoke is now ready to cook as desired.

Prepare artichoke hearts

1 Cut or pull away all of the leaves from the whole artichoke first, then cut the stalk from the base and discard.

2 With a sharp knife, cut off the soft middle cone of leaves just above the hairy choke. Rub the flesh with lemon to reduce browning.

3 Trim away the bottom leaves with a paring knife. Scoop out the hairy choke if you plan to cut the heart into pieces for cooking.

Prepare bell peppers

1 Place the pepper on its side and cut off the top and bottom. Stand on one of the cut ends and slice in half lengthways. Remove the core and seeds.

2 Open each section and lay them flat on the cutting board. Using a sideways motion, remove the remaining pale, fleshy ribs.

3 Cut the peppers into smaller sections, following the divisions of the pepper. Chop according to the preparation of your dish.

Roast and peel peppers

1 With a pair of tongs, hold the pepper over an open flame to char the skin. Rotate the pepper and char each side evenly.

2 Put each pepper into a plastic bag, seal, and allow the skins to loosen. When the peppers have cooled, peel away the charred skin.

3 Pull off the stalk, with the core attached, if possible. Discard the pepper seeds and slice the flesh into strips.

Deseed and cut chillies

1 Cut the chilli lengthways in half. Using the tip of your knife, scrape out the seeds and remove the membrane and stem.

2 Turn the chilli half flesh-side down and flatten with the palm of your hand. Turn it over again and slice it lengthways into strips.

3 For dice, hold the strips of cut chillies firmly together and carefully slice crossways to make equal-sized pieces.

Deseed, roast, and grind chillies

Scraping the seeds out of a chilli will lessen its heat. Cut in half lengthways, then scrape out the seeds with a knife or spoon.

To impart a smoky flavour to chillies, dry-roast in a heavy-based frying pan over a high heat. Remove when they begin to darken.

Use a mortar and pestle to grind dry-roasted chillies to a powder, or they can be soaked, sieved, and ground to a paste.

Roast potatoes

1 Peel and cut the potatoes into equal-sized pieces. Put in a pan with lightly salted cold water to cover, and boil for 10 minutes. Drain and set aside until they are cool enough to handle, then score them with a fork.

2 Heat a roasting pan with a thin layer of sunflower oil, goose, or duck fat in a hot oven at 200°C (400°F/Gas 6). Coat the potatoes in the hot fat and roast for 1 hour, or until crisp. Drain on kitchen paper.

Mash potatoes

1 Boil the potatoes until they are tender. Drain through a colander, then return them to the pan. Add butter, cream, salt, pepper, and nutmeg to taste. Re-cover the pan and leave for 5 minutes.

2 Using a potato masher, mash the potatoes until they are smooth and fluffy. Adjust the seasoning and add extra butter and cream, if desired. Keep hot until ready to serve.

Pan fry potatoes

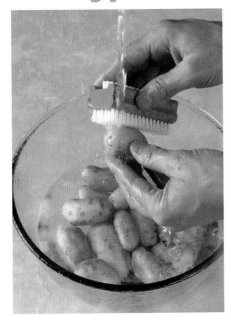

1 If using unpeeled potatoes, scrub them first by washing in water and lightly rubbing with a small vegetable brush to remove any dirt.

2 Heat a thin layer of sunflower or olive oil in a frying pan until hot. Over a medium heat, fry a single layer of potato slices for 10 minutes.

3 Using a fish slice or spatula and a knife, turn the slices over and fry until golden and tender. Drain on kitchen paper and season to taste.

Make chips

1 The first step to good, chunky chips is cutting large, floury potatoes into slices 1 cm (½in) thick and about 7.5cm (3in) long.

2 Heat oil for deep-frying to 160°C (325°F). Add the chips. Fry for 5–6 minutes, until soft, not brown. Remove and drain.

3 Reheat the oil to 180°C (350°F) and fry all the chips again for 2–3 minutes, until crisp and golden. Drain on kitchen paper.

Boil green vegetables

1 Bring a pan of salted water to the boil. Add the vegetables in small batches to avoid the water temperature being reduced.

2 Return the water to the boil, then reduce the heat and gently simmer the vegetables until they are just tender.

3 Drain through a colander and serve; or, to set the green colour and stop the vegetables cooking, rinse under cold running water.

Stir-fry vegetables

1 When the wok (or pan) is hot, add sunflower, rapeseed, or groundnut oil, tilting the pan to spread the oil, then toss in garlic or ginger.

2 Add the desired vegetables and use a spatula to toss continually. Add any meat first, and toss it more slowly to allow it to cook.

3 Some vegetables, such as broccoli, are best steamed for a few minutes. Add a couple of tbsp of water and cover until just tender.

Steam vegetables

1 Bring approximately 2.5 cm (1in) of water to the boil in the bottom pan of a steamer. Place the prepared vegetables in the upper basket and position it above the bottom pan.

2 When the steam rises, cover the pan with a fitted lid and cook until the vegetables are just tender. Test frequently with a knife to ensure that they are tender, but not overcooked.

Sauté firm vegetables

1 Set a sauté pan over a high heat. When it is hot, add a thin layer of oil or a small amount of clarified butter. As soon as this has heated, add the vegetables to the pan and keep turning them to cook evenly.

2 Continue turning and tossing the vegetables in the sauté pan. They should gradually take on a light golden brown colour and become tender. Remove from the heat and serve.

Herbs

BUY All herbs should look fresh, whether cut or growing in pots. Avoid any that look wilted or discoloured. Ideally, plant a herb garden or in a window box. Buy dried herbs in small quantities as they lose their fragrance once exposed to the air. Use sparingly as their flavour is concentrated. Also available frozen.
STORE Best picked and used fresh, but cut can be stored in a plastic bag in the refrigerator for a few days. Freeze sealed bags of cut herbs, whole or chopped, for up to 6 months.

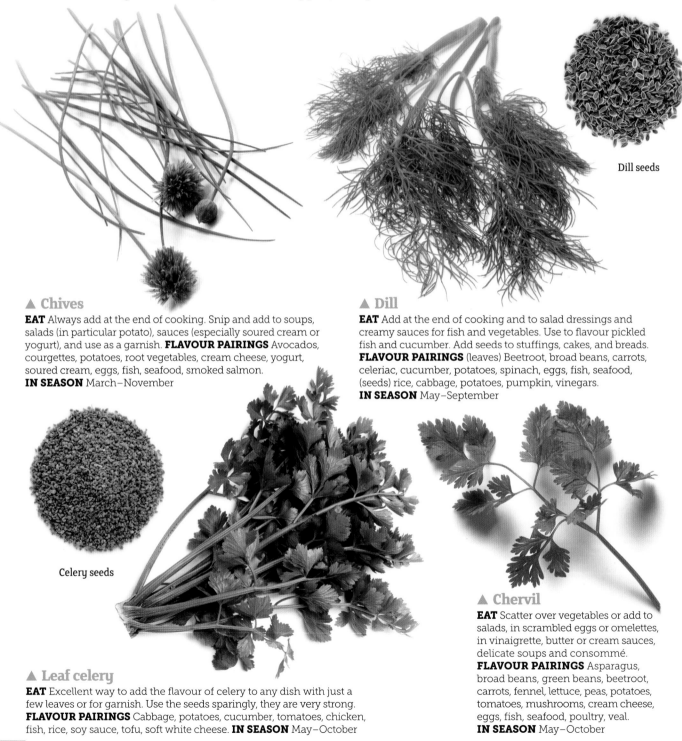

Dill seeds

▲ **Chives**

EAT Always add at the end of cooking. Snip and add to soups, salads (in particular potato), sauces (especially soured cream or yogurt), and use as a garnish. **FLAVOUR PAIRINGS** Avocados, courgettes, potatoes, root vegetables, cream cheese, yogurt, soured cream, eggs, fish, seafood, smoked salmon.
IN SEASON March–November

▲ **Dill**

EAT Add at the end of cooking and to salad dressings and creamy sauces for fish and vegetables. Use to flavour pickled fish and cucumber. Add seeds to stuffings, cakes, and breads.
FLAVOUR PAIRINGS (leaves) Beetroot, broad beans, carrots, celeriac, cucumber, potatoes, spinach, eggs, fish, seafood, (seeds) rice, cabbage, potatoes, pumpkin, vinegars.
IN SEASON May–September

Celery seeds

▲ **Leaf celery**

EAT Excellent way to add the flavour of celery to any dish with just a few leaves or for garnish. Use the seeds sparingly, they are very strong.
FLAVOUR PAIRINGS Cabbage, potatoes, cucumber, tomatoes, chicken, fish, rice, soy sauce, tofu, soft white cheese. **IN SEASON** May–October

▲ **Chervil**

EAT Scatter over vegetables or add to salads, in scrambled eggs or omelettes, in vinaigrette, butter or cream sauces, delicate soups and consommé.
FLAVOUR PAIRINGS Asparagus, broad beans, green beans, beetroot, carrots, fennel, lettuce, peas, potatoes, tomatoes, mushrooms, cream cheese, eggs, fish, seafood, poultry, veal.
IN SEASON May–October

◀ Coriander

EAT Except when used in curry pastes, best added at end of cooking. Use in curries, stir-fries, pesto, salsas, chutneys, relishes, and as a garnish. **FLAVOUR PAIRINGS** Avocados, sweetcorn, cucumber, root vegetables, onions, chillies, coconut milk, poultry, meat, fish, seafood, citrus, pulses, rice. **IN SEASON** May–October, imported all year

Tarragon ▶

EAT Use in moderation. Add to green salads or vinaigrette; in marinades; to flavour goat's cheese and feta, in egg dishes, herb butter, and vinegar. **FLAVOUR PAIRINGS** Artichokes, asparagus, courgettes, tomatoes, mushrooms, potatoes, salsify, fish, seafood, poultry, eggs, game, feta, and goat's cheese. **IN SEASON** May–October

▲ Horseradish

EAT Don't cook. As soon as it's grated, mix with lemon juice to preserve colour and pungency. Use in dressings, relishes, sauces, to glaze ham with apricot preserve or honey. Also available grated in jars. **FLAVOUR PAIRINGS** Sausages, beef, gammon, oily and smoked fish, seafood, avocados, beetroot, red cabbage, potatoes, celeriac, apples. **IN SEASON** October–December

Fennel seeds

▲ Fennel

EAT The leaves, flowers, and pollen give anise fragrance to cold soups, chowders, roast meats and vegetables, and in fish dishes. Add seeds to potatoes, breads, and pickles. **FLAVOUR PAIRINGS** Beetroot, beans, cabbage, leeks, cucumber, tomatoes, potatoes, duck, fish, seafood, pork, lentils, rice. **IN SEASON** May–September

▲ Lavender

EAT Infuse flowers in milk, syrup, cream, or wine for baking and desserts and add to jams, jellies, or fruit compôtes. Use chopped flowers and leaves to flavour roast lamb, rabbit, chicken, and pheasant. **FLAVOUR PAIRINGS** Berries, plums, cherries, rhubarb, chicken, lamb, rabbit, pheasant, chocolate. **IN SEASON** March–September

▲ Bay

EAT Add whole to flavour soups, stews, sauces, pickles, milk puddings, and marinades. Thread on kebabs, or use to top terrines or pâtés before baking. Remove before serving. **FLAVOUR PAIRINGS** Meat, poultry, offal, game, fish, chestnuts, citrus, haricot beans, lentils, rice, tomatoes, mushrooms. **IN SEASON** All year

▲ Lovage

EAT Use leaves and stalks instead of celery or parsley in salads, sauces, marinades, soups, stews, casseroles, or with just about any vegetable. **FLAVOUR PAIRINGS** Apples, root vegetables, potatoes, Jerusalem artichokes, courgettes, mushrooms, tomatoes, sweetcorn, Cheddar, Gruyère or cream cheeses, eggs, pulses, fish, meat, poultry, rice. **IN SEASON** May–September

▲ Garden mint

EAT Also called spearmint, the most common mint variety for cooking. Use in sweet and savoury dishes, to flavour and garnish. In some Mediterranean countries, dried is preferred to fresh. **FLAVOUR PAIRINGS** Lamb, duck, potatoes, peas, carrots, tomatoes, cucumber, currants, curries, chocolate, yogurt. **IN SEASON** March–October

▲ Sweet basil

EAT It loses flavour quickly, so add at the end of cooking or to cold dishes. It's the classic flavouring for tomato-based dishes, Genoese pesto, and French pistou. Best torn or rolled, then chopped. Look out for purple, Thai, and Greek basil too. **FLAVOUR PAIRINGS** Tomatoes, garlic, pine nuts, mozzarella and other cheeses, eggs, aubergines, haricot beans, courgettes, lemon, olives, peas, pizzas, potatoes, rice, raspberries, sweetcorn. **IN SEASON** June–September, imported all year

▲ Oregano

EAT Popular for flavouring everything from pizzas to baked fish, salads to Mexican bean dishes. **FLAVOUR PAIRINGS** Lamb, beef, chicken, pork, pulses, chilli, cumin, coriander leaf, garlic, tomatoes, aubergines, Cheddar, mozzarella, feta and halloumi cheeses, olives, peppers. **IN SEASON** March–October

▲ Sweet marjoram

EAT Similar to oregano but with a more delicate, sweet flavour. Use leaves and flower knots in salads, cream sauces, egg and delicate fish dishes, for marinating fresh cheeses, and as a garnish. **FLAVOUR PAIRINGS** Olive oil, fresh white cheeses, plaice, sole, red mullet, mushrooms, eggs, squashes. **IN SEASON** March–October

▲ Sage

EAT Use sparingly to flavour rich meats and offal, in toasted sandwiches, stuffings, and polenta. Good as a simple pasta sauce with olive oil, butter, and sea salt. Deep-fry leaves for a few seconds for a garnish. **FLAVOUR PAIRINGS** Pork, duck, goose, veal, chicken, liver, sausages, cheeses, beans, tomatoes, apples, bay leaf, caraway, onions, celery, garlic, lovage, marjoram. **IN SEASON** All year

Curly-leaf parsley

Flat-leaf parsley

▲ Parsley

EAT Flat-leaf parsley has a stronger taste for adding to dishes, but they are interchangeable. Add chopped at the end of cooking for best results. Use stalks for flavouring soups and stews. **FLAVOUR PAIRINGS** Eggs, fish, seafood, chicken, béchamel sauce, lentils, rice, lemon, tomatoes, garlic, onions. **IN SEASON** March–October, imported all year

▲ Common sorrel

EAT It has a lemony flavour. Good in salads (add a little honey to the dressing or use balsamic vinegar), shredded in omelettes, baked or scrambled eggs, in cream sauces, and with fish. **FLAVOUR PAIRINGS** Chicken, pork, veal, fish (especially salmon), mussels, eggs, lentils, leeks, lettuce, cucumber, tomatoes, spinach, watercress. **IN SEASON** March–November

▲ Thyme

EAT Use in stews, casseroles, stuffings, pies, sauces, pâtés, terrines, and marinades. The flowers make a pretty garnish in sweet and savoury dishes. Lemon thyme can be used in biscuits, breads, and fruit salads. **FLAVOUR PAIRINGS** Lamb, rabbit, chicken, turkey, pulses, aubergines, cabbage, carrots, leeks, wild mushrooms, tomatoes, onions, potatoes, sweetcorn. **IN SEASON** All year

▲ Summer savory

EAT Good in salads, soups, stews, casseroles and stuffings. **FLAVOUR PAIRINGS** Rabbit, chicken, oily fish, cheeses, eggs, broad and green beans, pulses, beetroot, cabbage, potatoes. **IN SEASON** May–October

▲ Rosemary

EAT Finely chop for soups, stews, casseroles, roast vegetables, meat and fish, in marinades, sautés, and grills. Also good in creams, bakes, and summer drinks. Use whole woody sprigs as skewers for kebabs or as basting brushes. **FLAVOUR PAIRINGS** Poultry, rabbit, pork, lamb, veal, fish, eggs, lentils, squashes, peppers, courgettes, cabbage, potatoes, onions, garlic, citrus, fruit, cream cheese. **IN SEASON** All year

Spices

BUY Buy spices in small quantities as they lose their fragrance and colour when exposed to the air. Avoid any that look dull or discoloured. Most are available from good supermarkets, but more unusual spices can be found in specialist food shops. For best flavour, grind (or grate as appropriate) whole spices as you need them, rather than using ready-ground. **STORE** Keep fresh spices in a sealed container in the refrigerator for up to 2 weeks. Dried, whole, and ground spices should be stored in sealed containers in a cool, dark place. Whole dried spices will keep for 1–3 years; ground ones for around 6 months.

Capers

Caperberries

▲ Galangal

EAT Similar to ginger, peel and grate, or chop. Soak dried slices then add to soups and stews. Remove before eating. Use in Southeast Asian curries, stews, sambals, satays, soups, and sauces. **FLAVOUR PAIRINGS** Chicken, fish, seafood, coconut milk, chillies, fennel, garlic, ginger, lemon grass, lemon, kaffir lime, shallots, tamarind.

▲ Capers and caperberries

EAT Both from the caper bush, capers are the pickled or salted buds, and caperberries are the pickled semi-mature fruit. Add towards the end of cooking, or put in cold sauces or dressings. Caperberries can be eaten like olives. **FLAVOUR PAIRINGS** Rich meats, poultry, fish, seafood, globe artichokes, aubergines, green beans, gherkins, olives, potatoes, tomatoes.

Black mustard seeds

White (yellow) mustard seeds

▲ Mustard seeds

EAT Black (and brown) seeds can be dry-roasted or heated in hot oil or ghee to enhance their nutty flavour. Use white (yellow) seeds for pickling and marinades. Powdered yellow mustard is best for rubs, barbecue sauce, and in savoury baking. Prepared mustards are usually served as a condiment, and in sauces, dressings, and glazes. **FLAVOUR PAIRINGS** Beef, rabbit, sausages, chicken, ham, fish, seafood, strong cheeses, cabbage, root vegetables, curries, dals.

▲ Paprika

EAT Available as sweet, hot, or smoked (pimentón). Use sweet or hot in goulash, tagines, soups, and as a garnish; smoked as a rub for grills and roasts, in braises, and pan-fries. **FLAVOUR PAIRINGS** Beef, veal, chicken, duck, vegetables (sweet/hot); pork, sausages, fish, onions, pulses, eggs (smoked).

▲ Chilli

EAT Use whole dried (there are many varieties, Kashmir shown above), flakes, chilli powder, chilli seasoning, or cayenne (the hottest powder) to add heat and colour.
FLAVOUR PAIRINGS Most spices, bay, coriander leaf, parsley, coconut milk, citrus, meats, poultry, fish, seafood, pulses, tomatoes, avocados, tropical fruits, chocolate.

▲ Cinnamon

EAT Good for flavouring fruity desserts, breads, cakes, and drinks, like coffee, chocolate, tea, mulled wine, and ale. Also good in meat and vegetable tagines and bakes. **FLAVOUR PAIRINGS** Lamb, poultry, aubergines, chocolate, coffee, rice, almonds, apples, apricots, bananas, pears, other sweet spices.

▲ Caraway seed

EAT Use to flavour rye breads, biscuits, cabbage (particularly sauerkraut), seed cakes, sausages, soups, and stews. It is also used in spice blends, such as harissa paste.
FLAVOUR PAIRINGS Duck, goose, pork, breads, apples, cabbage, potatoes, root vegetables, tomatoes.

▲ Coriander seed

EAT The basis for many spice blends. Use in vegetable dishes, stews, and French à la grecque dishes, for pickling, marinades, and court-bouillon. **FLAVOUR PAIRINGS** Cumin, chicken, pork, ham, fish, orchard fruits, citrus, mushrooms, onions, potatoes, pulses.

▲ Cumin

EAT Dry-roast before grinding, or fry in oil to use whole to enhance aroma. Add to soups, curries, and casseroles. Used in numerous spice blends, from Cajun spices to Indian curry powders.
FLAVOUR PAIRINGS Meats, poultry, cheeses, vegetables, pulses, coriander seed and leaf, chilli, oregano.

▲ Kaffir lime leaves

EAT If the fresh or dried leaves are to be eaten rather than removed before serving, discard the central rib and shred leaf finely before use. Use in Thai-style salads, curries, fishcakes, soups, and noodle dishes. **FLAVOUR PAIRINGS** Pork, poultry, fish, seafood, mushrooms, noodles, rice, green vegetables, coconut, tropical fruits.

◄ Preserved lemons

EAT Slice and roast with vegetables, meat, chicken, or fish, or chop and add to tagines. Use the salty preserving juice in salad dressings. **FLAVOUR PAIRINGS** Lamb, chicken, fish, rice, cardamom, cloves, allspice, pepper, ginger, cinnamon, coriander leaf, fennel, celery, olives.

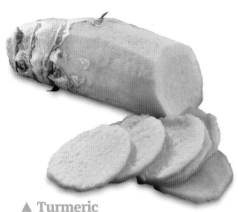

▲ Turmeric

EAT Use fresh, crushed, or ground turmeric in spice pastes for curries, stews, and vegetable dishes, and to flavour and colour rice and dals. **FLAVOUR PAIRINGS** Meat, poultry, fish, eggs, aubergines, beans, lentils, rice, root vegetables, spinach.

▲ Cardamom pods

EAT Lightly bruise and fry, or toast, then grind the seeds before adding to a dish. Split whole pods and add directly to rice. Also used in spice pastes, sweetmeats, pastries, puddings, breads, ice creams, tea, coffee, and chocolate. **FLAVOUR PAIRINGS** Apples, oranges, pears, sweet potatoes, pulses, cinnamon, star anise, cloves.

▲ Saffron

EAT Characteristic in Mediterranean fish soups and stews. Also popular in risottos, paellas, biryanis, pilafs, in baking, and to flavour ice cream. Infuse the strands and add early in cooking for a deeper colour; later for stronger fragrance. **FLAVOUR PAIRINGS** Chicken, game, fish, seafood, eggs, asparagus, leeks, mushrooms, spinach, squashes, mayonnaise (as rouille).

▲ Lemongrass

EAT Finely chop or slice to flavour curries, stews, and stir-fries. Pound with other spices and herbs for curry pastes. **FLAVOUR PAIRINGS** Beef, chicken, pork, fish, seafood, noodles, most vegetables, Thai or European basil, coriander leaf, chilli, galangal, cinnamon, cloves, turmeric, coconut milk.

▲ Star anise

EAT Use in Chinese and Vietnamese soups, stews, broths, and marinades. Also good for fish and seafood dishes, poaching fruit, and to enhance the sweetness of leeks, pumpkin, and root vegetables. **FLAVOUR PAIRINGS** Chicken, beef, oxtail, pork, fish, seafood, tropical fruits, figs, pears, leeks, pumpkin, root vegetables, chilli, cinnamon, coriander seed, fennel seed, garlic, ginger.

▲ Curry leaves

EAT Use in long-simmered South Indian and Sri Lankan curries, then remove or eat with the dish. Use also in a basic tadka to spoon over cooked dal. **FLAVOUR PAIRINGS** Lamb, fish, seafood, lentils, rice, most vegetables, cardamom, chilli, coconut, coriander leaf, cumin, fenugreek seed, garlic.

▲ Juniper berries

EAT Crush and add to marinades, stuffings, pâtés, and robust sauces. Also the classic flavouring in gin. **FLAVOUR PAIRINGS** Red meats, game, goose, apples, celery, cabbage, caraway, garlic, marjoram, rosemary, savory, thyme.

▲ Sumac

EAT It has a lemony taste, and brings out the flavours of foods, much as salt does. Use ground as a condiment. Rub on fish, vegetables, kebabs, and steaks before cooking. Use in chicken and vegetable casseroles, or mix with yogurt and herbs as a dip. **FLAVOUR PAIRINGS** Chicken, lamb, fish, aubergines, chickpeas, lentils, onions, pine nuts, yogurt, coriander leaf, mint, parsley.

▲ Poppy seed

EAT When baking, sprinkle on or add to breads, bagels, pretzels, and cakes. Use in dressings for noodles or to garnish vegetables. Grind to a paste with honey to fill pastries and sweetmeats. **FLAVOUR PAIRINGS** Aubergines, green beans, cauliflower, courgettes, potatoes, bread, honey.

▲ Nigella seed

EAT Often sold as black onion seed. Add to pilafs, curries, and pickles, or sprinkle alone or with other seeds on breads, savoury pastries, and vegetables before baking. **FLAVOUR PAIRINGS** Allspice, cumin, and sesame seeds, coriander leaf, star anise, pulses, rice, roots, and tubers.

▲ Allspice

EAT Allspice has long been used to preserve meat and fish, and is still used in pickled fish dishes, as well as in other pickles, chutneys, some sausages, and mulled wines and beers. Use in curries and pilafs, too. **FLAVOUR PAIRINGS** Aubergines, onions, squashes, root vegetables, white cabbage, tomatoes, most fruit.

▲ Peppercorns

EAT Use whole black to flavour cooking liquids, stocks, and marinades, and freshly ground for dressings, sauces, and cooked dishes. Mild pink and green peppercorns, often preserved in brine or vinegar, are good for steak au poivre or with chicken and veal (rinse before use). Use sharp white pepper for pale coloured sauces. **FLAVOUR PAIRINGS** Meat, poultry, game, fish, seafood, vegetables, oils, herbs, other spices, salts, some fruits (especially strawberries).

▲ Mace

EAT Similar but lighter than nutmeg. It lifts béchamel and onion sauces, clear soups, fish stock, potted meat, pâtés, terrrines, cheese soufflés, chocolate drinks, and cream cheese desserts. **FLAVOUR PAIRINGS** Chicken, lamb, veal, milk, eggs, cheeses, carrots, onions, pumpkin, spinach, sweet potato, other sweet spices, bay leaf, thyme.

◄ Nutmeg

EAT Good in many sweet and savoury dishes from vegetable purées, meat stews, and casseroles, to bread sauce, milk puddings, and fruit desserts. Best grated fresh, but can be bought ground. **FLAVOUR PAIRINGS** Chicken, veal, lamb, cabbage, onion, roots and tubers, squashes, spinach, cheese, eggs, milk, rice, couscous, semolina, cardamom, other sweet spices.

▲ Ginger

EAT Add freshly grated to Indian chutneys, relishes, and rice dishes, in stir-fries, soups, sauces, marinades, and tempura dipping sauce. Use pickled ginger with sushi, and fried as a garnish. Use ground ginger in baking for cakes and biscuits, and in desserts. It is also available preserved in syrup or candied. **FLAVOUR PAIRINGS** Fish, seafood, meat, poultry, most vegetables, chilli, coconut, garlic, citrus, soy sauce, orchard fruits, rhubarb.

▲ Tamarind

EAT Available in block, concentrate, or paste. For block, soak a small piece in hot water for 10 minutes. Stir, strain through a fine sieve, and use the liquid. It adds a sharp tang to curries, sambals, chutneys, marinades, and sauces, or mix with salt as a rub for meat. **FLAVOUR PAIRINGS** Chicken, lamb, pork, fish, seafood, lentils, mushrooms, peanuts, most vegetables, chilli, coriander leaf, cumin, galangal, garlic, ginger, turmeric, mustard, soy sauce, palm sugar.

▲ Fenugreek

EAT A bitter spice, widely used ground in vegetarian Indian cookery, in dals, fish curries, stews, and breads. The seeds are used in pickles, chutneys, and traditional spice blends. **FLAVOUR PAIRINGS** Green and root vegetables, chilli, garlic, fish, chicken, lentils.

▲ Sichuan pepper

EAT Best ground fresh. Remove the seeds from the berries, dry-roast briefly, then grind. Use as a condiment or to flavour meat or poultry for roasting, grilling, or frying, and stir-fried vegetables. One of the constituents of Chinese five-spice powder. Also available ground. **FLAVOUR PAIRINGS** Black beans, sesame oil and seeds, chilli, star anise, ginger, garlic, citrus, soy sauce.

▲ Cloves

EAT Use whole or ground with rich meats, in biscuits, pies, cakes, syrups, and preserves, and as a pickling and mulling spice. **FLAVOUR PAIRINGS** Ham, pork, duck, venison, orchard fruits, beetroot, red cabbage, carrots, onions, oranges, squashes, chocolate, cinnamon.

◀ Vanilla pods

EAT Use whole or split (with or without the seeds scraped into the dish) to flavour sugar, poached fruit, and desserts. Good with chicken and seafood, too. The pods can be rinsed, dried, and reused. Use pure vanilla extract in baking. **FLAVOUR PAIRINGS** Lobster, scallops, mussels, chicken, milk- and cream-based desserts, chocolate, apples, melons, pears, rhubarb, strawberries.

Salts

BUY Made up of crystals of sodium chloride, these salts can all be used as a condiment or seasoning, but for preserving, choose rock salt or pickling salt. Sea salt is unsuitable for this purpose because of the minerals it contains. It is, however, the one to use for cooking. Fine ground sea salt is labelled simply as cooking salt or *gros sel*. There are also speciality sea salts; see below. Avoid table salt or iodized salt for pickles, as they can cause clouding of the liquid, or darkening of the food. **STORE** Salts have an indefinite shelf life, but they should be kept in airtight containers as they will absorb moisture from the atmosphere and become lumpy. If this happens, spread evenly in a baking tray, dry in the oven, and break up the clumps. Iodized salt may turn yellow, but this is harmless.

▲ Rock salt crystals

EAT The commonest form of salt, with a plain, salty taste. It is mined rather than sourced from the sea. The best choice for pickling, and for putting in a salt grinder. **FLAVOUR PAIRINGS** Pickling onions, shallots, green beans, cauliflower, squashes, gherkins, cucumbers, red cabbage, green walnuts.

▲ Table salt

EAT All-purpose refined rock salt, milled to very small grains, with anti-caking agents added to stop it clumping. It has a straightforward salty taste. Use in a salt cellar and for general cooking. Some brands have added iodine. **FLAVOUR PAIRINGS** Meat, fish, vegetables, eggs, pastries, breads, biscuits.

▲ Sea salt flakes

EAT Made in Maldon, Essex, for over 200 years. Famous for its lack of bitterness and distinctive, fresh taste of the sea. It is strong, so use sparingly. Scatter over griddled vegetables with a drizzle of olive oil, over chips, or rub on the skins of jacket potatoes before baking. Also available smoked. **FLAVOUR PAIRINGS** All meat, fish, poultry, and vegetables (especially asparagus), aubergines, courgettes, peppers, potatoes.

▲ Fleur de sel sea salt

EAT The purest form of sea salt derived from the top layer formed in salt pans. The Guérande area of France is famous for it. Use like sea salt flakes and, again, sparingly, as it has a sharp, pure, salty taste. **FLAVOUR PAIRINGS** All meat, fish, poultry, vegetables, cheeses, grains, pulses, eggs.

▲ Celery salt

EAT Ground celery seeds mixed with table salt. It is strong-flavoured so use sparingly to season soups, stews, casseroles, quail's eggs, tomato, and cheese dishes. Good rubbed on the skin of chicken or fish before grilling. **FLAVOUR PAIRINGS** Chicken, fish, tomatoes and tomato juice, cheeses, mayonnaise, soured cream, yogurt.

▲ Garlic salt

EAT Powdered dried garlic mixed with table salt. Use judiciously to season soups, stews, casseroles, dips, and other dishes when not using fresh garlic. Onion salt can be used in the same way. **FLAVOUR PAIRINGS** Herbs, spices, chicken, meat, fish, cream cheese, yogurt, soured cream, avocados, tomatoes, unsalted butter.

Honey, sugars, and syrups

BUY The darker the honey, sugar, and syrup, the deeper the flavour. For honey, those high in fructose stay runny, those with more glucose, set. Choose "pure" honey. Multi-floral is cheaper than a mono-floral (a single-blossom one will be identified on the label). When using sugar, select the right one for the job. Brown sugars should be moist and soft. **STORE** Keep in a cool, dry, dark place. Clear honey and syrups may crystallize during storage; heat gently to dissolve. Sugars, honey, and sugar syrups (except corn) keep indefinitely. Fruit syrups will keep for about a year. Corn syrup is lighter and tends to ferment after around 6 months.

▲ Clear honey

EAT Use in place of sugar in many recipes, but it is sweeter, so try using less. Clear honey mixes easily, so good for drizzling, dressings, glazes, sauces, and syrups. **FLAVOUR PAIRINGS** All meats and poultry, vinegars, oils, tomato purée, garlic, shallots, Worcestershire sauce, soy sauce, mustard, nuts, yogurt, fruits, rosemary, mint. **IN SEASON** June–August (depending on the blossom), imported all year

▲ Set honey

EAT Good in biscuits and cakes, to spoon on fruit, or spread on meat or poultry as part of a glaze before baking. **FLAVOUR PAIRINGS** Poultry, game, gammon, bacon, pork, lamb, figs, pineapple, grapefruit, bananas, peanuts, walnuts, almonds. **IN SEASON** June–August (depending on the blossom), imported all year

▲ Comb honey

EAT A piece of honey-filled beeswax comb is the most natural way to eat honey. Don't use it for cooking, but it is delicious raw for breakfast or as a tea time treat. **FLAVOUR PAIRINGS** Warm crusty bread, toast, butter. **IN SEASON** June–August (depending on the blossom)

▲ Agave necter

EAT Sweeter than honey and yet suitable for vegans, this syrup is extracted from the agave plant, and is great poured over porridge or used to sweeten smoothies. Be careful to choose the pure variety. **FLAVOUR PAIRINGS** Oats, banana, lime, cinnamon, quinoa, sweet potato, chilli, mezcal and tequila, chocolate, coffee, cornmeal.

▲ Caster sugar

EAT A finer version of granulated sugar. White is refined sugar, golden caster is unrefined. Use both for general sweetening, frosting and candying, baking, and desserts. **FLAVOUR PAIRINGS** All fruit, nuts, tomatoes, chocolate, coffee, vanilla, eggs, cream, crème fraîche, yogurt.

▲ Icing sugar

EAT Finely ground refined sugar sometimes with anti-caking agent. Use for icings, frostings, sweet butters, delicate sweets, and to dust over cakes and desserts. **FLAVOUR PAIRINGS** Citrus and other fruits, eggs, vanilla, cinnamon, peppermint, almond, chocolate, coffee, cream cheese, caramel, brandy, rum.

▲ Demerara sugar

EAT Coarse crystal sugar traditionally used to sweeten coffee and for baking rich fruit cakes. Some is coloured refined sugar, look for unrefined. **FLAVOUR PAIRINGS** Coffee, mixed dried fruits, apples, pears, bananas.

▲ Muscovado sugar

EAT Dark and light unrefined, moist sugar (dark shown here). Use dark in rich fruit cakes, chutneys, and marinades; light in biscuits and crumbles. Soft brown sugars are refined, with added molasses. **FLAVOUR PAIRINGS** Fruits, vegetables, meats, sweet spices.

▲ Jaggery and palm sugar

EAT Jaggery (shown here) is blocks of unrefined palm or cane sugar. Palm sugar comes in blocks, sticky granules, or liquid. **FLAVOUR PAIRINGS** Vegetables, meats, fish, tropical fruits, spices, herbs.

▲ Golden syrup

EAT Sticky cane or beet syrup with a distinctive flavour. Classic ingredient of treacle tart and flapjacks. **FLAVOUR PAIRINGS** Ginger, cinnamon, mixed spice, chocolate, butter, oats.

▲ Blackstrap molasses

EAT Unrefined, almost black, thick, slightly bitter syrup for rich cakes and chutneys. **FLAVOUR PAIRINGS** Dried fruits, vegetables, stone and orchard fruits, chillies, spices.

▲ Black treacle

EAT Runnier than blackstrap molasses and slightly milder. Use in the same way, but also good for treacle toffee, parkin, and gingerbread. **FLAVOUR PAIRINGS** Ginger, cinnamon, cloves, nutmeg, mixed spice, allspice, nuts, oatmeal.

▲ Corn syrup

EAT Available as light or dark syrup, similar to golden syrup with a less distinctive taste. Use in the same way. **FLAVOUR PAIRINGS** Ginger, cinnamon, mixed spice, chocolate, butter, oats.

▲ Maple syrup

EAT Runny syrup from the sap of the maple tree, traditionally served with pancakes and waffles. Maple-flavoured syrup also available. **FLAVOUR PAIRINGS** American-style pancakes, waffles, pineapple, bananas, nuts, chocolate, coffee.

▲ Pomegranate syrup

EAT Thick, tangy, and sweet, also known as pomegranate molasses. Use in sweet and savoury dishes. **FLAVOUR PAIRINGS** Duck, chicken, fish, pork, game, soy sauce, pak choi, courgettes, salad leaves, tropical fruits.

Prepare spices

Before use, whole fresh spices such as lemongrass can be bruised with the flat side of a heavy knife and your hand.

Roots like ginger can be finely chopped by hand, but it's often easiest to grate them. Peel off the skin beforehand.

Scraping out the seeds from chillies lessens their heat. Wear a pair of rubber or plastic gloves to avoid irritation to your skin.

When spices are fried until lightly coloured, their flavour gets trapped in the oil. The oil can then be used along with the spices.

To dry-roast spices, place them in an oven preheated to 160°C (325°F/Gas 3), or fry them in a dry pan, until lightly browned.

Dried or dry-roasted spices can either be crushed by hand in a pestle and mortar or by machine in a spice mill.

Prepare herbs

A mezzaluna makes light work of chopping herbs. Rock it from side to side across them until they're chopped to your liking.

To strip the leaves of herbs with woody stalks, simply run the thumb and forefinger of one hand along the stalk.

For a classic soup flavouring, tie a sprig of thyme and parsley with a bay leaf. You could also include sage or rosemary.

1 To chop the leaves of herbs with tender stalks like basil, and avoid bruising them, roll the leaves together into a tight bunch.

2 Holding the bunch of leaves steady with one hand, slice across them with a sharp chef's knife to create fine shreds.

3 Using the knife in a rocking motion, chop the leaves finely, turning them by 90 degrees halfway through.

Extract vanilla seeds

1 Vanilla pods can be used whole, but the seeds look especially good in creamy desserts. To extract them, put the vanilla pod on a board and using the tip of a sharp knife, cut along the length of the pod.

2 Using the blunt side of a small knife or a teaspoon, scrape along the inside of the pod to collect the sticky seeds. The empty pod can then be used to flavour syrups and sugars.

Make lemon-zest julienne

1 Using a peeler, remove strips of the lemon zest, taking off as little of the bitter pith as possible. Try to select unwaxed lemons for this purpose, and always wash and dry the skin before you begin.

2 If any pith remains, use a sharp knife to slice it off by running your knife along the peel away from you. Then, using a rocking motion with your knife, slice the peel into strips.

Use gelatine

1 Soak the required number of leaves of gelatine in enough cold water, or other liquid, to cover them fully for at least 10 minutes. Squeeze out as much of the water as possible before using.

2 In a saucepan, warm some water or whatever liquid is specified in your chosen recipe. Add the gelatine, and stir to dissolve thoroughly before leaving the solution to cool.

Make a sugar syrup

1 Heat your measured amount of sugar and water over a low heat in a heavy-based pan, without stirring, until dissolved. Use a wet pastry brush to wipe the pan edge to stop grains of sugar sticking.

2 When the sugar has dissolved, bring the syrup slowly to the boil and boil for 2 minutes for basic syrup or to the correct temperature for your recipe, using a sugar thermometer.

Make caramel sauce

1 Warm 100ml (3½fl oz) liquid glucose in a heavy-based pan over a low heat. Do not boil. Add 125g (4½oz) caster sugar and heat gently until dissolved, then boil until golden. Cool the base of the pan for 1 minute in iced water.

2 While the syrup is still warm, whisk in 25g (scant 1oz) unsalted butter and 250ml (9fl oz) softly whipped cream. Return the pan to a low heat and bring gently to the boil until the sauce is smooth, thick, and creamy.

Make a ganache

1 Chop 100g (3½oz) dark chocolate by placing it on a work surface or chopping board. Select a knife with a serrated edge and use your hand to press down on the blunt side of the blade.

2 Melt the chocolate in a heatproof bowl over a pan of simmering (not boiling) water, ensuring the water does not touch the bowl. Stir with a wooden spoon and add the chocolate to 100ml (3½fl oz) boiling double cream. Stir again gently from the centre.

Prepare chocolate

Break the chocolate and chill in the freezer for a few minutes. Place on a board and, using a sharp knife, chop using a rocking motion.

For grating, rub chilled chocolate against the grater, using the widest holes. If it begins to melt, put it back in the freezer and repeat.

For curls, spread soft or melted chocolate onto a cool surface. Use the blade of a chef's knife to scrape the chocolate into curls.

Make professional glossy icing

1 Add 300g (10oz) chopped dark chocolate to a sugar syrup and stir until smooth. Heat to 120°C (225°F) – the mixture should form a "thread" if you dip your fingers in iced water, then the chocolate, and pull apart.

2 Brush the cake with apricot jam melted with a little water. Remove the icing from the heat and tap the pan to remove any air bubbles. Ladle it onto the cake and smooth it out with a warmed metal spatula.

Orchard fruits

BUY Choose fruit with no bruises. Brown russeting on the skin of some fruit is normal. Apples and Asian pears should smell fragrant. Loquats may have a few brown spots and should feel tender. Pears should give slightly at the stem end. Quinces have a downy skin that becomes smooth as they ripen (any left can be rubbed off). Medlars have a brown, wrinkled skin, and rarely ripen on the tree. Leave to "blet" in a paper bag in a cool, dark place for several weeks until soft. **STORE** Put in the fruit bowl as required. Loquats and pears should be eaten as soon as they are ripe. All can be prepared and frozen for up to 12 months.

▲ **Cox's Orange Pippin apple**
EAT With scented, crisp, sweet flesh and mottled skin, Cox's apples can be used for cooking as well as eating raw, but are best in salads. Good for juicing and drying.
FLAVOUR PAIRINGS White or red cabbage, walnuts, almonds, pine nuts, sunflower seeds, fresh and dried fruits, celery, lovage, mayonnaise, vinaigrette, ginger. **IN SEASON** August–February (best August–December)

▲ **Granny Smith apple**
EAT Good all-rounder with green skin and sharp, crunchy flesh. Use in pies, tarts, and cakes, for sauce, in fruit and savoury salads, meat, fish, and cheese dishes. **FLAVOUR PAIRINGS** Cinnamon, mixed spice, cloves, walnuts, almonds, raisins, sultanas, cabbage, cheeses, chicken, pork, duck, game, black pudding, cider, Calvados. **IN SEASON** Imported all year

▲ **Red Delicious apple**
EAT Large fruit with tough, crimson skin and sweet, crumbly flesh. Not good for cooking. **FLAVOUR PAIRINGS** All cheeses, celery, grapes, pork or duck pâté, nuts. **IN SEASON** Imported all year

▲ **Bramley apple**
EAT Large cooking apple that cooks to a fluffy pulp. Best for pies, sauce, baking, fritters, and all types of dessert. Good bottled or in chutneys. **FLAVOUR PAIRINGS** Citrus, almonds, berries, rhubarb, pears, quinces, dried fruit, cinnamon, cloves, mixed spice, nutmeg, vanilla, honey, syrup, demerara sugar, chocolate. **IN SEASON** All year (best October–December)

◄ Williams' pear

EAT Tender, juicy, and slightly musky, good raw or for preserving. **FLAVOUR PAIRINGS** Red wine, port, brandy, cinnamon, star anise, cloves, ginger, wine vinegar, white and demerara sugar, maple syrup, dried fruits. **IN SEASON** September–February, stored and imported all year

▲ Comice pear

EAT Eat raw or cooked in crumbles, pies, and savoury dishes. **FLAVOUR PAIRINGS** Pork, duck, goose, apples, raisins, cinnamon, cloves, ginger, walnuts, goat's and blue cheeses. **IN SEASON** September–March

▲ Conference pear

EAT Good raw or cooked in sweet and savoury dishes. For cooking, choose slightly under-ripe pears. Peel before use, if wished. Use over-ripe fruit in sauces and smoothies. **FLAVOUR PAIRINGS** Game, pork, Parmesan, blue cheeses, rocket, watercress, tarragon, celery, walnuts, almonds, cinnamon, ginger, star anise, cardamom, chocolate, butterscotch vanilla. **IN SEASON** September–February, stored and imported all year

▲ Asian pear

EAT Peel, if wished, core and slice, or chop. Use in fruit and savoury salads, spicy Asian dishes, or poach in syrup. In Japan they eat them sprinkled with salt. **FLAVOUR PAIRINGS** Beef, papaya, mango, lime, chilli, soy sauce, ginger, cardamom, star anise, rice vinegar, honey. **IN SEASON** July–October, imported most of the year

▲ Loquat (níspero)

EAT Halve, remove stone, and scoop out flesh or poach in syrup. Or peel, if liked, and quarter or chop for fruit for savoury salads, sauces, ice cream, cake fillings. **FLAVOUR PAIRINGS** Poultry, prawns, goat's cheese, vanilla ice cream, apples, pears, citrus, ginger, spirits. **IN SEASON** Imported April–June

▲ Quince

EAT Peel, core, and chop for sauces and meat dishes, tarts, pies, and crumbles. Purée for mousses and creams. Bottle or make into jams, jellies, or cheese. Use japonica quinces in the same way. **FLAVOUR PAIRINGS** Lamb, pork, chicken, game, hard cheeses (particularly Manchego), apples, pears, ginger, cloves, cinnamon. **IN SEASON** October–November

▲ Medlar

EAT When bletted (ripened), peel back the skin and suck or spoon out the flesh. Add pulp to a rich meat sauce or make into jelly, curd, or cheese. **FLAVOUR PAIRINGS** Meat, game, hard cheeses, cinnamon, nutmeg, mixed spice, star anise, red or white wine. **IN SEASON** October–November

Stone fruits

BUY Plums, gages, and sloes should have a slight bloom on the skin. They should all feel heavy for their size, and firm, but give slightly when gently pressed. They should never feel squashy. Avoid if rock-hard (they may never ripen), if split, wet, with any bruised patches, or with wrinkled skin (except dates, which may be semi-dried). **STORE** If a little firm, keep in a fruit bowl. If ripe, they will keep for a few days in the refrigerator in an open paper bag. All except dates can be bottled or frozen in dry sugar or syrup for up to 12 months.

▲ Victoria plums

EAT The classic British dessert plum. Delicious raw, or cooked in sauces, soufflés, pies, tarts, cakes, and puddings, or preserved as jam or chutney. **FLAVOUR PAIRINGS** Duck, lamb, pork, gammon, goose, game birds, chilli, Chinese five-spice powder, ginger, soy sauce, garlic, onions, pickling vinegar, almonds, cinnamon, custard, cream, eggs. **IN SEASON** August–October

▲ Red plums

EAT Various large red and purple varieties, mostly imported (Santa Rosa pictured). Red have a better flavour for cooking than purple. Eat fresh, in pies and crumbles, mixed with other fruit, diced in salsas, or as plum sauce. Available canned, and dried as prunes. **FLAVOUR PAIRINGS** Meat, game, avocados, tomatoes, red peppers, cucumber, spring onions, chilli, coriander leaf, lime, garlic, ginger, soy sauce, rice, vinegar, apples, pears, rhubarb, strawberries, custard, clotted cream, ground almonds. **IN SEASON** Imported all year

▲ Yellow plums

EAT Large imported yellow plums are best raw. Smaller ones, like Coe's Golden Drop (pictured) are good in crumbles, sweet and savoury salads, and salsas. **FLAVOUR PAIRINGS** Sweet peppers, spring onions, cucumber, light muscovado sugar, soft fresh cheeses. **IN SEASON** Imported all year

▲ Opal plums

EAT Sweet early-cropper. Good raw but excellent bottled whole in alcohol, and for pies, clafoutis, and desserts. **FLAVOUR PAIRINGS** Brandy, Kirsch, red wine, cream, clafoutis batter, light muscovado sugar, butter, almonds. **IN SEASON** August–October

▲ Greengages

EAT Sweet-scented fruit that can be used instead of plums in any dish. **FLAVOUR PAIRINGS** All rich meats and game, ground and flaked almonds, cinnamon, ginger, kirsch, amaretto, brandy, cream, custard. **IN SEASON** August

▲ Apricots

EAT Use the natural line on the fruit to cut in half and twist apart. Eat raw as a snack, or in fruit salads or platters. Poach in syrup or wine; purée for fruit sauce; or halve, stuff, and bake. Add to tagines, couscous, roasts, and stuffings. Also available canned, dried, and as jam. **FLAVOUR PAIRINGS** Chicken, lamb, pork, ham, yogurt, cream, custard, oranges, almonds, rice, ginger, vanilla, sweet white wine, amaretto. **IN SEASON** July–August, imported most of the year

▲ Damsons

EAT Sharp even when ripe, but excellent in desserts, jams, fruit cheese, soups, wine, and chutney. **FLAVOUR PAIRINGS** Sultanas, apple, garlic, light muscovado sugar, chilli, ginger, cinnamon, pickling vinegar, red wine, ice cream, custard, blackberries. **IN SEASON** August–September

Sweet cherries

Sour cherries

▲ Cherries

EAT Morello are sour cherries with a wonderful flavour for cooking, particularly when preserved in alcohol or syrup and in jam. Add sweet cherries whole or pitted to fruit salads, to decorate and fill cakes or in cold and iced desserts. Bake both in pies, tarts, clafoutis, and strudels. Use for soup, or in sweet and savoury sauces. Also sold canned and bottled, in syrup, brandy, cherry liqueur, and candied (glacé). **FLAVOUR PAIRINGS** Duck, game, almonds, sweet spices, chocolate, citrus, fromage frais, yogurt, brandy, Kirsch, grappa. **IN SEASON** June–August, sweet cherries imported most of the year

◀ Dates

EAT Medjool (pictured) is highly-prized. Eat raw, whole, or stuffed. Chop and add to rice, couscous, stuffings, stews, and relishes. Also available dried and as syrup. **FLAVOUR PAIRINGS** Poultry, lamb, bacon, cheeses, marzipan, nuts, clotted cream, yogurt, citrus, chocolate. **IN SEASON** Imported most of the year, best November–January

▲ Sloes

EAT Small black fruit of the blackthorn. Too sour to eat raw, but good in jam and jelly and to flavour gin or vodka. **FLAVOUR PAIRINGS** Juniper, cinnamon, vanilla, gin, vodka, apples. **IN SEASON** October–November

Yellow-flesh peach

Donut peach

White-flesh peach

▲ ▶ Peaches

EAT Flat donut, yellow- or white-fleshed can all be used in the same way. Best skinned before eating. Halve and grill to garnish savoury dishes; stuff and bake; slice or dice for fruit salads and salsas; purée for ice cream, sorbets, and sauces; make into jam or chutney. Also available canned and dried. **FLAVOUR PAIRINGS** Beef, duck, soured cream, yogurt, passion fruit, mangoes, berries, lime, mint, almonds, cinnamon, ginger, nutmeg, chilli, Champagne, sherry, amaretto. **IN SEASON** August–September, imported most of the year

Yellow-flesh nectarine

▲ ▶ Nectarines

EAT Similar to peaches (and used the same way) but with smooth skin. Delicious raw with cold meats and in salads and salsas, but also good stuffed and baked. **FLAVOUR PAIRINGS** Chicken, gammon, prosciutto crudo, soft white cheeses like mascarpone, walnuts, almonds, berries, chilli, cinnamon, vanilla, star anise. **IN SEASON** August–September, imported most of the year

White-flesh nectarine

Olives

BUY For best flavour, buy olives still with their pits – loose or in jars. Pitted olives can be useful for some dishes. In general look for plump, shiny specimens, although dry salt-cured ones are supposed to look shrivelled. **STORE** Always keep in the refrigerator in sealed containers. Loose ones, or those in salt or brine, should be used within a week or so. Those covered in olive oil will keep for months. If mould appears on the surface, rinse, dry, and cover with fresh oil.

▲ Manzanilla olives

EAT Large green, silky olives from Seville. Sold stuffed with pimento, too. Traditionally served with chilled fino sherry; also the perfect martini olive. Good sliced in fish, cheese, and pulse salads. **FLAVOUR PAIRINGS** Dry fino sherry, gin, dry martini, shellfish, chickpeas, white beans, chorizo, Serrano ham, squid, prawns, crab, Manchego cheese. **IN SEASON** Imported all year

▲ Kalamata olives

EAT From Greece, with a rich fruity flavour. Good with aperitifs, in salads, and also cooked in stews and casseroles. **FLAVOUR PAIRINGS** White cabbage, tomatoes, cucumber, red onions, sweet peppers, aubergines, feta cheese, halloumi cheese, red wine vinegar, olive oil, oregano, preserved lemons, pork, chicken, lamb, pasta, rice. **IN SEASON** Imported all year

◀ Dry salt-cured olives

EAT Shrivelled and salty with a strong, olive flavour. Pit and chop, then bake in bread, add to tapenade, pasta sauces, and meat dishes (whole or pitted). **FLAVOUR PAIRINGS** Beef, pork, lamb, spicy sausages, pasta, olive oil, cherry and sun-dried tomatoes, sweet peppers, basil, oregano, parsley. **IN SEASON** Imported all year

◀ Picholine olives

EAT Dusky green olives with a surprising amount of crisp, nutty flesh. Delicious served as an aperitif, but also good chopped in chicken, fish, and rabbit stews, and rice dishes. **FLAVOUR PAIRINGS** Chicken, white and oily fish, rabbit, tomatoes, rice, white wine, sherry, dry vermouth, peppers, white beans, oranges. **IN SEASON** Imported all year

▲ Stuffed green olives

EAT Small green olives are sold pitted and stuffed with pimento, anchovy, lemon, garlic, capers, celery, or almonds. Serve as appetizers or slice in salads. **FLAVOUR PAIRINGS** Fish, meat, poultry, cheeses, pasta, rice, peppers, tomatoes, onions, garlic, sweet spices, herbs. **IN SEASON** Imported all year

▲ Niçoise

EAT Small and nutty from Provence, France but also grown in Spain and Italy. Often preserved with herbs. Use in classics like pissaladière and salade niçoise. **FLAVOUR PAIRINGS** Tomatoes, onions, garlic, anchovies, eggs, green beans, new potatoes, courgettes, capers, caperberries, cinnamon, oregano, herbes de Provence. **IN SEASON** Imported all year

Tropical fruits

BUY Most should give slightly when lightly squeezed and have a fragrant aroma. Choose bananas according to personal preference. Avoid if soft and dark all over. All unripe fruit can be ripened at room temperature.
STORE Ripe fruit should be eaten as soon as possible after purchase. All except bananas (and pineapples, unless prepared then put in an airtight container) can be stored in a paper bag in the refrigerator for a few days (bananas go black if too cold). All except dragon fruit can be frozen for up to 12 months as purée (bananas discolour, so use for breads and cakes only and use within 6 months), or in syrup. Freeze passion fruit pulp in ice cube trays to add to ice creams and fruit salads.

▲ Kiwi

EAT Halve and spoon out for a snack. Peel and slice or dice for fruit salads and salsas, to decorate pavlovas, pastries, and cakes, or as a garnish. **FLAVOUR PAIRINGS** Gammon, chicken, guinea fowl, squid, salmon, chillies, orange, strawberries, other tropical fruit. **IN SEASON** Imported all year, best January–August

▲ Mango

EAT Peel and stone, then slice or chop for salads, salsas, or cakes. Purée for juices, smoothies, sorbets, mousses, and cream. Slice and bottle in syrup. Also available canned, dried, and as chutney. **FLAVOUR PAIRINGS** Chicken, smoked meats, fish, shellfish, green salads, avocados, lime, lemon, chillies, curry spices, coriander leaf, vanilla ice cream, sweet sticky rice, rum. **IN SEASON** Imported all year

▲ Passion fruit

EAT Halve and spoon out the pulp to add to fruit salads and desserts. Sieve to yield juice for dressings, ices, mousses, soufflés, sauces, smoothies, and drinks. **FLAVOUR PAIRINGS** Tuna, venison, game birds, cream, yogurt, custard, oranges, kiwi fruit, strawberries, bananas, peaches, light muscovado sugar, rum, white and sparkling wine. **IN SEASON** Imported October–June

▲ Papaya

EAT Peel, halve, and scoop out the seeds. Use in sweet and savoury salads, salsas, and desserts. The purée is an excellent meat tenderizer. When unripe, steam as a vegetable. Also available canned and dried. **FLAVOUR PAIRINGS** Meat, smoked meats, avocados, chillies, lime, lemon, coconut, ginger. **IN SEASON** Imported all year

▲ Pomegranate

EAT Use the juicy seeds in sweet and savoury salads, salsas, dressings, cold and iced desserts. Add the juice to soups, stews, desserts, and sauces. Also available as syrup (molasses). **FLAVOUR PAIRINGS** Prawns, lamb, chicken, duck, pheasant, aubergines, figs, almonds, pistachios, couscous, rice. **IN SEASON** Imported October–February

◀ Guava

EAT Add to sweet and savoury salads, purée for sauces, smoothies, and pancake fillings, sorbets, and ice cream. Poach or bake for compôtes, desserts, and savoury dishes. Also available canned and dried. **FLAVOUR PAIRINGS** Pork, pheasant, duck, seafood, chicken, cream cheese, apples, pears, lime, chillies, lemon, coconut, ginger, honey. **IN SEASON** Imported all year

Persimmon (Sharon fruit) ▶

EAT Eat whole, or cut off the top and scoop out flesh. Blend for smoothies, add to sauces, cold and iced desserts. If unripe, poach or chop and add to cakes, breads, and muffins. **FLAVOUR PAIRINGS** Ham, pork, game, lime, clotted cream, yogurt, fromage frais, walnuts, ginger, cinnamon, allspice, nutmeg, honey. **IN SEASON** Imported October–April

▲ Pineapple

EAT Peel and slice or dice for savoury and sweet salads, salsas, pastries, and desserts. Add pineapple juice to marinades, drinks, and smoothies. Also available canned, candied, and dried. **FLAVOUR PAIRINGS** Pork, ham, chicken, duck, fish, shellfish, cottage cheese, coconut, ginger, allspice, cinnamon, black pepper, Cointreau, rum, Kirsch. **IN SEASON** Imported all year

▲ Dragon fruit

EAT Do not cook. Best eaten chilled. Halve and scoop out the flesh. Add to fruit salads, or press the juice for sorbets, cocktails, and drinks. **FLAVOUR PAIRINGS** Lime, lemon, other tropical fruits, coconut, sugar, ginger. **IN SEASON** Imported all year

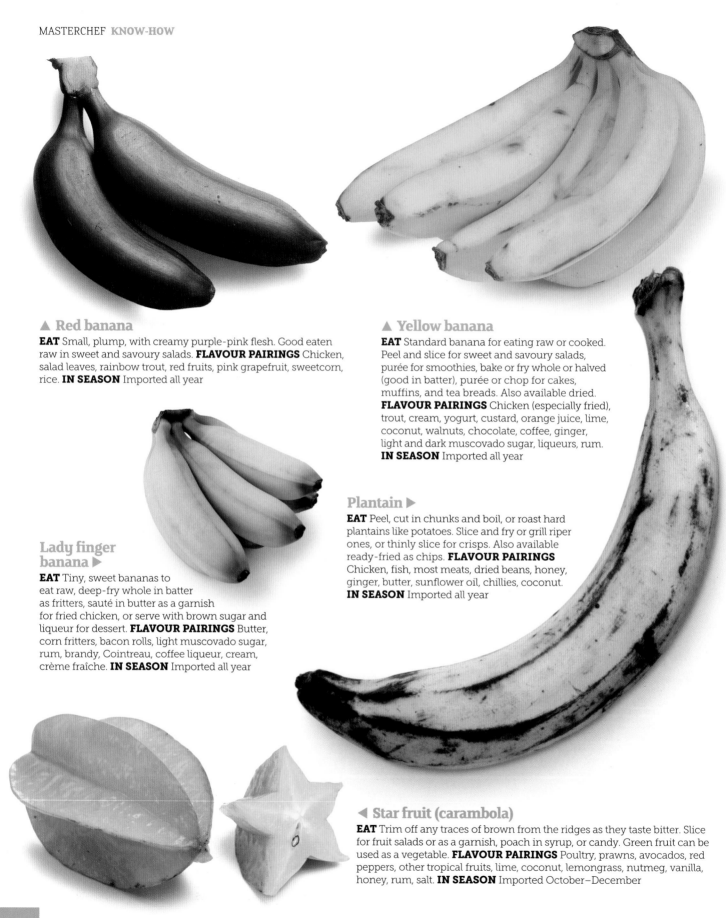

▲ Red banana

EAT Small, plump, with creamy purple-pink flesh. Good eaten raw in sweet and savoury salads. **FLAVOUR PAIRINGS** Chicken, salad leaves, rainbow trout, red fruits, pink grapefruit, sweetcorn, rice. **IN SEASON** Imported all year

▲ Yellow banana

EAT Standard banana for eating raw or cooked. Peel and slice for sweet and savoury salads, purée for smoothies, bake or fry whole or halved (good in batter), purée or chop for cakes, muffins, and tea breads. Also available dried. **FLAVOUR PAIRINGS** Chicken (especially fried), trout, cream, yogurt, custard, orange juice, lime, coconut, walnuts, chocolate, coffee, ginger, light and dark muscovado sugar, liqueurs, rum. **IN SEASON** Imported all year

Plantain ▶

EAT Peel, cut in chunks and boil, or roast hard plantains like potatoes. Slice and fry or grill riper ones, or thinly slice for crisps. Also available ready-fried as chips. **FLAVOUR PAIRINGS** Chicken, fish, most meats, dried beans, honey, ginger, butter, sunflower oil, chillies, coconut. **IN SEASON** Imported all year

Lady finger banana ▶

EAT Tiny, sweet bananas to eat raw, deep-fry whole in batter as fritters, sauté in butter as a garnish for fried chicken, or serve with brown sugar and liqueur for dessert. **FLAVOUR PAIRINGS** Butter, corn fritters, bacon rolls, light muscovado sugar, rum, brandy, Cointreau, coffee liqueur, cream, crème fraîche. **IN SEASON** Imported all year

◀ Star fruit (carambola)

EAT Trim off any traces of brown from the ridges as they taste bitter. Slice for fruit salads or as a garnish, poach in syrup, or candy. Green fruit can be used as a vegetable. **FLAVOUR PAIRINGS** Poultry, prawns, avocados, red peppers, other tropical fruits, lime, coconut, lemongrass, nutmeg, vanilla, honey, rum, salt. **IN SEASON** Imported October–December

▲ Rambutan

EAT Peel and eat fresh, use as a garnish, add to savoury or fruit salads, purée for ice cream or sorbet, or poach in syrup.
FLAVOUR PAIRINGS Pork, duck, avocados, chillies, cream, coconut, vanilla, ginger.
IN SEASON Imported May–September

▲ Tamarillo

EAT Also called tree tomato. Cut in half, sprinkle with sugar, chill overnight, then scoop out. Add to ice cream. Peel and stew in savoury dishes and for relishes. Bake or grill for dessert, or add to compôtes.
FLAVOUR PAIRINGS Roast meats, fish, chicken, curry spices, cream, kiwi fruit, oranges, light muscovado sugar.
IN SEASON Imported May–October

▲ Lychee

EAT Pop out of the shells for a snack. Stone and add to sweet or savoury salads, sweet and sour dishes, and stir-fries. Poach in syrup or purée for ice cream, smoothies, drinks, and dressings. Also available canned.
FLAVOUR PAIRINGS Pork, duck, chicken, seafood, chillies, avocados, raspberries, coconut, cream, lime, ginger. **IN SEASON** Imported April–June

▲ Mangosteen

EAT Cut off the top and scoop out the flesh; don't eat the pith. Use juice for drinks and sorbets. **FLAVOUR PAIRINGS** Other tropical fruits, strawberries, lemongrass, lemon.
IN SEASON Imported May–September

▲ Custard apple

EAT Remove the seeds and eat fresh, or use in pies, pancakes, stir-fries, and savoury sauces. **FLAVOUR PAIRINGS** Pork, chicken, citrus, yogurt, cinnamon, ginger.
IN SEASON Imported June–September

▲ Durian

EAT Famous for tasting delicious, but smelling awful! Split open and scoop out the pulp round the seeds. Eat with sugar and salt, or purée for shakes and smoothies, or add to cakes. Cook unripe fruit as a vegetable. Roast the seeds. **FLAVOUR PAIRINGS** Milk, cream, coconut, other tropical fruits, curry spices, chillies, sticky rice. **IN SEASON** Imported May–August

◀ Physalis

EAT Peel back the papery casing and eat raw, or dip in chocolate or fondant for petit fours. Poach in syrup, add to cakes and tarts, sauté briefly for savoury dishes, use as a garnish or make into jam. **FLAVOUR PAIRINGS** White fish, scallops, yogurt, other tropical fruits, nuts, lemon, tarragon, chocolate, Cointreau. **IN SEASON** Imported August–October

405

Grapes, rhubarb, and figs

BUY All should be unblemished. Grapes should have a slight bloom. Rhubarb stalks should be firm. The leaves of forced rhubarb should be pale yellow and fresh. Avoid if browning around the stalk end or wrinkling. Figs should feel heavy for their size and just yield without pressing; sugar beads around the stem indicate ripeness. **STORE** Keep in the refrigerator: rhubarb for a week or more, wrapped in moist kitchen paper in a plastic bag; grapes for up to 5 days in an open paper bag; ripe figs for a day or two, but best eaten quickly. If unripe, soften at room temperature. All can be frozen in syrup for up to 12 months.

▲ Red grapes

EAT A gourmet, seeded red variety is Muscat Rosada (pictured here). They have a rich, musky flavour. All red grapes (some are seedless) are best eaten fresh to round off a meal, or in fruit salads. **FLAVOUR PAIRINGS** Cheddar, Manchego, and Goat's cheeses, port, unblanched almonds, most fruits. **IN SEASON** Imported in spring

▲ Green grapes

EAT With or without seeds, eat whole or peel, if liked, halve and add to cream and white wine sauces, or to fruit salads. **FLAVOUR PAIRINGS** Chicken, poultry livers, rabbit, flat fish, melon, strawberries, cheeses, walnuts. **IN SEASON** Imported all year

▲ Black grapes

EAT Good colour and flavour. Halve, deseed, if necessary, and add to sauces and salads, or serve with cheeses, liver pâtés, and terrines. **FLAVOUR PAIRINGS** Beef, venison, game birds, cheeses, fruits, red wine, port. **IN SEASON** Imported all year.

▼ Rhubarb

EAT Forced rhubarb is tender and pink. Outdoor is coarser and may have tough skin. If so, pull off before cutting into short lengths. Also sold frozen and canned. Use in pies, crumbles, mousses, fools, ice cream, and sauces (particularly for oily fish). **FLAVOUR PAIRINGS** Ginger, cinnamon, vanilla, lavender, strawberries, oranges, plums, brown sugar, custard, mackerel, herring. **IN SEASON** Forced: February–April. Outdoor: April–July

Forced rhubarb

Outdoor rhubarb

▲ Fig

EAT Eat whole, including the skin if soft. Add to sweet and savoury salads, stuff for sweetmeats, poach in syrup, bottle, or make into jam. Also sold dried. **FLAVOUR PAIRINGS** Cured meats, yogurt, cream, cheeses, nuts, star anise, marzipan, fortified wine. **IN SEASON** August–September, imported May–December

Melons

BUY Winter and summer sweet melons and watermelons should all feel heavy for their size. Winter melons have smooth or finely ribbed yellow rind and pale flesh. Summer ones include those with a raised cross-hatch pattern of netting on the rind and have green through to orange flesh. They should yield to gentle pressure round the base and smell fragrant. Watermelons should give a ringing sound when tapped.
STORE Whole ones will keep in a cool dark place for up to 2 weeks. Keep cut fruits in a sealed plastic bag in the refrigerator for up to a week. Freeze balls or cubes in sugar or syrup for up to 6 months.

▲ Ogen

EAT Small summer melon with greenish-yellow skin and green flesh. Good halved and the seeds scooped out, then filled for starter or dessert. **FLAVOUR PAIRINGS** Prawns, crab, lobster, ginger wine, raspberries, framboise liqueur, sorbets, ice cream. **IN SEASON** Imported all year

▲ Honeydew

EAT The best known winter variety and the classic choice for melon-boat starters. Good in salads, soups, and jam.
FLAVOUR PAIRINGS Parma ham, other cured and smoked meats, ground ginger, orange, mint, rosemary, cucumber, herb bread. **IN SEASON** Imported all year

▲ Cantaloupe

EAT Summer melon with pale orange, very sweet flesh. Good for breakfast or in salads. Note Galia (not pictured) looks similar, but is oval and has light green flesh. **FLAVOUR PAIRINGS** Coconut (fruit and milk), lime, cucumber, mint, fresh cheeses like mozzarella. **IN SEASON** Imported all year

▲ Charentais

EAT The green ribs on the rind make it look like it comes ready-sectioned. Apricot-orange flesh and delicious fragrance. Excellent dessert summer melon, and good for sorbets and soup. **FLAVOUR PAIRINGS** Tropical fruit, raspberries, strawberries, mint. **IN SEASON** Imported all year

▲ Watermelon

EAT Serve chilled in wedges, add to a fruit platter or cube for salads and pickle, or make into jam. Roast and salt the seeds.
FLAVOUR PAIRINGS Chicken, prawns, crab, feta cheese, beetroot, sweet melon, apple, berries, lime, chillies, ginger, mint.
IN SEASON Imported all year

Citrus fruits

BUY Look for skins that are bright, taut, and glossy. Fruit should feel heavy for its size, and should smell aromatic. Avoid any fruits that look dry or mouldy, or have brown marks. Unwaxed fruit are best if you want to use the peel or zest. **STORE** Keep in a cool place, or uncovered in the refrigerator, for up to 2 weeks; use before the skins shrivel. Smaller fruits will not keep as long as large ones. Freeze peeled segments and slices, or whole small fruits, dry or in syrup for up to 12 months.

Pink grapefruit

▲ Pomelo

EAT Delicious in salads and salsas, but make sure you remove all the pith and membrane. Candy the goose-pimpled skin, or add it to marmalade. **FLAVOUR PAIRINGS** Shellfish, smoked fish, poultry, ham, pork, chicory, frisée, celery, spinach, chocolate, cloves, cardamom. **IN SEASON** Imported January–February

White grapefruit

Red grapefruit

Grapefruit ▲ ▶

EAT Halve or segment white, pink, or red grapefruit to eat alone or in salads. Squeeze the juice for drinks, sorbets, and sauces. Grill halves. Use in marmalade or candy the peel. **FLAVOUR PAIRINGS** Chicken, gammon, smoked meats, prawns, avocados, spinach, lemon, mint, ginger, nutmeg, coconut, honey. **IN SEASON** Imported all year

▲ Lime

EAT Squeeze the juice for dressings, salsas, marinades, and drinks. Use the juice and zest in desserts, pies, and baked goods. Also, make into pickles, chutneys, jams, jellies, and marmalade. Also available dried. **FLAVOUR PAIRINGS** Poultry, fish, shellfish, chillies, Tabasco, tomatoes, avocados, lemons, mango, melon, papaya, chocolate, rum, tequila, mint, coriander leaf. **IN SEASON** Imported all year

▲ Lemon

EAT Squeeze the juice for dressings, marinades, drinks, tarts, pies, soups, salsas, fish, curries, and emulsion sauces. Grate the zest for baking and desserts. Add pared zest to casseroles. Chop for marmalade and chutney. **FLAVOUR PAIRINGS** Chicken, veal, fish, shellfish, eggs, artichokes, garlic, olives, cream, sage, tarragon, coriander leaf and seeds, capers, olive oil, gin. **IN SEASON** Imported all year

▲ Kumquat

EAT Not a true citrus, but used in similar ways in the kitchen. Eat whole (including the soft skin) or cook with sugar, spices, or spirits to make compôtes and chutneys, or bottle in alcohol. **FLAVOUR PAIRINGS** Shellfish, smoked fish, poultry, ham, pork, duck, chicory, frisée, celery, spinach, chocolate, cloves, cardamom, vodka. **IN SEASON** Imported November–February

▲ Minneola

EAT A mandarin–grapefruit hybrid with sharp, juicy, seedless flesh. Eat as a refreshing snack or use in salads and desserts **FLAVOUR PAIRINGS** Shellfish, pork, duck, chicory, watercress, celery, rocket, chocolate, cloves, star anise, Cointreau. **IN SEASON** Imported December–February

▲ Ugli

EAT A Jamaican cross between a tangerine, Seville orange, and grapefruit. Halve and eat fresh, or segment and chop and add to rich meats, oily fish, salads, ice creams, and soufflés. Candy the peel. **FLAVOUR PAIRINGS** Oily fish, pork, duck, goose, chicory, frisée, rocket, cream, honey, Kirsch or sherry (over halves). **IN SEASON** Imported November–April

◄ Seville (bitter) oranges

EAT Used mostly for marmalade but also good with rich meats, in spicy fish dishes, desserts, and to flavour white spirits. **FLAVOUR PAIRINGS** Duck, pigeon, pheasant, pork, salmon, tuna, meaty white fish, pancakes, rhubarb, meringue, lemon, grapefruit, gin, vodka, white rum. **IN SEASON** Imported January–March

▲ Yuzu

EAT This Japanese cross between a mandarin and a lemon is very strongly perfumed, with exotic floral and spicy aromas. The juice and finely grated zest is great whisked into granitas, cocktails, and fruit curd, or made into marinades for fish, or stirred into a stunning vinaigrette or mayonnaise. **FLAVOUR PAIRINGS** Toasted sesame oil, sake, oysters, sashimi, fried squid, crab, poultry, cream, chilli, chocolate, ginger, butter, daikon, mirin, mango. **IN SEASON** November–January

Navel oranges

◄▲ Sweet oranges

EAT Valencia, then Navel are the two leading commercial varieties. Grate zest and segment fruit, or squeeze juice, for sauces, soups, with other fruits and vegetables, in casseroles, salads, and sorbets. Use the zest in cakes and biscuits. Also peel and eat raw, or poach in caramelized syrup. Candy the peel and dip in chocolate. **FLAVOUR PAIRINGS** Beef, duck, gammon, liver, scallops, tomatoes, beetroot, black olives, nuts, soy sauce, cloves, cinnamon, fennel, carrots, chicory, frisée, button mushrooms, chocolate, strawberries, brandy. **IN SEASON** Valencias: Imported February–October. Navels: Imported November–May

Valencia oranges

▲ Blood oranges

EAT Small oranges with red-flecked flesh that yield a dazzling ruby juice, essential for sauce maltaise – with egg yolks and melted butter – and sorbets. Use the segmented flesh in sweet and savoury salads. **FLAVOUR PAIRINGS** Egg yolks, butter, baby red chard, beetroot, spring onions, strawberries, raspberries, pineapple, bananas, lemon, lime, walnuts. **IN SEASON** Imported December–May

▲ Clementine

EAT Peel for a snack or add to salads. Squeeze the juice for smoothies and sorbets. Lightly sauté or grill segments as a side dish. **FLAVOUR PAIRINGS** Shellfish, pork, chicken, duck, spinach, carrots, sweet peppers, salad leaves, almonds, coriander leaf, chocolate, meringues, Grand Marnier. **IN SEASON** Imported all year

▲ Satsuma

EAT Slightly less sweet than clementines, satsumas can be used the same way but are also good preserved whole in syrup and caramel, with or without alcohol. **FLAVOUR PAIRINGS** Caramel, soft brown sugar, vanilla sugar, brandy, Grand Marnier, vodka, whisky. **IN SEASON** Imported most of the year, best November–January

▲ Tangerine

EAT Tangerines are varieties of mandarin and have distinctively fragrant, sweet, juicy flesh (Murcott, or honey tangerine, pictured here). Use the zest and juice in desserts, sauces, and for sautéed poultry, pork and fish, and the segments in fruit salads and coleslaw. **FLAVOUR PAIRINGS** Chicken breasts, pork fillet and chops, tuna, salmon, scallops, cabbage, carrots, shallots, cream, honey. **IN SEASON** October–April

Currants and berries

BUY Choose fruit that are uniformly ripe and unblemished. Avoid red or black fruits that are still green in patches. Currants and berries do not ripen further after picking. If buying in punnets, avoid any that are stained with juice as this is a sign that the fruit is past its best. **STORE** Better eaten the day of picking or purchase but can be stored in the refrigerator, preferably in a single layer, for a couple of days. Green gooseberries will keep for up to a week. All can be bottled or frozen in dry sugar or syrup for up to 12 months. They soften when thawed so then only use for cooked dishes and purées.

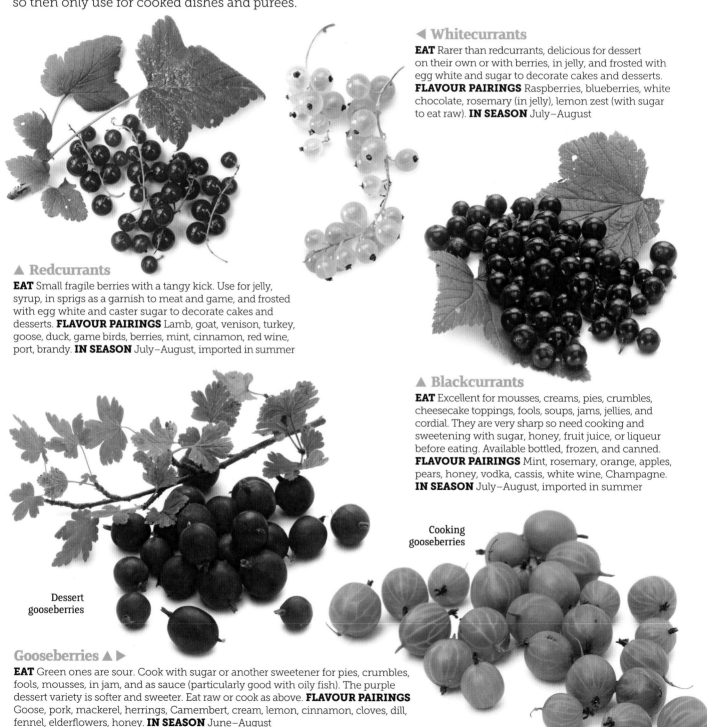

◀ Whitecurrants

EAT Rarer than redcurrants, delicious for dessert on their own or with berries, in jelly, and frosted with egg white and sugar to decorate cakes and desserts. **FLAVOUR PAIRINGS** Raspberries, blueberries, white chocolate, rosemary (in jelly), lemon zest (with sugar to eat raw). **IN SEASON** July–August

▲ Redcurrants

EAT Small fragile berries with a tangy kick. Use for jelly, syrup, in sprigs as a garnish to meat and game, and frosted with egg white and caster sugar to decorate cakes and desserts. **FLAVOUR PAIRINGS** Lamb, goat, venison, turkey, goose, duck, game birds, berries, mint, cinnamon, red wine, port, brandy. **IN SEASON** July–August, imported in summer

▲ Blackcurrants

EAT Excellent for mousses, creams, pies, crumbles, cheesecake toppings, fools, soups, jams, jellies, and cordial. They are very sharp so need cooking and sweetening with sugar, honey, fruit juice, or liqueur before eating. Available bottled, frozen, and canned. **FLAVOUR PAIRINGS** Mint, rosemary, orange, apples, pears, honey, vodka, cassis, white wine, Champagne. **IN SEASON** July–August, imported in summer

Cooking gooseberries

Dessert gooseberries

Gooseberries ▲ ▶

EAT Green ones are sour. Cook with sugar or another sweetener for pies, crumbles, fools, mousses, in jam, and as sauce (particularly good with oily fish). The purple dessert variety is softer and sweeter. Eat raw or cook as above. **FLAVOUR PAIRINGS** Goose, pork, mackerel, herrings, Camembert, cream, lemon, cinnamon, cloves, dill, fennel, elderflowers, honey. **IN SEASON** June–August

◀ Raspberries

EAT Many varieties. Eat raw for dessert, or purée for sauces, cold and iced desserts, soup, and smoothies. Add to savoury and sweet salads, tarts, pies, crumbles, summer pudding, and gâteaux. Use for jam, jelly, and to flavour vinegar and sweetened alcohol. **FLAVOUR PAIRINGS** Duck, goose, venison, game birds, chicken or duck livers, cream, crème fraîche, peaches, other berries, hazelnuts, meringue, almonds, oats, honey, vanilla, cinnamon, red wine, vodka, raspberry vinegar. **IN SEASON** July–November, imported all year

▲ Wild strawberries

EAT Also known as *fraises des bois*, they are found wild and cultivated (then called Alpine strawberries). Exquisite raw or as part of a special dessert, for wonderful flavoured vinegar or liqueur, or added to chilled still or sparkling wine. **FLAVOUR PAIRINGS** Champagne, white or rosé wine, vodka, Cointreau, cream, crème fraîche, eggs, custard, bitter chocolate, red wine or strawberry vinegar. **IN SEASON** June–August

▲ Strawberries

EAT Many varieties. Dip in melted chocolate, macerate in orange juice or liqueur, top cheesecakes, add to tarts, pies, summer pudding, gâteaux, and shortbread. Purée for coulis, cold and iced desserts, shakes, and smoothies. **FLAVOUR PAIRINGS** Cream, ice cream, curd and other soft white cheeses, cucumber, oranges, melon, rhubarb, other berries, almonds, vanilla, chocolate, black pepper. **IN SEASON** May–September, imported all year

▲ Blackberries

EAT Wild and cultivated. Add to salads, compôtes, pies, and crumbles. Use for jelly and flavoured vinegar. Purée for mousses, soups, and sauces. Bottle in syrup. **FLAVOUR PAIRINGS** Poultry, game, cream, yogurt, cream cheese, apples, pears, raspberries, almonds, oats, honey, vanilla, cinnamon. **IN SEASON** July–October, imported all year

▲ Rowanberries

EAT Gather after the first frosts, or pick when ripe and freeze for a couple of weeks to remove the bitterness. Must be cooked before eating. Use in sauces, pies, and crumbles, for jelly, wine, and liqueur. **FLAVOUR PAIRINGS** Lamb, mutton, goat, venison, poultry, apples, pears, red wine. **IN SEASON** August–October

▲ Loganberries

EAT Blackberry-raspberry hybrid with an intense flavour. Use in pies, tarts, summer pudding, and for jam. Purée for ice cream, sorbets, and smoothies. **FLAVOUR PAIRINGS** Apples, pears, bananas, rhubarb, cream, crème fraîche, soft white cheeses, yogurt, almonds. **IN SEASON** July–September

▲ Blueberries

EAT Serve as a snack or dessert alone, or with cereal for breakfast or in fruit salad. Purée for soups and smoothies. Bake in pies, tarts, crumbles, cobblers, cakes, and muffins. Stew for sweet and savoury sauces, in compôtes, or cheesecake toppings. **FLAVOUR PAIRINGS** Game, cream, crème fraîche, yogurt, citrus, almonds, pistachios, mint, cinnamon, allspice, plain and white chocolate. **IN SEASON** July–August, imported all year

▲ Cranberries

EAT Stew with sugar or honey for sauces and desserts. Add to pies, tarts, muffins, cakes, and parfaits as well as to pâtés, terrines, and stuffings for poultry and meat. Bottle alone or with apples or other berries. Make into jelly and jam. Also available frozen. **FLAVOUR PAIRINGS** Turkey, goose, pork, gammon, oily fish, apples, raspberries, blueberries, oranges, nuts, red wine, brandy, port. **IN SEASON** Imported November–March

▲ Mulberries

EAT Gather from the ground once they have dropped and are completely ripe. Eat whole, or purée for drinks, cocktails, ice cream, and sorbet. Make into jam or jelly, use to flavour vinegar, gin, white rum, or vodka **FLAVOUR PAIRINGS** Poultry, lamb, game, cream, pears, citrus. **IN SEASON** August–September

Elderberries ▶

EAT The fruit must be cooked. Add to pies, crumbles, or compôtes with other fruits, or purée for sauces and soups. Use to make cordial, wine, jam, or jelly. (Use elderflowers to flavour gooseberries, dip in batter as fritters, or to make cordial or Champagne.) **FLAVOUR PAIRINGS** Game, pork, apples, crab apples, strawberries, blackberries, lemon, walnuts, cinnamon, allspice, nutmeg, cloves. **IN SEASON** August–October

Dried and candied fruits

BUY Look for plump, unblemished, supple dried fruit (except banana chips, which are hard). Avoid if they appear leathery. Most are now sold ready-to-eat but check if they need soaking before use. They are sometimes treated with sulphur dioxide to preserve them further, or may contain added sugar, oil, flavourings, or additives. Check the labels. Candied fruit should be soft and moist. Available all year.
STORE Once a packet or pot is opened, place in an airtight container and store in a cool, dark, dry place. Dried fruits will keep for 6 months, candied fruit for a year.

▲ Raisins and sultanas

EAT Raisins are dried black grapes (pictured). Black manuka and muscatels have the best flavour. Sultanas are dried white grapes. Eat as a snack, add to breakfast cereals, in rice and couscous dishes, salads, tagines, curries, cakes, biscuits, muffins, puddings, and chutneys. **FLAVOUR PAIRINGS** Cinnamon, mixed spice, curry spices, coriander leaf, parsley, mint, oats and other grains, cabbage, honey, rum, cream, most fruits, chocolate, nuts.

▲ Dried cranberries

EAT Often sweetened when dried. Add to breakfast cereals, cakes, biscuits, muffins, sweet or savoury stuffings. **FLAVOUR PAIRINGS** Oats, wheat, barley, millet, rice, breadcrumbs, turkey, duck, goose, pork, chicken, pine nuts, rosemary, thyme, parsley, onions, honey, maple syrup.

▲ Dried blueberries

EAT Add to breakfast cereals, cakes, biscuits, muffins, trail mix, sweet and savoury salads. **FLAVOUR PAIRINGS** White and plain chocolate, vanilla, cinnamon, oats, rice, couscous, pistachios, almonds, walnuts, honey.

▲ Dried cherries

EAT Sour cherries are delicious as a snack, or add to breakfast cereals, puddings, pies, muffins, and ice cream. **FLAVOUR PAIRINGS** Almonds, oats and other grains, white soft cheeses, cream, Kirsch, amaretto, plain chocolate.

▲ Currants

EAT Dried small black grapes with an intense, slightly bitter flavour. Use alone or with other dried fruits for cakes, puddings, biscuits, and pastries. Also good in hot and cold rice and couscous dishes. **FLAVOUR PAIRINGS** Brown and white sugars, honey, soft white cheeses, other dried fruits, ginger, cinnamon, mixed spice, cardamom, cumin, turmeric, peas, apples, pears, citrus, mint, parsley, rosemary, coriander seed and leaf, basil.

▲ Dried mango

EAT They have a vibrant colour and chewy texture. Delicious as a snack. Chop and add to cakes, biscuits, tea breads, chutney, and jam. **FLAVOUR PAIRINGS** Coconut, lime, lemon, apples, pears, peaches, nectarines, strawberries, raspberries, blueberries, vanilla, ginger.

▲ Dried peach

EAT Eat for a snack, soak or poach in wine, fruit juice, or syrup, or chop and add to cakes, biscuits, desserts, savoury and fruit salads, and casseroles. **FLAVOUR PAIRINGS** Other dried fruits, hard cheeses, soft blues like Gorgonzola, mozzarella, feta, halloumi, ham, duck, game birds, rice.

▲ Dried dates

EAT Available whole or ready-chopped for baking. Pit whole ones and stuff with marzipan or walnuts and honey for a sweetmeat, chop and add to stuffings, cakes, tea breads, biscuits, breakfast cereals, puddings, relishes, and sauces. **FLAVOUR PAIRINGS** Marzipan, walnuts, honey, fruit syrup, golden syrup, molasses, ginger, sweet spices, cooking apples, pears, chocolate.

▲ Dried apricot

EAT Some need soaking before use. Eat as a snack, or add whole, halved, or chopped to casseroles and tagines, stuffings, couscous and rice dishes, sweet and savoury salads, desserts, cakes, biscuits, muffins, pies, and tarts. Unsulphured apricots have a brown colour and more intense flavour. **FLAVOUR PAIRINGS** Cinnamon, star anise, nutmeg, curry spices, almonds, brazil nuts, pistachios, walnuts, lamb, pork, chicken, turkey, goose, duck, game, soft cheeses, yogurt, cream, citrus.

▲ Dried pear

EAT Eat as a snack, or poach in wine, cider, fruit juice, or syrup. Chop and add to sweet and savoury salads, and serve with cheeses. **FLAVOUR PAIRINGS** Blue and sage-flavoured cheeses, Cheddar, walnuts, bananas, rice, pasta, peas, mushrooms, ice cream, custard.

◄ Prunes

EAT Dried plums, with or without stones. Some need soaking before use (cold tea is good). Eat as a snack, or wrap in bacon or pancetta and grill. Add whole, chopped, or puréed to soups, sauces, stews and casseroles, in stuffings, sweet and savoury pies, hot and cold desserts. Also available canned. **FLAVOUR PAIRINGS** Chicken, rabbit, pork, beef, venison, game birds, bacon, cheeses, spinach, other dried fruit, pears, apples, yogurt, cream, custard.

▲ Dried apple

EAT Nibble raw, add to casseroles and compôtes, soak and bake as a garnish with rich meats. Apple chips are excellent added to breakfast cereals. **FLAVOUR PAIRINGS** Pork, duck, goose, pheasant, honey, maple syrup, redcurrant jelly, cider, apple juice, dried pears, hard cheeses.

▲ Dried banana

EAT Slices are often coated with sugar or honey. Eat as a snack alone or with nuts, scatter on breakfast cereals, crush and add to biscuits. Small, whole, dried, brown, chewy bananas also available. Eat these as a snack, or chop and add to cakes, muffins, tea breads, stews, soufflés, and dried fruit salads. **FLAVOUR PAIRINGS** Yogurt, soft white cheeses, oats and other grains, walnuts, coconut, hazelnuts, other dried fruits, ginger, cinnamon, brandy.

Chopped mixed peel

◀ Dried fig

EAT Intense flavour. Eat as a snack or stuff for sweetmeats. Chop and add to hot and cold desserts, cakes, biscuits, tea breads, and shortbreads. Use in stuffings or casseroles with poultry and game birds. Soak and stew whole in syrup with or without alcohol and sweet spices. **FLAVOUR PAIRINGS** Pork, chicken, duck, goose, game birds, sausages, cheeses, fennel, rum, cider, Pernod, marzipan, star anise.

Citron peel

Flaked coconut

Desiccated coconut

▲ Candied peel

EAT Chopped, mixed, diced, or sliced candied peel is used in rich fruit and plainer cakes, biscuits, florentines, tea breads, and steamed puddings, particularly Christmas pudding. Candied citron peel is moist and sticky. Chop and use in cakes, marmalades, fruit relishes, jam, and as a sweetmeat. **FLAVOUR PAIRINGS** Angelica, glacé cherries, other dried fruits, chocolate, cinnamon, mixed spice, ginger, nutmeg, mace.

▲ Dried coconut

EAT Available sweetened and unsweetened, as shavings (chips), flakes, and shredded (desiccated). Use in baking, curries, breakfast cereals, cakes, biscuits, tuiles, or toppings for baked goods. **FLAVOUR PAIRINGS** Curry spices and spice pastes, pulses, all meats, poultry, fish, dried fruits, tropical fruits, cherries, citrus, oats and other grains, rice, noodles, cream.

417

Nuts and seeds

BUY Nuts are available in shells, or shelled whole, flaked, chopped, or ground, depending on variety. Buy nuts and seeds in smallish quantities as they have a high fat content so can go rancid. When buying in their shells, they should feel heavy. If light they may be rotten. Shake a coconut; you should hear the water inside. Avoid chestnuts and coconuts with any signs of mould or cracks. Seeds generally need no preparation, but both nuts and seeds can be toasted before use to enhance the flavour, or soaked for nutritious sprouting varieties. Look out for nut butters too. **STORE** Nuts in their shell will keep for several months. Keep ready-shelled nuts and seeds in airtight plastic or glass containers, in a cool, dark place and use within a few weeks.

▲ Almonds

EAT Available in shell or shelled, unblanched or blanched (raw, or roasted and salted), slivered or flaked, chopped, and ground. Eat whole as a snack, or in some baked dishes and salads. Use processed ones in cakes, biscuits, petits fours, meringues, pastries, desserts, praline, almond paste (marzipan), stir-fries, sauces, stews, and curries. **FLAVOUR PAIRINGS** Lamb, chicken, trout, honey, chocolate, apricots, cherries, plums, peaches, nectarines, dried fruits. **IN SEASON** Imported in shell October–January

▲ Brazils

EAT Excellent for snacks. Good chopped or ground in stuffings, biscuits, cakes, and confectionery. **FLAVOUR PAIRINGS** Bananas, dried fruits, chocolate, toffee, maple syrup, molasses. **IN SEASON** Imported in shell October–January, shelled all year

▲ Macadamias

EAT Highly prized roasted and salted as a snack with drinks, or add chopped to biscuits, cakes, pastries, confectionery, ice cream, sweet and savoury salads, and stuffings. **FLAVOUR PAIRINGS** Chicken, white fish, bananas, toffee, coconut, chocolate, maple syrup. **IN SEASON** Imported shelled all year

▲ Cashews

EAT A popular nibble, roasted, with or without salt, with drinks. Add raw whole or chopped in stir-fries, curries, stews, casseroles, sweet and savoury salads, biscuits, and confectionery. Grind for nut butter; also available ready-prepared. **FLAVOUR PAIRINGS** Chicken, beef, white fish, sweetcorn, chilli, smoked paprika, star anise, Thai curry pastes, lemongrass, galangal, ginger, orange, lime. **IN SEASON** Imported shelled all year

▲ Pistachios

EAT Roasted and salted in their shell, they are a popular nibble with drinks. Use blanched unsalted in desserts, cakes, biscuits, sweet pastries, ice cream, sweet sauces, in rice and couscous dishes, pâtés and terrines, sausages, and as a pretty garnish.
FLAVOUR PAIRINGS Chicken, fish, pork, veal, chocolate, vanilla, raspberries, blueberries, meringues, rice. **IN SEASON** Imported, with and without shells, all year

Cobnuts

Hazelnuts

▲ Hazelnuts and cobnuts

EAT Hazelnuts are the original wild variety, cobnuts are cultivated. Eat as a snack, or blanch and add whole, chopped, or ground to cakes, biscuits, meringues, sweet and savoury stuffings, pâtés, terrines, and salads.
FLAVOUR PAIRINGS Game birds, fish, pork, liver, apples, plums, raspberries, cinnamon, coffee, chocolate, cream cheese. **IN SEASON** Green: August. Brown: September–October, imported shelled all year

▲ Coconut

EAT Coconuts are not, technically, nuts but fruit. Snack on fresh chunks, drink the water. Grate fresh to add to cereals, salads, desserts, ice cream, sweetmeats, curries, biscuits, and cakes. Infuse the flesh to make coconut milk and cream, which is also available canned and powdered. The flesh is also available dried **FLAVOUR PAIRINGS** Chicken, shellfish, yogurt, chilli, curry spices, Thai curry pastes, rice, citrus, tropical fruits, cherries, vanilla, jaggery **IN SEASON** Imported all year

▲ Pine nuts

EAT Use extensively in sauces, sweet and savoury salads, roasts, bakes, soups, stews, stuffings, biscuits, cakes, pastries, and desserts. **FLAVOUR PAIRINGS** Chicken, fish, spinach, aubergines, basil, mint, coriander leaf, cinnamon, vanilla, rice, couscous, bulgur, chocolate, honey.
IN SEASON Imported shelled all year

▲ Chestnuts

EAT They have a high tannin content so should not be eaten raw. Roast in their shells, add whole or chopped in stuffings, casseroles, and braises, or with vegetables, or purée for soups, pastries, and desserts. Also available shelled and vacuum-packed, frozen and canned whole, puréed (sweetened and unsweetened), and candied. **FLAVOUR PAIRINGS** Chicken, turkey, game birds, venison, sausagemeat, Brussels sprouts, onions, nutmeg, vanilla, cinnamon, chocolate. **IN SEASON** September–December

▲ Pecan nuts

EAT Good raw, halved, or chopped, in breads, biscuits, muffins, cakes, pies, pastries, confectionery, ice cream, and in savoury dishes. Serve salted or spiced with drinks. **FLAVOUR PAIRINGS** Chicken, turkey, game birds, eggs, sweet potato, bananas, pears, cinnamon, maple syrup, chocolate, coffee. **IN SEASON** Imported in shell October–March, shelled all year

Green walnut

Dried walnut

▲ Peanuts

EAT Seeds of a legume, not nuts but used in the same way, raw or roasted and, salted as a snack, ground to a paste for peanut butter, or in sauces, soups, stews, curries, stir-fries, noodle dishes, and for biscuits, cakes, trail mix, and confectionery. **FLAVOUR PAIRINGS** Spring onions, wasabi, chilli, peppers, egg and rice noodles, sesame seeds, chocolate, caramel, light muscovado sugar, hard and soft cheeses. **IN SEASON** Imported all year

▲ Walnuts

EAT Sold in their shells and shelled halves and broken pieces. Add halves or chopped to breakfast cereals, salads, snack mixes, stuffings, breads, cakes, pastries, and to decorate sweetmeats. Grind for soups and sauces. Pickle green ones. **FLAVOUR PAIRINGS** Coffee, chocolate, bananas, pears, dried fruits, cream, blue cheeses, celery, apples, cabbage. **IN SEASON** Green June–July, dried September–January, imported shelled all year

▲ Sunflower seeds

EAT Enjoy raw, or toasted and salted, as a snack, on their own, or as part of a trail mix. Use raw or toasted to add flavour and texture to breakfast cereals, porridge, salads, sandwiches, bread, cakes, biscuits, pasta, and rice dishes. **FLAVOUR PAIRINGS** Oats, barley, rye, millet, rice, couscous, grated root vegetables, dried fruits, tropical fruits, honey, maple syrup, pomegranate syrup. **IN SEASON** Imported all year

▲ Linseeds

EAT Available as dark brown, reddish brown, or golden seeds. Use whole or cracked to add texture and colour. Grind or use the oil for maximum nutritional benefits. Add to porridge, breakfast cereals, flapjacks, biscuits, and bread. Use ground in smoothies. **FLAVOUR PAIRINGS** Oats, rye, rice, couscous, potatoes, almonds, dried fruits, honey, golden or corn syrup, mixed spice. **IN SEASON** All year

▲ Sesame seeds

EAT Used all over the world in sweet and savoury dishes. Add to rice and noodles, to coat foods before frying, sprinkle over salads and vegetables, add to salads, vegetables, breads, biscuits, pastries, and sweetmeats. Sesame seed paste (tahini) is used in dips, sauces, and dressings, in baking and sweetmeats. **FLAVOUR PAIRINGS** Chicken, fish, peanuts, chickpeas, spinach, carrots and other root vegetables, noodles, rice, parsley, mint, coriander leaf, chilli, honey, lemon, lime. **IN SEASON** Imported all year

▲ Pumpkin seeds

EAT Enjoy as a snack, toasted and salted, or spiced. Add raw or toasted to breakfast cereals, salads, stir-fries, pasta and rice dishes, cakes, biscuits, and breads. You can use seeds straight from the squash, fresh, or dry-roasted first. **FLAVOUR PAIRINGS** Oats, barley, wheat, apricots, pumpkin, chilli, cinnamon, ginger, maple syrup. **IN SEASON** Imported all year

Peel and prepare apples

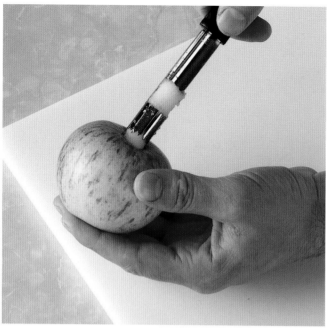

1 Remove the core of an apple by pushing a corer straight into the stalk of the apple and through to the bottom. Twist gently and loosen the core, then pull it out with the corer.

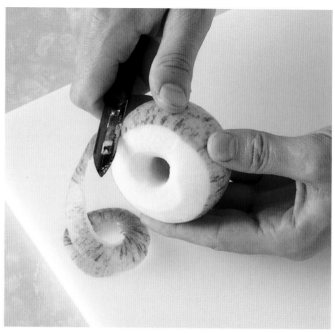

2 Using a peeler or small paring knife, gently remove the skin of the apple (and as little of the flesh as possible) by making a circular path around the fruit from top to bottom.

3 Place the cored apple on its side and hold it steady against a clean cutting board. Using a sharp knife, slice down through the apple. Repeat, making slices of an even thickness.

4 To chop: after slicing, stack the rings, a few at a time. Slice down through the pile, then repeat crossways in the opposite direction, making pieces of about the same size.

Cut a pineapple

1 With a sharp knife, cut the top and the base from the pineapple. Stand the pineapple upright and cut off the skin in strips from top to bottom. With a small paring knife, gouge out the brown "eyes".

2 To make the rings, turn the pineapple sideways and cut it into slices of an even thickness. Then use a round metal cutter to remove the hard, fibrous centre of each ring.

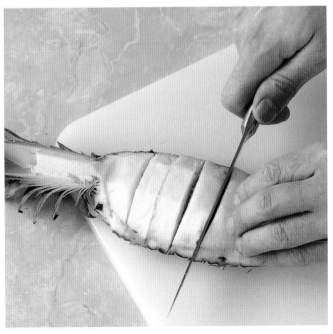

3 Quarter the fruit by cutting from plume end to base, then cut lengthways to remove the core at the centre of each piece. Beginning at the plume end, cut along between the flesh and the skin.

4 Hold the pineapple steady and cut the flesh crossways against the skin, making slices of an even width. Repeat the process, cutting the other quarters into slices.

Segment citrus fruit

1 With a sharp knife, cut off the top and bottom of the fruit so it can stand upright. Holding it firmly with a fork, slice down and around the flesh, following the contour of the skin. Try to remove as much of the bitter white pith as possible.

2 With one hand, hold the peeled fruit steady on the board, while you use a sharp knife to slice along the lines of the membrane which separates each slice. Repeat slicing between each membrane to remove the segments.

Prepare a mango

1 Standing the mango on its side, cut it by running your knife just to one side of the stone; repeat the cut on the other side, so that a single slice remains with the stone encased.

2 With the halves flesh-side up, cut the flesh into strips lengthways, then crossways, cutting to, but not through the skin. Invert the skin to expose the flesh. Run your knife along the skin to remove the segments.

Peel soft fruit

1 Starting at the base, make a shallow cut just through the skin. Then repeat the cut in the opposite direction to make an "x". Don't let your knife pierce the delicate flesh.

2 Place the fruit in a heatproof bowl and pour over boiling water, then using a slotted spoon, transfer the fruit to a bowl of cold water. When cool, remove the fruit from the water and pull the skin from the flesh.

Eggs

BUY Hen's eggs are sold graded according to weight, from small to extra large. Terms used to describe how laying birds are reared is confusing. "Farm fresh" and "barn" eggs have been reared in large industrial units with little or no space to move. "Free range" means the birds have an outside area to scratch around in. "Organic" means they are kept free-range and fed an organic diet. Avoid if cracked or dirty. **STORE** Eggs should be stored below 20°C (68°F) so are best kept in the refrigerator. It is best to freeze eggs and yolks separately in ice cube trays for easy measuring. Yolks need to be beaten with a pinch of salt or sugar to stabilize first (note which on a label!). Freeze for up to 6 months.

▲ Hen

EAT Boil, coddle, poach, fry, scramble, make into omelettes, or bake. Use whole for batters, to bind meat, fish, vegetable, or rice mixtures, in cakes, breads, and muffins. Hard-boil for salads, rice dishes, to stuff, or sieve for garnish. Use yolks for glazing, to enrich sauces, biscuits, and pastries, for mayonnaise, hollandaise, and custards. Use whites for glazing, meringues, soufflés, mousses, and ice creams (sometimes with the yolks added separately), or to clarify consommé. **FLAVOUR PAIRINGS** Cheese, cream, bread, rice, spices, herbs, most fruit and vegetables, potatoes, fish, sausages, cured meats. **IN SEASON** All year

▲ Duck

EAT Larger than hen's eggs, they have large, rich yolks and the whites are watery but protein-rich, giving great volume when whisked for meringues, soufflés, and mousses. Coddle rather than boil or they become tough. **FLAVOUR PAIRINGS** As hen's but particularly good with light muscovado sugar and vanilla (for brown sugar meringues), hard cheeses (for soufflés), chocolate, citrus or soft fruits (for mousses). **IN SEASON** All year

◀ Goose

EAT A seasonal delicacy, these large eggs (each one equivalent to 3 hen's eggs) have a strong flavour. Great for scrambled eggs, Yorkshire pudding, and intensely rich sponge cakes. **FLAVOUR PAIRINGS** Butter, smoked salmon, bacon, sausages, sage, onions, tomatoes, vanilla, chocolate, coffee, citrus. **IN SEASON** February–August

▲ Quail

EAT Tiny, delicately flavoured eggs. Delicious soft- or hard-boiled in salads, fried, or poached and served on tiny croûtes for an appetizer, as mini Scotch eggs, stuffed, or pickled. **FLAVOUR PAIRINGS** Asparagus, smoked fish, shellfish, caviar, sausagemeat, Parmesan, celery salt. **IN SEASON** All year

Dairy

BUY The mainstays for every cook. You may prefer sheep's, buffalo's, nut, rice, oat, or soy alternatives. Not all are as stable as dairy produce for cooking, so check the labels. Buy in usable quantities. **STORE** Unless UHT-treated, keep in the refrigerator and use within a few days. Freeze milk and commercial yogurt for up to 1 month (it may separate so, when thawed, thoroughly shake milk, or stir yogurt). Whip double cream partially or fully, then freeze for up to 3 months. Single cream won't freeze.

▲ Cow's milk

EAT Available whole (full-fat), semi-skimmed, or skimmed. Use according to preference in sauces, soups, batters, egg dishes, hot drinks, shakes, and to poach fish. For some rich custard dishes and milk puddings, whole milk is preferable. **FLAVOUR PAIRINGS** Cheeses, most vegetables, herbs, vanilla, cinnamon, chocolate, soft fruits, tropical fruits, grains, bread, honey.

▲ Pouring cream

EAT Single has a low fat content, not suitable for whipping or boiling (it will curdle). Stir in at the end of cooking or swirl to garnish soups or desserts on plates. Whipping and double cream are all-purpose, but double is thicker and better for cooking. **FLAVOUR PAIRINGS** most vegetables, fish, meat, poultry, game, all fruits, chocolate, coffee, all sugars and honey, vanilla, rosemary, bay, lavender.

▲ Clotted cream

EAT Traditional West Country cream, made by heating cow's cream. Rich, crusty, and sweet with a high fat content. Serve with desserts, or with scones, and add to toffee, fudge, and ice cream. **FLAVOUR PAIRINGS** White and muscovado sugars, fruit and plain scones, raspberry or strawberry jam, fresh fruit, apple pie, mince pies, Christmas pudding, chocolate desserts, vanilla.

▲ Crème fraîche and soured cream

EAT Both are cream with lactic acid added. Soured cream is lower in fat and should be added at the end of cooking. Crème fraîche can be cooked (not the half-fat variety). Serve on or in soups, in dressings, sauces, dips, spicy dishes, flans, tarts, desserts, cakes, and with fruit. **FLAVOUR PAIRINGS** Herbs, spices, beef, pork, chicken, fish, vegetables, eggs, honey, golden syrup, berries, stone fruits, chocolate.

▲ Yogurt

EAT Plain yogurt can be set, no-fat (not good in cooking), low-fat, whole-milk, or strained (Greek-style, often with added cream). Use for breakfast with fruit, in smoothies, or on breakfast cereals, in soups, curries, sweet and savoury baked dishes, desserts, scones, tea breads, dips, and marinades. Buttermilk (milk with lactic acid added) can be used for baking and sauces instead of yogurt. **FLAVOUR PAIRINGS** Lamb, beef, pork, chicken, fish, most vegetables, parsley, mint, chives, celery seeds, spices, fruits, cheese, eggs.

▲ Butter

EAT Available salted and unsalted (unsalted allows total control over the salt content of the dish). Use for its flavour and texture in everything from sauces to baking. When using for frying, add a dash of sunflower or olive oil to prevent burning. **FLAVOUR PAIRINGS** Eggs, white wine vinegar, citrus, herbs, garlic, all vegetables, meat, fish, poultry, game, pulses, cheeses, fruit, breads, crackers, scones, honey, jams, marmalades.

Cheeses

BUY There are, of course, hundreds of cheeses available, many that are delicious cooked, but we have only selected some of the most popular used for culinary purposes here. All cheese should look and smell fresh. Best to buy pieces freshly cut, when possible. Buy in quantities you can use quickly, but hard cheeses will keep much longer than fresh. **STORE** Keep each cheese separately, well-wrapped, in a sealed container with room to "breathe", in the refrigerator. Freeze full-fat fresh soft cheeses for up to 3 months (don't freeze low-fat varieties); hard, blue, and other soft cheeses for 6 months.

▲ Cheddar

EAT Choose a well-flavoured farmhouse one for cooking. Use in sandwiches, sauces, soufflés, salads, quiches, melted over potatoes, grated over vegetable dishes, and grilled. **FLAVOUR PAIRINGS** Crusty bread, pickles, chutneys, tomatoes, celery, beetroot, onions, apples, chillies, nuts, sage.

▲ Grana Padano and Parmesan

EAT Grana Padano (pictured) and Parmigiano Reggiano (Parmesan) are both hard and grainy with complex, salty flavours. Parmesan is considered superior. Freshly grate or shave over pasta, griddled vegetables, and salads, stir into risottos and soups, use to flavour pesto, or nibble to round off a meal. **FLAVOUR PAIRINGS** Pasta, ravioli, risotto rice, olive oil, butter, sage, basil, parsley, rosemary, garlic, pine nuts, balsamic vinegar, walnuts, pears.

▲ Pecorino

EAT A grainy, salty sheep's milk cheese. Use instead of Parmesan or Grana Padano. Particularly good with tomato-based sauces for pasta. **FLAVOUR PAIRINGS** Tomatoes, sun-dried tomatoes, onions, garlic, prosciutto, oregano, basil, white beans, pasta, olive oil.

▲ Gruyère

EAT One of many sweet, nutty, smooth-textured melting cheeses. Use for fondues, with pasta, gratins, salads, and sauces. Good mixed with other melting cheeses too. **FLAVOUR PAIRINGS** Crudités, Kirsch, white wine, potatoes, cauliflower, spinach, onions, garlic, tomatoes, leeks, crusty bread.

▲ Gorgonzola

EAT Smooth with a sweet, spicy tang. Use in salads, sauces, dips, mousses, soufflés, tarts, risottos, and on pizzas. **FLAVOUR PAIRINGS** Watercress, squashes, leeks, tomatoes, spinach, nuts, fruits, prosciutto, steaks, chicken.

▲ Stilton

EAT It mellows with age. Enjoy to round off a meal, or in soups, dressings, sauces, or potted. **FLAVOUR PAIRINGS** Red wine, port, walnuts, celery, fennel, leeks, potatoes, beetroot, squashes, cream, crème fraîche, unsalted butter, honey, sunflower oil, steaks, chicken, grapes, figs, orchard fruits.

Feta ▶

EAT Made with goat's or sheep's milk, crumbly, salty, and fresh. It does not melt completely when heated. Crumble or dice for salads, in stuffings, on vegetables, with olives as an appetizer. **FLAVOUR PAIRINGS** Lamb, chicken, tomatoes, onions, cucumber, cabbage, lettuce, aubergines, courgettes, broad beans, olives, olive oil, oregano, mint, thyme, watermelon.

▲ Mozzarella

EAT Buffalo mozzarella is the best, although it can also be made from cow's milk. Use for salads, to top pizzas, and with pasta. **FLAVOUR PAIRINGS** Tomatoes, avocados, artichokes, olives, Parmesan, basil, oregano, sage, rosemary, mushrooms, prosciutto, spicy sausages, bacon, olive oil, balsamic vinegar.

◀ Halloumi

EAT With the unique quality of being able to stand up to char-grilling without melting, halloumi's bouncy texture is lovely griddled or barbecued and served with a watermelon salad, or stuffed inside a burger bun with sweet chilli sauce, or paired with lentils and a citrus dressing. **FLAVOUR PAIRINGS** Pomegranate molasses, lemon, green chilli, beetroot, chilli, tomatoes, cucumber, aubergine, harissa, orange, watermelon, bell peppers, mint, red onion, olives, courgette.

▲ Mascarpone

EAT Smooth, rich, and creamy – the classic cheese for tiramisu. Also use for cheesecakes, with cream to fill gâteaux or accompany fruit, in pâtés, sweet and savoury stuffings, and pasta sauces. **FLAVOUR PAIRINGS** Tomatoes, artichokes, wild mushrooms, beetroot, stone fruits, berries, citrus, ginger, coffee, chocolate, coffee liqueur, brandy, amaretto.

◀ Ricotta

EAT Soft whey cheese with a touch of acidity and a delicate lemony aroma. Use in baked pasta dishes, sweet and savoury stuffings, and creamy desserts. **FLAVOUR PAIRINGS** Spinach, peppers, mushrooms, tomatoes, red onions, basil, sage, chilli, berries, stone fruits, figs, fresh dates, bananas, citrus, chocolate, coffee, honey, nutmeg, cinnamon.

Test an egg for freshness

FRESH To test if an egg is fresh, gently drop it into a glass of cold water. A really fresh egg will lie in a horizontal position at the bottom.

BORDERLINE If, after settling, the egg begins to rise in the water at one end, it is not completely fresh, but can still be used.

STALE If the egg bobs up towards the surface of the water in a vertical position, it is stale and should be discarded.

Separate yolks and whites

1 Break the eggshell by tapping it against the rim of the bowl. Insert your fingers into the break, and gently pry the two halves apart. Some of the white will escape into the bowl. Remove any shell that falls in too.

2 Gently shift the yolk back and forth between the shell halves, allowing the white to fall into the bowl. Take care to keep the yolk intact. Place the yolk in another bowl and set aside.

Whisk egg whites

1 Place the egg whites in a metal or ceramic bowl that is clean, free of any traces of grease, and completely dry. Begin whisking them slowly, using a small range of motion.

2 Continue whisking steadily, using larger strokes, until the whites lose their translucency and start to foam. The aim is to incorporate as much air as possible to make the whites expand and increase in volume.

3 Continue incorporating as much air as possible, increasing your speed and range of motion until the whites have expanded to the desired degree and are stiff, but not dry.

4 Test by lifting the whisk away; the peaks should be firm but glossy, and the tips should hang. Take care not to overwhisk the egg whites, or the air bubbles that have formed will collapse.

Soft- and hard-boil eggs

SOFT-BOIL EGGS The whites should be set and the yolks runny. Use a pan large enough to hold the eggs in a single layer. Cover them with at least 5cm (2in) of cold water and set over a high heat. Bring the water to the boil, then reduce the heat to a simmer for 2–3 minutes. Remove the eggs.

HARD-BOIL EGGS Both the whites and the yolks should be set. Use the method for soft-boiled eggs, but once the water has boiled, simmer them for 7–10 minutes. The less time you give them, the more moist the yolk will be. Then run cold water into the pan to stop the cooking process. Peel away and discard the shells when cool enough to handle.

Scramble eggs

1 Crack the eggs into a bowl, and remove any fallen shell. Beat the eggs with a fork and season with salt and black pepper.

2 Heat a non-stick pan over medium heat, and add a knob of unsalted butter if needed. When the butter melts, pour in the beaten eggs.

3 Using a wooden spoon, pull the setting egg from the edges into the centre. Continue doing so until it is set to your liking.

Poach eggs

1 Carefully crack an egg onto a small plate, then slide it into a pan of gently boiling water mixed with a drop of vinegar.

2 Using a slotted spoon, gently lift the white over the yolk until set. Adjust the heat to a gentle boil and poach for 3–5 minutes.

3 Before serving, place the eggs in another pan of gently simmering salted water for 30 seconds to remove the taste of the vinegar.

Bake a soufflé

1 Grease the inside of each soufflé dish and then coat with sugar, biscuit crumbs, or grated cheese. Use sugar or biscuit crumbs for a sweet soufflé, and grated cheese for a savoury soufflé.

2 Whisk the egg whites until holding stiff peaks: the soufflés will not rise if under-whisked. Fold into the base gently, to retain as much air as possible. Add a pinch of salt before mixing for savoury soufflés.

3 Run a finger around the soufflé mix, along the top edge of each ramekin just inside the rim, to give a professional "top hat" effect and help the soufflés rise up straight.

4 Cook the soufflés straight away, placing them on a thoroughly preheated baking tray. Doing this will heat the base of the ramekins so that the soufflés begin to rise as soon as you put them in the oven.

Make a classic omelette

1 Beat and season the eggs. Heat a non-stick frying pan over a moderate heat and melt a knob of butter. As soon as it begins to froth, add the eggs, tilting the pan so that the eggs can spread evenly.

2 Stir the eggs with a fork to distribute them evenly. Stop stirring the eggs just as soon as they are set. Fold the side of the omelette nearest to you halfway over itself.

3 To form a neatly rolled omelette, sharply tap the handle of the pan to encourage the other side of the omelette to curl over and slide to the edge of the pan.

4 When the omelette is cooked to your taste, tilt the pan over a serving plate until the omelette slides out of it onto the plate seam-side down. Serve immediately.

Make Italian meringue

1 Dissolve 250g (9oz) caster sugar in 75ml (2½fl oz) water over a low heat to 121°C (248°F). Whisk 4 egg whites until they form soft peaks. Pour the hot sugar syrup into the egg whites, whisking continuously.

2 Continue to whisk until the meringue is cold, with a very stiff, smooth, and satiny consistency. Transfer the meringue mixture into a piping or pastry bag fitted with a metal tip.

3 Twist the loose end of the bag to seal, then squeezing with one hand, pipe the meringue as required. You may find it easier to hold the tip end with your other hand to keep it steady.

4 Italian meringue is easy and quick to cook. Simply place under a preheated grill for a few minutes, or use a kitchen blowtorch, to lightly brown the top.

Make French meringue

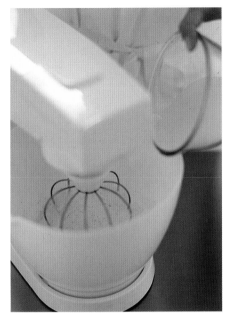

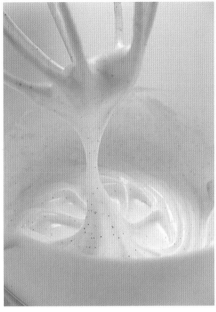

1 In a large mixing bowl, whisk 4 egg whites, half of 200g (7oz) caster sugar, and the seeds of 1 vanilla pod at moderate speed.

2 Continue whisking until the mixture becomes smooth, shiny, and firm. Draw the whisk away to check that there are soft peaks.

3 Using a rubber spatula, gently fold in the rest of the sugar. Bake until just golden, then leave to dry in the oven for at least 8 hours.

Shape meringue

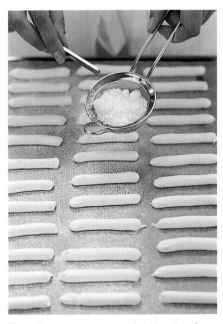

1 For discs, use a star tip to pipe the meringue in a spiral onto a parchment-covered baking tray. Bake for 1 hour 20 minutes, then let dry.

2 For shells, use a pastry bag with a round tip to pipe the meringue in equal-sized globes. Bake for 1 hour 10 minutes, then let dry.

3 For fingers, use a round tip to pipe the meringue into thin sticks and dust with icing sugar. Bake for 30–35 minutes, then let dry.

Whip cream

1 Remove the cream from the refrigerator and wait for it to reach 5°C (40°F). Set it in a large bowl over ice. Begin whipping slowly, at about 2 strokes per second (or the lowest speed on an electric mixer) until it starts to thicken.

2 To create soft peaks, increase the whipping to a moderate speed and for stiff peaks, continue beating the cream. Test by lifting the beaters or whisk to see if the cream retains its shape.

Fill a piping bag

1 Place your chosen piping nozzle in the bag and pull it through the opening until the bag is tightly surrounding the wider end of the nozzle. Then give the bag a twist to seal and prevent leakage.

2 Holding the bag just above the nozzle with one hand, fold the top of the bag over with your other hand, creating a "collar", and begin spooning in the cream.

Make crème pâtissière

1 Over a low heat, bring 250ml (9fl oz) full-fat milk, 25g (scant 1oz) cornflour, 2 split vanilla pods, and 30g (1oz) sugar to the boil, whisking.

2 Whisk 3 egg yolks with 30g (1oz) of sugar in a bowl. While whisking, add the hot milk, return to the pan and just before boiling, remove to cool.

3 While the pan cools, remove the vanilla pods. Then add 25g (scant 1oz) of unsalted butter pieces and whisk into the sauce until smooth and glossy.

Make custard

1 Bring 150ml (5fl oz) full-fat milk, 150ml (5fl oz) double cream, and ½ vanilla pod (and seeds) to the boil, remove, and chill overnight.

2 Discard the vanilla pod and bring the milk to the boil. Whisk 3 egg yolks and 25g (scant 1oz) sugar together. Pour in half the milk, whisking.

3 Return to the pan and whisk over a medium heat until thick, smooth, and coating the back of a spoon. Do not boil.

Rice and other grains

BUY Rice packets should be clear, showing unbroken grains. In ready-prepared mixes containing wild rice, the grains may be broken or pierced so they cook in a similar time to the other rice in the pack. For grains, choose those with the right amount of processing for the job in hand. For instance, you might want toasted buckwheat grains for adding to breakfast cereals and buckwheat flour to add flavour to your crêpes or pasta dough. **STORE** Wholegrain and polished rices will keep in a cool, dry cupboard for over two years. Fragrant varieties become less aromatic, though. Flaked and ground rice and rice flour can be stored for over a year in an airtight container. Most grains will keep in sealed containers in a cool, dark place for a year or more. Amaranth, millet, and buckwheat flour tend to go bitter after a few months, so buy in small quantities.

▲ White long grain

EAT Basic rice for side dishes, salads, and stuffings. **FLAVOUR PAIRINGS** Any meat, poultry, game, or fish, pulses, root vegetables, sweetcorn, cabbage leaves (for stuffing), peppers, aubergines, squashes, beans, peas, cheeses, salad vegetables, dried fruits, herbs, spices, soy sauce.

▲ Short grain rice

EAT There are superior risotto ones like Italian Arborio and Carnaroli, and basic short, round grain pudding rices. Use for risottos and rice desserts. **FLAVOUR PAIRINGS** Wild and cultivated mushrooms, truffles, peppers, aubergines, tomatoes, peas, squashes, saffron, herbs, onions, garlic, chicken, seafood, cheeses, citrus, white wine, caster sugar, milk, cream, unsalted butter, vanilla, nutmeg, dried fruits.

▲ Basmati rice

EAT Fragrant, long-grain variety. Use in biryanis, pilafs, stuffings, salads, and to accompany curries, casseroles, tagines, roast, and baked dishes. **FLAVOUR PAIRINGS** Curry spices, curry leaves, ginger, cinnamon, garlic, coriander leaf, parsley, mint, chives, all meats, poultry, seafood, vegetables, dried fruits, coconut milk, yogurt.

▲ Thai jasmine rice

EAT Slightly sticky and fragrant. Use to accompany Thai and Chinese savoury dishes. **FLAVOUR PAIRINGS** Thai curry pastes, lemon grass, galangal, ginger, nam pla, soy sauce, all meat, fish, shellfish, and poultry, all vegetables, coconut milk, tropical fruits, green tea.

▲ Red rice

EAT Speciality crops, one of the most famous being from Camargue, in Provence, France. Excellent for salads, stuffings and side dishes. **FLAVOUR PAIRINGS** Spring onions, garlic, leeks, puy lentils, fish, shellfish, chicken, courgettes, aubergines, feta cheese, olives, cherry and sun-dried tomatoes, cucumber, sweet peppers, mushrooms, peas, green beans, pine nuts.

▲ Black sticky rice

EAT Deep purple grains, with a fruity, grassy aroma. Used mostly boiled as a sweet breakfast cereal, in dumplings, stuffings, and for puddings. **FLAVOUR PAIRINGS** Coconut milk, palm sugar, peanuts, red onions, garlic, minced meat, dried prawns, oyster sauce, soy sauce, dried shiitake mushrooms, bananas.

▲ White sticky rice

EAT Also known as glutinous or sweet rice. Best steamed or it becomes mushy. Use for sushi. **FLAVOUR PAIRINGS** Rice vinegar, wasabi, pickled ginger, nori wraps (seaweed), fresh tuna or salmon, keta (salted salmon roe), prawns, avocados, beansprouts, cucumber, carrot, chicken.

▲ Paella rice

EAT Spanish rices (Bomba, the main variety, Calasparra, and Valencia, the best). Use for Paella. **FLAVOUR PAIRINGS** Chicken, shellfish, chorizo, pancetta, white wine, saffron, paprika, chilli, olive oil, onions, garlic, mushrooms, peppers, tomatoes, peas, green beans, parsley, thyme.

▲ Flaked rice

EAT Part-cooked before rolling into flakes. Good for milk puddings, or soaked, then fried in sunflower oil either with mirepoix, fresh chillies and spices, or seasoned and mixed with peanuts as a snack. **FLAVOUR PAIRINGS** Milk, cream, honey, citrus, vanilla, curry leaves, chillies, mirepoix, peanuts.

▲ Ground rice

EAT Slightly grittier than rice flour, use in puddings and mixed with wheat flour in baking to give a crisp texture to shortbread, pastry, and biscuits. **FLAVOUR PAIRINGS** Butter, milk, cream, vanilla, almond, lavender, chocolate, dried fruit, cinnamon, nutmeg, mixed spice.

▲ Rice flour

EAT White or brown, gluten-free with a slightly gritty texture. Good for coating before frying, and dusting work surfaces for rolling bread or pastry dough. Use, too, for gluten-free breads, cakes, and biscuits, on its own or with other gluten-free flours. **FLAVOUR PAIRINGS** Paprika, chilli, herbs, eggs, butter, honey, vanilla, mixed spice, cocoa, almonds, dried fruit.

▲ Wild rice

EAT The seeds of an aquatic grass. Can be eaten alone but often added to basmati, red, or long-grain rice. Also available ready-mixed with them. **FLAVOUR PAIRINGS** Game, poultry, salmon, shellfish, eggs, bacon, asparagus, celery, mushrooms, potatoes, squashes, mangoes, nuts.

▲ Brown rice

EAT Wholegrain unrefined rice with a chewy texture and nutty flavour. Available in many varieties from basic short-grain and long-grain to speciality rices like Basmati. Use instead of white rices but it takes longer to cook. **FLAVOUR PAIRINGS** Chicken, pulses, meat, fish, most vegetables and salad stuffs, dried fruit, curry spices, herbs, milk, cream, honey, vanilla, nutmeg.

▲ Barley

EAT Use pearl barley in soups, stews, and orzotto (barley risotto). Boil for pilafs and salads. Cook in milk like porridge and sweeten for breakfast or pudding. Pot barley is the whole grain variety. Barley flour and beremeal (a speciality Scottish flour) are best mixed with wheat flour for baking. **FLAVOUR PAIRINGS** Chicken, duck, prawns, beef, lamb, beer, mushrooms, most vegetables, coconut, herbs, spices, apples, blackberries, citrus.

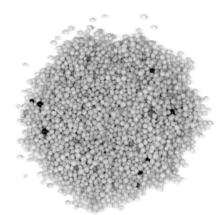

▲ Amaranth

EAT Highly nutritious, best toasted briefly before use. Boil, then use for pilafs, add to stews, or to rice puddings about 15 minutes before the end of cooking. Simmer in milk like porridge and add chopped fresh or dried fruit. Use the flour with wheat or rye flour for pastry, flat breads, and batters. **FLAVOUR PAIRINGS** Dried beans, cheeses, chicken, chillies, squashes, peas, mushrooms, coconut, corn, honey, chocolate.

▲ Farro

EAT The distinct hazelnut flavour of this grain makes it a great salad base. Stir into a warming vegetable soup with mushrooms and bacon, or make into a form of no-stir risotto. **FLAVOUR PAIRINGS** Tomatoes, olives, Florence fennel, red peppers, onion, aubergine, courgette, apple, soft goat's cheese, olive oil, basil, tarragon, chives.

▲ Buckwheat

EAT Strong-flavoured gluten-free grain. Use toasted and boiled for pilafs or salads, or add to rice for texture and flavour. The flour is used in Japanese soba noodles, and for blinis, crêpes, and pasta doughs (sometimes with wheat flour). **FLAVOUR PAIRINGS** Bacon, eggs, chicken, smoked salmon, caviar, ham, melting cheeses, cucumber, mushrooms, ginger, peanuts, cashews, parsley, soy sauce.

▲ Millet

EAT An excellent alternative to rice. Best toasted before boiling. Flakes make good porridge, or add to muesli or other breakfast cereals, flapjacks, and multigrain doughs. Use millet flour for gluten-free biscuits and crackers. **FLAVOUR PAIRINGS** Chicken, salmon, dried beans, eggs, spinach, mushrooms, soy sauce, dried fruit, nuts, oats, other grains, muscovado sugar.

Polenta

▲ Corn

EAT Many different varieties with different uses. Cornflour, a fine white powder, is used for thickening and dusting to prevent sticking. Cornmeal is coarser; use in baked goods, for crumb coatings, and tortillas. Polenta is very coarse yellow or white cornmeal (see p450). Also use for cornbread. **FLAVOUR PAIRINGS** Beef, bacon, chicken, pork, rabbit, cheeses, peppers, pulses, coriander leaf, parsley, citrus, mushrooms, pumpkin, tomatoes, butter, syrups.

▼ Oats

EAT Use rolled oats for porridge, muesli, flapjacks, biscuits, crumbles, and in bread dough. Use pinhead, coarse, and medium oatmeal for oatcakes, in soups and stews, haggis, or to coat fried fish. Use fine oatmeal for quick porridge, pancakes, pastry, and puddings. **FLAVOUR PAIRINGS** Ham, lamb, sausages, herrings, mackerel, onions, cabbage, stone and dried fruits, berries, cream, syrups, honey.

Wheat flours ▶

EAT Use strong white or wholemeal flour, high in gluten, for yeast cookery. Plain flour is for general baking and thickening; self-raising for quick bakes. Use pastry flour for puff and choux. Farina or Tipo "00" is for pasta, gnocchi, and fine cakes. **FLAVOUR PAIRINGS** Nuts, seeds, dried fruits, other grains, vanilla, chocolate, coffee, syrups, honey, jams, butter, oils, herbs, spices.

Spelt ▶

EAT Use wholegrains for soups, pilafs, salads, and risotto-type dishes. Farro is an Italian variety, often confused with spelt grain and can be used in the same way. Spelt flour is available as white and wholemeal, and is used as an alternative to common wheat. Often tolerated by people with wheat allergies.
FLAVOUR PAIRINGS Lamb, chicken, game, rabbit, fish, wild and cultivated mushrooms, most vegetables and salad stuffs, herbs, cinnamon, nutmeg, mace, caraway, poppy and nigella seeds.

◀ Freekeh

EAT This smoky, toasted green wheat comes cracked or whole, and makes a characterful change from bulgur. Use it in mixed salads, or as a side dish to simple grilled meats, or a stuffing for pheasant or partridge. **FLAVOUR PAIRINGS** Preserved lemons, pomegranate molasses, mackerel, game birds, mint, coriander, orange, mushrooms, olive oil.

▲ Quinoa

EAT High in protein and fat. An excellent alternative to rice, and quicker to cook.
FLAVOUR PAIRINGS Beef, chicken, pulses, cheeses, prawns, chickpeas, chillies, coriander leaf and seed, sweetcorn, nuts, squashes, sweet potatoes, citrus, grapes.

▲ Bulgur

EAT Whole wheat grains steamed, hulled, dried, and crushed. Traditional for tabbouleh, but good as a base for salads, pilafs, stuffings, soups, and as a side dish. Cracked wheat is similar, but not pre-cooked. Use it in multigrain breads, too. **FLAVOUR PAIRINGS** Tomatoes, cucumber, herbs, spring onions, garlic, cumin, cinnamon, lemon, olive oil, feta cheese, olives, dried fruit.

▲ Wheat berries

EAT Comprising the entire wheat kernel, these have a sweetness that gives amazing versatility. Toss them with oranges, feta, and watercress in a vitamin-rich salad, or stir into a spicy vegetarian chilli, or cook into a pilaf with vegetables and herbs.
FLAVOUR PAIRINGS Chilli, artichoke, onion, watercress, figs, orange, feta, poultry, lime juice, honey.

▲ Couscous

EAT Not technically a grain, as it's processed from wheat. Giant couscous and fregola have larger granules, roasted during manufacture, so are less sticky and chewier. Serve as a side dish, plain or with added flavourings, as a base for spicy main courses like Couscous Royale, in salads, stuffings, and cakes. **FLAVOUR PAIRINGS** Olive oil, lamb, chicken, chorizo, fish, chickpeas, coriander leaf, mint, thyme, bay leaf, oregano, garlic, onions, peppers, courgettes, aubergines, tomatoes, chilli, paprika, harissa paste, cumin, cinnamon, dried fruit.

▲ Rye

EAT Cook the grains for nutty pilafs, salads, in stuffings, bread doughs, and soups. Dark and light rye flour is good for baking, particularly bread, with or without wheat flour, and makes delicious Scotch pancakes. Rye flakes are also available for porridge, or adding to muesli, cracker, and bread doughs.
FLAVOUR PAIRINGS Cheeses, ham, crab, smoked salmon, fennel, sauerkraut, honey, maple syrup, oats, oranges, raisins.

Pulses (dried peas, beans, and lentils)

BUY If buying packets of pulses, inspect for signs of tearing where animals might have been at work. If buying in bulk, pulses should be clean and unbroken and free from dust, grit, or signs of spoilage. Sprouted beans should look crisp and fresh. Avoid if browning. Most kinds of pulses are sold ready-cooked in cans too. Some are sold frozen. **STORE** Keep indefinitely in sealed containers in a cool, dark place. The longer you keep them, the longer they'll need soaking before cooking. All except mung beans, lentils, and split peas should be boiled rapidly for 10 minutes to remove toxins, before simmering until tender. Can be frozen, cooked, for up to 6 months.

▲ Flageolet beans

EAT Integral to French cuisine, with a creamy texture and delicate flavour. Traditionally served with roast or braised lamb. Good in soups, stews, casseroles, and salads, or serve as a side dish. **FLAVOUR PAIRINGS** Lamb, delicate fish, veal, garlic, shallots, red onions, tomatoes, celery, carrots, fennel, paprika, parsley, sage, thyme.

▲ Cannellini beans

EAT Italian long white haricot bean, with nutty flavour and smooth texture. Good in salads, soups, and stews. Smaller round haricots are used for baked beans. **FLAVOUR PAIRINGS** Tomatoes, garlic, eggs, onions, fennel, cavolo nero, white wine, sage, thyme, bacon, pork, black pudding.

▲ Pinto beans

EAT Earthy flavour and floury texture, used for Mexican refried beans and in most chilli dishes. **FLAVOUR PAIRINGS** Eggs, beef, fresh, dried and pickled chillies, onions, garlic, coriander leaf, parsley, oregano, tomatoes, peppers, rice.

▲ Butter beans

EAT Large and floury, good for soaking up flavours in soups, stews, and braises, and for mashing. **FLAVOUR PAIRINGS** Gammon, pork, chicken, pheasant, chorizo and other sausages, garlic, onions, turmeric, cumin, cloves, turnips, carrots, kale, crème fraîche, tahini, parsley, coriander leaf.

▲ Chickpeas

EAT Smooth and buttery when puréed, ideal for dips and sauces, good in patties too. They also keep their shape, so good for long-cooked stews and casseroles. **FLAVOUR PAIRINGS** Garlic, cumin, turmeric, coriander seed and leaf, parsley, mint, chilli, sweet and smoked paprika, cinnamon, cloves, chorizo, tahini, tomatoes, onions, aubergines, peppers, squashes, mushrooms.

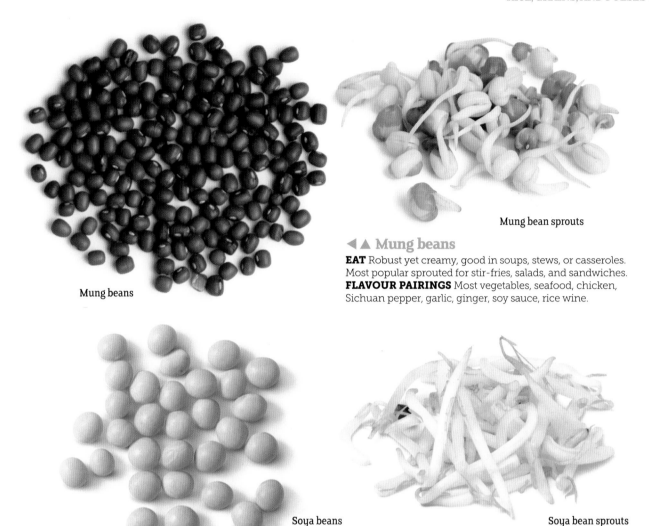

Mung bean sprouts

◀ ▲ Mung beans

EAT Robust yet creamy, good in soups, stews, or casseroles. Most popular sprouted for stir-fries, salads, and sandwiches.
FLAVOUR PAIRINGS Most vegetables, seafood, chicken, Sichuan pepper, garlic, ginger, soy sauce, rice wine.

Mung beans

Soya beans

Soya bean sprouts

▲ Soya beans

EAT Highly nutritious but lack flavour, so good used in spicy stews, terrines, and patties. Also used for making soya products like milk, tofu, miso, and soy sauce. Use the sprouts in stir-fries and salads. **FLAVOUR PAIRINGS** Beans: curry spices, herbs, mango chutney, chillies, mushrooms, root vegetables, kale, cavolo nero. Sprouts: oyster sauce, black bean sauce, hoisin, vinegar, honey, pineapple, peppers, spring onions, garlic, Chinese five-spice powder.

Adzuki bean sprouts

◀ ▲ Adzuki beans

EAT Nutty, slightly sweet and keep their shape when cooked. Good in pilafs, salads, stews, and patties. Use the sprouts in the same way.
FLAVOUR PAIRINGS Sweet peppers, squashes, sweet potatoes, rice, orzo, chilli, bay, basil, apples, pears, soy sauce.

Adzuki beans

445

▲ Red kidney beans

EAT Best known as an integral part of chilli con carne, but also excellent in soups, casseroles, and salads.
FLAVOUR PAIRINGS Beef, lamb, onions, tomatoes, garlic, cumin, chilli, coriander leaf, avocados, sweet peppers, pickled jalapeños, crisp lettuce, hard cheeses.

▲ Black beans

EAT Exceptionally good flavour and texture, used in both Central and South American and Asian cuisines, or fermented in black bean sauce.
FLAVOUR PAIRINGS Onions, garlic, chilli, ginger, rice, avocados, peppers, aubergines, beef, pork, chicken, oyster sauce, soy sauce, rice wine.

▲ Black-eyed beans

EAT Also known as black-eyed peas or cowpeas, a good all-rounder for serving hot and cold.
FLAVOUR PAIRINGS Rice, chilli (particularly hot sauce), pork, ham, cod, tuna, potatoes, spring onions, root vegetables, peppers, squashes, olive oil, citrus.

▲ Split peas

EAT Available green or yellow, they cook to a pulp so are good for purées (like dals), soups, vegetable bakes, and pâtés.
FLAVOUR PAIRINGS Ham, bacon, pork, beef, onions, garlic, leeks, potatoes, sweet potatoes, carrots, mint, parsley, mustards, cumin and coriander seeds, cardamom.

▲ Borlotti beans

EAT Classic Italian bean for soups, pasta dishes, and salads.
FLAVOUR PAIRINGS Onions, garlic, celery, fennel, root vegetables, squashes, mushrooms, chorizo, pork, lamb, squid, parsley, sage, thyme, rosemary.

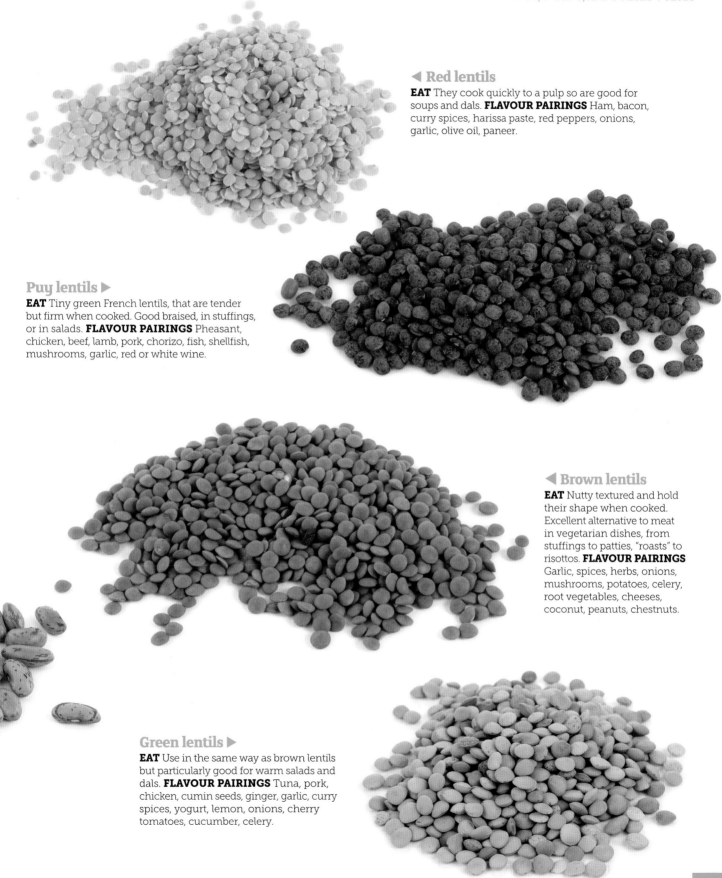

◄ Red lentils

EAT They cook quickly to a pulp so are good for soups and dals. **FLAVOUR PAIRINGS** Ham, bacon, curry spices, harissa paste, red peppers, onions, garlic, olive oil, paneer.

Puy lentils ▶

EAT Tiny green French lentils, that are tender but firm when cooked. Good braised, in stuffings, or in salads. **FLAVOUR PAIRINGS** Pheasant, chicken, beef, lamb, pork, chorizo, fish, shellfish, mushrooms, garlic, red or white wine.

◄ Brown lentils

EAT Nutty textured and hold their shape when cooked. Excellent alternative to meat in vegetarian dishes, from stuffings to patties, "roasts" to risottos. **FLAVOUR PAIRINGS** Garlic, spices, herbs, onions, mushrooms, potatoes, celery, root vegetables, cheeses, coconut, peanuts, chestnuts.

Green lentils ▶

EAT Use in the same way as brown lentils but particularly good for warm salads and dals. **FLAVOUR PAIRINGS** Tuna, pork, chicken, cumin seeds, ginger, garlic, curry spices, yogurt, lemon, onions, cherry tomatoes, cucumber, celery.

447

Cook rice by absorption

1 Put the rice and 1½ times its quantity of water into a saucepan. Bring to the boil, stir once, then simmer uncovered until the water is absorbed. Remove from the heat and cover with a clean tea towel and a lid.

2 Leave the rice to steam under the tea towel and saucepan lid for 20 minutes. Remove the tea towel and replace the lid. Leave to stand for 5 minutes, then fluff the rice with a fork and serve.

Rehydrate instant couscous

1 Place the couscous in a bowl and pour over twice as much boiling water. Cover with cling film and leave to stand for 5 minutes. Uncover the bowl and fluff up the grains with a fork, then cover again for 5 minutes.

2 Now remove the cling film. Enrich the couscous by adding 1 tbsp of olive oil or a knob of butter, and season to taste. Fluff up the grains again with a fork until they are light and separate. It is ready to serve.

Make risotto

1 Heat 900ml (1½ pints) stock in a saucepan to a simmer. In another, wide-based pan, heat 1 tbsp olive oil and 75g (2½oz) unsalted butter and soften 1 finely chopped shallot. Stir in 280g (10oz) risotto rice, coating the grains in the butter and oil.

2 Add one 75ml (2½fl oz) glass of white wine or dry vermouth and boil, stirring until absorbed. Then add a ladle of simmering stock and stir until absorbed. Continue adding the hot stock, one ladle at at time, and stirring constantly.

3 Continue adding the stock and stirring with a wooden spoon until the rice is tender, but retains a slight bite. Add a knob of butter, season with salt and pepper to taste, and remove from the heat.

4 The constant stirring releases the starch in the rice, so the risotto should now have a creamy texture. Cover the pan and leave the risotto to rest for about 2 minutes before serving.

Make soft and grilled polenta

1 Bring a large pan of salted water to the boil. Gradually pour in the polenta, whisking quickly and continuously to ensure there are no lumps and the mixture is smooth.

2 Reduce the heat to low. Continue cooking for 40–45 minutes, or until the polenta is coming away from the edge of the pan, whisking occasionally. Stir in butter and Parmesan cheese, and season to taste.

3 For grilled polenta, first make soft polenta, but without the butter and cheese. Once thickened, pour it onto a greased baking tray, spread with a spatula, then leave it to set. (Keep up to 4 days, chilled and covered.)

4 When ready to use, turn the tray out onto a board. Cut the polenta into the desired shapes and sizes. Brush the pieces with olive oil, then grill on a hot, ridged griddle pan for about 3–5 minutes on each side.

Make blinis

1 Sift 100g (3½oz) buckwheat flour, ¼ tsp baking powder, and ¼ tsp salt into bowl. Add 1 egg yolk and half of 100ml (3½fl oz) milk, and beat together. Add the remaining milk and when smooth, fold in 1 whisked egg white.

2 Heat a flat griddle pan and add a thin layer of vegetable oil. Spoon a few spoonfuls of batter into the pan to cook, turning them over with a spatula once bubbles appear on the surface and the edges are firm.

Make pancakes

1 Make a batter by whisking 200g (7oz) plain flour, 1 tbsp caster sugar, 2 large eggs, and 450ml (15fl oz) whole milk together. Melt a knob of butter in a frying pan, add a ladle of batter and tip it to cover the pan.

2 Cook the pancake for 30–45 seconds then use a metal spatula to peel the pancake loose and check it is golden brown. Then either turn it over by flipping in the air, or use the spatula to do the job.

Mix bread dough

1 In a bowl, whisk together 1½ tsp fresh yeast and 350g (12oz) tepid water (weigh both dry and liquid ingredients in a jug to keep the correct ratio of flour to water), until the yeast has completely dissolved.

2 In a separate bowl, combine 500g (1lb 2oz) strong white flour and 1 tsp salt. Then, using only your hand to stir, mix the yeast liquid together with the dry ingredients.

3 As quickly as possible, mix together to make a soft, sticky dough. Make sure that all the flour is thoroughly combined with the liquid by scraping your hand all around the bowl.

4 Cover the dough with a clean tea towel to keep it moist. Leave to stand for 10 minutes before beginning to knead it, as this should produce a more elastic dough that is easier to work.

Knead bread dough

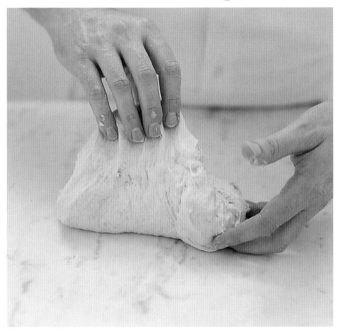

1 Try using a lightly oiled, rather than floured surface for kneading. Rub another 2 tbsp of oil over the dough ball, then fold it in half, bringing the top edge towards you. It will be very sticky and quite soft at this stage.

2 Use the thumb of one hand to hold the fold in place, then use the heel of your stronger hand to gently but firmly push down and away through the centre of the dough to seal the fold and stretch it.

3 Lift the dough and rotate it a quarter turn. Repeat the folding, pushing, and rotating process 10–12 times. Then place the dough in an oiled bowl seam-side down, cover with a cloth, and leave to prove for 10 minutes.

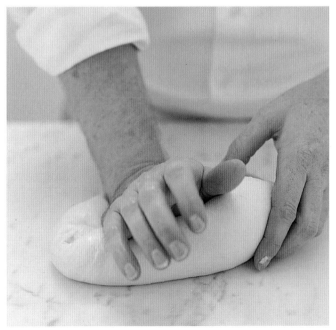

4 Knead the dough in this way again twice, with 10 minutes between each knead. Each time you do this it will require less oil. By the end, the dough will become noticeably more elastic and even silken.

Make a pizza base

1 In a bowl, dissolve 14g (½oz) fast-action dried yeast in 360ml (12fl oz) water and 2 tbsp olive oil. On a work surface, make a well in 500g (1lb 2oz) strong plain flour, add the liquid, and bring the flour into the centre.

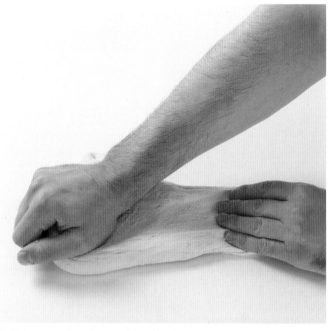

2 Using your hands, combine the flour and liquid and form it into a ball of dough. Knead the dough for 10 minutes, or until smooth. Set the dough aside in a bowl, cover with cling film, and allow to rise.

3 When the dough has doubled in size, turn it out onto a floured surface. Working from the centre outward, roll the dough into a circle. Flip the dough and repeat.

4 Roll the dough circle over the rolling pin and carefully transfer it to a lightly oiled and floured baking tray. Pinch the edges with your thumb and index finger to make a small rim.

Make brioche dough

1 In a bowl, mix 375g (13oz) strong white flour, 7g (¼oz) instant dried yeast, and 50g (1¾oz) caster sugar. Using a dough hook, mix on medium speed and gradually add 100ml (3½fl oz) warm milk and 3 lightly beaten eggs.

2 Mix until smooth, then add 1 more egg. Once the dough is mixed and begins to come away from the edges of the bowl, add salt and 175g (6oz) softened unsalted butter (cut into pieces). Mix again.

3 When the dough is smooth, transfer it to another large bowl. Cover with cling film and leave it to sit at room temperature for 2–3 hours, or until it doubles in size. The risen dough will be very sticky.

4 On a floured work surface, deflate the dough by punching it down. Return the dough to the bowl, cover with cling film and place in a refrigerator for 1¼ hours. Deflate once more, then shape and bake.

Shortcrust pastry

1 Sift 175g (6oz) plain white flour and a pinch of salt in a bowl. Add 85g (3oz) cold diced unsalted butter, margarine, or other fat. Lightly stir.

2 Using your fingertips, rub together the flour and butter until it forms coarse crumbs. Sprinkle over 2 tbsp iced water.

3 Use your fingers to gather the dough together and roll around to form a ball. Wrap in cling film and chill for 30 minutes before using.

Rough puff pastry

1 In a bowl, combine 250g (9oz) plain flour, 85g (3oz) cold unsalted butter, and 85g (3oz) vegetable fat with a knife. Add 150ml (5fl oz) iced water.

2 Add a squeeze of lemon juice, and stir with a knife to bind. Place the dough on a floured board and gently roll out.

3 Fold the top third of the pastry down, the bottom third up, and roll. Turn 90 degrees and repeat the process. Chill for 30 minutes before using.

Choux pastry

1 Bring 240ml (8fl oz) water and 115g (4oz) diced unsalted butter to the boil. Remove from the heat and add 140g (5oz) plain flour and 1 tsp sugar.

2 Beat until smooth, then return the pan to the heat and stir until the dough forms a ball and comes away from the sides of the pan.

3 Remove the pan from the heat. Add 4 eggs, one at a time, beating well. When the mixture easily drops off the spoon it is ready to use.

Sweet shortcrust pastry

1 Sift 200g (7oz) plain flour onto a work surface. Make a well in the centre and add 85g (3oz) unsalted butter, 4 tbsp sugar, and 3 egg yolks.

2 Using your fingertips, gradually work the flour into the butter and egg mixture to form very rough crumbs.

3 Gather the dough into a ball and knead it lightly until it is pliable. Wrap in cling film and chill for 30 minutes before using.

Shape choux pastry

1 Pipe neat and uniform globes onto a baking sheet, pressing the nozzle gently into the paste at the end to avoid forming a peak.

2 If peaks should form, dip a fork in a little beaten egg to gently flatten them. Lightly brush with beaten egg, then bake.

3 When cooked, the buns should be puffed and golden. Make a small slit in each of the buns to allow the steam to escape, then cool.

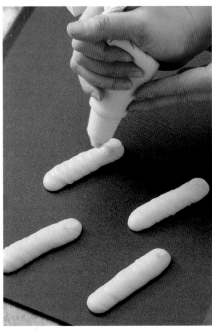

4 When cool, use the small slit in each bun to fill it, by piping in cream or chocolate using a large, plain nozzle.

5 To make éclairs, use a plain nozzle to pipe the choux paste in strips, making each "finger" identical in length. Bake, pierce, and cool.

6 To create rings, mark out circles of your chosen size on a baking sheet. Following the circles, pipe choux rings, bake, pierce, and cool.

Roll out puff pastry

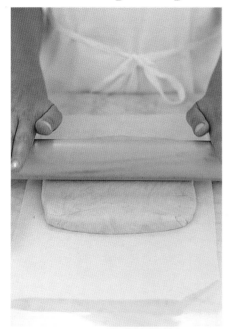

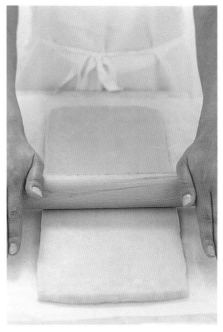

1 On a piece of baking parchment, on a cool, floured, work surface, roll out your pastry dough to a long rectangle.

2 Beat 100g (3½oz) chilled unsalted butter into a rectangle and encase it in the dough. Turn the parcel over and gently roll out again.

3 Using the edge of the baking parchment, fold both the top and the bottom ends of the dough inwards to meet in the centre (a "book fold").

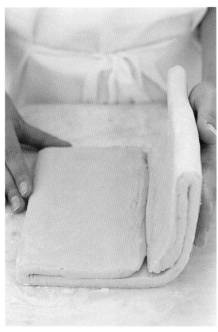

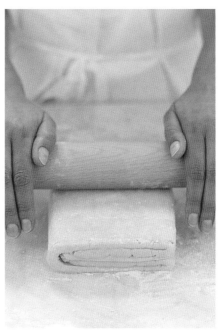

4 Turn the parcel 90 degrees and fold the dough in half at the centre. Using your hands, flatten the parcel slightly, and chill for 30 minutes.

5 Roll the pastry parcel out to a rectangle again, then fold and chill as before. Repeat the process once more.

6 Roll into a rectangle then fold one end to the middle and the other over it. Cover with cling film and chill for 30 minutes before using.

Line a tart tin

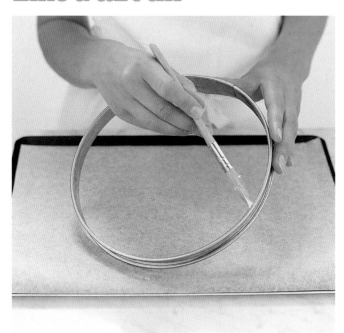

1 Using a pastry brush dipped in a little melted unsalted butter, grease the inside of a tart ring or a loose-bottomed tart tin. Place the ring on a large flat baking sheet covered with baking parchment.

2 Sprinkle a little flour on a cool work surface, then lightly dust the pastry ball with flour, and roll out the pastry into a circle larger than your tart ring. Keep rolling out until it is 3–5mm (⅛–¼in) thick.

3 Ensure that the pastry does not stick to the surface by sliding a flexible spatula underneath it after every few strokes with the rolling pin. Carefully brush away any surplus flour with a dry pastry brush.

4 Use the rolling pin to gather up the pastry by rolling the pastry halfway over it. Then carefully lift the rest of the pastry circle away from the surface to transfer it to the tart ring.

5 Dust off any surplus flour again, and gently unroll the pastry circle across the tart ring, making sure that there is plenty of excess pastry to cover the sides of the ring.

6 Carefully smooth the pastry from the centre of the circle then, using your thumbs and forefingers, gently press the pastry into the inside edge of the ring and and up the sides.

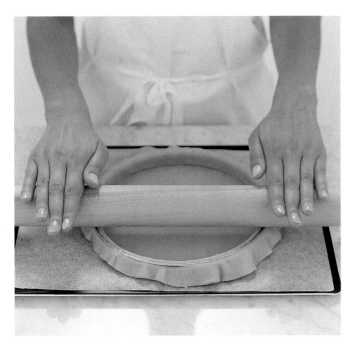

7 Now use your rolling pin to trim away the excess pastry and give a clean edge, by pressing the rolling pin over the top of the tart ring to cut away the pastry hanging over the top.

8 Using your thumbs, carefully press the pastry into and up the sides of the ring again to achieve a smooth fit. Prick the base all over with a fork to allow air to escape. Chill in the refrigerator for 30 minutes before using.

Blind bake

1 Cut a circle of baking parchment slightly larger than the flan ring or tart tin that you are using. Fold the disc in half several times, then clip the outer edge with scissors.

2 Place the pastry in the flan ring and and prick it with a fork, then cover the base and sides of the pastry with the parchment, taking the paper above the sides of the ring. Fill with baking beans or dried beans.

3 Place the shell in the oven and bake according to your recipe's instructions. For a fully baked case, remove the beans and paper, then return the shell to the oven for the required time.

4 Cool the pastry case on a wire rack. Lift off the flan ring (or remove from the tart tin) before or after filling, according to the recipe instructions.

Trim and decorate pastry

For a forked edge, press the dough to the rim of the dish using the prongs of a fork. Repeat around the edge in even intervals.

For a rope edge, pinch the dough between your thumb and the knuckle of your index finger. Place your thumb in the groove and repeat.

For a fluted edge, push a finger against the outside edge and pinch the pastry with the other finger and thumb to form a ruffle.

Seal and glaze pastry

Apply a melted jelly, jam, or light caramel over fruit before serving to give it a lustrous appearance.

For turnovers, brush with an egg wash (1 egg yolk, 1 tbsp water and a pinch of salt) before baking to give a rich, glossy glaze.

For a cooked sweet tart, thinly glaze the base of a cooled tart shell with melted plain or white chocolate and allow to set.

Prepare and line a cake tin

1 Melt unsalted butter and use a pastry brush to apply a thin, even layer all over the bottom and sides of the tin, including any corners.

2 Sprinkle a little flour into the tin, then shake and rotate the pan so the flour coats the bottom and sides. Tip away any excess flour.

3 If using a paper liner instead of flouring, place a fitted piece of baking parchment directly onto the greased bottom of the tin.

Roll a sponge roulade

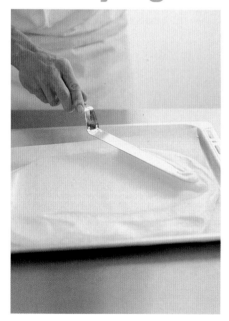

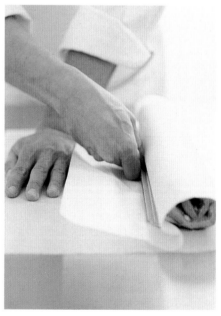

1 Spread the sponge mixture on a lined baking tray. Bake until golden, then put a piece of baking parchment on top and turn out the cake.

2 Slowly peel away the bottom layer of parchment. Fill, and roll, using the second piece of parchment to support the roulade.

3 Fold one half of the paper over the roulade, then push a ruler against the roll to shape it. Remove the paper, and trim the ends to serve.

Make a genoese sponge

1 Preheat the oven to 190°C (375°F/Gas 5). Sift 200g (7oz) plain flour and set aside. In a heatproof bowl over boiling water, place 6 eggs and 20g (¾oz) honey, and whisk until the mixture is a creamy, pale yellow.

2 Remove from the heat and whisk at a high speed until thick. Add grated zest of ½ unwaxed lemon, and whisk slowly for 15 minutes. Fold in the flour.

3 Whisk 2 tbsp of the butter into 60g (2oz) melted unsalted butter, then whisk it all together. Pour into a lined springform tin and bake at 180°C (350°F/Gas 4) for 30–40 minutes.

4 Remove the sponge from the oven and leave to cool for 10 minutes. Set on a wire rack and release the springform. To cut layers, place one hand on top of the cake and use a long-bladed, serrated knife to cut through.

Pasta

BUY Available fresh or dried, plain white, with egg, wholemeal, or coloured and flavoured with spinach, with olives, with black squid ink, and with tomato. Fresh is not always best; some sauces are better suited to dried pasta, and a quality brand will be superior to a cheap fresh pasta. A rough texture is a positive attribute, indicating that the pasta was made in small batches and that sauces will cling well to it. **STORE** Keep dried pasta in a sealed container in a cool dry place for up to a year. Freshly made pasta keeps for up to 3 days in the fridge, 3 months in the freezer. Bought fresh pasta keeps about a week in the refrigerator – check use-by date. Cooked pasta can be frozen for up to 2 months; it will be slightly softer on thawing.

◀ **Vermicelli**

EAT Very fine durum wheat pasta, like very thin spaghetti. Used in many cuisines outside Italy. Often cooked and layered with fish or vegetable mixtures and baked with a breadcrumb topping or broken into pieces to add to broth (available ready-cut too). **FLAVOUR PAIRINGS** Shellfish, sweet peppers, tomatoes, onions, aubergines, courgettes, olives, garlic, basil, oregano, thyme, breadcrumbs, olive oil, chicken, beef and vegetable broths.

▲ **Spaghetti**

EAT Long, thin, and round. Use with everything from a simple garlic, chilli, and olive oil dressing to cream or meat sauces. Made from durum wheat and also from alternative flours. Spaghettini is thin spaghetti; use in the same way. **FLAVOUR PAIRINGS** Meat ragùs, meatballs, pesto, olive oil, butter, cream, ham, pancetta, onions, garlic, tomatoes, chillies, shellfish, Parmesan.

◀ **Tagliatelle**

EAT Fresh tagliatelle is sold in strips; dried in nests. Good with rich meat and cream sauces. Dried nests are available in different colours and flavours. Best to choose complementary sauces e.g. black pasta is flavoured with squid or cuttlefish ink so best matched with seafood or vegetables. Fettuccine is a narrower version, sold in lengths. **FLAVOUR PAIRINGS** Cream, crème fraîche, eggs, ham, pancetta, mushrooms, peas, broad beans, fresh and smoked salmon, shellfish, broccoli, classic bolognese sauce, Parmesan.

▲ **Pappardelle**

EAT Thick ribbons with wavy or straight edges. Good with chunky meat or fish sauces. **FLAVOUR PAIRINGS** Olive oil, cream, veal, beef, chicken, chicken livers, monkfish, halibut, tuna, fresh and smoked salmon, sage, oregano, basil, parsley, olives, garlic, onions, tomatoes.

▲ **Orzo**

EAT Beads of pasta used in place of rice in soups, bakes or side dishes. **FLAVOUR PAIRINGS** Chicken, beef and vegetable broths, olive oil, tomatoes, onions, garlic, sweet peppers, olives, cavolo nero, carrots, turnips, mushrooms.

▲ **Macaroni**

EAT Smooth or ribbed, short or long pasta tubes. Use for macaroni cheese and other baked pasta dishes, such as timbales. **FLAVOUR PAIRINGS** Cheddar and blue cheeses, Italian hard cheeses, broccoli, tomatoes, mushrooms, spinach, sweetcorn, tuna, bacon, prosciutto crudo, breadcrumbs, butter.

▲ **Lasagne**

EAT Fresh or dried, usually layered with a chunky sauce and topped with béchamel sauce, then baked. Fresh lasagne can be cooked and folded on plates over a filling and served as open lasagne or open ravioli. **FLAVOUR PAIRINGS** Bolognese sauce, tomato sauce, fish and shellfish, mixed pulses, mushrooms, Mediterranean vegetables, broccoli, Italian hard cheeses, mascarpone.

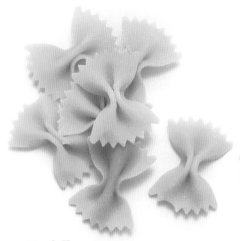

▲ Farfalle

EAT Resembling bow ties or butterflies, they're good with simple tomato, or cheese and ham sauces, or in salads and oven bakes. **FLAVOUR PAIRINGS** Tomatoes, onions, garlic, olive oil, basil, Gorgonzola, cream, Italian hard cheeses, cherry tomatoes, black olives, pesto, salmon, tuna, pine nuts, spinach.

▲ Fusilli

EAT Favourite spiral shape for coloured pasta and multigrain combinations (as well as plain). Good in salads and bakes and with chunky vegetable and creamy sauces. **FLAVOUR PAIRINGS** Olive oil, black olives, tomatoes, aubergines, red peppers, onions, garlic, capers, pine nuts, basil, cream, Gorgonzola, mozzarella, Parmesan.

▲ Rigatoni

EAT Large and satisfying, good with meat ragùs and chunky vegetables but also with smooth cream and cheese sauces. **FLAVOUR PAIRINGS** Beef, veal, chicken, ham, pig's liver, olive oil, butter, sage, basil, parsley, onions, tomatoes, sweetcorn, broccoli, beans, spinach, mozzarella, Italian hard cheeses, Gorgonzola.

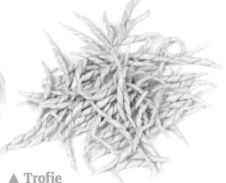

▲ Penne

EAT Pasta quills with smooth sides (*lisce*) or ribbed (*regate*). Classically paired with tomato and chilli sauces, and also good in salads and pasta bakes. **FLAVOUR PAIRINGS** Olive oil, butter, cream, onions, garlic, sweet peppers, mushrooms, shellfish, chicken, chorizo, beef, veal, tomatoes, fennel, sun-dried tomatoes, basil, parsley, thyme, chillies, Parmesan, mascarpone.

▲ Conchiglie

EAT Shells available in small (add to soups), medium (serve with sauces or in salads), and large (stuff). **FLAVOUR PAIRINGS** Chicken and vegetable broths, tomatoes, onions, garlic, anchovies, prawns and other shellfish, bacon, ham, chicken, sweetcorn, peas, spinach, squashes, rocket, olives, Parmesan, basil, sage.

▲ Trofie

EAT Speciality of Liguria, handmade with just Tipo "00" flour and water, traditionally served with pesto from the same region. **FLAVOUR PAIRINGS** Basil pesto, olive oil, butter, prawns, goat's cheese, lemon, artichoke hearts, wild mushrooms, courgettes, Parmesan.

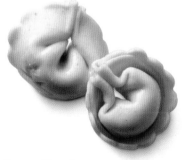

▲ Ravioli

EAT Stuffed square or round (*girasole*) pasta cushions, filled with meat, chicken, vegetables, mushrooms, fish, or spinach and ricotta cheese. Serve simply dressed, or with a sauce. **FLAVOUR PAIRINGS** Fresh tomato sauce, butter, olive oil, sage, thyme, parsley, Parmesan, mascarpone.

▲ Cappelletti

EAT Modelled on little hats worn in the Middle ages, usually stuffed with meat or cheese. **FLAVOUR PAIRINGS** Butter, olive oil, sage, parsley, garlic, Italian hard cheeses.

▲ Lunette

EAT "Little moons", sometimes flavoured with truffles, often stuffed with cheese, or mixtures like broccoli and almonds. **FLAVOUR PAIRINGS** Olive oil, butter, fresh herbs, truffles or truffle oil.

Noodles

BUY All these noodles cook quickly, so take care to follow packet instructions or they will become very soft. All are available dried. If you find a supplier of fresh noodles, make sure the shop has a high turnover of trade as they deteriorate quickly. **STORE** Fresh versions should be eaten on day of purchase but can be stored in the refrigerator in a plastic bag for a few days if necessary. Dried noodles will keep wrapped, in a cool, dry cupboard for several years.

▲ Flat rice noodles

EAT Also called rice sticks, they vary in width from 2mm (½in)–1cm (½in). Use in pad thai, add to stir-fries, or use with steamed dishes. **FLAVOUR PAIRINGS** Shallots, beansprouts, spring onions, chilli, coriander leaf, oyster sauce, nam pla, lime, peanuts, eggs, prawns.

▲ Rice vermicelli

EAT Very thin skeins of dried noodles. Use to add soft bulk and texture to many dishes including spring rolls and salads. Try deep-frying dried noodles to puff up and crisp as a garnish for salads, or soak, dry, then deep-fry for crunchy noodles to serve with stir-fries. **FLAVOUR PAIRINGS** Sesame oil and seeds, ginger, chilli, garlic, shiitake mushrooms, spring onions, cabbage, carrots, shellfish, chicken, beef, soy sauce, oyster sauce, beansprouts.

◀ Brown rice udon noodles

EAT Often made with wheat flour too, these give a more distinctive flavour and firmer texture to serve in soups, and with salads, stir-fries, steamed, or stewed dishes. **FLAVOUR PAIRINGS** Chilli, ginger, peanut butter, peanut oil, sesame oil, soy sauce, garlic, miso, coconut milk, spring onions, broccoli, carrots, daikon, pak choi and other leafy greens, baby corn, mangetout, green beans.

▲ Wheat udon noodles

EAT Plump white noodles with rounded or square-cut edges. Serve in broths and thick curry (katsu) sauces. **FLAVOUR PAIRINGS** Chicken, pork, prawns, garlic, onions, peppers, root and green vegetables, apples, bananas, curry spices, turmeric, honey, tomato ketchup, chicken broth, miso, nam pla, chilli, star anise.

▲ Fine rice noodles

EAT Thin, straight version of flat rice noodles, suitable for adding to soups and stir-fries. **FLAVOUR PAIRINGS** Chicken or beef broth, chicken, beef, prawns, crab, lobster, shiitake mushrooms, sweetcorn, spring onions, soy sauce, ginger, garlic.

▲ Chinese wheat noodles

EAT Round or flat, they are robust and versatile. Ideal for soups and stir-fries. **FLAVOUR PAIRINGS** Beef, poultry, pork, cashew nuts, peanuts, chilli, green peppers, miso, onion, oyster sauce, spinach, Chinese five-spice powder.

▲ Buckwheat (soba) noodles

EAT Japanese noodles, either exclusively buckwheat, or mixed with wheat flour (milder). Good hot or cold. **FLAVOUR PAIRINGS** Spring onions, shiitake mushrooms, asparagus, mangetout, carrots, celery, peppers, beansprouts, garlic, lime, soy sauce, peanuts, tahini, chilli, ginger, rice wine, rice vinegar, honey, chicken, prawns.

▲ Bean thread (cellophane) noodles

EAT Made from mung beans and tapioca, particularly good in salads. **FLAVOUR PAIRINGS** Peanut or sunflower oil, sesame oil, rice wine vinegar, soy sauce, chilli, ginger, garlic, cucumber, carrots, radishes, chicken, duck, prawns, lychees, mango, beansprouts.

▲ Chinese egg noodles

EAT Available in a variety of thicknesses. Famous in chow mein, but good in all stir-fries and steamed dishes. **FLAVOUR PAIRINGS** Beef, poultry, pork, prawns, sesame oil, soy sauce, dry sherry, rice wine, spring onions, peppers, Chinese five-spice powder, chilli sauce.

▲ Somen noodles

EAT Associated with Japanese summer time, they are often eaten cold with a dipping sauce. **FLAVOUR PAIRINGS** Tamari soy sauce, ginger, garlic, rice wine, chilli, spring onions, sesame oil, most vegetables, beef, chicken, pork, fish and shellfish.

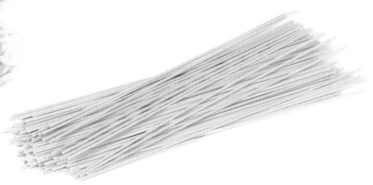

▲ Ramen noodles

EAT Japanese wheat noodles, similar to Chinese versions, served in soups and as an accompaniment. **FLAVOUR PAIRINGS** Chicken or beef broth, chicken, beef, shellfish, shiitake mushrooms, bamboo shoots, daikon, carrots, spring onions, miso, mustard greens, ginger, garlic, tamari soy sauce.

▲ Indian vermicelli

EAT Fine wheat noodles, sold plain or pre-toasted (as most recipes call for them to be browned in ghee before use). Used in some savoury dishes but mostly for milk puddings. **FLAVOUR PAIRINGS** Milk, sugars, honey, cardamom seeds, cumin seeds, saffron, raisins, cashew nuts, pistachios, butter or ghee.

Cook dried pasta

1 Bring a large pan of salted water to the boil and pour in the pasta. Stir once to prevent the pasta sticking to the bottom of the pan.

2 Boil with the pan uncovered, following the recommended cooking time on the pack, or until al dente (remove a spoonful to test).

3 Drain the pasta through a colander, shaking it gently to remove any excess water, and toss with a little oil to prevent it sticking together.

Boil noodles

1 To boil egg, wheat, or buckwheat noodles, bring a large saucepan of water to the boil. Add the noodles, allow the water to return to the boil, then cook until the noodles are softened (about 2 minutes).

2 Drain the noodles in a colander and place them under cold running water. Toss the noodles with a little oil to prevent them from sticking, then proceed with the desired recipe.

Make pasta dough

1 Pour the pasta flour onto a work surface, form a well in the centre and add the eggs, then gently break the yolks with a fork.

2 Beat the eggs lightly with the fork, then slowly begin to draw the flour into the centre to mix with the eggs a little at a time.

3 Once the eggs and the flour have been combined, push any remaining flour into the centre and use your hands to form the dough.

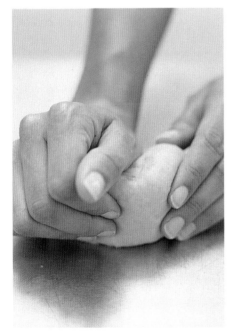

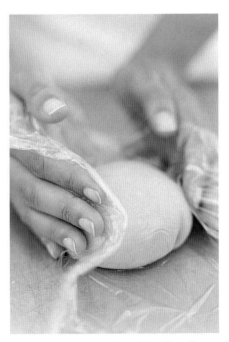

4 Now place the dough on a clean surface and knead it firmly with both hands until it feels semi-soft and holds together.

5 Continue to knead the dough, turning it as you go, for at least 4–5 minutes, or until it feels silky, smooth, and elastic.

6 Wrap the kneaded dough in cling film and place it in the refrigerator (but not the coldest part) to rest for up to an hour.

Use a pasta machine

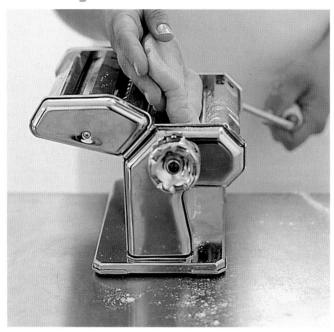

1 Flatten the pasta dough into a rectangle and pass tvhrough the pasta machine on the thickest setting 3 times. This will make the dough spread out to fill the full width of the machine.

2 Fold the pasta dough into thirds, then flatten it , and pass through the machine again. Repeat this process 6 times (lightly dusting the dough with flour once or twice to prevent it sticking).

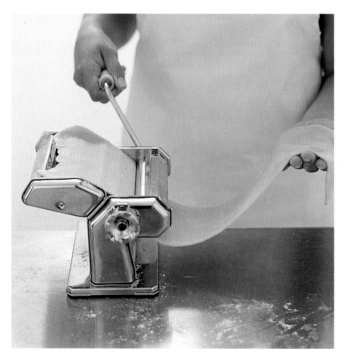

3 Continue to roll the pasta through the machine, decreasing the thickness setting each time. As you turn the handle with one hand, support the dough with the other, as it gradually becomes thinner.

4 To save time, press the edges of the pasta sheet together to create a loop. This will avoid the need to keep removing the dough from the machine and feeding it back in.

Cut pasta dough by hand

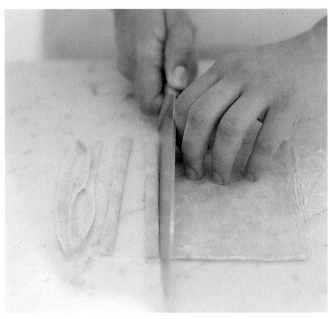

1 To make rectangular or square shaped pasta, cut the dough to the required size for your recipe. 12 x 15cm (5 x6 in) rectangles are the usual size for lasagne or cannelloni.

2 To make pasta noodles, fold the dough into thirds with the folds at the top and bottom, then cut it into strips. Pappardelle are usually 1cm (½in) wide; fettuccine are usually 5mm (¼in) wide.

Make gnocchi

1 Gnocchi are made by forming a rough dough out of cooked potato, eggs, and flour. Take each piece of dough and roll it back and forth on a floured work surface to form a cylinder. Ensure you handle it lightly.

2 When the cylinders are evenly formed (they should be about as thick as your forefinger), cut the dough into 3cm (1¼in) pieces, shape into crescents, and press onto the back of a fork to form the indentations.

Assemble ravioli

1 Using a pasta machine, roll out a thin sheet of pasta and divide it into two equal lengths. Take one sheet and mark out the number and shape of ravioli, as specified by the recipe, by scoring the pasta with a cutter.

2 Take teaspoonfuls of the filling mixture and carefully place them in the centre of each scored raviolo half. Brush on beaten egg or a little water, to help bind the edges of the ravioli.

3 Now take the second length of rolled-out pasta and carefully lift it over the first sheet, check for alignment, and then place on top. Gently shape round each dollop of filling, getting rid of any air bubbles.

4 Take the pastry cutter and run it around the outside edges of the ravioli sheet to form a neat edge, then cut out each individual raviolo. Lightly press around the edges with your fingertips to seal.

Shape tortellini

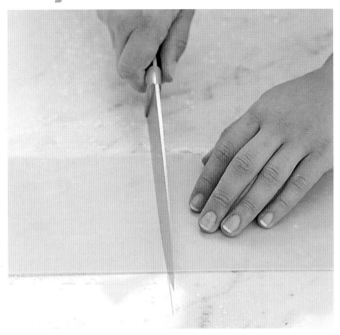

1 Roll the pasta dough until it is extremely thin. Lay out a sheet 12cm (5in) wide, then trim the edges. Cut the sheet into two equal lengths. Put one half aside and cover with a clean, damp tea towel.

2 Spread another damp tea towel on your work surface and lay the other dough sheet on top. Cut the pasta sheet in half lengthways, then cut across it at equal intervals to create 6cm (2½in) squares.

3 Take one square and turn it over onto the work surface, so that its damp side now faces upwards. Position it like a diamond, rather than a square. Place a teaspoon of filling into the middle of the diamond.

4 Now take the bottom corner up over the filling to the top corner, so that it forms a triangular shape. Press the edges together and then lift the left and right corners and pinch them together to seal.

Oils

BUY There are hundreds of oils on the market. It is important to use the right one for the job. Here's a selection of favourites used in cookery. Choose cold-pressed oils for flavour and nutritional value. Not all oils are suitable for frying. Those high in polyunsaturated fats have too low a smoking point. **STORE** Olive and seed oils will keep unopened in a cool, dark place for a year or more. However, nut oils should be used within 6 months. All open bottles should be used within 3 months.

▲ Extra virgin olive oil

EAT Highest-quality olive oil, the best is cold-pressed. Made from a single olive variety or a blend, filtered or unfiltered, producing a wide variety of flavour and colour, from olive green to greenish gold. Acidity must be less than 1 per cent. Use when flavour is all-important – as a condiment or drizzle, in dressings, dips, and marinades. Don't waste an expensive oil for frying. **FLAVOUR PAIRINGS** Asparagus, artichokes, aubergines, peppers, tomatoes, baby leeks, onions, shallots, garlic, fresh herbs, olives, capers, fresh cheeses, cured meats, fish, seafood, wines, vinegars, mustards, honey.

▲ Virgin olive oil

EAT Lower quality than extra virgin oil. Acidity must be less than 2 per cent. Use for everyday cooking, when you want a milder-flavoured dressing, or for grilling and sautéing. **FLAVOUR PAIRINGS** Wine, balsamic, and fruit vinegars, Dijon and wholegrain mustard, white and red wine, citrus, all meats, fish, seafood, poultry, game, vegetables, most dried and fresh fruits, herbs, chilli.

▲ Olive/light olive oil

EAT A blend of virgin olive oil and a cheaper refined oil to give a "lighter" flavour. Popular with those who aren't so keen on the pronounced flavour of extra virgin oil. Some like it for making mayonnaise. Light does not mean lower in calories. Use for general cooking or mix with a little nut or seed oil (like walnut or toasted pumpkin) in dressings. **FLAVOUR PAIRINGS** All meats, fish, poultry and game, egg yolks, mustard, vegetables, salad stuffs, wine, balsamic or fruit vinegars, lemon juice, honey, nuts, seeds.

▲ Groundnut oil

EAT The refined oil is almost tasteless and ideal when you don't want added flavour – for frying everything from chips to fritters, and general cooking. **FLAVOUR PAIRINGS** Roots and tubers, leafy greens, onions, meat, fish, poultry, robust herbs like parsley or sage (fried for garnish).

▲ Grapeseed oil

EAT Widely used in French cookery and in salad dressings, it has a delicate flavour. Can also be used for frying. **FLAVOUR PAIRINGS** Nuts, seeds, tomatoes, onions, root vegetables, garlic, balsamic, fruit, and herb vinegars, herbs.

▲ Rapeseed oil

EAT Also known as canola oil. Good for frying and baking. **FLAVOUR PAIRINGS** Meatballs, patties, burgers, fritters, fish and shellfish, choux pastry (for beignets), onions, potatoes, root vegetables, apples, pears, bananas, pineapple.

▲ Sunflower oil

EAT Suitable for all cooking and dressings. Cold-pressed is much earthier. Safflower is from the same family of seeds. Use in the same way. **FLAVOUR PAIRINGS** Meats, poultry, game, fish, vegetables, eggs, cream, vinegars, citrus.

▲ Pumpkin seed oil

EAT Toasted has best flavour. Good to finish soups, brush on roast meats, and in salad dressings. **FLAVOUR PAIRINGS** Pork, oily fish, squashes, balsamic, fruit, and wine vinegars, cherry tomatoes, cucumber, spinach, apples, berries.

▲ Sesame oil

EAT Nutty taste. Use for Chinese cookery and salad dressings. **FLAVOUR PAIRINGS** Sesame seeds, spring onions, garlic, soy sauce, honey, Sichuan pepper, beansprouts, peppers, cucumber, water chestnuts, chicken, fish, shellfish, beef, pork.

▲ Walnut oil

EAT Rich nut flavour and aroma. Use in dressings, drizzled over cooked vegetables, and for stir-fries. **FLAVOUR PAIRINGS** Nuts and seeds, pears, apples, cabbage, celery, root vegetables, spinach, blue and cream cheeses.

▲ Hazelnut oil

EAT Subtle flavour of hazelnuts. Delicious in dressings and desserts. Don't use for cooking, as it turns bitter. **FLAVOUR PAIRINGS** Beetroot, cherry tomatoes, shallots, baby leaves, fresh soft cheeses, raspberries, oats, rice, vanilla.

▲ Truffle oil

EAT White truffle oil is stronger. Drizzle over pasta, risotto, grills, and omelettes. Gently fry eggs in black truffle oil, then serve on bruschetta with the oil drizzled over. **FLAVOUR PAIRINGS** Eggs, pasta, risotto rice, fish, shellfish, game birds, fois gras.

▲ Chilli oil

EAT All chilli oils are pungent. Use whenever you want their spicy flavour in cooking and dressings. **FLAVOUR PAIRINGS** Tomatoes, mushrooms, onions, garlic, basil, oregano, cheeses, pasta, beef, pork, veal, chicken, seafood, citrus, tropical fruits.

▲ Garlic oil

EAT Use for a subtle garlic flavour. Good in dressings, marinades, and potato dishes. Don't use for frying. **FLAVOUR PAIRINGS** Potatoes, onions, mushrooms, rice, courgettes, pasta, couscous, fish, seafood, chicken.

▲ Herb oils

EAT Useful if a particular fresh herb is not available. Don't use for cooking at high temperatures. **FLAVOUR PAIRINGS** Most vegetables, pasta, rice, couscous, polenta, fish, seafood, meat, poultry, game, cheeses, tropical fruits.

Vinegars

BUY Each vinegar has its own particular flavour and is not usually interchangeable, so buy a selection from which to choose. Start with the ones you will use frequently, like, perhaps, basic wine vinegars and a good brown and white balsamic, and then add to the list as recipes call for them. **STORE** Most will keep almost indefinitely in a cool, dark cupboard (but fruit or herb vinegars usually only 2–3 years). Naturally produced wine vinegars that have not been pasteurized may grow a "vinegar mother" – a cluster of vinegar-producing bacteria. Just remove it and use it to make your own vinegar at home.

▲ White wine vinegar

EAT Delicately sour with fruity undertones. Use in dressings for delicate salads, to make mayonnaise, and to deglaze the pan before making cream sauces for steaks, chops, and cutlets. **FLAVOUR PAIRINGS** Shallots, baby salad leaves, artichoke hearts, avocado, cucumber, mushrooms, fennel, beef, lamb, pork, chicken, white fish, shellfish, white beans, cream, eggs, parsley, sage, lovage, chervil, olive oil, sunflower oil.

▲ Red wine vinegar

EAT Robust and fruity with a good depth of acidity. Use in most culinary applications, particularly stronger-flavoured salads, meat, game, and poultry stews and casseroles. It is also the French choice for making vinaigrette. **FLAVOUR PAIRINGS** Beetroot, carrots, red onions, green beans, mushrooms, beef, venison, pork, lamb, game birds, oily fish, pulses, tarragon, parsley, oregano, rosemary, bay, olive oil, herb oils, toasted seed oils.

▲ Sherry vinegar

EAT Matured for a number of years in wooden barrels. It is full of dried fruit flavours that are good for robust salads, and to marinate pork or veal loin before roasting. **FLAVOUR PAIRINGS** Pork, veal, chicken, duck, salmon, mackerel, sardines, root vegetables, spinach, sorrel, rocket, watercress, radishes, olive oil, nut oils.

▲ Muscat vinegar

EAT Strong aroma and taste of sweet Muscat grapes, from which it is made. Particularly good in fish and seafood dressings, desserts, and fruit sauces. **FLAVOUR PAIRINGS** Smoked mackerel, smoked salmon, lobster, prawns, olive oil, hazelnut oil, chicory, tropical fruits, apples, pears, strawberries, raspberries, nuts.

▲ Cider vinegar

EAT A strong aroma and flavour of apples. Use instead of red or white wine vinegar but particularly good with richer meats and fish. **FLAVOUR PAIRINGS** Duck, chicken, game birds, salmon, trout, mackerel, herring, sea bass and bream, orchard fruits, cabbage, shallots, olive, walnut, toasted sesame, and pumpkin oils.

▲ Pickling vinegar

EAT Usually malt vinegar-based, special blends of pickling spices are infused in it ready for making pickles. **FLAVOUR PAIRINGS** Onions, shallots, cucumbers, beetroot, plums, red and white cabbage, cauliflower, carrots, tomatoes, peppers, courgettes, beans, turmeric, mustard powder, garlic, bay leaf, cinnamon, muscovado and other brown sugars, granulated sugar, honey.

▲ Herb vinegar

EAT Made by infusing the chosen herb in wine vinegar (tarragon here). Use in dressings and marinades. **FLAVOUR PAIRINGS** Salads, peppers, avocados, mushrooms, fish, shellfish, carpaccios, fresh cheeses, chicken, olive oil.

▲ Fruit vinegar

EAT Strong flavour of featured fruit (raspberry here). Use for dressings, drizzles, and marinades. **FLAVOUR PAIRINGS** Duck, game, avocados, salad stuffs, beetroot, shallots, basil, rosemary, lavender, parsley, olive, hazelnut, and walnut oils.

▲ Balsamic vinegar

EAT Good balsamic from Modena contains no caramel or preservatives. Use for drizzles, dressings, savoury sauces, and with fresh and dried fruits. **FLAVOUR PAIRINGS** Cheeses, pulses, fruits, vegetables, duck, game birds, rich meats, fish, honey, olive oil.

▲ White balsamic condiment

EAT It's not a vinegar as it does not have a high enough acidity. It has a sweet, mildly acidic taste. **FLAVOUR PAIRINGS** Fish, shellfish, chicken, artichokes, white asparagus, chicory, celeriac, button mushrooms, olive, sunflower, and nut oils.

▲ Chinese white rice vinegar

EAT Tastes similar to white wine or malt vinegar. Use in sweet and sour dishes, pickles, and as a condiment. **FLAVOUR PAIRINGS** Pork, fish, prawns, chicken, peppers, spring onions, tomatoes, carrots, pineapple, cucumber, ginger, soy sauce.

▲ Chinese black rice vinegar

EAT Mellow, slightly salty, and smoky. Zhenjiang is the best. Use as a dim sum dipping sauce, or as balsamic vinegar. Red rice vinegar is similar but less sweet. **FLAVOUR PAIRINGS** Prawns, chicken, pork, beef, ginger, garlic, chilli, sesame oil, soy sauce.

▲ Japanese brown rice vinegar

EAT Mellow flavour. Use in dipping sauces and marinades. **FLAVOUR PAIRINGS** Fish, shellfish, chicken, cabbage, daikon, mizuna, lotus root, edamame, cucumber, peppers, corn, okra.

▲ Japanese rice vinegar

EAT Mix with salt and sugar for sushi vinegar. Add to tempura batter. **FLAVOUR PAIRINGS** Tofu, seafood, wasabi, ginger, soy sauce, sushi rice, nori, sesame seeds, cucumber, spring onions.

▲ Malt vinegar

EAT Strong and sour. Traditional condiment with fish and chips. Use for pickles and chutneys and in some sauces. **FLAVOUR PAIRINGS** Fish, tripe, potatoes, roots, beans, cauliflower, cucumbers, onions, peppers, fruits, bay leaves, pickling spices.

Flavouring sauces and pastes

BUY Check the labels and avoid those containing MSG or that have a long list of additives. For soy sauces, ensure they are authentically fermented from soya beans. For vegetable pastes, choose the longest use-by date. **STORE** Keep unopened in a cool, dark cupboard. Once opened, store in the refrigerator. Most will last 3–6 months.

▲ Tomato purée

EAT Intense tomato flavour. Use generally in soups, stews, casseroles, and sauces. Look for sun-dried tomato paste, passata (sieved tomatoes), and the condiment, tomato ketchup. **FLAVOUR PAIRINGS** All meats, poultry, game, fish, pulses, most vegetables, cheeses, herbs and spices.

▲ Worcestershire sauce

EAT A smooth sauce with a tangy flavour. Use in traditional British cookery and in a Bloody Mary. **FLAVOUR PAIRINGS** Tomato juice, vodka, celery salt, avocados, minced beef, bacon, mushrooms, mayonnaise, ketchup, Tabasco.

▲ Tabasco

EAT Thin, fiery sauce with a salty, sour taste. A green, milder one is also available. Use to spice up soups, stews, casseroles, and dips and add a few drops to a Bloody Mary. Slightly thicker yellow or orange hot chilli sauce can be used the same way. **FLAVOUR PAIRINGS** Most vegetables, poultry, meat, pulses, cheeses, tomato juice, vodka, parsley, coriander leaf, celery salt.

▲ Anchovy paste

EAT Intense anchovy flavour. Spread on toast or add a dash to enhance meat pâtés, casseroles, and fish dishes. Thinner anchovy essence also available. **FLAVOUR PAIRINGS** Beef, venison, pig's liver, all fish and seafood, tomatoes.

▲ Tahini paste

EAT Thick, smooth sesame seed paste. Essential in chickpea hummus, or use thinned with lemon juice as a dip with falafel. Good in sauces and dressings. **FLAVOUR PAIRINGS** Chickpeas and other pulses, olive oil, citrus, chilli, coriander leaf, mint, oregano, sesame seeds, yogurt.

▲ Miso

EAT Japanese white or red pastes made from fermented soy with wheat, barley, or rice. (Red miso shown here). Use in soups (with dashi – stock made with dried bonito flakes), dressings, sauces, stir-fries, stews, marinades, and glazes. Miso soup mix, too. **FLAVOUR PAIRINGS** Tuna, salmon, monkfish, veal, ham, poultry, most vegetables, ginger, chilli, garlic.

▲ Soy sauce

EAT Use dark soy in general Chinese cooking but particularly "red"-cooked dishes. Also good as gravy browning. Use light soy as a condiment and dipping sauce. **FLAVOUR PAIRINGS** Poultry, all meats, seafood, vegetables, noodles, rice, eggs, Sichuan pepper, ginger, rice vinegar.

▲ Tamari

EAT Japanese soy sauce. Use as a dipping sauce and in most savoury Japanese dishes. Often served with wasabi (the mustardy paste) as a condiment. **FLAVOUR PAIRINGS** Seafood, chicken, pork, beef, cabbage, daikon, mizuna, lotus root, edamame, cucumber, aubergine, peppers.

▲ Oyster sauce

EAT Only mildly fishy. Use to flavour Chinese meat and vegetable dishes, particularly stir-fries. **FLAVOUR PAIRINGS** Beef, pork, chicken, prawns, aubergines, bean sprouts, pak choi, onions, spring onions, shiitake mushrooms, bamboo shoots, water chestnuts.

▲ Black bean sauce

EAT Mild or fiery. Use in Chinese stir-fries and steamed dishes. Add towards the end of cooking. Use yellow bean sauce in a similar way. **FLAVOUR PAIRINGS** Beef, pork, chicken, most vegetables, garlic, soy sauce.

▲ Sweet chilli sauce

EAT Sweet and thick, good for dipping or in stir-fries. **FLAVOUR PAIRINGS** Chicken, beef, pork, fish and shellfish, most vegetables, noodles, rice, soy sauce.

▲ Mirin

EAT An essential ingredient in teriyaki sauce. Use it to balance the flavours of Japanese noodle broths, or stirred into a dipping sauce for tempura. **FLAVOUR PAIRINGS** Poultry, pork, beef, salmon, tofu, rice, noodles, soy sauce, spring onions, yuzu, sesame seeds.

▲ Nam pla

EAT Thai fish sauce; smells fishy, tastes salty. Add to dressings, stews, and curries. Asian shrimp paste is stronger, but use the same way. **FLAVOUR PAIRINGS** Curry pastes, galangal, coconut milk, beef, chicken, seafood, vegetables.

▲ Sambal oelek

EAT Strong, salty, and tangy chilli paste. Serve as a relish, in salsas, or to add a kick to many dishes. **FLAVOUR PAIRINGS** Chicken, seafood, pulses, root and green vegetables, bean sprouts, salad vegetables, rice vinegar, white balsamic condiment.

▲ Harissa paste

EAT Fiery chilli paste widely used in North African cookery. Use as a rub, in marinades, and dressings. **FLAVOUR PAIRINGS** Lamb, chicken, tuna, salmon, pulses, rice, edamame beans, broad beans, aubergines, courgettes, peppers, tomato purée.

Make fresh chicken stock

1 Roast chicken bones in the oven for 20 minutes at 200°C (400°F/Gas 6). This will intensify the flavour and colour of the broth.

2 Transfer the bones to a large saucepan. Discard the fat from the roasting pan, add 500ml (16fl oz) water, and bring to the boil.

3 Pour the boiling liquid from the roasting pan over the bones and add a further 2 litres (3½ pints) water.

4 Skim off the foam with a ladle or slotted spoon. Add stock vegetables and simmer for 3 hours, uncovered.

5 Ladle out the stock through a sieve into a bowl. When nearly all the stock has been removed, upend the bones and vegetables into the sieve to drain off their remaining liquid.

6 Leave the stock uncovered to cool, then use a ladle or spoon to skim off any fat that has settled on the surface. Freeze in portions.

Make chicken consommé

1 To make a clarification mixture, whisk 2 egg whites just enough to loosen them and form a few bubbles. Add 1 tsp tomato purée and mix.

2 Place finely chopped chicken meat, garlic, vegetables, and parsley in a bowl, add the egg white mixture, mix, and refrigerate.

3 Combine stock with the clarification mixture in a large saucepan. Heat slowly, and stir until the stock comes to the boil.

4 Once the stock reaches boiling point, reduce to a gentle simmer for 1 hour, or until a crust forms. Poke a knife through to check the clarity.

5 When the consommé is clear and the clarification ingredients cooked, strain the soup through a sieve lined with muslin.

6 Season the consommé with salt and white pepper to taste, then garnish with a sprig of fresh chervil and serve.

Make vegetable stock

1 Place chopped carrots, celery, onion, and a bouquet garni into a large stockpot. Cover with water and bring to the boil. Reduce the heat and gently simmer the stock for up to 1 hour.

2 Ladle the stock through a fine sieve, pressing the vegetables against the sieve to extract any extra liquid. Season to taste with salt and freshly ground white pepper, let cool, and refrigerate for up to 3 days.

Make fish stock

1 Over a low heat, melt a knob of unsalted butter in a large saucepan or stockpot. Add fish bones and stir until they smell of cooked fish, taking great care that they do not burn.

2 Add water, stock vegetables, and seasoning, and bring the liquid to the boil. Skim away any foam on the surface, and simmer for 30–40 minutes before straining through a fine sieve.

Make beef stock

1 Either use leftover bones from a rib of roast beef, or ask the butcher for a bag of beef bones. Tip the bones into a large roasting tin, add a handful of vegetables, and season. Roast for 30 minutes.

2 Add the roasted bones and vegetables to a large deep pan with some fresh stalks of thyme, rosemary, or a woody herb of your choice, then pour over enough cold water to cover completely.

3 Bring the liquid to the boil, then reduce to a gentle simmer. Cook with the lid half-on for about 1 hour, skimming any scum that may rise to the top of the pan, if necessary.

4 Remove the pan from the heat, then lift the beef bones from the saucepan and discard. Set a sieve over a large heatproof jug and pour the liquid through.

Make a classic vinaigrette

1 In a clean bowl, combine 2 tsp smooth Dijon mustard, 2 tbsp good-quality vinegar (red or white wine, herb, balsamic, or cider), and freshly ground black pepper.

2 Gradually whisk in 120ml (4fl oz) of extra virgin olive oil, until completely emulsified. Adjust the seasoning if necessary. Serve as a salad dressing, or in place of a heavier sauce for fish, poultry, or pasta.

Clarify butter

1 Cut unsalted butter into cubes and place them in a saucepan over a low heat. Keep watch over the butter and take care that it does not burn, as this will destroy the sweet flavour.

2 When the milk solids have completely separated from the fat, skim off any froth and remove from the heat. Carefully pour the clarified butter into a bowl, trying to keep the milk solids in the pan.

Make a velouté sauce

1 Sweat 4 finely chopped shallots in 15g (½oz) unsalted butter over a low heat. Add 300ml (10fl oz) white wine, and 75ml (2½fl oz) vermouth.

2 Bring to the boil, stirring, then reduce the heat and simmer, uncovered, for 25 minutes, or until the liquid has reduced by two-thirds.

3 Now add 600ml (1 pint) stock, stir, and return to the boil. Continue cooking it uncovered, over a high heat, for 20 minutes, or until reduced by half.

4 Add 375ml (13fl oz) double cream, and stir. Bring to the boil, then reduce the heat and cook until the sauce has reduced by over half.

5 The sauce should now be thick enough to coat the back of a spoon. If it is still too thin to do so, reduce for a further 5 minutes.

6 Strain the sauce through a fine sieve to remove the shallots, then serve, or keep warm in a bain marie or double boiler.

Make beurre blanc, noisette, or noir

1 Place 2 finely chopped shallots, 3 tbsp white wine vinegar, and 4 tbsp dry white wine in a small pan and bring to the boil.

2 Lower the heat and reduce the liquid until only 1 tbsp of it remains. It should now have a light, syrupy consistency.

3 Over a low heat, add 2 tbsp water, then whisk in 200g (7oz) chilled, cubed unsalted butter, a little at a time, until it has emulsified.

4 Season the sauce with salt, white pepper, and lemon juice before serving. For a smoother sauce, strain through a fine sieve.

5 For beurre noisette, heat 50–75g (1¾–2½oz) salted butter for 2 minutes until it turns nutty brown. Add a squeeze of lemon juice.

6 Beurre noir is made in the same way as a beurre noisette, but cook the butter in the pan for 20–30 seconds longer.

Make béchamel sauce

1 Push 4 whole cloves into a halved small onion. Place them in a pan with 600ml (1 pint) of full-fat milk and 1 bay leaf. Bring almost to the boil, then reduce the heat and simmer for 4–5 minutes. Allow to cool.

2 Melt 45g (1½oz) unsalted butter over a low heat in a separate pan. Add 45g (1½oz) plain flour, and cook gently for about 30 seconds, using a wooden spoon to stir the mixture into a pale roux.

3 Remove the pan with the roux from the heat. Add the cooled milk mixture through a sieve, and whisk until the sauce is smooth. Return to a medium heat and whisk continuously until the sauce comes to the boil.

4 Reduce the heat, and gently simmer for 20 minutes, or until the sauce is smooth, thickened, and glossy. Season to taste with salt, white pepper, and nutmeg. This recipe will make 600ml (1 pint).

Make mayonnaise

1 Whisk 2 egg yolks, 1 tsp Dijon mustard, and 1 tsp vinegar in a bowl. Pour in 250ml (8fl oz) olive oil, drop by drop, whisking all the time.

2 Gradually increase the speed of pouring to a steady stream. Once all the oil has been added, stir in 2 tsp freshly squeezed lemon juice.

3 If the mayonnaise "splits", place another egg yolk in a clean bowl, then trickle in the curdled sauce and whisk together (see below).

Save curdled mayonnaise

1 Curdling may happen because the egg yolks or the oil were too cold when mixed, too much oil was added, or it was done too hastily.

2 To save it, simply place 1 egg yolk into a clean mixing bowl, and very slowly, add in the curdled mayonnaise, whisking continuously.

3 Continue whisking after each ladleful until the curdled mixture is completely smooth and incorporated into the new egg yolk.

Make hollandaise

1 In a small pan, boil 2 tbsp vinegar, 2 tbsp water, and 1 tbsp of white peppercorns. Simmer for 1 minute, or until reduced by one-third.

2 Remove from the heat and leave to chill completely. Strain the liquid into a heatproof bowl, add 4 egg yolks, and whisk.

3 Place the bowl over a pan of simmering water. Whisk the mixture for 5–6 minutes, or until the sauce is thick and creamy.

4 Stand the bowl on a tea towel. Slowly pour in 250g (9oz) of clarified butter and whisk until the sauce is thick, glossy, and smooth.

5 Gently whisk in the juice of ½ lemon, and season to taste with freshly ground white pepper, a pinch of cayenne pepper, and salt.

6 The hollandaise is now ready, and should be served immediately. This recipe will make 300ml (½ pint).

Flavour pairings

In the following section you will find an easy reference guide to some of the ingredients and their flavour pairings featured in this book. It is an ideal at-a-glance guide to how you can combine textures and tastes to create wonderful dishes.

Fish

Fish always needs careful pairing because subtle flavours can be overpowered by strong accompaniments.

Anchovy Sherry vinegar, white wine vinegar, shallots, tomatoes, marjoram, oregano, sage, thyme, parsley, olive oil.

Barramundi Pak choi, lime, chilli, fresh herbs, white wine.

Bonito Sesame seeds, rice vinegar, mirin, cucumber, daikon, chilli, coriander leaf and seed, potatoes, onions, green peppers.

Brill Bacon, shallots, wild mushrooms, white wine, garlic, tomatoes, lemon, crab or prawn sauce.

Brown trout Bouquet garni (parsley, thyme and bay leaf tied together), watercress-flavoured hollandaise sauce, prawns.

Carp Paprika, butter, capers, dill, garlic, parsley, cornmeal, ginger, rice wine, sesame oil and seeds, fennel.

Catfish Cornmeal, sesame seeds, soured cream, mushrooms, spring onions, parsley, bay leaf, thyme.

Cod Dill, parsley, bay leaf, lemon, olive oil, tomatoes, olives, capers, garlic, breadcrumbs, butter, cheese sauce, cider, white wine.

Coley Butter, milk, beer batter, parsley, chives, bacon, Cheddar cheese.

Dab Shallot, prawns, mushrooms, parsley, tarragon, lemon, lime, capers, gherkins, anchovy butter.

Dover sole Butter, lemon, parsley, tarragon, cucumber, mint, shiitake mushrooms, truffle oil, white grapes.

Freshwater bream Thyme, rosemary, fennel, celery, nut oils.

Grey mullet Ginger, nutmeg, allspice, chillies, thyme, lemon, lime, anchovies, tomatoes, onions.

Haddock Parsley, milk, bay leaf, Cheddar cheese, tomatoes, pea purée, garlic, onions.

Hake Olive oil, smoked paprika, butter, lemon, onions, garlic, tomatoes.

Halibut Butter, beurre blanc, nutmeg, gherkins, capers, lemon, bacon, spicy sausages, charcuterie.

Herring Soured cream, dill, onions, oatmeal, bacon, horseradish, mustard, lemon, capers, parsley.

John dory Garlic, white wine, cream sauces, mushrooms, sage, capers, lemon, crème fraîche.

Kiln-smoked salmon Eggs, rocket, beetroot, soured cream, horseradish, cream, chilli, olive oil, lemon, dill.

Lemon sole Béchamel sauce, parsley, chives, lemon, butter, white grapes.

Ling Onions, garlic, potatoes, leeks, bacon, coriander leaf, parsley, sage, Cheddar cheese.

Mackerel Basil, olive oil, garlic, onions, horseradish, mustard, dill, rhubarb, gooseberries.

Monkfish Chorizo, prosciutto crudo, bacon, sage, rosemary, butter, olive oil, lemon, lime, chillies, capers, mushrooms.

Pike Butter, sage, lemon, cream, bay leaf, white wine.

Plaice Butter, lemon, parsley, sage, thyme, grapes, white wine, breadcrumb- or rice-based stuffing, chestnut mushrooms, potatoes.

Pollock Tomatoes, chilli, pancetta, basil.

Rainbow trout White wine vinegar, butter, lemon, chives, almonds, hazelnuts, Serrano ham, breadcrumbs.

Red gurnard Olive oil, chorizo, pancetta, garlic, leeks, onions, white wine.

Red mullet Citrus, chervil, tarragon, parsley, carrots, celery.

Salmon Lemon, butter, hollandaise sauce, dill, samphire, tarragon, ginger, harissa paste, soy, sesame seeds and oil, chilli, coriander leaf.

Salted dried anchovies Garlic, onions, tomatoes, olives, cheese, spinach, pine nuts, butter, olive oil, chilli.

Salt cod Olive oil, garlic, parsley, basil, olives, tomatoes, potatoes, citrus, capers, red peppers, chorizo.

Sardine or pilchard Olive oil, garlic, lemon, sultanas, pine nuts, parsley, oregano, thyme, tomatoes, peppers, chilli, lime, lemon.

Scad (horse mackerel) Chilli, ginger, soy sauce, Chinese five-spice powder, coconut milk, tomatoes, peppers.

Sea bass Black bean sauce, soy sauce, ginger, tomatoes, garlic, olive oil, red peppers, olives, aniseed flavours like fennel, caraway, Pernod.

Sea bream Fennel, Pernod, coriander leaf, lemon, saffron, parsley, garlic.

Sea trout Mayonnaise, watercress, hollandaise sauce, lemon, dill, parsley.

Skate and ray Beurre noisette/noir, capers, parsley, lemon, vinegar.

Smoked haddock Spinach, rice, eggs, mild curry powder, tomatoes, parsley, cheese sauce, poached eggs.

Smoked mackerel Horseradish, mustard, cream and crème fraîche, cream cheese, honey, sesame oil, dill, coriander leaf, beetroot, celeriac, waxy potatoes.

Smoked salmon Citrus, horseradish, dill, parsley, scrambled eggs.

Smoked trout Lemon, horseradish, waxy potatoes, rocket, watercress, dill, chives, cream, crème fraîche.

Sprat Beetroot, red and white wine vinegar, flat-leaf parsley, coriander leaf and seeds, lemon.

Sturgeon Horseradish, soured cream, beetroot, vinegar, butter, citrus.

Tilapia Chilli, palm sugar, nam pla (Thai fish sauce), shrimp paste, coriander leaf, coconut, galangal.

Tuna Sesame seeds and oil, teriyaki, rice wine vinegar, wasabi, pickled ginger; tandoori spices, tomatoes, garlic, olives, capers.

Turbot Mushrooms, Champagne, cream, butter, shellfish stock, lemon, prawns, Gruyère and Parmesan cheeses.

Whiting Tomatoes, chillies, basil, mushrooms, citrus, tartare sauce.

Shellfish

The sweet, intense flavours of some shellfish can take quite robust pairings, while others need more delicate treatment.

Abalone Shiitake mushrooms, sesame seeds and oil, soy sauce, ginger, garlic, butter, parsley, oyster sauce.

Brown crab Mayonnaise, chilli, lemon, parsley, dill, potatoes, butter, Worcestershire sauce, anchovies.

Brown shrimp Butter, lemon, nutmeg, mace, cayenne, Tabasco.

Clam Cream, onions, garlic, white wine, chives, parsley, oregano, thyme, bay leaf, tomatoes.

Cockle Malt vinegar, black pepper, salt, parsley, capers, gherkins, cucumber.

Fresh water crayfish Melted butter, salad leaves, mayonnaise, citrus.

Frogs' legs Butter, lemon, garlic, black pepper, Calvados, cream, apples, and mixed herbs.

Langoustine (Dublin Bay prawn) Mayonnaise, citrus, tomatoes, garlic, butter, tarragon, lovage, parsley, chives, tartare sauce.

Lobster Mayonnaise, brandy, white wine, sherry, citrus, Parmesan, cream, chilli, tarragon, parsley, chives, salad leaves, shallots.

Mussels White wine, cider, Pernod, butter, garlic, cream, shallots, ginger, fennel, lemongrass, chillies, parsley, coriander leaf, dill, rosemary.

North Atlantic prawn Mayonnaise, Marie Rose sauce, garlic, butter, citrus, chilli, avocados, melon, tomatoes, cucumber.

Octopus Red wine, onions, balsamic vinegar, parsley, sage, rosemary, paprika, chilli, olive oil, soy sauce, sesame oil, rice vinegar.

Oysters (Raw) red wine vinegar, shallots, Tabasco, lemon juice; (Cooked) anchovy essence, butter, spinach, cream, Parmesan cheese.

Periwinkle Chilli, vinegar, malt vinegar, salt, black pepper, lemon juice, garlic butter, watercress.

Razor clam Garlic, butter, parsley, coriander leaf, white wine, shallots, cream, chilli.

Scallops Bacon, chorizo, black pudding, red peppers, red onion, olive oil, sesame oil, black beans, spring onions, ginger, chilli, cream, bay leaf, parsley.

Sea urchin Lemon, black pepper, eggs, cream.

Snails Garlic butter with lemon or rosemary, olive oil with red wine vinegar and black pepper.

Squid Garlic, turmeric, black pepper, spring onions, chilies, other seafood, olive oil, breadcrumbs, lemon juice, tomatoes, mayonnaise.

Tiger prawn Mayonnaise, garlic, chilli, curry spices, capers, paprika, citrus, butter, tempura dipping sauce, soy sauce, coconut, sesame seeds.

Whelk Malt vinegar, salt, black pepper, garlic butter, parsley, tarragon, chives.

Meat, poultry, and game

From humble sausages to seasonal grouse, there are many exciting flavouring possibilities.

Beef and veal

Brisket Mustard, root vegetables, mushrooms, bay leaf, bouquet garni, rosemary, thyme, parsley.

Chuck or shoulder Onion, garlic, tomatoes, mushrooms, peppers, aubergines, carrots, celery, Indian curry spices, Thai red curry paste, star anise, chilli, cinnamon, ginger.

Fillet steak Any of the other steak flavourings, liver pâté, port sauce, oysters (stuff with, before grilling), soy sauce, oyster sauce, ginger, Cajun spices, garlic.

Oxtail Bacon, celery, parsnips, carrots, swede, onions, peppercorns, nutmeg, cumin, allspice, mustard, red wine, brown ale, soy sauce.

Rump steak Fried onions, potato chips, mushrooms, French mustard, red wine sauce.

Silverside Mustard sauce, carrots, parsnips, onions, red wine, cinnamon, olives, tomatoes.

Sirloin joint English mustard, horseradish sauce or relish, Yorkshire puddings, root vegetables.

Sirloin steak Peppers, onions, olives, savoury butters (see T-bone), green or black peppercorn sauce, béarnaise sauce.

T-Bone steak Savoury butters – anchovy, parsley, mixed herb and garlic, oregano, chilli.

Veal escalope Egg and breadcrumbs, Parmesan, ham and melting cheeses, cream, mushrooms, sorrel, spinach, gherkins, capers, tomato sauce, potato salad.

Veal loin chop Tarragon or parsley butter, garlic and rosemary, white wine, cream, brandy, lemon, shallots.

Veal osso buco Tomatoes, white wine, gremolata (chopped parsley, garlic, anchovy fillets, lemon zest), risotto alla milanese.

Lamb and goat

Goat, diced Yogurt, curry powder, fenugreek, chilli, vinegar, honey, soy sauce, spring onions, root vegetables.

Goat leg steak Cinnamon, cumin, ginger, allspice, jerk seasoning, onions, oranges, redcurrant jelly.

Goat, whole kid Red wine, olive and nut oils, chilli oil, cumin, cinnamon, garlic, honey, mint, oregano, onions, leeks.

Lamb kidney Cream, shallots, mushrooms, lemon, brandy, sherry, mustard, Worcestershire sauce, tomatoes, sausages, bacon.

Lamb leg Garlic, oregano and potatoes (Greek-style slow-roast), mint sauce/jelly, redcurrant jelly, roast onions or leeks, onion sauce, celery, carrots, paprika, flageolet beans.

Lamb loin chops Mint jelly, tomatoes, onions, garlic, oregano.

Lamb neck Mint, oregano, garlic, cinnamon, star anise, dried fruit, haricot beans, spring onions, dill, lemon.

Lamb noisettes Red wine, port, redcurrants, rosemary, lemon, garlic.

Lamb shank Turnips, carrots, celery, leeks, tomato purée, redcurrant or mint jelly, white, red, or rosé wine.

Lamb rack Garlic, rosemary, mint, honey, olives, harissa paste, aubergines, yogurt, baby spring vegetables.

Mutton shoulder Caper sauce (boiled mutton), turnips, carrots, leeks, onions, yogurt, aubergine, cinnamon, apricots, prunes, raisins, curry spices, oregano, mint, rosemary, pearl barley.

Pork

Belly Fennel or dill seed, garlic, juniper berries, wholegrain mustard, caramelized onions, red cabbage, raisins, cider, white wine, barbecue sauce, sweet and sour sauce.

Fillet Garlic, oregano, sage, chorizo, salami, prunes, apricots, spinach, mushrooms, spring onions, beansprouts, bamboo shoots, soy sauce, ginger.

Leg joint Apple sauce, sage and onion stuffing, English mustard, sweet and sour sauce, curry spices, vinegar, cabbage, caraway, dried beans.

Leg steak Egg and breadcrumbs (schnitzels), rosemary, sage, garlic, citrus, ham, cheese, lychees.

Liver Sage, onions, bacon, juniper berries, hazelnuts, watercress, brandy, mushrooms, red wine, cider, root vegetables.

Loin chop Apples, pears, plums, oregano, marjoram, cider, perry, or white wine, coriander seeds, wholegrain mustard, crème fraîche.

Ribs Barbecue sauce, chilli, soy sauce, honey, citrus, pineapple, Worcestershire sauce, tomato, Chinese five-spice powder.

Poultry

Chicken breast Thai green curry paste, coconut, nam pla, ginger, oyster sauce, black bean sauce, bacon/pancetta, chorizo, prawns.

Chicken breast quarter As for leg quarter, but also fried bananas, bacon rolls, and corn cobs.

Chicken drumstick Butter, olive oil, garlic, barbecue sauce, sweet and sour sauce, cumin, garam masala, curry paste, harissa paste, chilli, Worcestershire sauce, honey, lemon.

Chicken leg quarter Cajun or curry spices, thyme, tarragon, chives, garlic, lardons, red or white wine, mushrooms, tomatoes.

Chicken supreme Butter, herbs, garlic, cream, white wine, brandy, white grapes, mushrooms.

Chicken thigh Curry spices, pesto, olive oil, herbs, garlic, mirepoix.

Chicken, whole Sage and onion or parsley and thyme stuffing, lemon, honey, barbecue sauce, Cajun spices, tandoori spices, paprika, bread sauce, redcurrant jelly, cider, white wine.

Chicken wing Chinese five-spice powder, soy sauce, barbecue sauce, jerk seasoning, Cajun spices, garam masala.

Duck breast Berries, currants, pomegranate, baby leaves, cherry tomatoes, cucumber, red onion, olives, fruit vinegar, olive oil, pomegranate syrup.

Duck crown The same as for the whole bird, but try rubbing with smoked sea salt before cooking.

Duck leg portion As for duck breast, plus juniper berries, coriander seeds, thyme for confit.

Duck, whole Sage, onions, garlic, spring onions, apples, oranges, turnips, ginger, cherries, soy sauce, hoisin sauce, honey, vinegar, wine, peas, baby white onions, lettuce.

Goose, whole Apples, onions, red cabbage, tomatoes, white beans, spicy sausages, ginger, sage, oatmeal, almonds, apricots, prunes, soy sauce, red wine.

Poultry liver Butter, garlic, shallots, woody herbs, bacon, eggs, truffles, figs, prunes, Sauternes, sherry.

Poussin Bacon, garlic, shallots, tomatoes, mushrooms, lemon, lime, saffron, lemongrass, kaffir lime leaves, rosemary, thyme, tarragon, bay leaf, soy sauce, white wine, barbecue sauce.

Turkey crown As for whole bird, but also pancetta, garlic butter, tarragon butter, pesto, tapenade.

Turkey steak Ham, cheese (for topping), peppers, tomatoes, mushrooms, sage, tarragon, thyme, parsley, chives, oregano, redcurrant jelly.

Turkey, whole Chestnuts, cranberries, thyme, parsley, sage, tarragon, bacon, sausagemeat, root vegetables.

Game

Grouse Bacon, ham, celery, shallots, watercress, wild mushrooms, game chips, bread sauce, buttered crumbs, oranges, honey, juniper berries, redcurrants, cranberries, whisky, wine.

Mallard Ginger, garlic, mushrooms, onions, swede, coriander leaf, parsley, sage, apples, bitter oranges, plums, cherries, redcurrants, cider, red wine, soy sauce.

Partridge Bacon, cream, cabbage, watercress, lentils, shallots, wild mushrooms, grapes, citrus, pears, quinces, redcurrants, chestnuts, walnuts, turnips, kohl rabi, juniper berries, sage, chocolate, wine.

Pheasant Bacon, cream, celery, onions, cabbage, sage, apples, quinces, bitter oranges, prunes, walnuts, beetroot, Jerusalem artichokes, game chips, bread sauce, buttered crumbs, Calvados, brandy, wine.

Quail Bacon, butter, cream, sweet peppers, mushrooms, truffles, quinces, grapes, cherries, prunes, almonds, honey, cumin, cinnamon, brandy, white and red wine.

Rabbit, whole Bacon, carrots, fennel, celery, sweetcorn, mushrooms, tomatoes, olives, coriander leaf, parsley, rosemary, thyme, lemon, prunes, mustard, soy sauce, cider, white wine.

Teal Apples, bitter oranges, sage, thyme, white wine, peas, onions and lettuce (for braising), cider, spring onions, hoisin and plum sauce, soy sauce, ginger, garlic.

Venison fillet or tenderloin Bacon, pears, cream, fennel, red cabbage, pomegranate, red berries, pine nuts, red wine, vermouth.

Venison rolled haunch Guinness, red wine, port, redcurrant jelly, prunes, juniper berries, bay leaf, thyme, cream, chanterelle mushrooms.

Woodcock Butter, bacon, cream, shallots, garlic, watercress, ginger, bay leaf, parsley, thyme, nutmeg, lemon, apples, grapes, soy sauce, Madeira.

Wood pigeon Bacon, cream, red cabbage, mushrooms, spinach, chilli, garlic, orange, redcurrants, blueberries, juniper berries, chocolate, honey, soy sauce, red wine.

Cured and air-dried meats

Bacon Chicken, game, prunes, oysters, sausages, kidneys, liver, oily and white fish, scallops, prawns, eggs, cheese, cauliflower, potatoes, tomatoes, avocados, mushrooms, spinach.

Bresaola Olive oil, tomatoes, Parmesan, gherkins, olives, celeriac rémoulade, rocket, mozzarella, rustic bread.

Gammon/ham Eggs, pineapple, dried fruits, mustard, cloves, honey, onion, bay leaf, parsley sauce, butter beans, carrots, tomatoes, eggs, cheeses.

Jambon de Paris French and wholegrain mustard, Gruyère cheese, chips, buckwheat crêpes, eggs, tomatoes.

Jamón ibérico Fino sherry (chilled), rustic bread, asparagus, scrambled eggs, baby broad beans, tomato and garlic bread (pan con tomate).

Jamón serrano Olives, gherkins, manchego cheese, figs, rustic bread, nutmeg, eggs, red wine.

Pancetta Parmesan, asparagus, tomatoes, chilli, bacon, onions, garlic, eggs, cream, white beans.

Prosciutto crudo Parmesan, mozzarella, gherkins, figs, melon, asparagus, tomatoes, olives.

Sausages

Beef sausage Onions, root vegetables, tomatoes, peppers, red beans, oregano, paprika, chilli, cumin, coriander seed and leaf, brown ale, mustard, Worcestershire sauce, barbecue sauce.

Black pudding Scallops, halibut, turbot, lamb, pork, venison, rabbit, raisins, red wine, chickpeas, white beans, lentils, bacon, eggs, potatoes.

Boudin blanc Caramelized onions, red wine, brandy, port, tomatoes, wild mushrooms, spinach, black truffles, cream.

Boudin noir Walnuts, pears, apples, oranges, chestnuts, cabbage, white wine, red wine, Dijon and wholegrain mustards.

Chorizo Chicken, seafood, pork, mushrooms, peppers, aubergines, courgettes, pasta, white beans, chickpeas, rice, chimichurri sauce (parsley, sherry vinegar, oregano, chilli, olive oil).

Cumberland sausage Mustard, tomato sauce, barbecue sauce, chilli sauce, shallots, rosemary, red wine, white beans.

Pork sausage Potatoes, white beans, onions, apples, sage, mustard, tomato ketchup, cider, cabbage, tomatoes, mushrooms, Yorkshire pudding.

Salame di Genoa Parmesan, mozzarella, rocket, spinach, tomatoes, olives, gherkins.

Toulouse sausage White beans, belly pork, duck confit, celery, onions, tomatoes, garlic, cloves, bay leaf, flat-leaf parsley.

White pudding Batter, black pudding, tomatoes, eggs, bacon, toasted or fried bread, white beans, scallops, halibut or other meaty fish.

Vegetables

Vegetables add taste and texture themselves, but can also be complemented by exciting flavour combinations.

Cabbages, flowering, and leafy greens

Brussels sprouts Melted butter, chestnuts, walnuts, hazelnuts, toasted pine nuts, sausages, crispy bacon.

Calabrese Bacon, anchovies, pesto, chillies, cheese or béchamel sauce, lemon, garlic, pine nuts, olive oil.

Cavolo nero Garlic, onions, peppers, white beans, spicy sausages, pancetta, potatoes, tomatoes, olive oil, chilli.

Chinese broccoli Oyster sauce, soy sauce, ginger, garlic, cashew nuts.

Chinese leaves (napa cabbage) Spring onions, ginger, sambal oelek, garlic, sesame seeds, rice vinegar.

Chinese spinach Toasted sesame seeds, star anise, mushrooms, eggs, rice, prawns, coriander leaf, chillies, ginger, garlic.

Common cauliflower Brown butter, Gruyère, blue or Cheddar cheese (crumbled or in sauce), garlic, olive oil, parsley, lemon.

Kale Bacon, ham, venison, sausages, oily fish, clams, eggs, citrus, tomatoes.

Kohl rabi Parsley sauce, star anise, ginger, garlic, tomatoes, lamb, beef, game birds.

Mustard greens Fish, seafood, ham, pork, chicken, butter, garlic, soy sauce, rice vinegar, ginger, chillies.

Pak choi Prawns, pork, chicken, spring onions, water chestnuts, mangetout, cashew nuts, soy sauce, oyster sauce, coriander leaf.

Purple cauliflower Béchamel sauce, tomatoes, Parmesan (or other cheeses), bacon.

Purple sprouting broccoli Leeks, tomatoes, chillies, butter, olive oil, garlic, Parmesan, spring onions, citrus, hollandaise sauce.

Rainbow chard Nutmeg, spring onions, toasted almonds and pine nuts, butter, olive oil.

Red cabbage Vinegar, red wine, brown sugar, apples, pears, raisins, onions, fennel seeds, caraway seeds, bacon, ham, pork, liver.

Romanesco Olive oil and toasted flaked almonds (to dress), cherry tomatoes, olives, cream, Italian hard cheeses.

Round green cabbage Carrots, onions, celery, soy sauce, ginger, garlic, potatoes.

Savoy cabbage Bacon, celery, butter, onions, garlic, tomatoes, walnuts, hazelnuts.

Spinach Bacon, fish, anchovies, eggs, cheeses, yogurt, cream, butter, olive oil, garlic, onions, avocados, mushrooms, lemon, nutmeg, curry spices.

Spring greens Bacon, ham, lemon, onions, potatoes, salt pork, garlic, Chinese five-spice powder.

White cabbage Mayonnaise, wine vinegar, mustard, caraway seeds, smoked sausages, pork, ham, carrots, onions, nuts, apples, celery.

Salad leaves

Butterhead lettuce Peas, baby onions, anchovies, cheese, mayonnaise, olive oil, lemon juice, mustard, garlic.

Chicory Bacon, ham, prosciutto crudo, blue and Cheddar cheeses, nuts, garlic, watercress, olive oil, tomato salsa.

Cos (romaine) lettuce Anchovies, eggs, croûtons, garlic, Parmesan, chicken, onions, citrus, herbs, honey, mustard.

Curly endive (frisée) Olive oil, croûtons, smoked lardons, red onions, parsley, coriander leaf, chillies, Worcestershire sauce, poached or soft-boiled eggs.

Dandelion Bacon, cheese, garlic, onions, lemon, mustard, olive oil, wine or balsamic vinegar.

Escarole (batavia) Balsamic vinegar, fruit vinegars, olive oil, toasted nut and seed oils, mustard, croûtons, eggs, anchovies, avocados, pomegranate, raisins.

Iceberg lettuce Seafood, Russian salad, rice or pasta salads, tabbouleh, minced chicken, pork, veal or liver, soy sauce, ginger, garlic.

Lamb's lettuce (corn salad) Onions, croûtons, sweetcorn, honey, mustard, cherry tomatoes, toasted seeds, pears, avocados, lardons.

Little gem lettuce Mushrooms, spring onions, garlic, peas, bacon, Italian hard cheeses, cottage cheese, walnuts.

Lollo rosso Pears, apples, pomegranate, blueberries, cheeses, walnuts, toasted pine nuts, pumpkin seeds, olive oil, toasted nut oils, citrus, wine, sherry and cider vinegars, chorizo, salami.

Mizuna Pork, chicken livers, fish, shellfish, ginger, lemon, sesame oil, olive oil, toasted seeds, tamari.

Purslane Beetroot, broad beans, cucumber, spinach, potatoes, tomatoes, eggs, feta cheese, yogurt.

Radicchio Pancetta, hazelnuts, walnuts, pine nuts, pumpkin seeds, Italian hard cheeses, ricotta or feta cheese, balsamic vinegar, preserved lemons, anchovies.

Red oak lettuce Rocket, chicory, chervil, dandelion, purslane, olives, tomatoes, red onions, artichokes, avocados, beetroot, carrots, olive oil, citrus, fruit and wine vinegars.

Rocket Pine nuts, almonds, olive oil, citrus, garlic, hard and blue cheeses, tomatoes, onions, eggs, potatoes, thyme, basil, rosemary, oregano, lamb's lettuce, watercress.

Salad cress Eggs, salmon, sardines, tuna, Cheddar cheese, cream cheese, tomatoes, cucumber.

Watercress Cucumber, beetroot, goat's cheese, eggs, salmon, other oily fish, chicken, duck, oranges, potatoes.

White Swiss chard Ham, garlic, onions, chillies, olive oil, butter (leaves), hollandaise sauce (stalks).

Stems, shoots, and flowers

Cardoons Veal, anchovies, olive oil, hard cheeses, butter, cream, lemon, almonds.

Celery Béchamel or hollandaise sauces, cheeses, onions, cabbage, lemon, walnuts, apples, pears.

Florence fennel Cheeses, fish, seafood, veal, chicken, dried and cured meats, citrus, preserved lemon (roasted with), Pernod, Puy lentils, herbs, mayonnaise.

Globe artichokes Vinaigrette, butter, hollandaise sauce, herbs, cured and dried meats, anchovies, shellfish, tomatoes, chillies, mushrooms, cheeses, cream, garlic, lemon, white truffles.

Green asparagus Olive oil, butter, coarse sea salt, Parmesan or Grana Padano shavings, balsamic glaze or vinegar, hollandaise sauce, Mornay sauce, bacon, anchovies, salmon, pesto, vinaigrette, citrus, eggs.

Hearts of palm Cured and dried meats, shellfish, lime, vinaigrette, tomatoes, baby salad leaves, soy sauce, wasabi, sesame oil, ginger, avocados, tropical fruits.

White asparagus Vinaigrette, mayonnaise, garlic, quail's eggs, smoked salmon, hollandaise sauce.

Root vegetables and tubers

Anya potatoes Melted butter, pesto, parsley, thyme, mint, chives, olive oil, mustard, wine vinegar, shallots, grated citrus zest.

Beetroot Bacon, smoked oily fish, goat's and other cheeses, oranges, watercress, baby red chard, baby spinach and rocket, soured cream, nutmeg, horseradish, dill, caraway.

Carrots Beef, citrus, ginger, celery, chervil, fennel, thyme, parsley, coriander leaf, watercress, peas, pine nuts, cumin, cinnamon, mixed spice, other roots, particularly beetroot, honey.

Cassava Butter, garlic, citrus, coriander seeds and leaf, chilli.

Celeriac Bacon, beef, oily fish, cheeses, garlic, potatoes, parsley, dill, olive oil, mustard, tomatoes.

Charlotte potatoes Melted butter, mint, chives, parsley, mayonnaise, yogurt, olive oil, anchovies, citrus.

Desirée potatoes Cumin, cajun spices, nutmeg and seeds (to coat wedges), eggs, onions, mushrooms, butter, olive and nut oils.

Jersey Royal potatoes Melted butter, mint, parsley, chives, thyme, spring onions.

Jerusalem artichoke Béchamel or hollandaise sauce, butter, cream, ginger, nutmeg, lovage, parsley, lemon juice, spring onions, crispy bacon, pheasant and other game.

Jicama Chilli, lime, avocados, mangos, onions, tomatoes, coriander leaf.

King Edward potatoes Butter, milk, chives, rosemary, celeriac, leeks, onions, spring onions, garlic, olive oil, lemon, hard cheeses.

Lotus root Citrus, garlic, onions, coriander leaves, chervil, star anise.

Maris Piper potatoes Butter, chives, parsley, curry spices, mayonnaise, tomato ketchup, malt vinegar, sea salt.

Nicola potatoes Cream, crème fraîche, yogurt, garlic, nutmeg, Gruyère, Cheddar and blue cheeses, mayonnaise, French dressing, shallots, ham, bacon, pickled, salted and smoked fish.

Parsley root Chicken, fish, game, eggs, mushrooms, carrots, potatoes, turnips.

Parsnip Butter, curry powder, nutmeg, garlic, parsley, thyme, tarragon, potatoes, beef, walnuts.

Radish Smoked fish, cheese, potatoes, spring onions, chives, parsley, citrus, vinegar, chilli, star anise.

Salsify Italian hard cheeses, béchamel sauce, onions, shallots, olive oil, lemon, nutmeg, bacon.

Scorzonera White wine, hard cheeses, cream, breadcrumbs, parsley, Parma ham.

Swede Bacon, liver, onions, carrots, cream, butter, lemon, black pepper, nutmeg, thyme.

Sweet potatoes Apples, brown sugar, molasses, ginger, maple syrup, honey, citrus, chilli, nutmeg, Cajun spices, thyme.

Taro Sweet potatoes, chilli, star anise, cinnamon, cardamom, toasted sesame oil.

Turnip Lamb, bacon, duck, goose, game, cheese, apples, mushrooms, potatoes, sherry.

Water chestnut Prawns, beef, chicken, pork, pak choi, oyster sauce, soy sauce, ginger, garlic, sesame oil.

Yams Eggs, cheese, cream, curry powder, coconut, lime.

Squashes, cucumbers, and chayote

Acorn squash Cheddar, blue cheeses, Gruyère, eggs, garlic, ginger, maple syrup, honey, sage, thyme, apples, pears, quinces.

Bitter melon squash Pork, fish, shellfish, soy sauce, ginger, garlic, spring onions, black bean sauce, oyster sauce.

Bottle gourd Coconut milk, tamarind, mustard seeds, curry leaves, cumin, coriander seeds and leaf, ginger, chilli, star anise, tomatoes, onions, garlic, red lentils.

Burpless slicing cucumber Yogurt, mint, coriander leaf and seeds, toasted cumin seeds, garlic, spring onions, watercress, mayonnaise.

Butternut squash Goat's cheese, Cheddar, Gruyère, and blue cheeses, garlic, ginger, maple syrup, honey, apples, pears, sage, thyme, rosemary, beetroot.

Chayote Fish, shellfish, rice, garlic, onions, soft and hard cheeses, chillies.

Common greenhouse cucumber Vinegars, yogurt, dill, garlic, milk (for soup), anchovies, cream cheese, feta cheese, fennel, mint, mayonnaise, tomatoes, chillies, avocado, tropical fruits.

Courgettes Olive oil, coarse sea salt, sweet peppers, aubergines, onions, garlic, tomatoes, curry spices, basil, parsley.

Crookneck squash Olive oil, butter, cream, Cheddar, Gruyère, Parmesan, bacon, white beans, tomatoes.

Crown Prince squash Butter, eggs, nutmeg, cinnamon, mixed spice, muscovado sugar, sage, onions, ricotta cheese.

Gherkins (cornichons) Capers and caperberries, mayonnaise, parsley, thyme, tarragon, chervil, chicken, poultry and pig's livers, pork, salt beef, most fish.

Marrow Sausage, mince or rice and herbs for stuffing, tomatoes, melted butter, hard cheeses, béchamel sauce, thyme, oregano, sage, parsley.

Pattypan squash Melted butter, olive oil, garlic, cumin, coriander, thyme, basil, parsley, bacon, breadcrumbs, chickpeas, hard cheeses.

Pickling cucumber Rock salt, malt or white wine vinegar, coriander seeds, yellow mustard seeds, dried chillies, allspice, ginger, black peppercorns, bay leaf, dill, white onions.

Pumpkin Blue and Cheddar cheeses, toasted pumpkin oil, butter, pumpkin seeds, walnuts, sage, rosemary, thyme, ginger, nutmeg, cinnamon, cumin, tomatoes.

Red onion squash Red onions, chestnuts, garlic, olive oil, butter, nigella seeds, cinnamon, nutmeg, cloves.

Ridge cucumber Malt, balsamic, or red wine vinegar, black pepper, fish, shellfish, cheese sauce, soy sauce, garlic, ginger, cream cheese, root vegetables, spring onions.

Round squash As for courgettes, or try prawns or crab and rice stuffing with dill, parsley, and lemon zest.

Spaghetti squash Fresh tomato sauce, bolognese sauce, olive oil, melted butter, Parmesan, anchovies, mushrooms.

Turk's turban squash Butter, olive oil, Cheddar or goat's cheeses, breadcrumbs, rice, onions, sage, thyme, cream, bacon, ham.

Onions, shallots, leeks, and garlic

Baby leeks Olive oil, chillies, Parmesan, anchovies, toasted pine nuts, almonds and pumpkin seeds, sun-dried tomatoes, basil, thyme, parsley, olives.

Banana shallot Butter, balsamic vinegar, white balsamic condiment, red wine, white wine, cream, wild mushrooms, sorrel, thyme, parsley, mussels and other fish and seafood, chicken.

Brown onions Bacon, liver, sausages, steak, lamb, pork, game, fish, curry spices, herbs, tomatoes, all vegetables, cheeses.

Dry garlic Any meat, poultry or game, fish, shellfish, pulses, most vegetables, herbs, spices, mayonnaise, cheeses, soured cream, yogurt, walnuts, pine nuts.

Elephant garlic Olive oil, coarse sea salt, butter, wine, cream, mushrooms, thyme, parsley.

French grey shallot Red wine vinegar, oysters, mussels, beef, chicken, red wine, lardons, carrots, celery, cream, white wine, sherry, fennel, parsley.

Green garlic Tomatoes, soft cheeses, mayonnaise, yogurt, crème fraîche, soured cream, olives, basil, pine nuts, white wine, white balsamic condiment, olive oil, fresh chillies.

Leeks Fish, lamb, chicken, cream, cheese, parsley, potatoes, lemon, olive oil, sage, thyme, fennel, chillies.

Pickling/pearl onions Malt, white or balsamic vinegar, coriander seeds, yellow mustard seeds, dried chillies, black peppercorns, bay leaf, milk, cream, red and white wine, beef, lardons, chicken, pork, lamb, game, fish, peas, cheese, ham.

Red onions Fresh and sun-dried tomatoes, peppers, aubergines, squashes, avocados, bacon, lentils, chickpeas, cheeses, oily fish, basil, thyme, bay leaf.

Round shallot Malt or balsamic vinegar, coriander seeds, yellow mustard seeds, black peppercorns, cinnamon, chillies, bay leaf.

Spring onions Thai red and green curry pastes, galangal, lemon grass, nam pla, eggs, potatoes, meat, chicken, fish, most cheese.

Tree onion (Egyptian onion) Beef, chicken, game, cheeses, celery, bay leaf, sage, parsley, pickling spices, malt and red wine vinegar.

White onions Tempura and beer batters, veal, chicken, lamb, sage, parsley, thyme, risotto rice, white beans, white wine, spinach, tomatoes.

White salad onions Cream cheese, cottage cheese, soured cream, crème fraîche, yogurt, radishes, cherry tomatoes, chicken, fish, shellfish.

Wild garlic Olive oil, pine nuts, Parmesan, parsley, thyme, potatoes, onions, sorrel, rocket, tomatoes, water chestnuts, beansprouts, soy sauce, ginger.

Peas, beans, and other pods

Baby corn Baby vegetables, sesame oil, soy sauce, chicken, fish, duck, gammon, garlic, butter, olive oil.

Broad beans Bacon, ham, fish, lamb, chicken, game, spinach, onions, cream, béchamel sauce.

Edamame beans Coarse sea salt, harissa paste, lamb, chicken, fish, soy sauce, ginger, garlic, chillies.

French beans Eggs, shallots, red wine vinegar, olive oil, tomatoes, garlic, olives, oily fish, new potatoes.

Garden peas Bacon, ham, fish, duck, baby onions, lettuce, mint, thyme, chervil, mushrooms.

Helda beans Citrus, melted butter, walnuts, nut oils, toasted sesame seeds, tomatoes.

Mangetout Almonds, chicken, mushrooms, soy sauce, garlic, ginger, sherry, rice wine, Chinese five-spice powder.

Okra Butter, garlic, chillies, curry spices, coconut, green peppers, tomatoes.

Runner beans Bacon, mushrooms, onions, tomatoes, red wine vinegar, honey, olive oil, cashew nuts.

Sugar snap peas Toasted sesame seeds, chillies, sesame oil, ginger, soy sauce, soft cheeses, oyster mushrooms, radishes, mint.

Sweetcorn Bacon, potatoes, butter, cheese, cream, chillies, citrus.

Yellow wax beans Tomatoes, garlic, onions, olive oil, chorizo, mushrooms.

Vegetable fruits

Aubergine Ham, lamb, beef, mozzarella, feta, hard cheeses, garlic, mushrooms, tomatoes, sweet peppers, lemon, oregano, mint, thyme, chillies, olive oil, cinnamon, curry spices.

Avocado Parma ham, mozzarella, bacon, prawns, tomatoes, spinach, grapefruit, lime, mango, lemon, pineapple, sugar, balsamic vinegar, chillies.

Beefsteak tomatoes Mozzarella, Parmesan, eggs (bake inside), olives, anchovies, pesto, pine nuts, almonds, rustic bread, green garlic, peppers, courgettes, aubergines, avocados, basil, oregano, marjoram, chervil.

Bell peppers Chicken, lamb, beef, pork, anchovies, garlic, onions, sweetcorn, tomatoes, olives, capers, cheeses, rosemary, oregano.

Cherry tomatoes Salad leaves, cucumber, celery, olives, pumpkin and sunflower seeds, red onions, basil, oregano, olive oil, balsamic vinegar, goat's cheese, mozzarella, rocket.

Hungarian hot wax chilli Beef, pork, lamb, chicken, seafood, cream cheese, hard cheeses, thyme, sage, tomatoes.

Jalapeño chilli Beef, spicy sausages, noodles, sweet peppers, courgettes, aubergines, peanuts, cashews, tomatoes, mozzarella, cream cheese, sheep's cheese.

Pimientos de Padrón Olive oil, sea salt, crusty bread.

Plum tomatoes Basil, oregano, bay, chervil, onions, garlic, bacon, olive oil, oranges, celery salt.

Romano peppers Chorizo and other spicy sausages, soft cheeses, chilli, garlic, basil, parsley, chives, capers.

Scotch bonnet chilli Chicken, beef, squashes, potatoes, sweet potatoes, yam, spring onions, garlic, spinach, allspice, bay leaf, coconut milk, lime.

Serrano chilli Sweet peppers, potatoes, onions, garlic, dried chipotle chillies, avocados, tomatoes, coriander leaf, prawns, steak.

Standard globe tomatoes Bacon, eggs, fish, mushrooms, cheese, parsley, thyme, oregano, sage, cinnamon, garlic, onions, chilli, Thai red curry paste, coconut milk.

Thai (bird's eye) chillies Most spices, coriander leaf, bay leaf, coconut milk, lime, nam pla, palm sugar, galangal, spring onions, chicken, beef, pork, lamb, fish.

Mushrooms and truffles

Black (Périgord) truffles Spaghetti, chicken, rabbit, game birds, celeriac, meaty white fish, shellfish, pancetta.

Brown crimini or chestnut mushrooms Oregano, parsley, marjoram, chives, parsley, coriander leaf and seeds, curry spices, Thai spices, red wine, garlic, bacon, onions.

Cep (porcini) mushrooms Risotto rice, pasta, cream, brandy, white wine, leeks, onions, garlic, Parma ham, Parmesan, truffle oil, beef, chicken, game, scallops.

Cultivated white button mushrooms Onions, garlic, tomatoes, coriander seeds and leaf, parsley, oregano, lemon, cream, crème fraîche, yogurt, white wine, sherry, steaks, chicken.

Enoki mushrooms Chicken, prawns, crab, chicken and fish broth, cucumber, celery, carrot, soy sauce, garlic, beansprouts, peppers.

Field mushrooms Bacon, eggs, sausages, steak, venison, risotto rice, cream, crème fraîche.

Morel mushrooms Butter, olive oil, garlic, asparagus, leeks, cream, white wine, brandy, eggs, chicken, beef, veal, halibut, turbot, monkfish.

Open cup or flat mushrooms Garlic, cream, white wine, herb stuffings, cheese, pâté, bacon, eggs, parsley.

Oyster mushrooms Eggs, chicken, fish or vegetable broth, noodles, beef, chicken, pork, prawns, crab, spring onions, Chinese five-spice powder, soy sauce, rice wine vinegar.

Portobello mushrooms Butter, garlic, cream, herbs, white or rosé wine, halloumi and soft cheeses, cider, tomatoes, spring onions.

Shiitake mushrooms Pork, chicken, beef, prawns, noodles, rice, soy sauce, ginger, garlic, spring onions, bamboo shoots, water chestnuts, beansprouts, chillies, rice wine, oyster sauce.

White (Alba) truffles Eggs, risotto rice, pasta, game birds, scallops, halibut, monkfish, foie gras, potatoes, olive oil, garlic, Parmesan.

Wood blewit (Pied Bleu) mushrooms Cream, crème fraîche, brandy, white wine, rice, pearl barley, lasagne, Italian hard cheeses, thyme, parsley, marjoram.

Herbs

Herbs add fabulous fragrance to dishes, but it is important to choose the right ones for the job.

Basil Tomatoes, garlic, pine nuts, mozzarella and other cheeses, eggs, aubergines, haricot beans, courgettes, citrus, olives, peas, pizzas, potatoes, rice, raspberries, sweetcorn.

Bay Beef, chicken, game, lamb, ham, offal, fish, chestnuts, citrus, haricot beans, lentils, rice, tomatoes, mushrooms.

Chervil Asparagus, broad beans, green beans, beetroot, carrots, fennel, lettuce, peas, potatoes, tomatoes, mushrooms, cream cheese, eggs, fish, seafood, poultry, veal.

Chives Avocados, courgettes, potatoes, root vegetables, cream cheese, yogurt, soured cream, eggs, fish, seafood, smoked salmon.

Coriander leaf Avocados, cucumber, root vegetables, sweetcorn, coconut milk, fish, seafood, beef, lamb, pork, poultry, citrus, pulses, rice, chillies, onions.

Dill (leaves) Beetroot, broad beans, carrots, celeriac, courgettes, cucumber, potatoes, spinach, eggs, fish, seafood; (seeds) rice, cabbage, onions, potatoes, pumpkin, vinegar.

Fennel Beetroot, beans, cabbage, leeks, cucumber, tomatoes, potatoes, duck, fish, seafood, pork, lentils, rice.

Garden mint Lamb, duck, potatoes, peas, carrots, tomatoes, cucumber, currants, curries, chocolate, yogurt.

Horseradish Apples, beef, baked gammon or ham, sausages, oily and smoked fish, seafood, avocados, beetroot, red cabbage, potatoes.

Lavender Berries, plums, cherries, rhubarb, chicken, lamb, rabbit, pheasant, chocolate.

Leaf celery Cabbage, potatoes, cucumber, tomatoes, chicken, fish, rice, soy sauce, tofu, soft white cheeses.

Lovage Apples, root vegetables, potatoes, Jerusalem artichokes, courgettes, mushrooms, tomatoes, sweetcorn, Cheddar, Gruyère, and cream cheeses, eggs, pulses, fish, meat, poultry, rice.

Marjoram Olive oil, feta, mozzarella and halloumi cheeses, plaice, sole, red mullet, mushrooms, eggs, squashes.

Oregano Lamb, beef, chicken, pork, pulses, chilli, cumin, coriander leaf, garlic, tomatoes, aubergines, Cheddar, mozzarella, feta, and halloumi cheeses, olives, peppers.

Parsley Eggs, fish, seafood, chicken, béchamel sauce, lentils, rice, lemon, tomatoes, garlic, onions.

Rosemary Poultry, rabbit, pork, lamb, veal, fish, eggs, lentils, squashes, peppers, courgettes, cabbage, potatoes, onions, garlic, citrus, fruit, cream cheese.

Sage Pork, duck, goose, veal, chicken, liver, sausages, cheeses, beans, tomatoes, apples, bay leaf, caraway, onions, celery, garlic, lovage, marjoram.

Sorrel Chicken, pork, veal, fish (especially salmon), mussels, eggs, lentils, leeks, lettuce, cucumber, tomatoes, spinach, watercress.

Summer savory Rabbit, chicken, oily fish, cheeses, eggs, broad and green beans, pulses, beetroot, cabbage, potatoes.

Tarragon Artichokes, asparagus, courgettes, tomatoes, mushrooms, potatoes, salsify, fish, seafood, poultry, eggs, game, feta and goat's cheeses.

Thyme Lamb, rabbit, chicken, turkey, pulses, aubergines, cabbage, carrots, leeks, wild mushrooms, tomatoes, onions, potatoes, sweetcorn.

Spices

For subtlety or a big kick, spices used judiciously add an extra sensational dimension to many dishes.

Allspice Aubergines, onions, squashes, root vegetables, white cabbage, tomatoes, most fruit.

Capers and caperberries Rich meats, poultry, fish, seafood, globe artichokes, aubergines, green beans, gherkins, olives, potatoes, tomatoes.

Caraway seeds Duck, goose, pork, breads and cakes, apples, cabbage, potatoes, root vegetables, tomatoes.

Cardamom pods Apples, oranges, pears, sweet potatoes, pulses, cinnamon, star anise, cloves.

Chilli Most spices, bay leaf, coriander leaf, parsley, coconut milk, citrus, meat, poultry, fish, seafood, pulses, tomatoes, avocados, mangoes, papayas, chocolate.

Cinnamon Lamb, poultry, aubergines, chocolate, coffee, rice, almonds, apples, apricots, bananas, pears, other sweet spices.

Cloves Ham, pork, duck, venison, orchard fruits, beetroot, red cabbage, carrots, onions, oranges, squashes, chocolate, cinnamon.

Coriander seeds Cumin, chicken, pork, ham, fish, orchard fruits, citrus, mushrooms, onions, potatoes, pulses.

Cumin Coriander seeds and leaf, chilli, oregano, chicken, lamb, hard and soft cheeses, most vegetables, pulses.

Curry leaves Lamb, fish, seafood, lentils, rice, most vegetables, cardamom, chilli, coconut, coriander leaf, cumin, fenugreek seed, garlic.

Fenugreek Green and root vegetables, chillies, garlic, fish, chicken, lentils.

Galangal Chicken, fish, seafood, chilli, coconut milk, fennel, garlic, ginger, lemongrass, lemon, kaffir lime leaves, shallots, tamarind.

Ginger Fish, seafood, meat, poultry, most vegetables, chilli, coconut, garlic, citrus, soy sauce, orchard fruits, rhubarb.

Juniper berries Red meats, game, goose, apples, celery, cabbage, caraway, garlic, marjoram, rosemary, savory, thyme.

Kaffir lime leaves Pork, poultry, fish, seafood, mushrooms, noodles, rice, green vegetables, coconut, tropical fruits.

Lemongrass Beef, chicken, pork, fish, seafood, noodles, most vegetables, Thai or European basil, coriander leaves, chilli, galangal, cinnamon, cloves, turmeric, coconut milk.

Mace Chicken, lamb, veal, milk, eggs, cheeses, carrots, onions, pumpkin, spinach, sweet potatoes, other sweet spices, bay leaf, thyme.

Mustard seeds Beef, rabbit, sausages, chicken, fish, ham, seafood, strong cheeses, cabbage, root vegetables, curries, dals.

Nigella seed Allspice, cumin and sesame seeds, coriander leaf, star anise, pulses, rice, roots and tubers.

Nutmeg Chicken, veal, lamb, cabbage, onions, roots and tubers, squashes, spinach, cheeses, eggs, milk, rice, couscous, semolina, cardamom, other sweet spices.

Paprika (sweet/hot) Beef, veal, chicken, duck, vegetables; (smoked) sausages, pork, fish, onions, pulses, eggs.

Peppercorns Meat, poultry, game, fish, seafood, vegetables, oils, herbs, spices, salts, some fruits (especially strawberries).

Poppy seed Aubergines, green beans, cauliflower, courgettes, potatoes, bread, honey.

Preserved lemons Lamb, chicken, fish, rice, cardamom, cloves, allspice, pepper, ginger, cinnamon, coriander leaf, fennel, celery, olives.

Saffron Chicken, game, fish, seafood, eggs, asparagus, leeks, mushrooms, spinach, squashes, mayonnaise (as rouille).

Sichuan pepper Black beans, chilli, citrus, garlic, ginger, sesame oil and seeds, soy sauce, star anise.

Star anise Chicken, beef, oxtail, pork, fish, seafood, tropical fruits, figs, pears, leeks, pumpkin, root vegetables, chilli, cinnamon, coriander seed, fennel seed, garlic, ginger.

Sumac Chicken, lamb, fish, seafood, aubergines, chickpeas, lentils, onions, pine nuts, yogurt, coriander, mint, parsley.

Tamarind Chicken, lamb, pork, fish and shellfish, lentils, mushrooms, peanuts, most vegetables, chilli, coriander leaf, cumin, galangal, garlic, turmeric, mustard, soy sauce, palm sugar.

Turmeric Meat, poultry, fish, eggs, aubergines, beans, lentils, rice, root vegetables, spinach.

Vanilla pods Lobster, scallops, mussels, chicken, milk- and cream-based desserts, chocolate, apples, melons, pears, rhubarb, strawberries.

Fruit

Fruit complements so many sweet and savoury foods, adding colour, texture, and depth of flavour.

Orchard Fruits

Asian pears Beef, papaya, mango, lime, chilli, soy sauce, ginger, cardamom, star anise, rice vinegar, honey.

Bramley apples Citrus, almonds, berries, rhubarb, pears, quinces, dried fruit, cinnamon, cloves, mixed spice, nutmeg, vanilla, honey, syrup, demerara sugar, chocolate.

Comice pear Pork, duck, goose, apples, raisins, cinnamon, cloves, ginger, walnuts, goat's and blue cheeses.

Conference pear Game, pork, blue cheeses, Parmesan, rocket, watercress, tarragon, celery, walnuts, almonds, cinnamon, ginger, star anise, cardamom, chocolate, vanilla, butterscotch.

Cox's Orange Pippin apples White or red cabbage, walnuts, almonds, pine nuts, sunflower seeds, fresh and dried fruits, celery, lovage, mayonnaise, vinaigrette, ginger.

Fig Cured meats, yogurt, cream, cheeses, nuts, star anise, marzipan, fortified wine.

Granny Smith apples Cinnamon, mixed spice, cloves, walnuts, almonds, raisins, sultanas, cabbage, cheeses, chicken, pork, duck, game, black pudding, cider, Calvados.

Loquat (Nisperos) Poultry, prawns, goat's cheese, vanilla ice cream, apples, pears, citrus, ginger, spirits.

Medlar Meat, game, hard cheeses, cinnamon, nutmeg, mixed spice, star anise, red or white wine.

Quince Lamb, pork, chicken, game, hard cheeses (particularly Manchego), apples, pears, ginger, cloves, cinnamon.

Red Delicious apples All cheeses, celery, grapes, pork or duck pâté, nuts.

Williams' pear Red wine, port, brandy, cinnamon, star anise, cloves, ginger, wine vinegar, white and demerara sugar, maple syrup, dried fruits.

Stone fruits

Apricots Lamb, pork, chicken, ham, yogurt, cream, custard, oranges, almonds, rice, ginger, vanilla, sweet white wine, amaretto.

Black grapes Beef, venison, game birds, cheeses, fruits, red wine, port.

Cherries Duck, game, almonds, sweet spices, chocolate, citrus, fromage frais, yogurt, brandy, Kirsch, grappa.

Damsons Sultanas, apples, garlic, light muscovado sugar, cinnamon, chilli, ginger, pickling vinegar, red wine, custard, blackberries.

Dates Poultry, lamb, bacon, cheeses, marzipan, nuts, clotted cream, yogurt, citrus, chocolate.

Dry salt-cured olives Beef, pork, lamb, spicy sausage, pasta, cherry and sun-dried tomatoes, olive oil, bell peppers, basil, oregano, parsley.

Green grapes Chicken, poultry livers, rabbit, flat fish, melon, strawberries, cheeses, walnuts.

Greengages All rich meats and game, ground and flaked almonds, cinnamon, ginger, Kirsch, amaretto, brandy, cream, custard.

Kalamata olives White cabbage, tomatoes, cucumber, red onions, sweet peppers, aubergines, feta cheese, halloumi cheese, red wine vinegar, olive oil, oregano, preserved lemons, pork, chicken, lamb, pasta, rice.

Manzanilla olives Dry fino sherry, gin, dry martini, chickpeas, white beans, chorizo, Serrano ham, squid, prawns, crab, Manchego cheese.

Nectarines Chicken, gammon, prosciutto crudo, soft white cheeses like mascarpone, walnuts, almonds, berries, chilli, cinnamon, vanilla, star anise.

Niçoise-Coquillos olives Tomatoes, onions, garlic, anchovies, eggs, green beans, new potatoes, courgettes, capers, caperberries, cinnamon, oregano, herbes de Provence.

Opal plums Brandy, Kirsch, red wine, cream, clafoutis batter, light muscovado sugar, butter, almonds.

Peaches Beef, duck, soured cream, yogurt, passion fruit, mangoes, berries, lime, mint, almonds, cinnamon, ginger, nutmeg, chilli, Champagne, sherry, amaretto.

Picholine olives Chicken, white and oily fish, rabbit, tomatoes, rice, white wine, sherry, dry vermouth, peppers, white beans, oranges.

Red grapes Goat's cheese, Cheddar, Manchego, port, unblanched almonds, most fruits.

Red plums Meat, game, avocados, tomatoes, red peppers, cucumber, spring onions, chilli, coriander leaf, lime, garlic, ginger, soy sauce, rice, red wine or malt vinegar, apples, pears, rhubarb, strawberries, custard, clotted cream, ground almonds (for crumble topping and in strudels).

Sloes Juniper, cinnamon, vanilla, gin, vodka, apples.

Stuffed green olives Fish, meat, poultry, cheeses, pasta, rice, peppers, tomatoes, onions, garlic, sweet spices, herbs.

Victoria plums Duck, lamb, pork, gammon, goose, game birds, chilli, Chinese five-spice powder, ginger, soy sauce, garlic, onions, pickling vinegar, almonds, cinnamon, custard, cream, eggs.

Yellow plums Sweet peppers, spring onions, white balsamic condiment, cucumber, light muscovado sugar, soft fresh cheeses, fromage frais.

Currants and berries

Blackberries Poultry, game, cream, crème fraîche, yogurt, soft white cheeses, apples, pears, hazelnuts, raspberries, almonds, oats, honey, vanilla, cinnamon.

Blackcurrants Mint, rosemary, oranges, apples, pears, honey, vodka, cassis, white wine, Champagne.

Blueberries Game, cream, crème fraîche, yogurt, citrus, almonds, pistachios, mint, cinnamon, allspice, plain and white chocolate.

Cranberries Turkey, goose, pork, gammon, oily fish, apples, oranges, raspberries, blueberries, nuts, red wine, brandy, port.

Elderberries Game, pork, apples, crab apples, strawberries, blackberries, lemon, walnuts, cinnamon, allspice, nutmeg, cloves.

Gooseberries Goose, pork, mackerel, herrings, Camembert, cream, lemon, cinnamon, cloves, dill, fennel, elderflowers, honey.

Loganberries Apples, pears, bananas, rhubarb, cream, crème fraîche, fromage frais, soft white cheeses, yogurt, almonds.

Mulberries Poultry, lamb, game, cream, pears, citrus.

Raspberries Duck, goose, venison, game birds, chicken or duck livers, cream, crème fraîche, peaches, other berries, hazelnuts, meringue, almonds, oats, honey, vanilla, cinnamon, red wine, vodka, raspberry vinegar.

Redcurrants Lamb, goat, venison, turkey, goose, duck, game birds, raspberries, strawberries, loganberries, mint, cinnamon, red wine, port, brandy.

Rowanberries Lamb, mutton, goat, venison, poultry, apples, pears, red wine.

Strawberries Cream, ice cream, curd and other soft white cheeses, cucumber, oranges, melon, rhubarb, other berries, almonds, vanilla, chocolate, black pepper.

Whitecurrants Raspberries, blueberries, white chocolate, rosemary (in jelly), lemon zest (with sugar to eat raw).

Wild strawberries Champagne, white and rosé wines, vodka, Cointreau, cream, crème fraîche, eggs, custard, bitter chocolate, red wine and strawberry vinegars.

Citrus fruits

Blood orange Egg yolks, butter, baby red chard, beetroot, spring onions, strawberries, raspberries, pineapple, bananas, lemon, lime, walnuts.

Clementine Shellfish, pork, chicken, duck, spinach, carrots, sweet peppers, salad leaves, almonds, coriander leaf, chocolate, meringue, Grand Marnier.

Grapefruit Chicken, gammon, smoked meats, prawns, avocados, spinach, lemon, mint, ginger, nutmeg, coconut, honey.

Kumquat Shellfish, smoked fish, poultry, ham, pork, duck, chicory, frisée, celery, spinach, chocolate, cloves, cardamom, vodka.

Lemon Chicken, veal, fish, shellfish, eggs, butter, artichokes, garlic, olives, cream, sage, tarragon, coriander leaf and seeds, capers, olive oil, gin.

Lime Poultry, fish, shellfish, chillies, Tabasco, tomatoes, avocados, lemons, mangoes, melons, papayas, chocolate, rum, tequila, mint, coriander leaf.

Minneola Shellfish, pork, duck, chicory, watercress, celery, rocket, chocolate, cloves, star anise, Cointreau.

Pomelo Shellfish, smoked fish, poultry, ham, pork, chicory, frisée, celery, spinach, chocolate, cloves, cardamom.

Satsuma Caramel, soft brown sugar, vanilla sugar, brandy, Grand Marnier, vodka, whisky.

Seville (bitter) orange Duck, pigeon, pheasant, pork, salmon, tuna, meaty white fish, pancakes, rhubarb, meringue, lemon, grapefruit, gin, vodka, white rum.

Sweet orange Beef, duck, gammon, liver, scallops, tomatoes, beetroot, black olives, nuts, soy sauce, cloves, cinnamon, fennel, carrots, chicory, frisée, button mushrooms, chocolate, strawberries, brandy.

Tangerine Chicken breasts, pork fillet and chops, tuna, salmon, scallops, cabbage, carrots, shallots, cream, honey.

Ugli Oily fish, pork, duck, goose, chicory, frisée, rocket, cream, honey, Kirsch, or sherry (over halves).

Yuzu Toasted sesame oil, sake, oysters, sashimi, fried squid, crab, poultry, cream, chilli, chocolate, ginger, butter, daikon, mirin, mango.

Melons

Cantaloupe Coconut (fruit and milk), lime, cucumber, mint, fresh cheeses like mozzarella.

Charentais melon Tropical fruit, raspberries, strawberries, mint.

Honeydew melon Parma ham, other cured and smoked meats, ground ginger, orange, mint, rosemary, cucumber, herb bread.

Ogen melon Prawns, crab, lobster, ginger wine, raspberries, framboise liqueur, sorbet, ice cream.

Watermelon Chicken, prawns, crab, feta cheese, beetroot, sweet melons, apple, berries, lime, chillies, ginger, mint.

Tropical fruits

Custard apple Pork, chicken, citrus, yogurt, cinnamon, ginger.

Dragon fruit Lime, lemon, other tropical fruits, coconut, sugar, ginger.

Durian Milk, cream, coconut, other tropical fruits, curry spices, chillies, sticky rice.

Guava Pork, pheasant, duck, seafood, chicken, cream cheese, apples, pears, lime, chillies, lemon, coconut, ginger, honey.

Kiwi Gammon, chicken, guinea fowl, squid, salmon, chillies, oranges, strawberries, other tropical fruit.

Lady Finger banana Butter, corn fritters, bacon rolls, light muscovado sugar, rum, brandy, Cointreau, coffee liqueur, cream, crème fraîche.

Lychee Pork, duck, chicken, seafood, chillies, avocados, raspberries, coconut, cream, lime, ginger.

Mango Chicken, smoked meats, fish, shellfish, green salads, avocados, lime, lemon, chillies, curry spices, coriander leaf, vanilla ice cream, sweet sticky rice, rum.

Mangosteen Other tropical fruits, strawberries, lemon grass, lemon.

Papaya Meat, smoked meats, avocados, chillies, lime, lemon, coconut, ginger.

Passion fruit Tuna, venison, game birds, cream, yogurt, custard, oranges, kiwi fruit, strawberries, bananas, peaches, light muscovado sugar, rum, white and sparkling wine.

Persimmon (sharon fruit) Ham, pork, game, lime, clotted cream, yogurt, fromage frais, walnuts, ginger, cinnamon, allspice, nutmeg, honey.

Physalis White fish, scallops, yogurt, other tropical fruits, nuts, lemon, tarragon, chocolate, Cointreau.

Pineapple Pork, ham, chicken, duck, fish, shellfish, cottage cheese, coconut, ginger, allspice, cinnamon, black pepper, Cointreau, rum, Kirsch.

Plantain Chicken, fish, most meats, dried beans, honey, ginger, butter, sunflower oil, chillies, coconut.

Pomegranate Prawns, lamb, chicken, duck, pheasant, aubergines, figs, almonds, pistachios, couscous, rice.

Rambutan Pork, duck, avocados, chillies, cream, coconut, vanilla, ginger.

Red banana Chicken, salad leaves, rainbow trout, red fruits, pink grapefruit, sweetcorn, rice.

Star fruit (carambola) Poultry, prawns, avocados, red peppers, other tropical fruits, lime, coconut, lemongrass, nutmeg, vanilla, honey, rum, salt.

Tamarillo Roast meats, chicken, fish, curry spices, cream, kiwi fruit, oranges, light muscovado sugar.

Yellow banana Chicken (especially fried), trout, cream, yogurt, custard, orange juice, lime, coconut, walnuts, chocolate, coffee, ginger, light and dark muscovado sugar, liqueurs, rum.

Dried and candied fruits

Candied peel Angelica, glacé cherries, other dried fruits, chocolate, cinnamon, mixed spice, ginger, nutmeg, mace, light and dark muscovado sugar.

Currants Dark and light muscovado sugars, honey, soft white cheeses, other dried fruits, ginger, cinnamon, mixed spice, cardamom, cumin, turmeric, peas, apples, pears, mint, rosemary, parsley, coriander seed and leaf, basil, rice, citrus.

Dried apple Pork, duck, goose, pheasant, honey, maple syrup, redcurrant jelly, cider, apple juice, dried pears, hard cheeses.

Dried apricots Cinnamon, star anise, nutmeg, curry spices, almonds, Brazil nuts, pistachios, walnuts, lamb, pork, chicken, turkey, goose, duck, game, soft cheeses, yogurt, cream, citrus.

Dried banana Yogurt, fromage frais, oats, soft white cheeses, wheat, barley, millet, walnuts, coconut, hazelnuts, other dried fruits, ginger, cinnamon, brandy.

Dried blueberry White and plain chocolate, vanilla, cinnamon, oats, rice, couscous, pistachios, almonds, walnuts, honey.

Dried cherry Oats and other grains, white soft cheeses, almonds, Kirsch, amaretto, cream, plain chocolate.

Dried coconut Curry spices and spice pastes, pulses, all meats, poultry, fish, dried fruits, tropical fruits, cherries, citrus, oats and other cereals, rice, noodles, cream.

Dried cranberry Oats, wheat, barley, millet, rice, breadcrumbs, turkey, duck, goose, pork, chicken, pine nuts, rosemary, thyme, parsley, onions, honey, maple syrup.

Dried dates Marzipan, walnuts, honey, fruit syrup, golden syrup, molasses, ginger, cinnamon, allspice, mixed spice, mace, cooking apples, pears, chocolate.

Dried fig Pork, chicken, duck, goose, game birds, sausages, cheeses, rum, cider, Pernod, marzipan, star anise, fennel.

Dried mango Coconut, lime, lemon, apples, pears, peaches, nectarines, strawberries, raspberries, blueberries, vanilla, ginger.

Dried peach Other dried fruits, cheeses, particularly Gorgonzola, mozzarella, feta and halloumi, ham, duck, game birds, rice.

Dried pear Blue cheeses, sage-flavoured cheeses, Cheddar, walnuts, bananas, rice, pasta, peas, mushrooms, ice cream, custard.

Prunes Chicken, rabbit, pork, beef, venison, game birds, bacon, cheeses, spinach, other dried fruit, pears, apples, cream, custard.

Raisins and sultanas Oats, wheat, chilli, cinnamon, star anise, mixed spice, curry spices, coriander leaf, parsley, chives, mint, honey, rum, cream, most fruits, cabbage, nuts.

ACKNOWLEDGMENTS

SECOND EDITION
Project editor Lucy Bannell
Editor Amy Slack
Senior art editor Sara Robin
Designer Philippa Nash
Jacket designer Steven Marsden
Pre-production producer Rebecca Fallowfield
Print producer Luca Bazzoli
Creative technical support Sonia Charbonnier
Recipe photography David Loftus
Food stylist Julia Azzarello
Managing editor Stephanie Farrow
Managing art editor Christine Keilty
Art director Maxine Pedliham
Publisher Mary-Clare Jerram

DK India
Project editor Janashree Singha
Project art editor Vikas Chauhan
Managing editor Soma B. Chowdhury
Managing art editor Arunesh Talapatra
Pre-production manager Sunil Sharma
Senior DTP designer Pushpak Tyagi

This edition published in 2017
First published in Great Britain in 2011 by
Dorling Kindersley Limited
80 Strand, London, WC2R 0RL

A Penguin Random House Company
10 9 8 7 6 5 4 3 2 1
001–306728–Oct/2017

A CIP catalogue record for this book is available
from the British Library.
ISBN: 978-0-2413-0726-7

Acknowledgments
Shine TV and Endemol Shine Group would like to thank:
Frances Adams, David Ambler, Katie Attwood, Alice Bernardi, Martin Buckett, Claire Burton, Harriet Cary, Bev Comboy, Kerisa Edwards,
Jessica Hannan, Ozen Kazim, Angela Loftus, Lou Plank, Lyndsey Posner, Franc Roddam, John Torode, and Gregg Wallace.

MasterChef alumni whose recipes and quotes are reproduced in this book:
Dhruv Baker, Natalie Brenner, Susie Carter, Alix Carwood, Larkin Cen, Ping Coombes, Jane Devonshire, David Coulson, Lisa Faulkner, Mat Follas,
Chris Gates, Helen Gilmour, Daniel Graham, Steve Groves, Christine Hamilton, Angela Kenney, Andrew Kojima, Tim Kinnaird, Claire Lara,
Jack Lucas, Marianne Lumb, Liz McClarnon, Hannah Miles, Daksha Mistry, James Nathan, Andy Oliver, Luke Owen, Shelina Permalloo,
Wendi Peters, Tony Rodd, Alex Rushmer, Dennice Russell, Nadia Sawalha, Emma Spitzer, Stacie Stewart, Dick Strawbridge, Iwan Thomas,
Jaye Wakelin, Steven Wallis, Dale Williams, and Simon Wood.

Dorling Kindersley would like to thank:
Rosamund Cox for editorial assistance, Elizabeth Bray for recipe testing, and Vanessa Bird for indexing.
First edition shoot team: William Reavell, Fergal Connolly, and Jane Lawrie.

British vegetables – what's in season when

Key: ■ = peak season (dark) · ▤ = available (grey) · blank = not in season

	JAN	FEB	MAR	APR	MAY	JUN	JUL	AUG	SEP	OCT	NOV	DEC
asparagus				▤	▤	▤						
aubergines						■	■	■	■	■		
beetroot	▤	▤				■	■	■	■	■	■	■
bell peppers							■	■	■	■		
broad beans					▤	▤	▤	▤				
broccoli							■	■	■	■	■	■
brussels sprouts	▤	▤	▤								▤	▤
butternut squash									■	■	■	■
cabbages	▤	▤	▤	▤	▤	▤	▤	▤	▤	▤	▤	▤
carrots	■	■							■	■	■	■
cauliflower	▤	▤	▤	▤	▤	▤	▤	▤	▤	▤	▤	▤
celeriac	■	■	■							▤	▤	▤
celery	▤								▤	▤	▤	▤
chicory	■	■	■	■						■	■	■
courgettes					▤	▤	▤	▤	▤	▤		
cucumbers						▤	▤	▤	▤	▤		
fennel						▤	▤	▤	▤	▤		
garlic					■	■	■	■				
globe artichokes						▤	▤	▤	▤			
jerusalem artichokes	■	■	■							■	■	■
kale	▤	▤	▤						▤	▤	▤	▤
kohlrabi							■	■	■	■	■	
leeks	▤	▤	▤	▤					▤	▤	▤	▤
lettuce	■	■	■	■	■	■	■	■	■	■	■	■
marsh samphire						▤	▤	▤	▤			
onions	■	■	■	■					■	■	■	■
parsnips	▤	▤	▤							▤	▤	▤
peas						■	■	■	■	■		
potatoes	▤	▤	▤	▤	▤	▤	▤	▤	▤	▤	▤	▤
pumpkins									■	■	■	
rocket	▤	▤	▤	▤	▤				▤	▤	▤	▤
runner beans							■	■	■	■		
sorrel		▤	▤	▤	▤	▤	▤	▤	▤	▤		
spinach	■	■	■	■	■	■	■	■	■	■	■	■
spring greens		▤	▤	▤	▤							
swede	■	■	■	■	■					■	■	■
sweetcorn								▤	▤	▤		
swiss chard								▤	▤	▤	■	■
tomatoes							▤	▤	▤	▤		
turnips	■	■	■	■	■	■	■	■	■	■	■	■
watercress	▤	▤	▤	▤	▤	▤	▤	▤	▤	▤	▤	▤
wild mushrooms									■	■	■	■